UNDERSTANDING AUTISTIC RELATIONSHIPS ACROSS THE LIFESPAN

Understanding Autistic Relationships Across the Lifespan is an accessible overview of autistic relationships from the early years through to old age. This much-needed book combines the latest research findings with first-hand accounts to offer insight into the relationships of autistic people and how they differ to those of non-autistic people in a range of ways.

Felicity Sedgewick and Sarah Douglas delve into life's stages and their challenges, revealing how navigating relationships can lead to misunderstandings, rejection, and trauma – but also to genuine connection, support, and joy. Illustrated throughout with extracts from interviews, and with extended narratives from Sarah, it explores key topics including relationships in the early years, childhood friendships, teenage friendships and romance, adult romantic and sexual relationships, LGBTQ relationships, finding community, family relationships, and issues in the later stages of life. The authors explore a wide range of emotions and life situations, examining the social world of autistic people and the strategies they use to navigate it.

Understanding Autistic Relationships Across the Lifespan offers practical recommendations for both autistic and non-autistic people on how to have the healthiest and most satisfying relationships possible. It is essential reading for all those working with autistic people and studying autism, as well as autistic individuals and those close to them.

Felicity Sedgewick is Senior Lecturer in Psychology of Education at the University of Bristol, with a research specialism in the relationships of autistic women, girls, and non-binary people. She has worked with autistic people in a variety of settings, with these experiences driving her research interests and helping shape her desire to do work with a positive real-world impact.

Sarah Douglas is an autism study advisor who has contributed to much-needed areas of research such as education, self-harm, suicidality, anxiety, intimate partner violence, and sexual assault. She is also currently volunteering for SARSAS, supporting survivors of all genders, and is a member of their Autism and ID Advisory Group.

UNDERSTANDING AUTISTIC RELATIONSHIPS ACROSS THE LIFESPAN

Family, Friends, Lovers and Others

Felicity Sedgewick and Sarah Douglas

LONDON AND NEW YORK

Cover image: Getty Images/Sean Gladwell

First published 2023
by Routledge
4 Park Square, Milton Park, Abingdon, Oxon OX14 4RN

and by Routledge
605 Third Avenue, New York, NY 10158

Routledge is an imprint of the Taylor & Francis Group, an informa business

© 2023 Felicity Sedgewick, Sarah Douglas

The right of Felicity Sedgewick and Sarah Douglas to be identified as authors of this work has been asserted in accordance with sections 77 and 78 of the Copyright, Designs and Patents Act 1988.

All rights reserved. No part of this book may be reprinted or reproduced or utilised in any form or by any electronic, mechanical, or other means, now known or hereafter invented, including photocopying and recording, or in any information storage or retrieval system, without permission in writing from the publishers.

Trademark notice: Product or corporate names may be trademarks or registered trademarks, and are used only for identification and explanation without intent to infringe.

British Library Cataloguing-in-Publication Data
A catalogue record for this book is available from the British Library

ISBN: 978-0-367-49101-7 (hbk)
ISBN: 978-0-367-49103-1 (pbk)
ISBN: 978-1-003-04453-6 (ebk)

DOI: 10.4324/9781003044536

Typeset in Bembo
by Apex CoVantage, LLC

CONTENTS

Acknowledgements	*vii*
Preface	*viii*

Introduction	1
1 First steps – relationships in the early years	12
2 Moving on up – childhood friendships	32
3 Big school – adolescent friendships	55
4 Teenage dreams – adolescent dating	83
5 With a little help from my friends – adult friendships and finding community	106
6 Well, hello there – sexual and romantic relationships in adulthood	139
7 A family affair – adult families	170
8 Getting older – older adulthood	197
9 Toxic – problematic relationships and victimisation	214

vi Contents

10 Tips and tricks for good relationships with autistic people   242

11 Conclusion   245

Recommended reading list   *247*
Index   *249*

ACKNOWLEDGEMENTS

During the two years of writing this book, we have gone through family divorces, family deaths, employment tribunals, long-term sickness, being disabled out of work, ADHD diagnoses, long-distance relationships, an engagement, buying a house, moving house, wedding planning . . . and a pandemic. It's been a huge journey, and, despite it all, we have created something we are proud of.

We could not have done it on our own. We both owe huge thanks to our contributors, who gave us their time and their trust in sharing their experiences here and letting us write about them. This book genuinely could not be what it is without them. We also want to thank the publisher, Routledge, for believing in us, and specifically thank Helen Pritt and Shreya Bajpai for the support they have provided – and for not chasing too hard as the deadlines zoomed past!

Felicity personally wants to thank the brilliant man who will, by the time this is published, be her husband, Tim. The 'difficult second book' has definitely lived up to the stereotype at times, and Tim's love, patience, and speed at producing cups of tea has been unerring. And Felicity sends him thanks for sorting out all the headings! She would also like to thank her parents and brother, and all her friends. They looked at her like she was mad when she announced that she was doing another one right away, and then proceeded to support her anyway. If this book shows anything, it is that the relationships we have with other people are what can make life brilliant, and her relationships absolutely make her life the best it can be.

Sarah would like to thank her many wonderful loved ones who have helped her to discover who she truly is and to like, love, and see herself as they do. Special thanks and so much love goes to her boys Kyle and Rob and her fam-friends the Lampylanders, Helen and Rebecca; the Hubbucks; and the Lucy's, Hannah, Heidi, Kelly, Ricky, and Adam. In truth, there are too many to mention, but they have all taught her how to live, love, and be loved in return. They may well have learned some things from Sarah as well. With so much info-dumping over the years, something must have stuck!

PREFACE

This book cannot tell you everything you want to know about the relationships of autistic people. We (Felicity and Sarah) know that it seems odd to start our book by telling you what it can't do, instead of what it can, but it is important to be honest. This book is designed to give you a brief insight into some of the most common relationships autistic people will experience over their lifespans, both in their own words and according to what the research tells us. That is not the same as being a comprehensive review of every possible relationship or social situation, and it cannot speak for the individual experiences of every autistic person. We are talking here in commonalities, averages, and generalities. Every autistic person is unique and will have unique experiences, but there are patterns to autistic relationships, and these are what we are describing.

The idea for this book came from our own long-standing friendship, and the life experiences we have shared during chats over hot chocolate, cake, and wine. There are so many similarities in our relationships as humans, but there are also differences. Aspects of being autistic make social relationships different (sometimes harder), and, equally, the world is set up to think about relationships from a very neurotypical perspective, which can end up disadvantaging or even harming autistic people, whether intentionally or unintentionally. This has not been helped by a history of autism research which has assumed – for reasons we will discuss in detail later – that autistic people were not capable of, did not have, and were not interested in relationships with other people. The life stories of autistic people, and emerging research, show categorically that this is not true, and this is what we are going to explore.

Felicity is an autism researcher and lecturer at the University of Bristol who is interested in autistic people's relationships and mental health, along with gender differences on these fronts. She originally intended to be an archaeologist, but got sidetracked when learning about cultural differences in child development as part of her archaeology and anthropology degree, and took a new path into developmental and social psychology. She is now the programme director for the conversion masters she took nearly a decade ago, which was the gateway into her psychology career. Her projects are co-produced with autistic people, and she prioritises doing work that can have a positive impact in the real world.

Sarah is a late diagnosed autist who describes herself as also something of a late developer, currently emerging in her early fifties from decades of poor mental and physical health and a series of jobs that can only be described as careering, rather than an actual career. Over the last five years she has used her lived experiences of being neurodivergent to support the autistic community by advising participatory autism research study teams and being involved in autism training/education. She has recently completed a 20-week stint of mentoring for NDSA, a non-profit organisation set up by autistic people for autistic people. Sarah is currently volunteering on the emotional support line for SARSAS, Somerset and Avon Rape and Sexual Abuse Service, and is also a member of their Autism and Learning Disability Advisory Group.

We are hoping that this book forms a useful overview and starting point into autistic people's relationships at different stages of their lives. It is split into ten chapters, each of which contains quotes from a range of autistic people we interviewed to get a variety of perspectives into the book. We have spoken to 25 people from the age of nine into their sixties, from different parts of the world – people of different genders, different sexualities, different ethnicities, those who have additional physical and mental health conditions, those who use non-verbal communication . . . everyone we could think of and who had time to talk to us! We are deeply grateful for their time and the trust they have placed in us to tell parts of their stories, and we hope we have done them justice. Any errors are made by us, and should not reflect on our contributors.

So, to give an overview of what to expect in the book ahead:

The *Introduction* is where we will take a brief tour through the history of autism and autism research, looking at how early assumptions and biases became built into later work and how they are now being challenged to reshape our ideas about autistic relationships.

Chapter 1: First Steps looks at family relationships in the early years of life, such as how autistic children are known to relate to their parents and siblings, and to other caregivers in settings like nursery education.

Chapter 2: Moving On Up talks about friendships as children move into primary school – the importance of these relationships, how they are made and maintained, some of the difficulties autistic children can face, but also the positive experiences they have.

Chapter 3: Big School looks at how friendships change as children turn into adolescents, moving from primary to secondary education. This is often a major life transition on many fronts, and this has an impact on friendships. Here we will also consider emerging research into online friendships for autistic adolescents, and the ways in which these can be both an opportunity and a risk.

x Preface

Chapter 4: Teenage Dreams is the first chapter to look at a different type of relationship – romantic relationships. Adolescence is when most people, autistic and non-autistic, start to develop romantic and sexual urges and relationships. It is also when sexuality starts to come to the fore in terms of our developing identity, so this chapter also discusses LGBTQ identities on the autism spectrum.

Chapter 5: With a Little Help from My Friends moves to exploring what is known about autistic adult's friendships and how these change as people mature. This chapter also looks at some of the research about how an adult diagnosis can impact people's relationships both with other people and with their own sense of self.

Chapter 6: Well, Hello There goes on to look at sex, sexuality, and romantic relationships in adulthood. From early assumptions to the most recent research, we look at what is known about autistic people's approaches to these relationships and the ways this plays out in everyday life.

Chapter 7: A Family Affair moves on to looking at how family relationships change as people get older, from becoming parents to starting to look after parents as they become elderly.

Chapter 8: Getting Older explores the relationships of autistic people as they move into their later years, the challenges of ageing, and how these are similar and different to the experiences of non-autistic people of the same age.

Chapter 9: Toxic looks at some of the ways in which relationships can go wrong or be harmful. This can apply to any kind of relationship, from family members to friends to romantic partners, and we will look at examples of all of these.

Chapter 10: Tips and Tricks for Good Relationships with Autistic People does what it says on the tin – we will give you some of our top tips for positive autistic relationships. These are often not age- or life-stage specific, hence we put them together rather than as a section in each chapter.

Finally, we have a short *Conclusion* to the book, and send our thanks to our contributors.

INTRODUCTION

Autism, and autistic people, have been around as long as humans have. It is likely there were ancient humans with behaviours, cognitive patterns, and sensory sensitivities that would meet clinical diagnostic criteria (though that would be taking the game of historical diagnoses too far!). Autism, and other neurodevelopmental conditions, are part of the natural range of human biodiversity. This belief is known as the neurodiversity paradigm, and it is the framework within which we are writing this book. We take the approach that autistic people (see the language note that follows) are valid in their way of being in, experiencing, and relating to the world, and hope to help them and others understand some of these differences, rather than arguing that they are somehow 'wrong' or need changing to be more like non-autistic people. This book is not about the definitions or evolution of neurodiversity, but if you would like some further reading on the topic, we would recommend looking at the book list we provide at the back!

Throughout the book, we will be using the terms 'autistic people' and 'non-autistic people'. This is known as identity-first language, and has been shown to be the preference of the majority of autistic people who take part in research on the topic (Kenny et al., 2016). This is different to the way a lot of clinicians, professionals, and researchers have historically talked about autistic people, as they have tended to use 'people with autism' or say someone 'has autism' – known as person-first language. Originally this was used because it was thought to emphasise the person rather than the condition (Kenny et al., 2016), and in some cases it is the preferred language of people affected themselves (e.g. in eating disorder research, people are described as 'having anorexia'). However, recent research in the autism field has shown that person-first language can increase the stigma against autistic people and has a dehumanising rather than humanising effect on how others think about them (Cage et al., 2022). Combined with the stated preference of many autistic people, therefore, we use identity-first language in our writing,

DOI: 10.4324/9781003044536-1

2 Introduction

whilst recognising that a proportion of autistic people prefer person-first language. We have no wish to intimidate a minority within a minority and are following majority preference for simplicity.

Autism has both a very complex and a very simple history, depending on how you look at it. The simple version is that two psychologists in the 1940s, Kanner in the United States and Asperger in Austria, independently noticed that they were seeing children who had a shared set of characteristics – difficulties with social interaction (to varying degrees), a preference for routine and sameness, and challenges with everyday living skills. Kanner called this 'autism' (a preference for oneself or being alone), and Asperger called it 'Aspergers' (a preference for showing off his ego). The two did not know about each other's work, and autism became the dominant diagnosis as Kanner published in English, whereas Asperger published in German (which was not the way to make your work popular in 1940s Europe, for obvious reasons. It may also have had something to do with the fact that Asperger worked with the Nazis in highly problematic ways.).

These diagnoses were unchanged over the next 40 years or so, until Lorna Wing and Judy Gould, in 1980s South London, did a large-scale population level study and realised that the children with these two diagnoses were actually part of the same spectrum, as were lots of children who had not been given a formal diagnosis of either. This is where the term 'the autism spectrum' comes from, and it was designed to create a broader and more inclusive sense of what being autistic meant and could look like. This pair of researchers also invented 'the triad of impairments', which, while not the terminology we use today, revolutionised how autistic people were recognised and opened up diagnosis and support for more of those who needed it. This triad was made up of difficulties with:

- *Imagination and executive function* (things like guessing what other people were thinking, or being able to make a plan based on imagining what will happen next)
- *Social communication* (things like being non-verbal, not following standard 'rules' of communication like turn taking in conversation, or struggling with eye contact)
- *Repetitive behaviours and restricted interests* (things like repeated physical movements such as hand flapping, or having intense special interests)

The rise in autism diagnoses following this expansion of the diagnostic criteria from the strict ones set out earlier, especially removing the need for co-occurring learning difficulties Kanner used, was significant. This coincided with the rolling out of the MMR vaccine; and a highly questionable researcher called Andrew Wakefield used this correlation to publish his idea that the vaccine was causing autism in children. What he did not publish was that he was paid by the rival vaccine company, had faked his results, and the blood samples he 'used' had been collected without parental consent from children at a birthday party. If you want a fuller idea of just how wrong his work was, there are literally thousands of academic papers proving it – but these tend not to make such good Facebook memes, and hence we have the anti-vaxxer movement.

Regardless of that particular issue, autism diagnoses have generally continued to rise. This is because we are getting better at spotting when someone is autistic, our diagnostic tools have improved, and we are starting to recognise that autism can present in an even wider variety of ways than we thought in the 1980s. It is also because there is now a recognition that we can – and should – diagnose adults who were missed in childhood, for a variety of reasons. For a long time, if someone was not diagnosed before the age of about 14, they were highly unlikely to get a diagnosis at all, because autism was thought to be a 'childhood condition'. The fact that autistic children grow into autistic adults was somehow lost on a lot of the early researchers.

In 2013, on the basis of evidence from autistic people and clinicians, *sensory sensitivities* (being under/hypo- or over/hyper-sensitive on one of the five senses) were added to the diagnostic criteria. Similarly, there is growing research into and awareness of how autism can look different in those who internalise a lot of their experiences and those who externalise them – which is more what is considered 'classically autistic'. A lot of these more nuanced ideas about what autism is have come from the autism community itself, with autistic advocates and academics driving change and increasing societal awareness. There is still plenty of work to do, but the direction of movement seems positive.

There is also, as we said, a much more complex story which can be told about autism and how autism research has developed over time. That isn't the focus of this book (though it is the focus of *Neurotribes*, by Steve Silberman), and so we won't try to tell it all here. What is relevant for the current book is the focus on social difficulties, which have characterised autism research and stereotypes from the earliest days, back in the 1940s, and the assumptions this led people to make about autistic relationships until very recently.

Most autism research, researchers, and parents of autistic people, for most of the last 80 years, have functioned based on the assumption that because autistic people had difficulties with making and maintaining friendships and relationships, had different social interaction patterns, and did not show distress about these things in the ways they expected . . . that autistic people did not want friends or romantic relationships . . . that these were just things autistic people were hardwired not to value, or be interested in at all. Avoiding eye contact was seen as a sign of not wanting to engage with the person who was speaking; not inferring someone's true intentions was seen as a failure to understand that other people have minds (yes, really); and not making friends at school was assumed to be because the child did not want friends and was happier on their own.

A whole academic discipline of autism studies, with corresponding theories, was built upon the basis of these observations of social difficulty (along with the other two parts of the triad). A few examples of these theories follow.

4 Introduction

Theory of Mind

ToM; Baron-Cohen et al., 1985

This theory begins with the idea that everyone has something called a Theory of Mind (ToM) – the ability to understand what other people are thinking and feeling without them telling you explicitly, based on what you know about the situation and what you know that they know about the situation. Baron-Cohen et al. argued that autistic people lack this skill, and that this is what causes their difficulties with social interaction – if you can't work out how the other person feels, then it makes it hard to react as they are expecting, which leads to negative responses from them. This theory was expanded to argue that autistic people also lack empathy, meaning that they cannot feel for other people, and this point has been used to argue that autistic people themselves do not feel emotions in the same way as non-autistic people (Nuske et al., 2013; Rueda et al., 2014). Some have even tried to argue that autistic people do not feel emotions at all. There have been lots of studies which showed that autistic children find ToM tasks harder than non-autistic children, with autistic children giving similar answers to much younger non-autistic children (Baron-Cohen, 2000). There have also been studies where autistic adults score lower on ToM tasks than non-autistic adults, when they are asked to do things like guess someone's emotions from just a picture of someone's eyes (Baron-Cohen et al., 2001).

Extreme Male Brain Theory

EMB; Baron-Cohen, 2002

Another Baron-Cohen theory. This time, he started with the idea that men have logical, systematising brains, and women have emotional, empathising brains (yes, really). From that starting point, he argued that everyone has an Empathising score and a Systematising score (measured using his E-S scale) and that men will score higher on S and women will score higher on E. He then gave the test to lots of autistic people (mostly autistic men) and found that autistic men scored even higher on Systematising than many non-autistic men did – therefore, he concluded being autistic must be like having an Extreme Male Brain, and that is what he called the theory. There are several research studies which have found that autistic people do score higher on Systematising than non-autistic people on this test, and later studies even managed to include autistic women. These studies also found that autistic women score higher on Systematising than non-autistic women, and similarly to non-autistic men – but lower than autistic men (Baron-Cohen, 2010).

This theory was originally used to support the low rates of diagnosis for autistic women, on the basis that if it was a 'male brain thing' then it made sense that not many women 'had it', and later to suggest that autistic women may somehow be 'less than' non-autistic women because of their 'male brains'. (I hope the number of quotation marks here show the extent of our scepticism towards these claims.)

The under-diagnosis of autistic females, partly as a result of these kinds of theories, is now a well-recognised issue (Gould & Ashton-Smith, 2011). While the knowledge that it is harder for girls and women to get a diagnosis is widespread in both the autism community and amongst researchers, this has not yet led to changes to diagnostic criteria or tools, which means that the difficulty continues for many. A recent study showed that women with high levels of empathy and social functioning are the least likely to have a formal diagnosis, even when they have high levels of autism traits. Instead, they were likely to have had multiple mental health diagnoses, especially borderline personality disorder (Belcher et al., 2022) – precisely the kind of misdiagnosis which was being talked about a decade earlier, but is still being given in many cases.

Weak Central Coherence Theory

Happe et al., 1994

This theory is not really based on the social behaviours of autistic people; it is more about something called executive function, but it is important to include here because of the proposed consequences for social behaviours. Executive functions are the things our brain does to help us organise ourselves and the way we think. They are usually broken down into cognitive flexibility (the ability to switch between things you are thinking about or doing), working memory (how many things you can hold in your head at once or how long you hold information 'at the front of your mind'), and self-control (the ability to choose to act or not act on an impulse). Studies have long shown that autistic people have more difficulties with all three areas of executive function than non-autistic people (South et al., 2007). Based on this, and some other experiments, Professor Francesca Happe came up with the theory that autistic people have 'weak central coherence' – that they tend to focus on disparate details of the task in front of them, rather than pulling these together into a central and coherent whole idea. There is evidence that this is something autistic brains tend to do – focus on details rather than the bigger picture – from studies which show that autistic people are significantly faster at tasks such as finding Wally in Where's Wally images. When we expand this concept to apply to social interaction, you can see how this idea might help to explain some of the differences in autistic interactions. Focussing on just one part of the face, such as the mouth, might lead you to get a different – and more literal – interpretation of what someone means when they talk, because you aren't comparing their words with their overall facial expression to check for a mismatch that means they are being sarcastic, for example (and this is something autistic people do – Mathersul et al., 2013; Sedgewick et al., 2018). It might also mean that you are more likely to take someone 'at face value', because you treat each interaction as an individual event rather than building up a picture of how this person has treated you over time – something called a lower reliance on priors – which it has also been shown autistic people do (Pellicano & Burr, 2012).

6 Introduction

Social Motivation Theory

SMT; Chevallier et al., 2012

The interest, or lack of it, in having social interactions or relationships is called social motivation. There are questionnaires that try to measure how much social motivation someone has, and this score is assumed to be indicative of how they behave in real life – and autistic people tend to score lower on these measures. The Social Motivation Theory (SMT) starts with the observation that autistic people struggle with social interactions, seem to be less interested, and score lower on these measures to conclude that autistic people lack – or at least have less – social motivation than non-autistic people. It argues that this lack of social motivation is present from birth, because autism is a neurodevelopmental condition which is present from birth. They then construct an image of a sort of 'negative spiral' for autistic people which goes like this:

- Autistic people have less social motivation
- So they find social interactions less rewarding
- So they seek out fewer social interactions
- Which means they get less practice at social skills
- So the interactions they do have tend to go less well (this is called negative feedback)
- So they feel anxious about how future social interactions will go
- Which means they avoid even more social interactions
- So they have even less practice at social skills
- So the interactions they have continue to go differently/worse than they hope . . .
- And so on and so on, across the whole of an autistic person's life

When you look at it from that perspective, things like research finding high levels of isolation among autistic people (Locke et al., 2010), high levels of social anxiety in all autistic people (Lever & Guerts, 2016), and low numbers of autistic adults having friends or partners (Howlin et al., 2004) seems to make perfect sense.

But are any of these theories the whole story? Are they even right?

Spoiler alert: some of them are definitely not; some of them have useful bits.

There is evidence for each of the social difficulties just described, in research and in everyday life. Autistic children and adults do tend to avoid eye contact in the traditional way. They can appear to struggle with understanding what someone else is thinking or feeling and how it is driving their responses. Lots of autistic people of all ages struggle to make friends.

What these concrete observations are not actually evidence of, however, is *why* these things are happening. The theories just explained are almost entirely based on (almost always neurotypical) academics making up their own explanations for the things they saw autistic people doing, rather than asking the autistic people themselves. This is a long-standing flaw in a lot of autism research, which luckily is starting to be corrected by a new generation of autistic and non-autistic academics who value participatory research practices and consciously strive to include and elevate autistic voices in their work.

The insights and improvements to our knowledge about autistic people which have come from this change are invaluable. Who knew asking the people you are interested in about their lives would tell you new and important things, let alone letting autistic people themselves lead the way in autism research? (More sarcasm.)

From this, a new set of theories of autism have developed which do a better and more inclusive job of describing what is going on for autistic people. We will lay out a few of these next, largely chosen because they are in some way direct responses to the ones we described earlier; but this is not an exhaustive list, and there are new ideas coming out all the time. There is a Recommended Reading List at the end of the book – have a look at that for where to find more information on these.

Double Empathy Theory

Milton, 2012

Damian Milton is an autistic sociologist who took issue with the Theory of Mind discussed earlier (as many people have before and since). Thinking about the way the situation is presented, he noted that it is always portrayed as the autistic person failing to understand the people around them – but he knew from his own and other autistic people's experiences that the people they met weren't always that great at understanding them either. He therefore wrote his Double Empathy Theory, which argues that it is actually a two-way failure of understanding and empathy which underlies much of the social interaction difficulties which are seen as so classically autistic. This idea immediately chimed with many in the autism community, who had been talking for years about the fact that autistic people often find socialising with each other perfectly straightforward, and that they were routinely misunderstood or misinterpreted by non-autistic people. While it took a few years for research papers to be published testing the theory, there is now a wealth of evidence to back up Milton's point. For example, there are studies showing that non-autistic people are bad at interpreting the emotions of an autistic person from their facial expressions (Brewer et al, 2016) – just as autistic people struggle with the task with the eyes mentioned previously. There are studies showing that non-autistic people judge autistic people as less likeable and less desirable to work with, simply based on a couple of seconds of video footage – and that autistic people rate other autistic people more highly based on the same thing (DeBrabander et al., 2019). This is very much an issue on both sides of the interaction, not just one, as was historically assumed – an assumption which had formed the basis for a lot of theories, research studies, policies, and interventions such as social skills training (more on that later).

8 Introduction

Diverse Social Intelligences

Crompton et al., 2020

This point is not officially a theory, yet, though we suspect that a coherent theoretical framework could and will be built based on the insights it is raising, which is why we are including it. The Social Intelligences Project is based around exploring the practical implications of the Double Empathy Theory for how autistic and non-autistic people interact. Taking the idea that it is a two-way communication problem, the team from the University of Edinburgh set out to test how well different pairs of people worked together. The task involved chains of people in three conditions: all autistic, all non-autistic, and alternating autistic and non-autistic. They showed the first person how to make a model, and then asked them to teach the next person in the chain to do it. That person then taught the next one, and so on, to a chain six people long. What they found was that all autistic chains and all non-autistic chains actually passed on the information to a similar level of accuracy and efficiency to each other. Where there were problems, and where communication broke down, was when the chain alternated between autistic and non-autistic people. This really does emphasise that the assumptions built into the Double Empathy Theory are correct – non-autistic people were just as poor at accurately passing on information from and to autistic people as vice versa. There are other studies that support this, such as the finding that autistic children and young people build their own unique 'social communication norms' for how to talk to each other while they are gaming (Heasman & Gillespie, 2019), and that autistic adults feel more comfortable with each other than with non-autistic adults, sharing more information about themselves, even without being told the other person's neurotype (Crompton et al., 2021).

Monotropism

Murray et al., 2005

Monotropism is a theory which was developed by autistic academic and activist Dinah Murray as a reply and a challenge to all the 'cognitive dysfunction' based theories about autistic people. This includes things like the aforementioned Weak Central Coherence Theory and many others. Murray argued that rather than focussing on the outputs (the test scores, the forgotten appointments, etc.) it was more valuable to focus on the *inputs* autistic people were experiencing, and that this might explain more about their behaviour. She conceptualised autistic differences as being based in attention, rather than executive function. Monotropism is the idea that some people, especially autistic people, have a strong tendency to focus on one thing at once, with that one thing taking up all or nearly all of their attention capacity – they are *monotropic*. In contrast, non-autistic people are *polytropic*, or able to pay attention to several things at once relatively easily. This does not mean that non-autistic people are all multitasking geniuses, but instead that they can be thinking about the email they are writing and hear the doorbell ring at the same time. Autistic people are more likely not to hear the doorbell because it is not part of what their attention is focussed on. Or, they will hear the doorbell and this will totally disrupt their attention on the email, so that they forget to finish it, or struggle to know how to finish it when they do come back to it because they have lost that train of thought and their attention now wants to focus on something entirely different. Murray posited that attention is a finite resource which our brains have to choose how to allocate, and that our brains will naturally allocate more attention to the things we like, and less attention to things which are less rewarding. Non-autistic people can give most of their attention to something while retaining some spare for other things, such as sensory stimuli. Autistic people tend to give all of their attention to one thing, so that they ignore other stimuli, or if their attention shifts, they are then totally immersed in that new thing. This singular hyperfocus of attention on different stimuli, tasks, or topics can potentially explain a lot of autistic behaviours, including many of the diagnostic criteria.

For example – Murray does not argue that autistic people do not have different levels of social motivation or interest, but argues instead that other things interest them more, and therefore get priority for attention over the social interaction. This would, understandably, lead to autistic people appearing to be less interested in socialising than non-autistic people, but does not rely on the same assumption of total disinterest as Social Motivation Theory. Equally, the overwhelming nature of some autistic people's sensory experiences makes sense in the light of monotropism. If your brain generally focusses all your attention on one thing at a time, and at this moment in time that thing is the pain that the strip lighting in the shopping centre is causing you, to the point where your brain (and body) genuinely cannot focus on or think about or process anything else – well, having a meltdown or a shutdown becomes a logical response to your experience. Added to this, there is emerging research evidence that autistic people may have higher perceptual capacity than non-autistic people (they may be able to take in and process more information at once), as it has been shown on tasks which test this that they are more likely to hear the 'distractor' information and the 'target' information, whereas non-autistic people are more likely to miss the 'target' (Remington & Fairnie, 2017). If this finding holds up, it suggests that autistic people are not only focussing on one thing instead of many, they are focussing on that one thing harder than a non-autistic person would be. With all that, it is easy to see why finishing a relatively boring work email could get forgotten for a week or three!

Chapter conclusion

These new theories, combined with the work of the autistic community and emerging research findings, combine to paint a new picture of autism. It is a picture which aims to accurately represent the differences between autistic and non-autistic people in a co-produced way, rather than autistic people being told what they are like. It does not pretend that these differences cannot sometimes lead to difficulties – it absolutely accepts, acknowledges, and centres the lived experiences of autistic people, including the tough ones. But what it wants to do with that information

10 Introduction

is find ways to understand and support autistic people, helping them to work out what they want out of life and relationships and how to achieve that in ways which are manageable and positive. It challenges the old stereotypes about autistic people, their lives and their relationships, in important ways. The new approach to autism – based in the neurodiversity paradigm – does not blame autistic people, or tell them that there is something wrong with them. And neither will we, as we go through the book.

References

Baron-Cohen, S. (2000). Theory of mind and autism: A review. *International Review of Research in Mental Retardation, 23,* 169–184. https://doi.org/10.1016/S0074-7750(00)80010-5

Baron-Cohen, S. (2002). The extreme male brain theory of autism. *Trends in Cognitive Sciences, 6*(6), 248–254. https://doi.org/10.1016/S1364-6613(02)01904-6

Baron-Cohen, S. (2010). Empathizing, systemizing, and the extreme male brain theory of autism. *Progress in Brain Research, 186,* 167–175. https://doi.org/10.1016/B978-0-444-53630-3.00011-7

Baron-Cohen, S., Leslie, A. M., & Frith, U. (1985). Does the autistic child have a "theory of mind"? *Cognition, 21*(1), 37–46. https://doi.org/10.1016/0010-0277(85)90022-8

Baron-Cohen, S., Wheelwright, S., Hill, J., Raste, Y., & Plumb, I. (2001). The reading the mind in the eyes test revised version: A study with normal adults, and adults with asperger syndrome or High-functioning autism. *Journal of Child Psychology and Psychiatry, 42*(2), 241–251. https://doi.org/10.1111/1469-7610.00715

Belcher, H. L., Morein-Zamir, S., Steven. S. D., & Ford, R. M. (2022). Shining a light on a hidden population: Social functioning and mental health in women reporting autistic traits but lacking diagnosis. *Journal of Autism and Developmental Disorders 2022,* 1–15. https://doi.org/10.1007/S10803-022-05583-2

Brewer, R., Biotti, F., Catmur, C., Press, C., Happé, F., Cook, R., & Bird, G. (2016). Can neurotypical individuals read autistic facial expressions? Atypical production of emotional facial expressions in autism spectrum disorders. *Autism Research, 9*(2), 262–271. https://doi.org/10.1002/aur.1508

Cage, E., Cranney, R., & Botha, M. (2022). *Brief report: Does autistic community connectedness moderate the relationship between masking and wellbeing?* https://doi.org/10.31234/OSF.IO/P6BT5

Chevallier, C., Kohls, G., Troiani, V., Brodkin, E. S., & Schultz, R. T. (2012). The social motivation theory of autism. *Trends in Cognitive Sciences, 16*(4), 231–239. https://doi.org/10.1016/J.TICS.2012.02.007

Crompton, C. J., Fletcher-Watson, S., & Ropar, D. (2021). *I never realised everybody felt as happy as I do when I am around autistic people: A thematic analysis of autistic adults' relationships with autistic and neurotypical friends and family.* https://doi.org/10.31219/OSF.IO/46B87

Crompton, C. J., Ropar, D., Evans-Williams, C. V. M., Flynn, E. G., & Fletcher-Watson, S. (2020). Autistic peer-to-peer information transfer is highly effective. *Autism, 24*(7), 1704–1712. https://doi.org/10.1177/1362361320919286

DeBrabander, K. M., Morrison, K. E., Jones, D. R., Faso, D. J., Chmielewski, M., & Sasson, N. J. (2019). Do first impressions of autistic adults differ between autistic and nonautistic observers? *Autism in Adulthood, 1*(4), 250–257. https://doi.org/10.1089/aut.2019.0018

Gould, J., & Ashton-Smith, J. (n.d.). *Missed diagnosis or misdiagnosis? Girls and women on the autism spectrum.* October 18, 2018 www.ingentaconnect.com/content/bild/gap/2011/00000012/00000001/art00005

Grossman, R. B. (2015). Judgments of social awkwardness from brief exposure to children with and without high-functioning autism. *Autism, 19*(5), 580–587. https://doi.org/10.1177/1362361314536937

Happé, F. G. E. (1994). An advanced test of theory of mind: Understanding of story characters thoughts and feelings by able autistic, Mentally handicapped, and normal children and adults. *Journal of Autism and Developmental Disorders, 24*(2), 129–154. https://doi.org/10.1007/BF02172093

Heasman, B., & Gillespie, A. (2019). Neurodivergent intersubjectivity: Distinctive features of how autistic people create shared understanding. *Autism: The International Journal of Research and Practice, 23*(4), 910–921. https://doi.org/10.1177/1362361318785172

Howlin, P., Goode, S., Hutton, J., & Rutter, M. (2004). Adult outcome for children with autism. *Journal of Child Psychology and Psychiatry, 45*(2), 212–229. https://doi.org/10.1111/j.1469-7610.2004.00215.x

Kenny, L., Hattersley, C., Molins, B., Buckley, C., Povey, C., & Pellicano, E. (2016). Which terms should be used to describe autism? Perspectives from the UK autism community. *Autism, 20*(4), 442–462. https://doi.org/10.1177/1362361315588200

Lever, A. G., & Geurts, H. M. (2016). Psychiatric co-occurring symptoms and disorders in young, middle-aged, and older adults with autism spectrum disorder. *Journal of Autism and Developmental Disorders, 46*(6). https://doi.org/10.1007/s10803-016-2722-8

Locke, J., Ishijima, E. H., Kasari, C., & London, N. (2010). Loneliness, friendship quality and the social networks of adolescents with high-functioning autism in an inclusive school setting. *Journal of Research in Special Educational Needs, 10*(2), 74–81. https://doi.org/10.1111/j.1471-3802.2010.01148.x

Mathersul, D., McDonald, S., & Rushby, J. A. (2013). Understanding advanced theory of mind and empathy in high-functioning adults with autism spectrum disorder. *Journal of Clinical and Experimental Neuropsychology, 35*(6), 655–668. https://doi.org/10.1080/13803395.2013.809700

Milton, D. E. M. (2012). On the ontological status of autism: The "double empathy problem." *Disability and Society, 27*(6), 883–887. https://doi.org/10.1080/09687599.2012.710008

Murray, D., Lesser, M., & Lawson, W. (2005). Attention, monotropism and the diagnostic criteria for autism. *Autism, 9*(2), 139–156. https://doi.org/10.1177/1362361305051398

Nuske, H. J., Vivanti, G., & Dissanayake, C. (2013). Are emotion impairments unique to, universal, or specific in autism spectrum disorder? A comprehensive review. *Cognition & Emotion, 27*(6), 1042–1061. https://doi.org/10.1080/02699931.2012.762900

Pellicano, E., & Burr, D. (2012). When the world becomes 'too real': A bayesian explanation of autistic perception. *Trends in Cognitive Sciences, 16*(10), 504–510. https://doi.org/10.1016/J.TICS.2012.08.009

Remington, A., & Fairnie, J. (2017). A sound advantage: Increased auditory capacity in autism. *Cognition, 166*, 459–465. https://doi.org/10.1016/J.COGNITION.2017.04.002

Rueda, P., Fernández-Berrocal, P., & Schonert-Reichl, K. A. (2014). Empathic abilities and theory of mind in adolescents with asperger syndrome: Insights from the twenty-first century. *Review Journal of Autism and Developmental Disorders, 1*(4), 327–343. https://doi.org/10.1007/S40489-014-0026-5/TABLES/2

Sedgewick, F., Crane, L., Hill, V., & Pellicano, E. (2018). Friends and lovers: The relationships of autistic and neurotypical women. *Autism in Adulthood, 1*(2), 112–123. https://doi.org/10.1089/aut.2018.0028

South, M., Ozonoff, S., & Mcmahon, W. M. (2007). The relationship between executive functioning, central coherence, and repetitive behaviors in the high-functioning autism spectrum. *Autism, 11*(5), 437–451. https://doi.org/10.1177/1362361307079606

1

FIRST STEPS

Relationships in the early years

The very first people we form relationships with are our early caregivers, usually our parents. While there might not be much two-way conversation going on at this point in our lives, these earliest bonds help to set our expectations and patterns for a lot of our relationships going forwards. That means that they are vitally important, even if the first 12 months of communication mostly consist of crying, and the next few years consist of learning the words to try to get one's point across.

The importance of early relationships has not always been considered so obvious. Way back in history, children were thought to be 'blank slates' for their parents to simply 'write' their preferred personalities, identities, and outcomes onto, rather than individual and complete humans. At other points in time, children were treated as small adults from ages we find shockingly young nowadays, with six- and seven-year-olds having jobs outside the home, or caring responsibilities inside it.

The term used in psychology for early relationships with caregivers is generally 'attachment' or 'attachment bond'. So, how is this defined? It is usually summed up as a strong emotional bond with a caregiver which results in proximity-seeking behaviour and distress upon separation, and which builds a model for future relationships. It is also important to note that this is built through what is called an experience-expectant model. What this means is that based on their previous experiences with their caregiver, a child builds up an idea of how they expect their caregiver to behave, and this sets their expectations for how most people they encounter will behave.

Attachment develops and changes over time, and babies are not born with an inherent attachment to their caregivers. Instead, there is the 'pre-attachment' phase, where they will seek care indiscriminately from those around them – although there is evidence that babies prefer their mothers and those they have skin-to-skin contact with. Recognition of familiar people happens from early on, after just a few weeks, and clear-cut attachment happens between then and up to about

DOI: 10.4324/9781003044536-2

First steps **13**

15 months old. This is when babies and toddlers have clearly preferred people who they will choose to go to for comfort, their needs, and to share things they are excited about. After this point, children tend to develop multiple attachments to other people – not just family adults, but siblings, peers, and people at their nursery or school for example.

Theories of attachment

The earliest theory of attachment was created by Bowlby in 1958. This had two main principles – first, that babies need their mothers to survive, and, second, that the emotional caregiver bond is what justifies the high level of care babies require from their mothers. He argued that the attachment bond provides a feeling of safety by encouraging the child, when distressed (being hungry or cold or sad, for example), to reduce their distance from their mother who then responds to that distress by reducing it (they feed them, put a blanket on them, or comfort them).

Through this process, a child learns that they can trust their mother to make them feel better, which builds their relationship with her. It also helps them learn to regulate their emotions, as trusting that their distress will be soothed helps to reduce the intensity of the distress when a similar thing occurs – if a child knows someone will comfort them when they are scared by a dog barking, for example, hearing the dog bark the next time feels less scary and threatening, and the child is more able to manage their reaction to the noise.

Bowlby's attachment theory is known as an ethological theory of survival. This means that the theory is based on evolutionary psychology, in that it posits attachment as something which is adaptive and aimed at increasing chances of survival. It also emphasises that attachment between a child and their mother is an active process, rather than a passive dependence. It acknowledges that children learn to communicate that they want to be close to their mother, that they communicate their needs to that mother, and that they engage in rewarding behaviours such as showing affection when their mother responds to them. He said that the first three or four years of life are the critical period for forming attachments, as this is when children are the most dependent on their mothers for care and survival. Bowlby further argued that this early attachment to the mother forms an internal working model for later relationships in life, as it sets the expectations for how other people will respond to your distress or affection, and for how things like affection should be displayed behaviourally.

If you've been reading closely, you will have noticed something in the preceding paragraphs – we have only talked about mothers, not parents or caregivers.

This is not because we believe that mothers are the only people who children can form early attachments to – but Bowlby basically did. Throughout his writing, Bowlby focussed on early attachment to mothers and argued that the lack of constant and consistent maternal care in early life led to poor development, maladjustment, delinquency, and even criminality. He believed that 'maternal deprivation' caused cognitive and behavioural issues in children, based on his work in

14 First steps

care homes for troubled teenagers and on children's wards in hospitals. (This was a time when parents were discouraged from visiting children in hospital, so very unwell children could go long periods of time without seeing their families.) These are obviously not standard experiences or situations for children to grow up in, but Bowlby believed that these 'disrupted' childhoods could give insights into the importance of a good attachment relationship with the mother in early life.

The reason Bowlby was so focussed on mothers was partly because he was a man writing in the 1950s, with all the assumptions about gender roles which were prevalent at the time, and partly because he was paid to be. During World War II, lots of women had gone into jobs and workplaces which had previously been the domain of men, as the men were off fighting. When the war ended, lots of men returned, and the government wanted them back in their old jobs, but that meant justifying the removal of women (above and beyond the general belief that men deserved jobs more for being men). Bowlby's work was therefore picked up and further funded on the understanding that he emphasise the importance of it being women – mothers – who were doing childcare at home, rather than anyone else. And his findings were framed in such a way as to make women feel that by being 'absent mothers' with jobs, they were letting down their children and also society. In a lot of ways this 'propagandised' version of the results was very successful, and the idea that someone was a bad mother for having a job was greatly reinforced across not just Great Britain but also places like America and other countries. Of course in the real world, a mother is rarely the only caregiver, and there are often other people who are a child's primary caregiver, or caregiving may be shared between multiple people.

There are other issues with Bowlby's work – he assumed that children were physically able to maintain closeness to their caregivers, ignoring the challenges with mobility that very young babies have or which disabled children may have. Yet attachment begins before children are independently mobile, and disabled children are more than capable of having warm and reciprocal relationships with their caregivers. He also assumed that the primary caregiver was a secure base for the child, and consistently acted in a positive, supportive, and reassuring way. Sadly, this is not always the case, and even well-meaning parents can have inconsistent or less than reassuring parenting styles which result in children having very different internal working models for their relationships.

Types of attachment

This naturally leads on to considering types of attachment, which was what Mary Ainsworth did in the late 1960s and 1970s. While she was working in a childcare clinic in Ethiopia, she began to wonder about the different patterns of relationships she was seeing between children and their parents. When she and her husband returned from his posting, she worked in Baltimore on developing a way to test and classify children's attachments to their caregivers. This test is the Strange Situation, and it is still used today all over the world.

The Strange Situation is a short observational experiment in which the researcher watches how a child reacts to being with their mother, then being left alone with

First steps **15**

a stranger, then being with their mother again, then being on their own, and then their mother returning for the final time. Each phase lasts a couple of minutes, and the focus is to observe the levels of child separation distress, their reaction to the stranger, and their reaction to their mother's return. It is based on ideas of both proximity and protection (following Bowlby) and that the mother forms a secure base for exploration for the child (Ainsworth's own idea).

Ainsworth's work led to her identifying three types of attachment which most children could be categorised as falling into, and which are associated with different broad-level patterns of parenting behaviour:

Type A, or Avoidant Attachment: these children would explore the space without returning to their mother to 'check in' for reassurance, showed little distress when she left the room, and deliberately ignored her when she came back. Parents of these children (mothers were still the focus of her work, as with Bowlby) tended to be slow to respond to the distress of their children, were uncomfortable with close physical contact with their child, reported often or consistently feeling angry or frustrated with their baby, and tended to be both rigid and overly interfering in their interactions with their child.

Type B, or Secure Attachment: these children used their mother as a 'secure base' for exploring the room, coming back to her to show her things they liked or when they found something scary. They showed some distress when their mother left the room, and had a positive and excited response to her returning. Mothers of these children were responsive to their child's needs and distress, were emotionally expressive and psychologically accessible when interacting with their children (they showed and talked about having emotions as normal and positive, and modelled how to manage them), and tended to be flexible and co-operative when interacting with their child rather than trying to control what was happening minutely.

Type C, or Resistant/Ambivalent Attachment: these children were reluctant to explore the room even when their mothers were present, showed extreme distress when she left the room, and when she returned they ran to her but then refused to be comforted by contact with her, instead staying extremely upset. When looking at parenting styles, it was found that the mothers of these children were inconsistent in how they responded to child distress, sometimes helping and sometimes ignoring them. They also tended to be 'inept' in physical interactions, being visibly uncomfortable with physical affection from their child and rarely exhibiting spontaneous affection. When playing with their child, they showed occasional interference, sometimes being overbearing, sometimes being flexible and responsive, and sometimes ignoring them.

Later work from a team led by Solomon identified a further fourth type of attachment:

Type D, or Mixed Attachment: these children did not show any consistent strategies when interacting with their mothers, and in fact showed different

16 First steps

strategies with different adults. They are normally found to have an underlying predisposition to one of the three main types, but if they feel that this often fails then they switch between approaches while feeling 'let down' by the adults they are trying to interact with. They often have confused or fearful expectations of their caregiver, arising from inconsistent reactions from that person, including ones which increase their distress rather than decrease it. Type D is common among children who have severely disordered family lives, especially those with mothers who themselves have childhood trauma and attachment issues and therefore lack internal working models of secure attachment.

There are some critiques of Ainsworth's work. She assumes a certain set of home life experiences based on child behaviour rather than extended observations of the parent and child interacting, based her ideas of good parent–child attachment on her own Western ideas about families, and the test is very much lab based rather than being about how children interact with their mothers in natural everyday contexts. Despite these issues, her work still forms the underlying basis for a lot of how we understand early attachment, including how researchers have interpreted attachment amongst very young autistic children.

Sarah's Earliest Relationships

I am the youngest of three autistic siblings, a sister to two older brothers, born in the late 60s into an aspirational, white middle-class family in the South East of England. I don't have many very early memories, just snap-shots really. I have a vague impression of being in a pram under a tree and then screaming loudly as I trapped my finger in a Wendy house door at nursery, but not much else, apart from the following scene.

I had an altercation with one of the school gerbils that my brothers were looking after, early in the morning before anyone else was awake in the house. I had taken it out of its cage to play with it and it clearly wasn't happy with that arrangement, as I ended up being badly bitten and with my hands covered in blood. I went into my parents' bedroom crying, but they didn't help me and instead told me off for disturbing them. I then remember being upset, stuffing some random clothing into a small bag and shouting out that I had had enough and was leaving home. All I could hear was laughter. I was being mocked by my family, but I don't recall exactly who was mocking me. I then left and ran down the road, but was not able to go any further as I had reached the main road and I wasn't allowed to cross it. Being a child who needed rules and certainty I had nowhere to go but to retrace my steps back to the house. I can still feel the strength of the emotion of my younger self as I am writing this now. I did not want to go back to face more shaming, but had no choice. What four-year-old does? I returned, unpacked, and as I cannot recall anyone offering me any sense of comfort or reassurance, I'm guessing that none was offered.

This may well be my first memory of an autistic meltdown. I didn't ever have many and I suspect that I learned from an early age to internalise and shut down emotionally as any outbursts or distress would either not have been tolerated or derided. I know that meltdowns are involuntary; they happen to autistic people when completely overwhelmed and stressed out. They are not manipulative tantrums; they are the explosive outpouring of an overloaded sensory and emotional system, but for a young, undiagnosed autistic child living in a cold and sterile environment who needed to learn any behaviour that could earn approval and love, a meltdown wasn't going to help with this. Overwhelm is powerful, but so is shame and I think that it was this that caused me to turn inward over time and learn to shut down instead. I guess my family had unconsciously developed its own form of Applied Behavioural Analysis (ABA), utilising shame to rid me of behaviours that were deemed unacceptable or not to the required standard.

This is all that I can recall of my very early years. Growing up I had a close relationship with the oldest of my two brothers as our characters and the way we experienced our then unknown autism were similar. Doug and I were loud and rambunctious, and he was protective of his little 'sis', whereas our middle brother was quieter and more solitary. I do not remember having had any sense of warmth, closeness, or emotional connection from either parent, and therapy undertaken as a middle-aged adult revealed a development of unhealthy early attachments, which included elements of Dismissive Avoidant and Anxious Preoccupied styles with Fearful Avoidant being my dominant modus operandi. I recognise a combination of these three insecure attachment styles in my familial, friendship, and romantic relationships well into adulthood, which have thankfully now developed into more secure ones. My relationships were characterised by high levels of fear of rejection and clinginess, especially with boyfriends in my teens. My first marriage was disastrous, as we both had unhealthy attachment styles, and although there was a sense of escaping our difficult pasts by being together, we ended up damaging and hurting each other further.

It would be easy to apportion blame to my parents for not fulfilling my emotional needs from an early age. However, intergenerational trauma as well as autism runs through my family and I have come to the conclusion that they simply didn't have the tools to be warm, loving caregivers and that this, in all likelihood, stems in part from their own early childhood experiences, a lack of healthy supportive attachment with their own parents, and, I suspect, the additional trauma of growing up undiagnosed autists themselves.

18 First steps

Attachment, autism, and early parent relationships

Attachment between autistic children and their parents has had quite a lot of attention from researchers, particularly between (roughly) the mid 1980s and the late 1990s. This was a time when a lot of attachment research was happening in general, and autistic children were of interest because of the known differences – and assumed difficulties –in their relationships. This means that there are actually a lot of studies out there we can look at for evidence from the literature, covering everything from prevalence of types of attachment among autistic children to how parents think about their relationship with their autistic child.

The note of caution this comes with is linked to the time period when the majority of this work was done. This was a point when the neurodiversity movement had not emerged into general academic consciousness, when research was very much something done 'to' or 'about' autistic people rather than with them, and when many researchers (and people in general) believed in and perpetuated deficit-focussed narratives about autism. These papers, now, make for difficult and potentially distressing reading, and anyone wanting to follow up on what we say here by reading them should be prepared for that. Throughout this chapter, and the book overall, we will attempt to minimise this as much as possible by rephrasing problematic language and giving critical reflections on research, but we cannot go back and change what was done or concluded, and there is not currently much neurodiversity-informed work being done in the area which we can refer to instead.

The consistent and key message from all the research, even the older work, is that autistic children *can* and *do* form secure attachments. Reviews of studies which did the Strange Situation with autistic young children have shown that around 47% of autistic children were classified as having a secure attachment style (Teague et al., 2017), which means that they are slightly more likely to be insecurely attached than non-autistic children. Some studies have also suggested that autistic toddlers are more likely to display a disorganised attachment style, but this may be because they seem to have a lower stress response to the Strange Situation test and therefore react differently (Naber et al., 2007). Parents who are warm and supportive are more likely to have a child who is securely attached, regardless of neurotype, and the differences in parenting approach were still recalled by our contributors when they were well into adulthood:

> I drove my parents crazy as a small child because I always used to ask, "why?" Neither of my parents could manage me but the good thing about my Dad was that he just let me be who I was, whereas my Mum was always trying to mould me into this, "you'll never get on if you don't do this".
>
> *(anonymous, 48, trans man)*

It is possible that the Strange Situation itself may be more distressing for autistic toddlers than non-autistic toddlers, because autistic people are more likely to find unexpected changes such as a separation from their mother distressing. This concern has led to the development of an adapted version of the experiment which only has one period of separation, rather than several, and this is usually used in research along with the Attachment Behaviour Form. The idea that autistic children may display different behaviours during the Strange Situation has been looked at in a few studies, with findings that they tend to be less obviously reciprocal in their relationship with their mother (still almost universally the target adult in these studies) and having differences in joint attention to, and sharing of, toys with their mother in that portion of the experiment. Autistic children have also been shown to be more avoidant of the stranger when they are alone than non-autistic children (Filippello et al., 2015), which makes sense in the context of the higher levels of anxiety and lower levels of social confidence that are typical for autistic people.

Along with research into what type of attachment autistic children display, there has been a whole range of studies which try to identify what factors lead to more secure attachments for autistic children. In non-autistic children, parenting is seen as a key component of attachment type development, as we discussed earlier in the chapter. This has also been looked at among the parents of autistic children. For example, it has been shown that mothers who actively try to imagine and understand how their autistic child is experiencing the world, and who are accepting of their child's diagnosis, are more likely to have a secure attachment bond with their child (Oppenheim et al., 2009). It would have been incredibly interesting if these researchers had asked whether the mothers themselves were autistic, or looked at whether there was a link with mother's autism traits, but sadly they did not do so. More recent work around autistic parenting of autistic children has suggested that autistic mothers feel they are better able to understand their child and therefore support them and bond with them more effectively than some non-autistic mothers do (Adams et al., 2021). This shows why it is important to include measures of maternal autism in studies into autistic child-parent relationships, as there may be a whole world of insights which are currently missing from the literature.

Indeed other studies into autistic child-parent attachment, and adult perceptions of that attachment, have shown that how non-autistic parents perceive their attachment relationship with their autistic child is strongly linked to their overall parenting experiences. It has generally been shown that these parents feel that their autistic child is less attached to them than parents of children with other disabilities do (i.e. Sakaguchi & Beppu, 2007). For fathers in particular – in one of the few studies which included them, and then looked at differences between fathers and mothers – it was shown that the more stressful they found parenting their autistic child, the less they felt their child was attached to them (an interesting commentary perhaps on the idea that being 'easy' or obedient is associated with being 'loving' for some parents). The same study also showed that both fathers and mothers felt that a child who had lower levels of independent functioning was less attached to them, suggesting a link between the (lack of) traditional performance of affection and the perception that this means there is a lack of affection at all (Goodman & Glenwick, 2012).

20 First steps

As mentioned frequently in this chapter, most attachment work focusses on children's relationships with their mothers. One study which looked at attachment to fathers, however, raised an interesting point – it found that autistic children had a much stronger dislike of being laughed at than non-autistic children, and that this had a negative impact on their attachment to their fathers, but not mothers (Wu et al., 2015). This suggests that the different types of interactions which are often typical of fathers and mothers, whereby mothers tend to be calmer and fathers tend to be the ones who engage in more boisterous play (the type more likely to result in laughing with or at a child), can lead to differences in attachment style with each parent. The researchers do make some caveats clear – this is not necessarily 'an autism thing' but can be an individual personality thing, and different cultures have different levels of 'normal' amounts of being laughed at/laughing at others, which may mean that this relationship does not hold true outside the Taiwanese setting of the study. This chimes with the memories of one of our contributors of his relationship with his father, where rather than having the 'traditional' playful relationship, it was tense:

> He is not a remotely patient person. He just seemed to be angry all the time. My perception as a child is that I was the one who made him angry the most, which looking back is an interesting thing because he probably found me a frustrating and strange child. I know he said to my eldest brother recently that he doesn't think he has ever had much in common with me.
>
> *(anonymous)*

Attachment does not end in early childhood. (The next section of this chapter, 'Long-term Impact of Attachment', rather proves that point!) There have also been a few studies looking at the attachments of older autistic children, such as work with a group of 8- to 12-year-olds, which found that autistic children were just as likely to have secure attachment in middle childhood as their non-autistic peers, and that both children and parents rated their attachment as similarly strong and supportive (Chandler & Dissanayake, 2014). While this may feel like an obvious conclusion to many of our readers, it is important because it shows that autistic children's attachments and relationships develop in similar ways to those of non-autistic children, and therefore we are justified in some of the extrapolations we may make from one group to the other, and in the types of social development we are interested in exploring more deeply with autistic people.

It has been argued that the reliance on questionnaires both in this and other studies of attachment in middle childhood is flawed, as this relies on the child completing it being able to reflect on and recognise their attachment relationships, and on them interpreting the questionnaires in the way which non-autistic researchers designed them to be interpreted (Giannotti & de Falco, 2021). It has been shown in other areas of autism research that this assumption around shared interpretations can be problematic, such as the findings from Sarah Cassidy and her team at the University of Nottingham that mental health and suicidality measures need to be adapted for autistic people in order to accurately capture their state of mind and risk level (Cassidy et al., 2020). If measures are not adapted to be specific for autistic people, this can lead to missed or misdiagnoses. For example, one paper has argued that it is important to make sure that attachment measures can distinguish between autistic children and children with reactive attachment disorder (RAD), a condition where, due to early childhood abuse, children form disorganised and indiscriminate superficial attachments rather than genuine long-term stable bonds. At first glance, the attachment behaviours of the two groups can look similar, because autistic children display their attachments in different ways than expected, just as children with RAD do. However, the researchers found that autistic children had significantly fewer 'indiscriminate friendliness' behaviours than those with RAD, along with differences in how high quality their social interactions are, something which was only clear during structured observations rather than from questionnaires (Davidson et al., 2015). This emphasises the need for research to go beyond statistical analysis of written measures, and to spend time with autistic children and young people, including listening to their own stories of their experiences – something we have done throughout this book.

Long-term impact of attachment

Considering the widely acknowledged importance of early attachment for everyone, regardless of neurotype, it should come as no surprise that there has also been research into whether and what effect this might have on people longer term. It turns out – quite a lot.

When talking about the impact of early attachment on friendships, for example, it has been shown that children who have a secure attachment style have more, and better, friends than those who are insecurely attached (Raikes & Thompson, 2008). This is because they tend to be more emotionally stable and are more able to manage their emotions when things go wrong with friendships, meaning that they are more capable of negotiating solutions to whatever the problem is – and therefore they are more likely to keep the friendship. In contrast, children with an insecure avoidant attachment style tend to have a high level of fear of rejection, which can lead to both clinginess and aloofness and contribute to poor peer relationships, as these tend not to be desirable behaviours for other children (Groh et al., 2014). They are also likely to have friends who also have an insecure attachment style, as their behaviours are more understandable or acceptable to each other (Hodges et al., 1999). Looking at the final main attachment style, research into the friendship experiences of children with an insecure resistant/ambivalent attachment style has shown that they tend to have the most behavioural issues of the groups, and are likely to 'act out' for attention from peers and adults. They often display very high intensity emotions – similar to the extreme distress they showed when their mother left in the Strange Situation experiment – and are likely to be bullied by their peers because they are therefore easy to get a reaction from. While these children obviously can and do have friends, their friendships may be more tempestuous than

22 First steps

those of securely attached children, which can be hard for any child to make sense of – especially as their reactions will often not be conscious choices but immediate responses.

Moving beyond friendships and attachment, originally lifespan work around attachment was actually interested in how romantic relationships in adulthood were related to early experiences. Ainsworth herself saw 'pair bonds' between adults as the equivalent of adult attachment bonds, because within that relationship the two people (generally) seek proximity with each other (want to be close), feel secure within the relationship (we hope!), dislike separation, share things they are excited about with each other, and display 'a mutual fascination with one another'.

In a famous study of attachment and adult relationships, Hazan and Shaver in 1987 found that all three attachment types can be seen in adults, with behaviour in adult relationships mimicking that seen in the Strange Situation. For example, adults who reported warm and positive relationships with their parents (securely attached) endorsed the statement "I find it relatively easy to get close to others and am comfortable depending on them and having them depend on me. I don't worry about being abandoned or about someone getting too close to me". Adults who reported more inconsistent or emotionally unpredictable relationships with their parents (insecurely resistant/ambivalent attached) instead were more likely to endorse the statement "I find that others are reluctant to get as close as I would like. I often worry that my partner doesn't really love me or won't want to stay with me. I want to get very close to my partner, and this sometimes scares people away". They found that with this (admittedly very simple) measure, roughly 60% of adults classified themselves as securely attached, 20% as insecure avoidant, and 20% as insecure resistant/ambivalent – similar to the percentages seen in Ainsworth's work with young children, and which have been replicated elsewhere.

Researchers have found that securely attached adults are self-confident, seek emotional intimacy with their partners, and tend not to be neurotic about their relationships, whereas insecurely attached adults had higher levels of neuroticism (worrying about their partner and the relationship) and lacked self-confidence both in forming relationships and about keeping their partner (Feeney & Noller, 1990). Building on this study, it has been found that people with insecure resistant/ambivalent attachment can be impetuous and demanding of their partners, wanting repeated displays and reassurances of affection – in line with the emotional intensity seen in young children with this attachment type (Crittenden, 1995). Adults with an insecure avoidant attachment style, similarly, had behavioural patterns which echo those seen in children in the Strange Situation, avoiding intimacy with their partners or caregiving roles, often because they expect a negative emotional response such as being chastised for relying on someone or because they expect to be rejected by their partner (Collins et al., 2003).

Following on from Hazan and Shaver's work, researcher Kathy Brennan worked to explore the aspects of adult attachment in more detail. She and her team found two key dimensions: attachment-related anxiety and attachment-related avoidance. Those high in attachment-related anxiety often worry about whether or not their partner is truly interested, available, and committed to them, whereas people low in attachment-related anxiety are more trusting in the responsiveness and genuine affection of their partner. Looking at attachment-related avoidance, people who have high levels of this are generally reluctant to rely on or open up to other people, whereas those with low levels of avoidance are more likely to be comfortable both with relying on others and others relying on them. This results in a categorisation of four types of attachment style in adults:

	Low avoidance	*Low anxiety*
High avoidance	Secure	Avoidant
High anxiety	Preoccupied	Resistant/ambivalent

These two key dimensions have more recently been explored and identified in young children too, which further emphasises that patterns of attachment are consistent across the lifespan – even as our theories are refined and improved, the finding that the same things are found in childhood and adulthood remains. This has been statistically tested by Fraley as well, with small to moderate correlations between parental attachment and romantic attachment styles – meaning that the more securely attached someone is to their significant parent, the more likely they are to be securely attached to their romantic partner.

This has important consequences. It shows just how central our early attachment experiences are for our relationships over the lifespan. While people with any predominant attachment style are more than capable – and likely – to have relationships, this can require more or different work from both partners depending on each person's situation. Having strong and similar communication styles is an especially good predictor of relationship success, even for those with different attachment styles (O'Connell Corcoran & Mallinckrodt, 2000).

How this plays out for autistic adults has, as with many aspects of what this book covers, been less researched, but what we know so far is discussed in later chapters.

Siblings

Parents, of course, are often not the only people young children spend a lot of time with at home. Most will have siblings, and just as attachment bonds form with parents, so they form with brothers and sisters. Our siblings are usually our first 'practice ground' for learning skills like negotiation, perspective taking, and communication skills with peers. There is research that shows that children actually spend more time with their siblings than with their parents after the first year or so of life (and then more time with peers at school than with family, but this is discussed in the next chapter). This means that, just as parents have a significant impact on how someone thinks about relationships, so do their interactions with their siblings.

24 First steps

This influence can be seen in a whole range of areas of development. Good sibling relationships have been shown to be associated with better self-concept and self-esteem, as you get positive reinforcement from your early interactions with a peer who is usually emotionally important to you. This is especially the case with older siblings, who often take on a kind of 'teaching' role for their younger brothers and sisters (Howe & Recchia, 2005) and therefore are held in higher esteem due to the skills they pass on (and often because the younger sibling thinks they are cool!). Having a supportive sibling and a warm relationship with them is associated with fewer behavioural and mental health issues, and better long-term adjustment and well-being overall (Waldinger et al., 2007). Siblings have an important impact on how many areas of our identity develop – it has been shown, for example, that they have as much impact on our gender identity as parents do, that having an older sibling 'speeds up' gender identity development (because you have a close age-mate to model from), and that the cooler your older sibling is, the more influence they have over this identity development.

The process of identity development is not straightforward, though, and while many siblings will intentionally or unintentionally develop to be like each other in a lot of ways, this is not always the case (obviously). De-identification theory (Whiteman et al., 2007) argues that some people, consciously or unconsciously, work to differentiate themselves from their siblings – whether this is on the grounds of hobbies, interests, or life choices. This helps individuals to establish a unique space and role within the family, thereby reducing sibling rivalry and allowing for more positive relationships overall.

Autism and sibling relationships

A major complicating factor for autistic children developing their identity within a family system, though, is masking. Masking, or camouflaging, has been defined in research as "a mismatch between external behaviours and internal state" regarding autism traits (Lai et al., 2017). How autistic people talk about it is a bit more accessible – for them, it is the process of consciously trying to hide or suppress their natural autistic behaviours so that they stand out less to other people, and therefore can try to avoid some of the stigmatising and negative attitudes they can encounter. (We're biased, but we would recommend you look at Felicity's other book for a summary of both research and lived experience around autism and masking, as it goes into more detail and has contributions from a range of autistic people who have different experiences – *Autism and Masking*, Sedgewick, Hull & Ellis, 2021.) The thing is, if you are masking these aspects of your authentic autistic self, and consciously copying other people to try to 'get it right' socially and behaviourally – it is easy to end up copying aspects of their identity as well, and this can make it hard to understand what is truly 'you' and what is the 'mask' you are putting on. We will talk about masking a lot elsewhere in the book, and the impact it has long term on autistic people, but even in childhood it plays a role in how autistic children develop – one that has not yet really been researched.

It has traditionally been assumed that one child being autistic will disrupt sibling relationships in some way, with a focus on the potential negative impacts on things like closeness or even the social development of the non-autistic child. For example, non-autistic siblings report finding their autistic brother or sister more difficult than a non-autistic sibling is typically rated, and that they are less close, with fewer positive interactions (Kaminsky & Dewey, 2001). It had also been assumed that, because our siblings act as practice for wider social interactions, those with autistic siblings would get less of this practice and themselves have challenges interacting with peers outside the family. When looking at the impact on the development of the non-autistic sibling, studies originally found that these children were more likely to have behavioural problems (Rodrigue et al., 1993). However, as researchers started to come to autism work with a more open mind as to how having an autistic sibling could impact a non-autistic child and look beyond the traditionally expected negatives, they found a whole other side of the story. For example, even in the early 2000s, a study showed that the siblings of autistic children were well-adjusted, were not lonely, and generally felt that they had good social support in their lives (Kaminsky & Dewey, 2002). Equally, many of our contributors had good early relationships with their siblings in some social contexts and these helped their development:

> All the neighbourhood kids were younger and I could be my playful self with them. My brother and sister were there too, but that was fine. When we were in the group, play was easy and fun and I'd get along with my siblings.
>
> *(Eleanor, autistic woman)*

Among families where at least one child is autistic, a lot of research into sibling relationships initially focussed on the views of non-autistic children and young people on having an autistic sibling, and how this affected family dynamics as they aged and potentially took on caring roles. The findings on what characterises autistic/non-autistic sibling relationships has been mixed – as should probably be expected, considering how varied sibling relationships can be even between non-autistic pairs. One study found that the relationship tended to have less aggression but also less involvement between the siblings and more avoidance of each other (Walton & Ingersoll, 2015). It has been shown that the more behavioural issues an autistic child has, the less close their relationship with their sibling is likely to be – though the study which gives this result only asked the non-autistic sibling, so we do not know what the autistic children in the study thought about their relationship (Hastings & Petalas, 2014).

A different study by some of the same people, however, explicitly focussed on asking autistic teenagers how they felt about their siblings – although it should be noted that the sample was 11 boys and one girl, so there is a lack of the views of autistic girls still (Petalas et al., 2015). What they found was that autistic adolescents talked about basically having a lot of very typical interactions with their siblings – both things like in-jokes and playing together on the positive side, and things like

26 First steps

fights over not sharing or an inability to 'get' each other's interests on the negative side, for example. Alongside this, though, autistic teenagers acknowledged that some of their interaction with their siblings was influenced by them being autistic, such as the greater difficulty they had with controlling their emotions and how this could lead them to lash out and hurt a sibling without meaning to, or how it meant that they had different social interaction styles which could lead to conflict – either arguments, or one of the siblings feeling 'unwanted' by the other due to mismatched desires for spending time together. This finding, though, again puts the lie to the Social Motivation Theory that we mentioned in Chapter 1 – autistic children would not be upset or hurt by their sibling not wanting to spend time with them right now if they lacked social motivation, as that theory suggested.

Some recent research into the sibling relationships of autistic children and young people, however, rather than emphasising difficulty and dependency, has shown how strong and positive these often are. Some of the key work in this area has come from Dr Georgia Pavlopoulou, who worked with nine girls between the ages of 10 and 14 who had autistic brothers and sisters (Pavlopoulou & Dimitriou, 2019). She used a novel methodology – not just questionnaires or adults observing the siblings together and coming up with their own interpretations of what was going on. She used something called Photovoice, which asks the participants to take photos of things that are important to them or relevant to the topic (such as their relationship with their autistic sibling) and then the researcher has a conversation with them about the photos they have taken, and analyses what everyone chooses and why to look for patterns. The title of the paper this study is reported in sums up the key message: 'I Don't Live with Autism, I Live with My Sister'. Sisters of autistic children emphasised the importance of the sibling relationship over the importance of the diagnosis. Other themes did acknowledge the impact having an autistic sibling had – things like being asked to help with caring for their sibling, and the feeling that society 'doesn't care' about them and their families, for example. The participants talked about how much they loved their sibling, and how much they enjoyed time spent doing things together, despite being aware of and struggling with these challenges, which at times caused frustration. Overall, the picture was positive and of children who are happy to have the siblings they have, regardless of any difficulties.

Our contributors' stories also emphasise the ways in which siblings can be a really positive presence in the lives of young autistic children. For example, Kenzi's mum talked about him and his sister, and how his sister supported him when he was young and struggled to communicate his needs:

> Kenzi relied a lot on his older sister Leah as she was the one who would do a lot of the talking for him. She just seemed to know what he wanted. So she just tended to tell people what he wanted and he didn't interact much with other people.
>
> *(Kenzi, 13, autistic male)*

When these relationships are positive, it has been suggested that it can be worthwhile to include siblings in interventions for autistic children, with positive outcomes for both children – the autistic child seems to engage more with their brother or sister than an adult, and it builds a more positive relationship as they are spending time together doing something which is (usually) designed to be fun (Ferraoilo et al., 2012). Of course, it is important not to make siblings the only or main people involved in any intervention – having the chance to have as normal a sibling relationship as possible is better for both children than most interventions can be shown to be.

Sibling relationships do not always go smoothly, especially for the oldest child who can feel like they are losing out to the new baby. This is true for autistic older siblings as much as non-autistic children, though it has not been explored in the literature:

> When I was three my little brother was born and when I was five my little sister was born. It was difficult for me because I felt like my parents had no attention left for me. My sister was our mother's favourite and my brother was my father's favourite. The only role I seemed to have left was to be the good kid.
>
> *(Eleanor, autistic woman)*

Early years care

For many, if not most, young children, family members are not their only caregivers. It is very common for children to spend some time in structured childcare settings outside the nuclear family, whether this is other relatives, nursery, a childminder, or communal childcare, as is common in many cultures outside the West. This means that there are a whole other set of adults and children which they regularly interact with and are likely to form affectionate relationships with. For many children this is a space and time which is a lot of fun, as they make their first friends. One of our contributors, remembering going to nursery for the first time, said this:

> I do have a clear memory of being in preschool and having this weird curiosity around other people and other kids. Even that far back I knew that my interaction with other people was different to how they interacted amongst those without me and I felt different and outside the group, right back as far as aged 3 I suppose.
>
> *(anonymous, 54, autistic woman)*

Before focussing on childcare and attachment, it is worth a brief review of research into what time in childcare does for children's development more broadly as well, as this is an important context for everything else we are interested in. Cognitive development, social development, mental health and self-esteem, and temperament – all have been the focus of a range of investigations. Children's early years, and their time in childcare, is an area of significant investment in most countries globally, and there is a corresponding amount of research we could look at. The key takeaway

28 First steps

points though, are that time in group childcare can help with social and emotional development, because it gives children a chance to interact with their peers and practice skills like sharing, playing together, and making friends. It can help with academic development and school readiness, because children get to do activities which they wouldn't necessarily at home, and because the day follows a similar pattern to school, getting them used to listening to teachers for example. There have been some suggestions that too much time in childcare can have a negative impact on very young children, if it interferes with them developing secure attachments with their primary caregivers for example, but this is when looking at children who spend several long days a week there, which is generally unusual.

Moving back to attachment with adults, which is the main focus of this chapter, it has been shown that non-autistic children do indeed form responsive and individual relationships with preferred individual carers – a reasonable proxy for attachment bonds in this setting. This is especially the case when they are seeing a regular child minder in a small group setting versus being in a larger nursery where there is often high turnover of staff and less time with any specific adult. Staff turnover can disrupt relationships with the children, which sounds like an obvious statement, but this comes from the change in overall dynamics of the childcare setting as well as the more absolute ending of the bond with the staff member who has left. Also important when thinking about this is that few early years staff receive much (if any) training about attachment and relationships, so while they are doing their best to be warm and supportive and emotionally available for the children, they are doing this without knowing best practice. It can also be emotionally demanding for staff to try to build these relationships with multiple very young children, who themselves often pass through each stage of early years care with high frequency, which can lead some members of staff to 'check out' on that side of their job (Page & Elfer, 2013). It has also been pointed out that the increasingly 'risk-averse climate' of early years education may discourage some professionals from being overly demonstrative with the children they care for, even if they would like to feel more confident doing so. This is likely having a negative impact, not only on their ability to care for young children well but also on the children's feelings about spending time with those adults. However, there is a general consensus that children can and do form positive relationships with early years staff, and that these relationships help with their learning and general social development.

Autism and early years care

There are no studies of whether these same patterns and problems occur for autistic children in early years settings. This is largely because it is usually too early in life for a child to have been diagnosed as autistic, and so we cannot study whether their relationships with staff are different to non-autistic children. There may well be some autistic children included in the preceding samples, but we don't know for sure and we can't do any comparisons. Attachment testing of young children isn't common enough for us to look at their relationships retrospectively after diagnosis either. We can make some reasonable guesses – that autistic young children find it harder to build these kinds of relationships with staff members, and that they are more distressed by the rapid turnover of staff due to their preference for predictability and familiarity, for example. Hopefully, though, their primary attachments are strong and secure, and therefore their relationships with adults at nursery have minimal impact on their overall social development.

Chapter conclusion

It can be easy to assume that because young children do not yet have the same understanding of the world as older children or adults their experiences will not affect them as much. When it comes to relationships, the opposite can be true – because they cannot rationalise their feelings the same way, they can become more impactful. From early caregiver attachments to sibling and peer relationships, young children are learning about other people for the first time, and they carry those lessons with them for the rest of their lives – autistic children just as much as anyone else.

References

Adams, D., Stainsby, M., & Paynter, J. (2021). Autistic mothers of autistic children: A preliminary study in an under-researched area, *3*(4), 339–346. https://doi.org/10.1089/AUT.2020.0078

Cassidy, S., Bradley, L., Cogger-Ward, H., & Rodgers, J. (2020). *Development and validation of the suicide behaviours questionnaire-autism spectrum conditions in autistic, Possibly autistic and non-autistic adults.* https://doi.org/10.21203/rs.3.rs-48455/v1

Chandler, F., & Dissanayake, C. (2014). An investigation of the security of caregiver attachment during middle childhood in children with high-functioning autistic disorder. *Autism, 18*(5), 485–492. https://doi.org/10.1177/1362361313486205

Cozzarelli, C., Karafa, J. A., Collins, N. L., & Tagler, M. J. (2003). Attachment style stability stability and change in adult attachment styles: Associations with personal vulnerabilities, Life events, and global construals of self and others. *Journal of Social and Clinical Psychology, 22*(3), 315–346.

Crittenden, P. M. (1995). Attachment and risk for psychopathology. *Journal of Developmental & Behavioral Pediatrics, 16*(3), 12–16. https://doi.org/10.1097/00004703-199506001-00004

Davidson, C., O'Hare, A., Mactaggart, F., Green, J., Young, D., Gillberg, C., & Minnis, H. (2015). Social relationship difficulties in autism and reactive attachment disorder: Improving diagnostic validity through structured assessment. *Research in Developmental Disabilities, 40*, 63–72. https://doi.org/10.1016/J.RIDD.2015.01.007

Feeney, J. A., & Noller, P. (1990). Attachment style as a predictor of adult romantic relationships. *Journal of Personality and Social Psychology, 58*(2), 281–291. https://doi.org/10.1037/0022-3514.58.2.281

Ferraioli, S. J., Hansford, A., & Harris, S. L. (2012). Benefits of including siblings in the treatment of autism spectrum disorders. *Cognitive and Behavioral Practice, 19*(3), 413–422. https://doi.org/10.1016/J.CBPRA.2010.05.005

Filippello, P., Flavia, M., Sorrenti, L., Marino, F., & Chilà, P. (2015). Attachment and social behavior in children's autistic disorders. *Life Span and Disability XVIII, 1*, 101–118. www.researchgate.net/publication/279525695

Giannotti, M., & de Falco, S. (2021). Attachment and autism spectrum disorder (without intellectual disability) During middle childhood: Search of the missing piece. *Frontiers in Psychology, 12.* https://doi.org/10.3389/FPSYG.2021.662024

Goodman, S. J., & David, G. S. (2012). Correlates of attachment perceptions in parents of children with autism spectrum disorders. *Journal of autism and developmental disorders, 42*(10), 2056–2066. https://doi.org/10.1007/s10803-012-1453-8

Groh, A. M., Fearon, R. P., Bakermans-Kranenburg, M. J., van Ijzendoorn, M. H., Steele, R. D., & Roisman, G. I. (2014). The significance of attachment security for children's social competence with peers: A meta-analytic study. *Attachment & human development, 16*(2), 103–136. https://doi.org/10.1080/14616734.2014.883636

Hastings, R. P., & Petalas, M. A. (2014). Self-reported behaviour problems and sibling relationship quality by siblings of children with autism spectrum disorder. *Child: Care, Health and Development, 40*(6), 833–839. https://doi.org/10.1111/CCH.12131

Hodges, E. V. E., & Perry, D. G. (1999). Personal and interpersonal antecedents and consequences of victimization by peers. *Journal of Personality and Social Psychology, 76*(4), 677–685. https://doi.org/10.1037/0022-3514.76.4.677

Howe, N., & Recchia, H. (2005). Playmates and teachers: Reciprocal and complementary interactions between siblings. *Journal of Family Psychology, 19*(4), 497–502. https://doi.org/10.1037/0893-3200.19.4.497

Kaminsky, L., & Dewey, D. (2001). Siblings relationships of children with autism. *Journal of Autism and Developmental Disorders, 31*(4), 399–410. https://doi.org/10.1023/A:1010664603039

Kaminsky, L., & Dewey, D. (2002). Psychosocial adjustment in siblings of children with autism. *Journal of Child Psychology and Psychiatry, 43*(2), 225–232. https://doi.org/10.1111/1469-7610.00015

Lai, M.-C., Lombardo, M. V, Ruigrok, A. N., Chakrabarti, B., Auyeung, B., Szatmari, P., Happé, F., Baron-Cohen, S., & Consortium, M. A. (2017). Quantifying and exploring camouflaging in men and women with autism. *Autism, 21*(6), 690–702. https://doi.org/10.1177/1362361316671012

Naber, F. B. A., Swinkels, S. H. N., Buitelaar, J. K., Bakermans-Kranenburg, M. J., Van IJzendoorn, M. H., Dietz, C., Van Daalen, E., & Van Engeland, H. (2007). Attachment in toddlers with autism and other developmental disorders. *Journal of Autism and Developmental Disorders, 37*(6), 1123–1138. https://doi.org/10.1007/S10803-006-0255-2/TABLES/7

O'Connell Corcoran, K., & Mallinckrodt, B. (2000). Adult attachment, self-efficacy, perspective taking, and conflict resolution. *Journal of Counseling & Development, 78*(4), 473–483. https://doi.org/10.1002/J.1556-6676.2000.TB01931.X

Oppenheim, D., Koren-Karie, N., Dolev, S., & Yirmiya, N. (2009). Maternal insightfulness and resolution of the diagnosis are associated with secure attachment in preschoolers with autism spectrum disorders. *Child Development, 80*(2), 519–527. https://doi.org/10.1111/J.1467-8624.2009.01276.X

Page, J., & Elfer, P. (2013). The emotional complexity of attachment interactions in nursery. *European Early Childhood Education Research Journal, 21*(4), 553–567. https://doi.org/10.1080/1350293X.2013.766032

Pavlopoulou, G., & Dimitriou, D. (2019). 'I don't live with autism; I live with my sister'. Sisters' accounts on growing up with their preverbal autistic siblings. *Research in Developmental Disabilities, 88*, 1–15. https://doi.org/10.1016/J.RIDD.2019.01.013

Petalas, M. A., Hastings, R. P., Nash, S., & Duff, S. (2015). Typicality and subtle difference in sibling relationships: Experiences of adolescents with autism. *Journal of Child and Family Studies, 24*(1), 38–49. https://doi.org/10.1007/S10826-013-9811-5/TABLES/3

Raikes, H. A., & Thompson, R. A. (2008). Attachment security and parenting quality predict children's problem-solving, attributions, and loneliness with peers. *Attachment & human development*, *10*(3), 319–344. https://doi.org/10.1080/14616730802113620

Rodrigue, J. R., Geffken, G. R., & Morgan, S. B. (1993). Perceived competence and behavioral adjustment of siblings of children with autism. *Journal of Autism and Developmental Disorders*, *23*(4), 665–674. https://doi.org/10.1007/BF01046108

Sakaguchi, M., & Beppu, S. (2007). Structure of stressors in mothers of preschool children with autism. *Japanese Journal of Special Education*, *45*(3), 127.

Sedgewick, F., Hull, L., & Ellis, H. (2021). *Autism and masking: How and why people do it, and the impact it can have*. Jessica Kingsley Publishers.

Teague, S. J., Gray, K. M., Tonge, B. J., & Newman, L. K. (2017). Attachment in children with autism spectrum disorder: A systematic review. *Research in Autism Spectrum Disorders*, *35*, 35–50. https://doi.org/10.1016/J.RASD.2016.12.002

Waldinger, R. J., Vaillant, G. E., & Orav, E. J. (2007). Childhood sibling relationships as a predictor of major depression in adulthood: A 30-year prospective study. *American Journal of Psychiatry*, *164*(6), 949–954. https://doi.org/10.1176/AJP.2007.164.6.949/ASSET/IMAGES/LARGE/R821T4.JPEG

Walton, K. M., & Ingersoll, B. R. (2015). Psychosocial adjustment and sibling relationships in siblings of children with autism spectrum disorder: Risk and protective factors. *Journal of Autism and Developmental Disorders*, *45*(9), 2764–2778. https://doi.org/10.1007/S10803-015-2440-7/TABLES/5

Whiteman, S. D., McHale, S. M., & Crouter, A. C. (2007). Competing processes of sibling influence: Observational learning and sibling deidentification. *Social Development*, *16*(4), 642–661. https://doi.org/10.1111/J.1467-9507.2007.00409.X

Wu, C. L., An, C. P., Tseng, L. P., Chen, H. C., Chan, Y. C., Cho, S. L., & Tsai, M. L. (2015). Fear of being laughed at with relation to parent attachment in individuals with autism. *Research in Autism Spectrum Disorders*, *10*, 116–123. https://doi.org/10.1016/J.RASD.2014.11.004

2
MOVING ON UP

Childhood friendships

Our friendships are some of the most important, long-lasting, and often defining relationships of our lives. This is even true, in many ways, for those who feel that they do not have friends, because the lack of friendship is often as important to how someone feels about themselves as its presence. Friends help us develop social, emotional, and behavioural skills; they help us do better in school; they support good mental health. Both girls and boys, men and women, garner these benefits from having friends, and the best part is that it is mutual – friendship is a win–win situation for all involved.

Friendships are reciprocal relationships between two people, where those two people spend time together voluntarily and stay in contact to some degree when not together. The relationship is usually characterised by emotional warmth and closeness, security, trust, helpfulness, and a lack of conflict. This is a very academic way of saying that our friends are people we like, we choose to spend time with, we trust, and we feel comfortable around.

Friendships are also among the most defining relationships of our lives, as we just said. Children show an interest in each other from as early as three months old, and show preferences for playing with specific other babies from as young as 11 or 12 months old. This shows both just how instinctive it can be to make friends, and that for most people, from all cultures and of all neurotypes, doing so starts with playing together. Early friendships are absolutely defined by who wants to and enjoys playing with who, to the extent that play behaviours are usually the key thing being observed by interested researchers.

They have, in fact, created a whole hierarchy of play behaviours which describes the level of imagination, interaction, and creativity which is involved in different types of play. This is Parten's Stages of Play:

DOI: 10.4324/9781003044536-3

Moving on up **33**

1 Unoccupied play: this is typical of very young babies, and is mostly about exploration of things around the child. Think of a baby picking up both a plastic toy and their parents car keys, and putting both in their mouths or banging both against the floor. This is about learning to hold and move and manipulate items, learning some self-control, and learning about the world around them.

2 Solitary play: this is when children are keeping themselves entertained, without involving other people in any way – this can be to the point of ignoring or not acknowledging other children or adults. This is also about learning motor skills, working out how different things fit together or can work together. It is very normal for children to play on their own – at many stages of life – and is not something adults should be worried about even though we tend to think of 'play' as an activity with more than one person.

3 Onlooker play: this is when a child is watching other people play without taking an active part in it themselves. Again, this is a very normal part of child behaviour and development – watching other people does not automatically mean that a child is lonely or being left out. All humans learn by watching others (this is called Social Learning Theory and comes from the work of a psychologist called Bandura, who did a famous experiment with Bobo dolls), or simply find watching other people interesting and entertaining.

4 Parallel play: when children are playing next to each other but not really interacting to create a shared game, this is called parallel play. One example could be two children both building towers with blocks – they are both playing the same game, but independently, focussing on their own construction rather than building together. This enables children to start to practice skills at being together while they play without the full intensity and pressures of social integration.

5 Associative play: a major change in how children play comes when they move towards associative play. This is defined as becoming more interested in the other child or children in the game, rather than the game or toys themselves. This stage of play is almost like a practice for playing with other people, starting to combine the motor skills learned in earlier activities with the social skills and requirements of being around other people while you play.

6 Co-operative play: the final stage, which is usually seen as the 'highest' level of play, is co-operative play. This means that the game is co-created between the children involved, with shared understandings of the rules and the goals, rather than being a solo or parallel activity. Co-operation of this kind is a complex skill, and can be very difficult – it often involves a lot of conflict as you work out those shared rules and behaviours in the game, or when things don't go how one participant wanted or when turns are involved. Young children can struggle to manage their emotions, especially when frustrated, and there is a lot of scope for that to happen in a shared game. However, this style of play builds social skills, cognitive skills, and actually helps to build the emotional regulation which then makes it easier to play such games in the future.

34 Moving on up

While we won't explore stages of play in non-autistic and autistic children in detail, it is important to note that autistic children do have a greater propensity towards solitary and parallel play than their same-age peers tend to (Barbu et al., 2011). This doesn't mean that they do not do associative and co-operative play; they absolutely do. Autistic children can and do have rich internal creative and imaginative lives. This is a key element of cooperative play, and this should not be downplayed by the tendency to also play alone more often, for example on the playground (Bauminger et al., 2008). This can be due to their different communication styles, or their increased need for time alone to 'decompress' from social interaction, something which autistic adults have talked about in studies about self-soothing, or friendships, for example. It is also the case that autistic people of all ages find solace and restoration through immersing themselves in their special/intense interests, which helps them to regulate their emotions, anxiety, and social overwhelm. Eleanor talked about how her play preferences as a child were different to those around her, but that these made her happy:

> I used to love playing with pots and pans as a toddler. I would get everything out of the drawer and start banging around. It was my favourite activity.
>
> *(Eleanor, autistic woman)*

Similarly, finding ways to play which made sense to an autistic way of thinking, such as following structures or rules, was what made Louise happiest – and she was confused if the other children wanted to do other things or focus on chatting instead:

> I liked being around other people and children and feeling like I was part of a group, but I couldn't understand why that wasn't enough for them. They always wanted to be talking to each other and doing things with each other and some of those things didn't align with what I wanted to do. They seemed like boring things, and I didn't appear to get a say. So then I would leave them to it and do the things I wanted to do instead. It felt nice when they shared things with me or showed me things that I could relate to or we played games with proper rules like Cluedo.
>
> *(Louise, autistic woman)*

Key social skills

There are some key social skills that go into all our interactions. Things like taking turns to talk in a conversation, knowing how to express your interest in what someone else is saying and how to work out whether they are interested (or bored) by what you are saying, being able to recognise and understand what someone's body language might mean, and how yours might come across, to name but a few. Having the level of these skills your peers expect of you is important for fitting in and making friends, but is something our contributors talked about struggling with from being young:

I really struggled to fit in socially because it was obvious that I was clever, but not in social ways and that created a separation from the start that I just didn't have the skills to overcome.

(Sarah O, autistic woman)

It has consistently been found in research that autistic people, of all ages, perform differently on tests of all these skills. We have already talked about differences in theory of mind, how this led to assumptions about autistic people's ability to feel empathy, and the problems this has embedded into popular conceptions of autism. While this is the most well-known and glaring error that has arisen from research driven by a myopic focus on neurotypicality-as-superior, it is not the only one.

Other studies have looked at things like autistic children's ability to recognise emotions, both in images and in videos of other people. There have been lots of studies which looked at autistic emotion recognition, because it is one of the things which can either be a major barrier or major facilitator for relationships. This makes sense – if you are good at recognising how someone else is feeling, you can change your own reactions to be sympathetic to them, which tends to improve how they think of you and make for a better long-term relationship. Equally, if you are bad at recognising other people's emotions, you will struggle to account for them in your interactions, and this can cause problems if someone is perceived as uncaring or unsympathetic. Research studies have suggested that among autistic children and young people, fewer difficulties with emotion recognition are associated with better social functioning, as well as tending to increase with age – so there is a real-world impact of this skill, and it seems to be one that autistic people learn over time, possibly on a bit of a delay compared to non-autistic people (Trevisan & Birmingham, 2016).

Reviews of the work into autistic emotion recognition (there are dozens, possibly hundreds of reviews, which tells you how many individual studies there are!) have suggested that the overall picture of whether autistic children are good at emotion recognition or not is . . . mixed. Most studies find that they are significantly worse than non-autistic children, some that they are about the same, some that they may even be slightly better (though this is a very rare finding). The reviews emphasise that the wide variety of methods used to carry out investigations into emotion recognition, and very different sample sizes and compositions, are probably to blame for the lack of clarity in results (Wieckowski et al., 2020). Alongside the need for standardisation around measures, there are calls for longitudinal work to try to help us understand how emotion recognition develops over time, rather than just brief snapshots.

It should be remembered, though, that recognising emotions is not automatically the same as responding to them in the way that the other person is expecting, and responding differently than expected is not the same as not caring how they feel. Responsive behaviour is usually used as a proxy for emotion recognition and empathic capacity, but this depends on a lot of assumptions about the 'right' response to the other person. One international research

36 Moving on up

team (which Felicity was part of) specifically looked into this nuance around empathy in young autistic and non-autistic adolescents (Rieffe et al., 2020). As part of a larger set of tasks, at one point the experimenter pretended to trap their finger in the closing rings of a ring binder, saying "ouch" and looking at the part of their hand they had 'hurt' in front of the child. The interaction was video and audio recorded, and the team then coded how adolescents reacted to this scenario. What they found was that all the young people, autistic and non-autistic, paid the same amount of attention to the injured researcher, but autistic boys and girls tended to show less visible emotional responses (often seen as an indication of less affective empathy). Despite this, they offered comfort to the researcher at the same rate, showing that they understood her pain and were affected by it, regardless of how traditionally they expressed their empathy for her situation. Autistic boys tended to respond by suggesting practical solutions to the problem, for example how to close the folder safely, whereas girls (autistic and non-autistic) tended to focus on the emotions of the researcher, for example trying to comfort her and make her feel better. This study showed that even when there are differences in the expression of empathy, it is still present, and highlights the kinds of nuance that much modern neurodiversity-informed research is focussing on, rather than creating a narrative of empathic deficit in autistic people which has been common previously.

Some of the autistic people we talked to for this book talked about the ways in which empathy works for them in friendships – often being something they gave even to those who had been mean or bullied them:

> I'm really loyal and I don't drop people. When my bossy friend was alone after falling out with her friends, I would be friends with her again. I would go back to her because I don't like it when people are alone and ostracised because I know how hard that hurts. So I would invite her in again and I did my best to help her patch it up with the girls because I felt that it was not fair. Which meant that afterwards, she'd drop me like a stone again. They didn't have any empathy for me, but I had empathy for them.
>
> *(Eleanor, autistic woman)*

The team in the aforementioned empathy study also discussed the idea that some of the gender differences they saw between the autistic boys and girls may partially be due to the impact of socialisation. Generally, boys and girls are taught different social skills, and autistic girls tend to have higher levels of social motivation than boys do (Head et al., 2014), so it makes sense that they would have a similar responsive strategy to non-autistic girls. The team also presented the hypothesis that camouflaging may have a role in the observed gender differences, because there is evidence that while autistic people of all genders engage in masking, girls and women tend to do this more (Hull et al., 2019), and this may lead them to react to scenarios in ways which fit with how they think other people expect them to, more so than autistic boys do.

This section shows how there are a whole range of social skills which go into social interactions, the key building blocks of friendship formation and maintenance.

The skills that are needed are complex, change from moment to moment, and are somewhat dependent on the reactions of the other person (and therefore on the ability to understand the reactions of that person). When you break it down and think about it, spending time with other people is hard work!

Children's early friendships

Despite the hard work involved in social interactions, pretty much everyone on the planet does it. (There may be some hermits in remote parts of the world who no longer interact with others, but even they had to spend some time with other people to get to that point – and have some ongoing interactions in order to get food deliveries!) We automatically want to share our lives with other people, and contrary to the assumptions of much autism work historically, this is true for autistic people too.

(On a side note: Felicity and Sarah have previously had conversations wondering whether some of the mediaeval religious hermits, recluses, and anchorites – female hermits – could have been people on the spectrum. A preference for time alone, reduced sensory input, an affinity for nature, an intense passion for a particular subject which comes with an encyclopaedic knowledge of the topic, but often idiosyncratic interpretations which deviate from doctrine . . . it is relatively easy to debate some potential retrospective diagnoses! Especially as committing yourself to religion was one of the few acceptable ways for someone of either sex to avoid getting married and having children, something which does not automatically appeal to everyone and especially may not have appealed to those on the spectrum in the middle ages, for a variety of reasons.

For example, Julian of Norwich, a 14th-century mystical anchorite and the first female author in England that we can name, is one of Sarah's current interests, and because she feels a close affinity with her, despite there being 700 years distance between them, she does wonder if Julian could well have been autistic. Although Julian possibly did have the experience of having been a wife and mother prior to her mystical revelations, she fits the pattern of intense experience, need for withdrawal, and an extraordinary ability to challenge patriarchal church doctrines whilst appearing to conform. How she managed to avoid the heresy-curing (!) flames is a mystery in itself and her non-normative approach and insights reach through the centuries and resonate with Sarah's understanding and experience of being autistic in the here and now, so much so that her most recent tattoo (also a current interest!) is an homage to one of Julian's key themes, that "All Shall Be Well".

There have also been modern-day instances of autistic people becoming religious or spiritual hermits, and you can easily Google these to read about their experiences.)

Back to the point . . .

Most friendships for children begin in school – this is the first time children spend a lot of time together independently of adults or with much less-intense adult supervision.

38 Moving on up

Moving even from a preschool setting, where there is usually somewhere around one adult for every two to eight children, to a school setting where the ratio moves to one adult to around 30 children, results in a very different set of child-to-child interactions. With these comes an increased capacity for building relationships, both of preference and dislike, with peers. These early friendships can in many cases last a lifetime, or at least for many years – often being stable throughout the school years, due to a mix of geographic closeness and shared experiences and memories which enable people to feel warmly towards each other for long periods of time. Of course, it is also possible that knowing someone this well and for this long can result in deeply entrenched dislike as well, but luckily this tends to happen less often.

Children, particularly young children, tend to focus on companionship when defining or naming their friends – the people who they like to do things with and who they find fun to be around. Most of us say that our friends are people we find fun, regardless of how old we are, but the things that make someone fun change, and adolescents and adults tend to focus more on how important it is to be able to trust a friend, be open and honest, be yourself, and share emotional bonds, rather than children who are interested in the fun of playing together (Rose & Asher, 1999). Although . . . the amount of time many adults spend on group games, from World of Warcraft, to Dungeons and Dragons, to Farmville, to escape rooms, board games, and paintballing, suggests that this doesn't go away entirely!

So how do children choose their friends? How do they work out who is 'fun to play with'? The principle that applies most broadly is called homophily – that is, we instinctively like people who are like us more than we like people who are not like us. This can be on the basis of gender, ethnicity, values, hobbies, neighbour- hood . . . all sorts of things, and it applies to how both children and adults choose who they want to spend time with and form friendships and relationships with. An interesting other factor that it has been shown children especially pay attention to is prosocial and antisocial behaviour. For boys in particular, this plays a significant role in how they choose friends and make friendship groups – they look for other people who have a similar level of these behaviours. This is how we end up with groups of 'the naughty boys' in a class or school, as the boys who want to be more mischievous or are more comfortable breaking rules find each other and then rein- force that behavioural norm within their group. It can also be the case, though, that these boys (and it is more often boys) end up spending time together because they have fewer other options, as most children do not choose to make friends with those who display more antisocial behaviour than they do.

This is an example of a process which researchers have called social deselection, which pretty much does what it says in the title. Whereas earlier we described some of the points on which people select who to be friends with, social deselection covers the factors on which people choose who not to be friends with. Levels of antisocial behaviour are often important, as we have said, and so are things like being of very different class background or levels of academic motivation. It is also the case that those who have developmental conditions have been shown to be more likely to be 'socially deselected' than their neurotypical peers. Although they are often included in the social networks of their classrooms when very young, such as at preschool, this can change as children grow up and their peers start to be more aware of their differences. This results in them being less likely to be chosen as friends, and more likely to be 'dropped' as friends, as they move into middle childhood. Social deselection can happen very rapidly, even for quite young children – one study showed that within just a few hours of being in a 'class' together, a group of seven- and eight-year-old children had established clear patterns of preference and dislike within themselves (Rubin et al., 1994). It can be hard to change these once they begin, although it is definitely possible, and children can move from being less preferred to being more preferred based on a wide range of things that change over time, as they and their peers mature, or as circumstances change. We will talk a bit more about social inclusion and exclusion later on, as it is a complex picture that often has a strong gendered component for autistic young people. Therefore, it makes sense to look at what we know about gender differences in friendships before we get to that.

Gender differences in friendships

A quick note to start this section, because it is important and will be relevant in a lot of the later writing as well – sex and gender are two different things. A person's sex is defined by their chromosomes (XX for female, XY for male, and there are a range of other options which result in intersex individuals), and is usually identified by genitalia at birth (though this is not always as simple as just 'male or female', as we said before). A person's gender can match with their biological sex, or it cannot – it usually does, but this statistical probability does not mean that people who do not identify with their gender assigned at birth are in some way wrong. Gender is made up of a variety of factors. One important factor is the gender a person feels (gender identity), which is often influenced by hormones, interpretation of oneself within the gender norms of the culture, and the degree to which a person identifies with a single gender, both genders, or no gender. The other key element talked about a lot both in research and in society is the way one presents oneself in terms of dress or hairstyle or make-up (gender expression), and what this says about how a person fits in with the cultural expectations for 'looking' male or female within a society. Sexual orientation is separate to all these things – this is about who a person is attracted to, romantically and physically, which is not dependent on one's gender identity or one's biological sex (and for some people, not dependent on these things in the other person either).

Having said all that, people still mostly identify as male or female in line with the gender they were assigned at birth (there are a growing number of openly non-binary and trans people, but they are still a statistically very small group), and historically in the West these have effectively been the only 'options' available for those who did not want to be totally ostracised from society. This means that we have a cultural history which sees people as male or female, and this has led to gender stereotypes based on this binary model.

There are a wealth of stereotypes about gender differences in our culture: 'men are from Mars, women are from Venus'; men like sports, women like make-up;

40 Moving on up

'boys will be boys' (synonymous usually with bad behaviour, especially towards girls and women); boys are strong leaders but girls are bossy shrews; men are doctors and women are nurses; he's a ladies man but she's a slut; boys like maths and science, girls like English and textiles . . . we could go on. Those reading closely, or even passingly familiar with our basically patriarchal society, will notice that these stereotypes generally frame the male side of things as better, stronger, smarter, higher status, and (when they are behaving in harmful ways) deserving of more understanding and forgiveness for any discretions than the female partner to it. Feminism has tried, and is still trying, to counteract these stereotypes and build new, more equal narratives which emphasise the value in a range of skills and approaches, and which tell men that they can be empathetic, emotional, and into sewing just as much as it tells women that they can be logical coders who have no interest in children.

Gender stereotypes can be seen in the attitudes of people of all ages, including very young children. Gender-typed play can be seen in babies as young as just 12 months old, with boy babies tending to play with toys we think of as 'male' (cars, trucks, building blocks) and girl babies more often choosing 'female' toys (dolls or prams) (Serbin et al., 2016). This gender-typing in play, and in assumptions about what it means to be male or female, are firmly formed and testable by two and a half years old, something which has been found consistently for decades. Our gender stereotypes are also remarkably stable over childhood – the attitudes we see at three or four are still present at seven, ten, and fourteen (Ruble, 1983). Indeed, they are often carried all the way into adulthood, where they are reproduced through being passed on to the next generation – parents are one of the strongest influences for where we get our knowledge and assumptions about gender from.

Generally, parents prefer and reward gender-typical play from their children – they are more engaged and positive when a boy plays with a car than a doll, or a girl with a doll than a car – and children pick up on this positive reinforcement and internalise the message it is sending about what being a 'proper' or 'good' boy or girl is (Caldera et al., 1989). These differences even emerge in how parents talk to their children, using far more 'emotion' words with girls than with boys, which helps to model thinking about and understanding both their own and other people's emotions, thereby building the empathy that is supposedly 'typical' of girls more than boys (Aznar & Tenenbaum, 2020). This shows some of the ways in which the gendered behaviours and attributes upon which many stereotypes are based can be both true – they are observable – and false – they are created by being part of a society which holds and therefore reinforces them.

These patterns are stronger in boys than girls – they are less likely to choose 'cross-gender' toys than girls are, meaning a girl is more likely to play with a car than a boy is to play with a doll. This is because across the lifespan, engaging in play or behaviour which is not considered gender typical tends to hold more social risk and punishment for boys than for girls. Boys who are into dolls, or ballet, are often accused of being homosexual (which has historically been given negative connotations, though this is happily changing) or of wanting to be a girl – which, as we have discussed, is seen as inherently 'lesser' than wanting to be, or being, a boy. Indeed, in one frankly distressing study, seven-year-olds were asked to imagine they had to be the opposite sex for a period of time, and were asked what they would do or what would be good about it. The girls all started talking about the adventures they could go out and have (which reminds us all too much of the threads which do the rounds on Twitter occasionally: "Women, what would you do if you were a man for a day?" "Walk outside at night"). The boys? Well, they said that it would be boring to be a girl, it would be stupid, there would be nothing good or interesting about it. One boy – and this child was only *seven years old* – said that being a girl would be so awful he would kill himself (Feder-Feitel, 1993). That is truly shocking, and shows just how strong and how ingrained these attitudes towards gender can be.

That diversion aside, and having probably made our personal views on the topic of gender stereotypes more clear than we should, there are some stereotypes about gender and friendship that it is worth mentioning before we go on.

These stereotypes say that girls and women are more sociable than boys and men, generally having more friends, spending more time with them, and spending that time differently. Think about almost any sitcom – the women tend to be depicted as talking to their friends about their life and emotional problems (usually focussed on the men in the piece) over coffee, food, or alcohol, whereas men are more often depicted as being focussed on an activity while they socialise – playing a sport, watching a sport, going on a trip, for example. The same stereotypes apply to how children are shown in media as well, with boys tending to get more active storylines and girls usually having the conflict they face being more about interpersonal issues.

Now, the next sentence is controversial, so brace yourselves – and wait for us to explain.

There is some truth in those stereotypes.

Girls do tend to have more friends than boys – at least, when asked to list their friends, they tend to give more names, they tend to have more reciprocal nominations (where both children say that they are friends), and they have more connections within their classroom networks than boys do. Girls talk more about their best friends and their wider friends, whereas boys discriminate less between 'levels' of friendship and tend to have more equal relationships with each of their friends. Boys are more likely to spend their time with friends on structured activities, saying that the people who are good to play with are their friends. In contrast, when asked who is a good friend and why, even from a relatively young age, girls are more likely to give answers that focus on someone being a good listener, emotionally available, and trustworthy – not someone who tells other people the things you have shared with them. Boys tend to play rougher, more physical games than girls, and in early and middle childhood the two genders don't like playing with each other because of this difference. Before puberty, boys and girls actually spend minimal time socialising with each other, instead forming single-sex groups.

All of this, obviously, is based on the assumption of there being just two genders, and sadly there is very little research on the friendships and relationships of non-binary and trans people before adolescence. This is mostly because many people do not express a gender other than that assigned at birth until they are a bit older, for a variety of reasons. The picture in terms of lived experience is currently in the process of

42 Moving on up

significant change – it is becoming much more common for children to discuss their gender identity much younger, and for parents to be more supportive and affirming of this – but it takes research a while to catch up to these kinds of things. Even if a study started today, it is usually a process that takes several months to get ethical approval, collect data, and analyse it, and then publication can take between three and twelve months in and of itself. (If you think this is frustrating, try being the researcher with data you want to be able to share with the world!) So, we can hope that there will be studies published by the time we get to write a second edition of this book.

Until that time, we can only report on what is out there already, which is basically about the differences in friendships based on two genders. And that research, as just explained, actually supports a lot of the stereotypes we hold as a society. Whether that is because they are inherent, or because children learn that this is how they are meant to behave, or a mix, is the kind of debate social and developmental psychologists have been having for a hundred years now, and we aren't the ones to be able to give a conclusive answer. We lean towards 'a mix', as most things seem to ultimately be.

Sarah's childhood friendships

I remember more details and social interactions as I moved on to primary school and the first of two middle schools following family moves from Essex to West Sussex. I don't remember much about these moves, but my older siblings have told me how each time they were each presented with a box and told that anything they wanted to bring with them had to fit into it. This then involved a lot of heart-rending decisions about what to take and what to throw away and just how painful it was to have been parted from their treasured possessions every few years.

Friendships during this time in Worthing were either brief or non-existent. There was a family who lived next door who had a girl who was younger than me. I remember her persuading me to copy her by taking all my clothes off and running naked around the garden and sliding down the slide. I can visualise the scene and re-experience the discomfort of not feeling secure being naked coupled with a nagging sense of coercion, but yet at the same time laughing and behaving as though I was having fun and being free. This may well be my first memory of autistic masking, but in any case, the potential friendship came quickly to an end as I was discovered at the top of the slide, sans clothing, by my mother, roundly told off for behaving like a 'savage' and not being allowed to go next door to play again.

There was another family who lived around the corner whose daughter was the same age as me and we did play together, although I do not remember much about what we did. What I do remember is suddenly not being allowed to spend time with her or her family, which I found out later was because they were not considered to be good enough for us by my father. So that was that. Some older girls who lived across the road occasionally tolerated me and I remember reading girls comics with them, but that is as far as that interaction went.

Encouraging me to develop friendships wasn't a priority for my parents, which given their preoccupations, isn't surprising. I also wasn't naturally obedient or submissive and remember to this day the shock and pain of being smacked so hard around the face by my father on one occasion that I saw stars. I had answered back during a family dinner time and as this was the reward for having an autonomous opinion I learned not to have one very often. However, what I did do is begin developing self-harming behaviours, mental health conditions, and phobias from this early age that are still with me now 45 years later.

At primary school I mainly remember playing by myself during break time. There was a tree on the playing field and I used to love picking catkins from it. I can still feel their sensory softness and texture and I enjoyed stripping them down to their core and storing them in the exposed tree roots so that the fairies could have something to eat. I had a rich imaginative inner life, but a solitary one and even though school reports consistently equated my loud and boister-ous character with popularity, the reality is that the opposite was true.

I was academically bright and enjoyed escaping into books. I loved read-ing anything to do with dinosaurs and was delighted that there was one named after me (TriSARAHtops . . . obviously 1☺). Although I was gener-ally solitary, I did attend a dance school and did tap, modern, and ballet. I was the chubby one at the edge of the group photos, but I was really quite a good dancer and won medals in dance competitions. I didn't pur-sue it as I became older though, as I was bullied by some of the other danc-ers for being overweight and consequently felt that dancing wasn't for a larger person like me. I also went to Brownies, but did not feel liked there either, although I did enjoy being on stage in the Gang Show.

The move from Elm Grove to West Park Middle School didn't improve my friendship options and I was bullied regularly, particularly about the clothes that I was made to wear. My mother made most of my clothes, and she always chose the style and fabric that they were made from. I didn't have a choice in the matter and it felt as though my mother saw me as a doll that she wanted to dress in a certain way. I really didn't like dolls and I certainly didn't like being dressed like one. The school uniform summer dress she made me was a ghastly voluminous stripey tent affair with a stand-up collar. It made me a prime target for mockery, particularly at break times, when I recall being surrounded by classmates laughing at me and my awful dress. Non-school uniform days were even worse, as I had no fashionable clothes to wear and I dreaded them as I knew that I would be ridiculed mercilessly.

I did however have a brief moment of respite when I was trying to get out of wearing a turquoise and pink crocheted monstrosity to Sunday School. A few minutes before being due to leave I managed to fall over in the cupboard under the stairs and injure my elbow which then needed to be x-rayed. A chipped elbow felt like a small price to pay for the relief that I felt at avoiding going to church in that frock. Small wonder that clothes and, most importantly, my choice of apparel is so important to me now.

Autistic children's friendships

Autistic children – and adults – seem to follow the same principles when they are choosing who they do and do not want to be friends with (so some of what we say here applies in all the following chapters as well). Autistic children like to do similar things with their friends as non-autistic children do, following the same gendered patterns in terms of how they spend their time together as mentioned earlier. Nearly all autistic children liked watching TV and movies with their friends, just as non-autistic children do (this is from a review paper which summarised, compared, and consolidated the findings from lots of individual smaller papers). Autistic boys, however, like to *do* things together which give them an external focus and structured format, especially things like video games and board games, and autistic girls like to talk to their friends or play with shared created worlds (Petrina et al., 2014). Basing friendships on who you play with is common in childhood, as we said, and also applies for our interviewees, even if this changes as the autistic child gets older.

> He liked PC games, Pokemon and cars and preferred playing on a one to one basis with children who had a 'no-nonsense' approach to his favourite themes. He wasn't trying to be one of the gang or popular and the other kids liked him for being quiet and not a loudmouth or bragger. These could be intense relationships and he struggled when his themes did not vary much as he was growing older when the other kids did have new interests. I guess that this was a disappointment to him and the more that the (trusted and approved) child moved on to new interests, the weaker the contact got.
>
> *(anonymous, 61, female)*

Interestingly, autistic boys – who made up roughly 80% of all participants in these studies – were found to have better friendships overall when they played video games with their friends than when they did not. This is an important finding, considering the widespread concern about children spending (too much) time on screens or playing (potentially violent) video games and the impact this could have on development, and the ways in which these concerns have often been treated as more relevant or impactful for autistic children. When we look at teenage friendships we will talk a bit about access to the internet, online friendships, and the concerns and opportunities contained within these, but it is worth highlighting that even for relatively young autistic children, technology can mediate and facilitate strong friendships, rather than undermining them. This is something which Kenzi talked about a lot:

> I play quite a few different games like Minecraft. I've recently got back into Fortnite. People I can play games with I have stronger friendships with them. When you are playing games you interact with them a lot. It helps that.
>
> *(Kenzi, 13, autistic male)*

Most of the research, though, as ever, has looked at the ways in which autistic children struggle to make and keep friends, and has focussed on boys under the age of 14. The picture is starting to expand, which is good news, but still is not comprehensive in terms of who is included, so we can only talk about what is known so far and can't necessarily speak to all the possible experiences people have from a research perspective – which is why the words of our contributors are so important.

Narratives of difficulty

For a long time, the picture of autistic children's friendships which emerged from research literature was fairly negative – one fairly recent paper looked at autistic children in preschool (ages two to five) and suggested that only 20% of the (admittedly small) sample had what the observers classified as friends (Chang et al., 2016). Autistic children have generally been found to have fewer friends (if any), and those they nominated as friends in their classrooms were less likely to nominate them in return, meaning that their friendships were one-sided (Bauminger & Kasari, 2000). Autistic children are more likely to be on the periphery of social networks, for example at school, than they are to be tightly integrated into them – they are less likely to be listed by other children as someone they want to work and play with, and this is what happens in practice as well (Kasari et al., 2011). Unsurprisingly, in light of these findings, autistic children reported both being and feeling lonelier than their non-autistic peers, spending more time alone in general and especially in unstructured breaks during the school day. Louise and an anonymous contributor, for example, struggled to keep friends because the expectations differed, regardless of what made them happy:

> There were times when children approached me in a friendly way, but I don't think I reciprocated in the way they expected. They wanted to play a game that I didn't want to play. I would want to talk about things but they would say, "we talked about that last time". They would just drift away and it didn't really happen.
>
> *(Louise, autistic woman)*

> There was a very strong sense of expectation around making friends and having friends, and I think I would have been a lot happier if that hadn't been imposed on me.
>
> *(anonymous, 54, autistic woman)*

46 Moving on up

Autistic children also define friendship differently in many studies, talking about their friends as people they do things with, rather than people they shared their thoughts and emotions with – something which non-autistic children of the same age tended to talk about much more (O'Hagan & Hebron, 2017). This mismatch in expectations of friendships can lead to further difficulties in addition to those created by communication differences, because if you value different things in a friendship, it is easy for one or both people to be upset by something the other person has done, even when unintentional. The friendships of autistic children tend to be less long-lasting than those of non-autistic children, with a variety of reasons having been proposed for this – weaker emotional connections to friends overall; more difficulty with emotional regulation leading to arguments; difficulties with social information processing speed meaning that autistic children struggle to 'keep up' with non-autistic friends, to name just a few (Mendelson et al., 2016). For example, Sarah talked about the change through primary school and how being autistic made it more difficult to maintain friendships:

> I think things definitely felt easier in the lower years of primary school and those connections with people were really simple and as the world of the child becomes more complex and interests become more complex then it got harder and then people got better at social performing whereas I stayed worse.
>
> *(Sarah O, autistic woman)*

One of the ways in which autistic children's differences, and how they link to friendship, has been investigated is through looking at facial expressions. Non-autistic adults and children were asked to watch short videos of autistic and non-autistic children, then score them for how expressive they were (adults) and what they thought the child in the video would be like as a friend (children). Nobody knew whether the child in the video they just watched was autistic or not, so that it was an unbiased rating. The adults consistently rated the autistic children as less expressive than non-autistic children, and the children rated them lower on all the different elements of the friendship questionnaire (Stagg et al., 2014). Considering that these were short videos, this suggests that even when only meeting for a short time, it is possible that autistic children are immediately perceived as less friendly, or at least as less desirable friends, by their peers, and that this has an impact on how they are treated by other children.

Partly because of those differences, autistic children can find it harder to make and maintain friendships, and may experience more difficulties with their peer relationships in general. Making friends in the first place is often described as the most difficult bit, especially for autistic boys, as they feel anxious about approaching someone, especially if they are aware of the social hierarchy in their school and are unsure how to make friends without upsetting this balance (Daniel & Billingsley, 2010). This social hierarchy is something which girls are also aware of, though it seems to become more relevant for girls as they move into adolescence, something we will talk about in the next chapter.

These challenges in making and keeping friends can lead to feeling (and being) isolated, and to being vulnerable to bullying. Most of the autistic people we talked to had been bullied, often from being young, and struggled to get support with this:

I was bullied from Reception onwards by loads of different groups. Being bullied by the girls, being bullied by the boys.

(Sarah O, autistic woman)

I had read in books that if you're bullied you're not supposed to tell the adults because it will get worse and everyone will get mad at you. I was all alone, it was me against the world. I was in my head most of the time, daydreaming. I had my books. I had my friends a year older, some younger. I was surviving.

(Eleanor, autistic woman)

I was trapped, shamed, bullied.

(Imane, 15, autistic girl)

We know that in non-autistic children, having friends is a protective factor against being bullied, and the same has been found for autistic children as well. However, as outlined earlier, making those protective friendships can be harder for autistic children, and they are among the most-bullied groups of children in schools overall, with autistic children being more likely to be bullied than those with a range of other special educational needs, such as deaf or blind children (Rowley et al., 2012). The majority of autistic children report having been actively bullied at some point in their school careers, and the numbers may actually be even higher than thought – one study found that when presented with a list of concrete bullying behaviours, rather than just asked about being bullied, more autistic children said that those things had happened to them in comparison to when asked the general question (Humphrey & Symes, 2010). Interestingly, it seems that autistic children who have more social skills and higher IQs are more likely to be bullied than autistic children with co-occurring learning difficulties (LD). This may be because autistic children without LD appear more neurotypical than they are at times, so when they then do something which makes them stand out to the other children, it is more 'unusual' and therefore more likely to be noticed and then they are picked on for it.

As you can imagine, the combination of the research findings and autistic people's own difficult experiences with friendships as children have resulted in a general view that autistic people do not really have, and often do not want, friends or relationships. The next section, however, shows us that this isn't exactly true.

A more positive picture

In the last decade or so – that same time frame again where understandings of autism have shifted (and are shifting) dramatically – it has been increasingly recognised that autistic people can, and do, have positive, meaningful, reciprocal friendships. This should not have come as the surprise it did to many in academia, education, and healthcare.

48 Moving on up

As autism researchers have become better at listening to autistic people, there has been a shift in the way they investigate early friendships. Resulting from these changes in viewpoint and methods, there is now a growing number of studies which show that autistic children have many positive friendship experiences in their primary school years, especially when their needs are respected in that friendship, such as a need for time alone as well as together (Calder et al., 2013; Sosnowy et al., 2019). Autistic children have been found to expect similar things from their friends as non-autistic children do in terms of trustworthiness, loyalty, support, and fun (Bottema-Beutel et al., 2019), and they choose their friends in similar ways – focussing on people who share their interests, values, and preferences for amount and type of contact (Finke et al., 2019). Once they have chosen their friends, autistic children do similar things with them to non-autistic children, playing games together, talking about things they are interested in, visiting each other or sitting together at lunchtime in school. Interestingly, we see similar gendered patterns of activity between autistic and non-autistic children – boys are more likely to play video games, girls are more likely to play make-believe games, for example (Kuo et al., 2013).

Most importantly, it has been shown that autistic children are equally as happy with their friendships as non-autistic children are (Petrina et al., 2017). There is not something lacking in these friendships simply because a child is autistic, and they are not inherently incapable of forming and enjoying those friendships. Some of our interviewees talked about making good friends which they kept for the rest of their lives:

> I found friendships in primary school ok. I had some really good lifelong friendships that I've kept for over 20 years. We remained friends throughout as we went to brownies and guides outside of our secondary schools. We basically stayed in contact by doing things together. We still had a connecting factor, and saw each other once or twice a week but we didn't go to school together.
>
> *(Krysia, 30)*

> I was mainly ok with not being friends with the girls because they all seemed really cliquey to me even from a really young age, and we didn't have things that we could talk about. . . . I think I felt mainly ok with it because I was doing friendship the way I thought friendship worked.
>
> *(Sarah O, autistic woman)*

Following from the findings about the double empathy problem and improved same-neurotype communication, some people have argued that autistic people, including autistic children, should be encouraged to mostly (or even, in extreme cases, only) have friendships and relationships with other autistic or neurodiverse people. While it is crucially important for autistic people to have autistic role models, to see themselves represented, and to be able to build positive self-identity as autistic through being around people who understand them, we would argue that the best way to do this is not for autistic people, including autistic children, to be cut off from the potential joys of cross-neurotype friendships (such as ours). Indeed, it is likely almost impossible to do so, as the majority of people in the world are not autistic and so we can't imagine a way where you could remove all interaction with non-autistic people from someone's life!

It is not just about practicality though. First, as we said, there is a lot of joy to be had in cross-neurotype friendships, just as there is in same-neurotype friendships. Learning to understand someone else's point of view, developing empathy, and finding the differences which make you laugh together is a lovely thing. This is something autistic people talked to us about:

> Not all my friends are autistic or neurodivergent and they will know when not to say, "oh well, I have it harder than you" and they say the right thing at the right time and be good at listening. And I think it's because they are genuinely nice people. . . . I have a couple of non-autistic friends but they are quite good allies. They've always been quite good at listening and validating what I say and not being annoying, not overstepping and just accepting me as I am without trying to correct or use me as a pet project or anything. It is a two way interaction.
>
> *(Krysia, 30)*

Indeed, the team led by Petrina (who has come up a lot in this chapter) did a study where they found that among 5- to 11-year-olds, half of autistic children said their friend was another autistic child, and half said that their friend was a non-autistic child – and these were reciprocal nominations, so the other child agreed that they were friends (although the reciprocation rate was slightly lower when asked if the other child was your "best" friend instead of just a friend) (Petrina et al., 2016). Second, there is evidence that cross-neurotype friendships actually are beneficial for autistic children. For example, a relatively early Israeli study found that in mixed autistic/non-autistic friendships, both children were more responsive and attentive to each other, had more developed language skills, and engaged in more complex play together than in non-mixed pairs. This means that there were benefits for both children, not just the autistic child, as many researchers at that time would have predicted (Bauminger et al., 2008). It is worth noting that the team did not investigate autistic-autistic friendships, considering autistic-disabled to be the equivalent of a non-mixed pairing for the autistic children, so we don't know what the impact of same-neurotype friendships are on the same measures, but it is still a more positive view than many studies of the time. It has also been shown that autistic children who build cross-neurotype friendships (all friendships, really) through taking part in group activities they enjoy have lower levels of internalising problems like anxiety and depression, that they feel these activities help them to develop their social skills through practising in a 'safe' environment, and that this in turn builds their social confidence (Dovgan & Mazurek, 2019). This becomes a positive spiral or cycle, in contrast to the negative social skills spiral theorised by Chevallier in the Social Motivation Theory. As someone gets to practice their skills, they improve those skills, they get more positive responses from their peers, so they

50 Moving on up

become more confident, so they put themselves into more social situations, practising their skills more . . . you can see how it goes.

Interventions around friendships

Historically, it has been incredibly common for families and professionals to want to, and try to, intervene in ways that they think will help autistic children do 'better' in terms of their social development. Indeed, when parents were asked to rank the most important outcomes for their children (aged five to ten), social skills was number one, emotional skills were number two, and friendships were number three, although all the results were very close (Petrina et al., 2014). The ways in which people try to teach or impart these skills are usually called social skills interventions.

Social skills interventions are the most common interventions offered to families for their autistic children, because difficulties with socialising are seen as one of the biggest challenges for succeeding in life for autistic people. These range from teaching conversational skills like turn taking, to making scripts for different social situations, to buddy programmes – if you can think of a social skill, there is an intervention out there aimed at autistic children (and it is almost always children and young people under 18, not adults: this can lead to issues later in life, but most professionals have tended to worry less about this historically because of that attitude of autism being a 'childhood issue' that we mentioned).

These interventions are delivered in nearly as many ways as they have 'target' skills. Some are done by professionals like clinical psychologists, some by teachers, some by parents, some by video or robot, and some by other children (called peer-delivered interventions). These all have different pros and cons – clinical psychologists are unlikely to have the time to spend working with individual children really closely, but have lots of experience with adapting to different children; parents know their child personally very well so can help them, but may not have much training so can struggle to deliver the intervention as intended; other children are likely to be who an autistic child most wants to be friends with, so they will be motivated, but there are obvious issues with how genuine that friendship may be if it comes in the form of a tracked and observed intervention rather than naturally. These are just a few examples – there are many more, which are usually acknowledged and discussed in papers which present interventions to their readers.

We are not going to discuss all the possible interventions out there in this book – there isn't space to do it in detail or give each one a full and balanced consideration. We will talk about a few as we go through, when it is appropriate and in line with what else we are talking about in that section.

One key friendship intervention aimed at autistic children is called PEERS. This stands for Program for the Education and Enrichment of Relational Skills, and it was developed by UCLA (a university in America) in 2015. This is a structured programme of weekly sessions which aim to help autistic children develop and improve their social skills, using things like supported get-togethers and lessons about choosing friends, how to approach people, and how to respond to rejection by peers. These lessons include a wide range of activities such as role play and social modelling, and then the actual social events give autistic children the chance to try to put those skills into practice. It has generally been found to have a positive impact on the social skills autistic children display, with increases in things like how often they approach or engage with other people, and seems to help them become more integrated with the social world of their peers – children were invited to more social events after the intervention than they were before it, for example (Hill, 2017). It is worth noting, though, that the evaluation of this programme has only been done from observer and parent perspectives, not asking for the views of the autistic children themselves, so we are missing important voices in understanding what it is like to take part in the programme.

Despite that, this kind of model is prevalent for social skills interventions across the board – some more structured teaching, some role play, some practical testing out of the skills which are meant to be being learned by the autistic children. And generally, research suggests that doing this kind of targeted intervention does have at least small- to medium-size effects on the skills which are the focus. That doesn't always mean, however, that these effects are generalised to a child's everyday life outside of the programme, which is probably meant to be the eventual goal. Some children do show generalisation of the skills, but this needs to be built into any intervention (on anything, not just social skills) for it to happen for the majority of participants.

It is worth remembering, though, that not all children get to take part in these interventions and opportunities equally. Autistic children and young people with intellectual disabilities are often excluded from both the activities themselves and the research about the activities and interventions. This can be for a variety of reasons, but the outcome is that they are not able to benefit either directly from the skills being imparted, or indirectly from the social interactions and friendships built during the programme (Taheri & Minnes, 2016). This means that it is a priority for anyone conducting or developing these kinds of interventions to find ways to make them accessible to those with intellectual disability, to those who may have limited verbal communication, and to any children and young people who would benefit, not just those who are easy to reach and easy to include. Sabrina, another non-speaking autistic person who answered questions about her experiences with friendships, summed up this need for better inclusion:

> I find it painful to talk about friendship because of lasting damage from years of not being able to connect. Respect above kindness is critical assistance when creating opportunities for connection for non-speakers. . . When aiming to facilitate friendship it is important that one identify ways of playing all can enjoy. Anytime kids can join in the play of a disabled child it feels glorious. Try typing with non-speakers. It is wonderful to dialogue with another speller.
>
> *(Sabrina, 10, autistic girl)*

Neurodiversity-informed schools

One of the ways we could help to ensure that children have a good time at school, both educationally and socially, is to make more schools neurodivergent-friendly. If school staff and children know more about neurodiversity, neurodivergence, and

52 Moving on up

the different ways that different brains experience the world, the chances are that stigma and prejudice towards neurodivergent children will decrease. This would reduce the bullying and social trauma that many autistic people go through, and increase the number of people who are able to be understanding and supportive in their lives, potentially reducing mental health issues later on and reducing the need for therapeutic services in adulthood.

Creating a genuinely inclusive environment is a brilliant goal for schools, and would improve things for students and teachers alike (because there are neurodivergent teachers out there too!). One project which is working to help make that a reality is the LEANS (Learning About Neurodiversity at School) project in Edinburgh. The team, led by Dr Alyssa Alcorn and Prof Sue Fletcher-Watson, worked to create a free resource pack where, over the course of a school term, a classroom teacher has everything they need to work through teaching children about neurodiversity and neurodivergent classmates (link at the end of the book). Everything was co-designed with autistic people, educators, and autistic educators, and has been thoroughly tested to make sure it is easy to understand and gets the intended messages across. So far it has been tested in a handful of Scottish schools, where it has gone well, and it is now available for anyone to use – so if you work in a school, have a look. You could make a really concrete and positive difference to the children you work with!

Chapter conclusion

Friendships are central and formative relationships for any child, autistic children included. They help form our identities, they support our emotional development, they help set us up for success or difficulty as we grow up – they are important in so many ways. Autistic children have historically been thought to really struggle with friendships, to the point of not having them even, but we know that isn't true. It certainly isn't the whole picture, and hopefully we have shown you that as best we can here!

References

Aznar, A., & Tenenbaum, H. R. (2020). Gender comparisons in mother-child emotion talk: A meta-analysis. *Sex Roles*, *82*(3–4), 155–162. https://doi.org/10.1007/S11199-019-01042-Y/TABLES/1

Barbu, S., Cabanes, G., & le Maner-Idrissi, G. (2011). Boys and girls on the playground: Sex differences in social development are not stable across early childhood. *PLoS One*, *6*(1), e16407. https://doi.org/10.1371/JOURNAL.PONE.0016407

Bauminger, N., & Kasari, C. (2000). Loneliness and friendship in high-functioning children with autism. *Child Development*, *71*(2), 447–456. https://doi.org/10.1111/1467-8624.00156

Bauminger, N., Solomon, M., Aviezer, A., Heung, K., Brown, J., & Rogers, S. J. (2008). Friendship in high-functioning children with autism spectrum disorder: Mixed and non-mixed dyads. *Journal of Autism and Developmental Disorders*, *38*(7), 1211–1229. https://doi.org/10.1007/S10803-007-0501-2/TABLES/3

Bottema-Beutel, K., Malloy, C., Cuda, J., Kim, S. Y., & MacEvoy, J. P. (2019). Friendship expectations may be similar for mental age-matched children with autism spectrum disorder and typically developing children. *Journal of Autism and Developmental Disorders*, *49*(10), 4346–4354. https://doi.org/10.1007/S10803-019-04141-7/TABLES/6

Calder, L., Hill, V., & Pellicano, E. (2013). Sometimes i want to play by myself: Understanding what friendship means to children with autism in mainstream primary schools. *Autism*, *17*(3), 296–316. https://doi.org/10.1177/1362361312467866

Caldera, Y. M., Huston, A. C., & O'Brien, M. (1989). Social interactions and play patterns of parents and toddlers with feminine, Masculine, and neutral toys. *Child Development*, *60*(1), 70. https://doi.org/10.2307/1131072

Chang, Y. C., Shih, W., & Kasari, C. (2016). Friendships in preschool children with autism spectrum disorder: What holds them back, child characteristics or teacher behavior? *Autism*, *20*(1), 65–74. https://doi.org/10.1177/1362361314567761

Daniel, L. S., & Billingsley, B. S. (2010). What boys with an autism spectrum disorder say about establishing and maintaining friendships. *Focus on Autism and Other Developmental Disabilities*, *25*(4), 220–229. https://doi.org/10.1177/1088357610378290

Dovgan, K. N., & Mazurek, M. O. (2019). Relations among activity participation, friendship, and internalizing problems in children with autism spectrum disorder. *Autism*, *23*(3), 750–758. https://doi.org/10.1177/1362361318775541

Feder-Feitel, L. (1993). How to avoid gender bias. *Creative Classroom*, *8*, 27–28.

Finke, E. H., McCarthy, J. H., & Sarver, N. A. (2019). Self-perception of friendship style: Young adults with and without autism spectrum disorder. *Autism & Developmental Language Impairments*, *4*, 239694151985539. https://doi.org/10.1177/2396941519855390

Head, A. M., McGillivray, J. A., & Stokes, M. A. (2014). Gender differences in emotionality and sociability in children with autism spectrum disorders. *Molecular Autism*, *5*(1), 19. https://doi.org/10.1186/2040-2392-5-19

Hill, T. L., Gray, S. A. O., Baker, C. N., Boggs, K., Carey, E., Johnson, C., Kamps, J. L., & Enrique Varela, R. (2017). A pilot study examining the effectiveness of the peers program on social skills and Anxiety in adolescents with autism spectrum disorder. *Journal of Developmental and Physical Disabilities*, *29*(5), 797–808. https://doi.org/10.1007/S10882-017-9557-X/FIGURES/1

Hull, L., Lai, M.-C., Baron-Cohen, S., Allison, C., Smith, P., Petrides, K. V, & Mandy, W. (2019). Gender differences in self-reported camouflaging in autistic and non-autistic adults. *Autism*, 136236131986480. https://doi.org/10.1177/1362361319864804

Humphrey, N., & Symes, W. (2010). Perceptions of social support and experience of bullying among pupils with autistic spectrum disorders in mainstream secondary schools. *European Journal of Special Needs Education*, *25*(1), 77–91. https://doi.org/10.1080/08856250903450855

Kasari, C., Locke, J., Gulsrud, A., & Rotheram-Fuller, E. (2011). Social networks and friendships at school: Comparing children with and without ASD. *Journal of Autism and Developmental Disorders*, *41*(5), 533–544. https://doi.org/10.1007/s10803-010-1076-x

Kuo, M. H., Orsmond, G. I., Cohn, E. S., & Coster, W. J. (2013). Friendship characteristics and activity patterns of adolescents with an autism spectrum disorder. *Autism*, *17*(4), 481–500. https://doi.org/10.1177/1362361311416380

Mendelson, J. L., Gates, J. A., & Lerner, M. D. (2016). Friendship in school-age boys with autism spectrum disorders: A meta-analytic summary and developmental, process-based model. *Psychological Bulletin*, *142*(6), 601–622. https://doi.org/10.1037/bul0000041

54 Moving on up

O'Hagan, S., & Hebron, J. (2017). Perceptions of friendship among adolescents with autism spectrum conditions in a mainstream high school resource provision. *European Journal of Special Needs Education, 32*(3), 314–328. https://doi.org/10.1080/08856257.2016.1223441

Petrina, N., Carter, M., & Stephenson, J. (2014). The nature of friendship in children with autism spectrum disorders: A systematic review. *Research in Autism Spectrum Disorders, 8*(2), 111–126. https://doi.org/10.1016/J.RASD.2013.10.016

Petrina, N., Carter, M., Stephenson, J., & Sweller, N. (2016). Perceived friendship quality of children with autism spectrum disorder as compared to their peers in mixed and non-mixed dyads. *Journal of Autism and Developmental Disorders, 46*(4), 1334–1343. https://doi.org/10.1007/S10803-015-2673-5/TABLES/5

Petrina, N., Carter, M., Stephenson, J., & Sweller, N. (2017). Friendship satisfaction in children with autism spectrum disorder and nominated friends. *Journal of Autism and Developmental Disorders, 47*(2), 384–392. https://doi.org/10.1007/S10803-016-2970-7/TABLES/3

Rieffe, C., O'Connor, R., Bülow, A., Willems, D., Hull, L., Sedgewick, F., Stockmann, L., & Blijd-Hoogewys, E. (2020). Quantity and quality of empathic responding by autistic and non-autistic adolescent girls and boys. *Autism, 25*(1), 199–209. https://doi.org/10.1177/1362361320956422

Rose, A. J., & Asher, S. R. (1999). Children's goals and strategies in response to conflicts within a friendship. *Developmental Psychology, 35*(1), 69–79. https://doi.org/10.1037/0012-1649.35.1.69

Rowley, E., Chandler, S., Baird, G., Simonoff, E., Pickles, A., Loucas, T., & Charman, T. (2012). The experience of friendship, victimization and bullying in children with an autism spectrum disorder: Associations with child characteristics and school placement. *Research in Autism Spectrum Disorders, 6*(3), 1126–1134. https://doi.org/10.1016/J.RASD.2012.03.004

Rubin, K. H., Lynch, D., Coplan, R., Rose-Krasnor, L., & Booth, C. L. (1994). Birds of a feather . . .: Behavioral concordances and preferential personal attraction in children. *Child Development, 65*(6), 1778–1785. https://doi.org/10.1111/J.1467-8624.1994.TB00848.X

Serbin, L. A., Poulin-Dubois, D., Colburne, K. A., Sen, M. G., & Eichestedt, J. A. (2016). Gender stereotyping in infancy: Visual preferences for and knowledge of gender-stereotyped toys in the second year. *International Journal of Behavioral Development, 25*(1), 7–15. https://doi.org/10.1080/01650250042000078

Sosnowy, C., Silverman, C., Shattuck, P., & Garfield, T. (2019). Setbacks and successes: How young adults on the autism spectrum seek friendship. *Autism in Adulthood, 1*(1), 44–51. https://doi.org/10.1089/aut.2018.0009

Stagg, S. D., Slavny, R., Hand, C., Cardoso, A., & Smith, P. (2014). Does facial expressivity count? How typically developing children respond initially to children with autism. *Autism, 18*(6), 704–711. https://doi.org/10.1177/1362361313492392

Taheri, A., Perry, A., & Minnes, P. (2016). Examining the social participation of children and adolescents with intellectual disabilities and autism spectrum disorder in relation to peers. *Journal of Intellectual Disability Research, 60*(5), 435–443. https://doi.org/10.1111/jir.12289

Trevisan, D. A., & Birmingham, E. (2016). Are emotion recognition abilities related to everyday social functioning in ASD? A meta-analysis. *Research in Autism Spectrum Disorders, 32*, 24–42. https://doi.org/10.1016/J.RASD.2016.08.004

Wieckowski, A. T., Flynn, L. T., Richey, J. A., Gracanin, D., & White, S. W. (2020). Measuring change in facial emotion recognition in individuals with autism spectrum disorder: A systematic review. *Autism, 24*(7), 1607–1628. https://doi.org/10.1177/1362361320925334

3

BIG SCHOOL

Adolescent friendships

As people move from childhood to adolescence, friendships change dramatically. The expectations of peers significantly increase and shift as everyone grows up – friendship groups expand, shifting from mostly one gender to being mixed gender; the social politics become more complex; and the level of social skill and emotional regulation people are expected to display increases. All these things take some time to get used to and work out how to navigate, but this is likely even more complex for autistic young people. Having learned one set of social rules and done their best to implement them successfully to make friends, these change suddenly and nobody explains the new ways they are expected to behave. This transition, which coincides with the move to secondary school (at least in England and Wales), is when we know a lot of autistic adolescents hit a real crisis point, especially autistic girls. The combination of moving to larger and more overwhelming school situations at the same time as the social scene utterly changes can be too much for many autistic teenagers, and this is when previously hidden difficulties become unmanageable.

In early adolescence, there is usually lots of change in friendship groups, at group and individual levels, as adolescents meet new people in secondary school, try out different friendships, and have new opportunities outside of education as well. As they get older, teenagers' friendships settle down into much more stable groups and close friendships within those groups (Poulin & Chan, 2010). These friendships become much more focussed on emotional sharing and bonding, rather than playing together, which is usually listed as the key sign of a friend by younger children. Because of these closer bonds, and the greater level of trust which comes with them, teenagers tend to be more selective in their friends as well – they name smaller numbers of people as friends than younger children, and have more sense of differentiation between 'levels' of friends – those who are closer and those who are less so. Also because of this increase in the emotional investment in friendships,

DOI: 10.4324/9781003044536-4

56 Big school

adolescents prioritise saving the relationship over proving that they were 'right' in the situation – at least most of the time (Bukowski & Sippola, 2005). This reflects the increasing social skill which people acquire over the course of the teenage years, becoming subtler and more nuanced both in their social behaviour and the way that they think about their friendships and relationships.

Secondary school, or 'big school', involves being surrounded by far more people than primary school ever does. Individual classes may well be bigger, but even if they aren't, the corridors have more students in them, the lunch hall is larger and louder, there are bells and shouting and pushing in ways there aren't at primary school, one is changing room and teacher and subject every hour or so, and so on. The sensory and executive challenges of secondary school can be too much, and it is easy to see why. In fact, this is one of the main things autistic teenagers talk about when they discuss why they avoid school or work to be moved to alternative provision (Sproston et al., 2017). The other major thing they talk about are the difficulties with their relationships we have hinted at – either because they are being bullied (Ochi et al., 2020), or because they feel isolated and like they don't have friends who they want to see at school, so they aren't motivated to attend by the social aspect, like lots of non-autistic teenagers are (Munkhaugen et al., 2017). Building good relationships, with staff and peers, can help get autistic adolescents back into regular school attendance though (O'Hagan et al., 2022). This emphasises just how important friendships can be, both for well-being and mental health, which we will talk about more later, and for simply for educational engagement and achievement – after all, the child who is going to school is likely to do better on their exams than one who isn't, with lifelong consequences.

Seeing the impact of friendships in high school for autistic teenagers is actually how Felicity first realised that she wanted to study this for her PhD. She used to work as a teaching assistant in a large secondary school, specifically working supporting an autistic girl (plus a couple of other students) in Year 9 (14 years old, for those whose schools use different systems). Despite being academically smart, this girl dropped a subject she enjoyed because she had an argument with a friend she shared the class with – she was so anxious about seeing someone after that it was better for her to stop a lesson she enjoyed than try to work out how to fix the friendship, which she thought was irrevocably broken. Wanting to try to help her, Felicity went looking for resources . . . and found basically nothing on friendship for autistic teenagers, rather than children, and definitely nothing available for girls. So, she decided to develop an intervention for her PhD . . . only to find out there was no evidence out there on which to base it. So, her thesis ended up being about understanding the friendship experiences of autistic girls and women with the longer-term plan of developing some kind of support programme. That part hasn't happened just yet, but we will discuss her research and the findings about gender differences in autistic teenage friendships later in this chapter.

For now, let's start with a more general overview of what we know.

Autistic friendships in secondary school

There have been times so far in the book where we have said that we don't have a huge amount of research, but generally there is at least something on the different relationships of autistic children we have looked at. Autistic adolescents have been much less researched than younger children, and as we go through from this point on, you will see that basically, the older an autistic person is, the less we know about their lives full stop, and their relationships particularly. Saying that, there is still plenty of research into the social experiences of autistic teenagers, both with friends and their wider peers.

As you will see time and again throughout this book, early autism researchers assumed that autistic young people did not really have friends, because this didn't fit with their theoretical models and they didn't really bother talking to anyone who was autistic. A lot of work focussed on the loneliness of autistic young people, presenting them as socially isolated and as trying to work with definitions of friendship which did not match those of their same-age non-autistic peers, focussing on shared activities rather than emotional closeness, and therefore failing to build true relationships (Baumnger et al., 2000; Bauminger et al., 2008). Even into the early 2000s, the accepted wisdom was that autistic adolescents were not connected to the social networks around them in the same way as their non-autistic peers, usually being on the periphery of these structures, if they were included at all (Chamberlain et al., 2007; Locke et al., 2010). Making friends was often highlighted as the most difficult thing for autistic teens, especially for those who were aware of social hierarchies and did not want to violate these in some way (Daniel & Billingsley, 2010). Of course, the thinking went, if you struggle to make friends then there aren't going to be many friendships for us to investigate in terms of things like how good they are, how long they last, and what people think about them. It is true that many of the people we talked to had difficulties with friendships as teenagers:

> I seemed to be able to make friends initially and there would be something kind of positive going on, but then something would go wrong or somebody more interesting would come along or somebody that they had more in common with.
>
> *(Louise, autistic woman)*

> I found it really difficult to make friends and then visiting CAMHS [Child and Adolescent Mental Health Services] three times a week which was a bit much. It became difficult to keep up with school work and keep up with friendships and so I just ended up throwing myself into my subjects instead of friendships.
>
> *(Sarah O, autistic woman)*

The assumptions that autistic teens had inherently poor friendships changed the way that results of studies were interpreted by researchers, so that even when there seemed to be a positive finding, it was taken as a sign of difficulty. For example,

58 Big school

there was some recognition of the fact that autistic adolescents reported having more friends than their parents said they did (Orsmond & Kuo, 2011), but this was often interpreted as the teenagers overestimating their friendships because they did not 'really' understand what a friend was. Autistic people (this study included people from 14 to 37 years old, so a very broad spread of ages!) do seemingly tend to give a less complex definition of friendship when asked (Platos & Pisula, 2021). That does not necessarily mean that they are wrong though, which is how this was presented. Similarly, a study which showed that autistic teenagers had insight into the expected qualities of a friendship, such as affective sharing and emotional intimacy, and that those with friends had better self-esteem and lower levels of loneliness (Bauminger et al., 2003). This finding was interpreted, though, as showing that autistic teens could only at best achieve friendships which would be like those of their non-autistic peers, and probably wouldn't, rather than seeing the positives and emphasising that many did in fact do this.

Updated knowledge about autistic adolescents' friendships

Luckily, there has been a rising tide of evidence which undermines those interpretations of autistic adolescents' friendship experiences. That new evidence actually overlaps somewhat with the older work in terms of when it started to be published, but the difference is driven by researchers who took a more neurodiversity-informed position, and who worked more cooperatively with autistic people, rather than seeing them just as subjects to study.

This newer work emphasises that autistic teenagers have friends and best friends, sometimes in ways that look different to non-autistic teenagers, but in ways which are genuine (Cresswell et al., 2019; Sedgewick et al., 2018). Autistic adolescents tend to rate reliability, trustworthiness, kindness, help, and reciprocity most highly in their friendships, with the amount of personal disclosure being least important to them (Bottema-Beutel et al., 2019). These rankings were very similar to those of the non-autistic adolescents in the study, although autistic participants rated kindness more highly than their non-autistic peers. Autistic teenagers and their friends are happy with the relationships they build with each other – mixed pairs are as satisfied with their friendships as non-mixed pairs, and generally the two teenagers show a high level of agreement as to how good the friendship is (Petrina et al., 2016). This shows that even allowing for the mismatch in communication styles described by the Double Empathy Theory, it is absolutely possible for autistic and non-autistic teenagers to build strong, mutually enjoyable friendships. That shouldn't be considered news, as this is essentially a quick summary of what we would expect for most people's friendship experiences in adolescence. But against the backdrop of the research presented earlier, it really was.

The friendships which were most successful for autistic teenagers were the ones where their autistic behaviours were normalised, rather than made a big deal out of or seen as something which needed to be suppressed or altered. Finding people who shared their interests, and who did not mind things like them monologuing on the topic, worked especially well, because then their deep knowledge was actively appreciated by their friends (Sosnowy et al., 2019). This is something several of our interviewees discussed, for example:

> My friendships were a bit better or kind of deeper and more meaningful just because I was with people who had some of the same interests as me and we could talk about things more . . . the boys who were into computers and stuff and girls who were shunned because they had atypical characteristics, not wearing make-up to school or thinking constantly about beauty and things.
>
> *(Sarah O, autistic woman)*

One of the shared activities which has been researched . . . well, not thoroughly, but more than once, which is enough to make it stand out in the autism field, are role-playing games, online and offline. Playing massive multiplayer online games, such as World of Warcraft or League of Legends, is a common hobby for lots of people. Asking autistic teenagers and young adults what they get out of this, beyond fun, shows that making friends through this kind of game works well for autistic teenagers, that they are motivated to talk frequently to friends through the game, and that it helps them to learn the rules of socialising and how they differ online and offline (Gallup & Serianni, 2017). These gaming friendships aren't perfect, of course, because it can be easy to be misunderstood online, but generally they were positive, and the same is true for the people we talked to as part of writing the book:

> I see my mates outside of school virtually to game. They all like their own bedrooms to interact from. Working it out on their terms as they need to do it.
>
> *(Kenzi, 13, autistic male)*

Similarly, looking at tabletop versions of similar games (things like Dungeons and Dragons, for example), it has been shown that the semi-structured nature of the gameplay helps autistic adolescents learn social skills in a supportive setting, where going 'off track' is often rewarded or seen as part of the fun by the group, and that this helps build a really important sense of belonging to the community (Parks, 2021). Similarly, autistic teenagers also talk about how good it is to find other autistic people their age at school, if they can, because it gives them someone to talk to about things, someone who gets what they are going through without them having to explain in detail (Crompton et al., 2022). Being understood, and talking to peers about neurodiversity, can help to build a stronger sense of identity as an autistic person, and this is a good thing. That sense of acceptance and reward for being yourself is central to building good friendships, and good mental health.

Those autistic teenagers who take part in more out-of-school activities (offline and online) tend to have more friends – because they have more opportunities to meet people who enjoy the same things they do, which is how anyone naturally makes friends (Dovgan & Mazurek, 2019). Autistic teenagers look for similar things in their friends as non-autistic teenagers do: someone to have fun with, who enjoys the same things, and someone who wants to use their time to maintain their

60 Big school

current friendships rather than always making new friends, for example (Finke et al., 2019). They were less likely than non-autistic teenagers to say they wanted friends who acted as confidants, who held the same values in life, or who wanted to be physically close a lot of the time; and they were more likely to find an activity they were interested in doing, then think of the friend to do it with, rather than seeing their friend and then finding something to do.

So there are differences in how autistic teenagers approach friendships, and we don't want to deny that. Those differences do matter, and can impact the success – or not – of a fledgling friendship.

Autistic teenagers tend to be more functional in their communication with friends, for example, contacting friends to make arrangements rather than just to chat. They also tend to focus on finding practical solutions if their friend has a problem, rather than talking through the feelings involved in the situation (something Felicity has personal experience of with her friend – if she sends me a link to a relevant policy to an issue I've told her about, I know that is her way of showing she cares, not a hidden message that she thinks I'm too silly to find it myself!). Autistic teenagers are also more likely to say that if they have a problem with a friend, they would have to end that friendship – a response which zero non-autistic participants gave (Finke, 2022). This is something Felicity has seen in her work with autistic teenage girls too – they tend to describe having very all-or-nothing responses to conflict with their friends, so if they fell out, it was either entirely up to the autistic girl to fix it, or entirely up to the other person – and if they didn't try to fix it the way the autistic girl thought they should, they would end the friendship (Sedgewick et al., 2018). The next section looks at some of the ways friendships and peer relationships can be less positive for autistic teenagers.

Sarah's friendships as a teenager

My family moved from Worthing to the Isle of Wight and I went to my second middle school and then high school in Sandown. Older childhood and adolescent home and school life and friendship experiences were difficult both for me and my brothers. My oldest brother was in the middle of his A Levels when we moved, which was a wrench, and my other brother was left behind in Worthing with neighbours so that he could complete his O Levels and join us when he had finished them. Why one set of exams were deemed to be more important than another is beyond me, but that is the decision that was made, again with no input from my brothers or explanation or discussion with our parents. The move did not improve their marriage and towards the end the tension in the household was unbearable.

At middle and high school the popular girls hunted in packs and some of them were incredibly cruel. Being overweight, academically clever, and wearing glasses made me an easy target even without adding my undiagnosed autistic weirdness into the mix. I existed on the periphery of friendship groups and didn't have any close friends although I appeared to my teachers, as reflected in my school reports, as being popular and bubbly. I developed a persona of being 'jolly' and someone who laughed off the taunts of bullies, but I was painfully lonely and traumatised by my school experience. One particularly awful memory involves me being at Guide Camp, sharing a tent with two of my worst bullies and being constantly subjected to songs that they made up about my weight. I couldn't escape them, but at least the internet wasn't a thing in the 80s. My heart goes out to all the neurodivergent kids who are bullied round the clock, even when they are not in anyone else's physical company.

By the time my parents eventually separated, both brothers had been shipped off to university and my mother and I moved into a small house near the high school. Like everything else of relational importance, their divorce was badly handled and devoid of communication. My older brother wasn't even aware that our parents were divorcing and was belatedly and grudgingly told that he had better come and stay with his mother during the summer holidays. It was like he had been completely forgotten about and it came as no surprise that he fell mentally ill during his time at university and was shipped off to our paternal grandparents to recuperate.

I can still picture the scene in the kitchen where my father promised my tearful mother and I that he would still be around and then promptly disappeared off the scene for months. My mother helpfully informed me that it was because he didn't love me. It was probably a throwaway comment made by a rejected woman sunk in her own misery, but I internalised it and added it to my already well-developed sense of worthlessness and unacceptability. My mother had said it, therefore it must be true because parents were always right. If I was going to be loved, I would have to obey the rules and try harder to be lovable. I had by this stage fully taken on board the messages that women existed to serve men; that obeying men and their needs was a woman's role in life and that in order to obtain any love from my father I had to strive to please him.

As a result, I worked hard at school, was top in most subjects apart from PE but had no real friends. I was a bullied swot, who felt far safer studying than socialising, the rules of which were a mystery to me. Trying desperately to fit in, but usually failing, I copied my peers and masked everything with loudness, bubbliness, and apparent confidence. I had no idea of how to behave or how to recognise social cues and floundered through my teens, judged as weird and feeling lost and lonely. I existed on the periphery of friendship groups, but was rarely included, and I remember feeling devastated when most of the girls in the class had been to see Duran Duran but had excluded me from the event. My mental health also continued to be poor, but hidden, apart from the very obvious development of extreme panic and obsessional fear of nuclear war that seemed to be constantly in the news in the 1980s. I remember calculating how long it would take for a nuclear strike in Portsmouth to reach the Isle of Wight and burn me alive and I couldn't sleep alone for several months.

I did well in my O Levels and went up to the Sixth form to study A Levels. I had become interested in sewing and costume design and started off by doing needlework, English literature, and geography. I met one of the newer girls at school who was friendly and kind and she introduced me to her family who were welcoming and included me in their lives far more than my own family did. I was lonely, lost, and desperately needing warmth and affection, so when they took me along to their church I wholeheartedly embraced what they were offering. This was probably one of the biggest mistakes of my life, as although this gave me certainty and structure, their love was very conditional on me obeying all their rules and my involvement in this, what can only be described as a cult, has left deep psychological and spiritual scars that I am still healing from now.

The male leadership was deeply controlling and didn't allow make-up, jewellery, trousers, or women speaking in church or having any kind of leadership role or opinion. Head coverings were insisted upon in services, and music of any kind, other than classical, was frowned upon, as was going to nightclubs or pubs or associating with other Christians from 'questionable' denominations. As well as these utterly crushing, sexist expectations, there were far more sinister undercurrents. I knew one female member who, when her car broke down, was too terrified to go into the pub down the road for assistance, as it was a 'godless' place which she could not associate with. What sort of belief system would put female safety at such a potential risk? The sort that preaches hellfire, damnation, and the terrors of being left behind in the Rapture at every opportunity, but also allows for male behaviour that says, "She's a good looking one. We'll have trouble with her" as part of my introductory greeting. Or another male church member who, when he had broken his leg, thought that it was appropriate to ask me, a young female who was alone in the room with him, to accompany him into the toilet and help him off with his trousers so that he could relieve himself.

Of course, I know now that all of this was deeply abusive. The warped theology, male-dominated control, and insistence of maintaining distance from 'the world' only served to isolate me even further from my peers. One very painful memory that stands out was a lunch break performance by one of the Sixth Form bands where one of the songs was about a religious hypocrite. The title of this song was 'Sarah'. Everybody but me knew that this was going to happen and I was utterly crushed by it, although there was more than an element of truth in the lyrics. I was living a double life – outwardly behaving in the way that the Elders wanted me to, while at the same time having sexual relationships with boyfriends. I wanted love and acceptance and behaved in ways that I thought would give me that with the people I was with at the time. It was classic people pleasing, masked behaviour that was rooted in the toxic misogynistic messages I had internalised growing up, and it was deeply damaging.

My home life had deteriorated to the point where I ran away from the flat where I lived with my mother and stepfather. I went to the 'cult' family, as I had nobody else. There were no real friends that I could turn to and neither my mother nor father were prepared to let me stay in their households. It was the same old story – no discussion or explanation, just a decision made on my behalf. I stayed with them for a few weeks while benefits and a room to live in could be organised so that I could restart, complete my A Levels and achieve the holy grail of getting to university. I had to attend the benefits appointments alone, had weeks of anxiety chasing the delayed housing benefits, and then when I filled out a form incorrectly a few months before my A Level exams, my benefits stopped and I was homeless again.

I don't know what would have happened had my oldest brother not stepped in and offered me a home when, yet again, neither parent was willing to house me. I found out quite recently that my uncle had actually contacted my father offering me a place to stay, but that this was refused. I will never fully understand my parent's treatment of me, but will always be grateful for my brother's kindness and living with him was fun. We did sailing and pub and cribbage nights together and being with him gave me the security that I needed. Travelling to school was a three-hour round trip which was exhausting, but I managed to get the B in English and the C in history that I needed to get into university. Quite an achievement after the years of turmoil, but all my father could offer when I told him my grades was, "Is that all?" He did, for once, apologise after being told off by my stepmother for his insensitivity, but the damage was done. Again.

Negative peer experiences of autistic adolescents

While it is obviously possible, and likely, that autistic teenagers will have friends, their social experiences are rarely universally positive. (Though really, whose are?) Autistic children and adolescents are more likely to be bullied than non-autistic children, and more likely to be bullied than children with other forms of specific

64 Big school

educational needs such as visual or hearing impairment, or those with Down's syndrome (Rowley et al., 2012). Between 6% and 46% of autistic adolescents in special schools report having been bullied (van Roekel et al., 2010), and this number is higher for those in mainstream settings, where up to 94% say they have been bullied (Hebron & Humphrey, 2014). It seems as though those autistic adolescents with milder social skills difficulties are more likely to be bullied than those with more obvious differences, possibly because their peers expect more of them and therefore are more socially sanctioned when they do not live up to those expectations. That may also be why autistic adolescents in inclusive education are more likely to be bullied than those in special education settings, and why those who have higher anxiety are targeted as 'easier marks' than other young people (Park et al., 2020). This is supported by the fact that autistic teens tend to be more subject to social bullying than physical bullying, facing things like being called names, being excluded, and being tricked into situations where other people will laugh at them (Kloosterman et al., 2013). Young people who have fewer friends at school are more likely to be victims of all types of bullying, and this may partly be because they don't have people around who can help defend them from these kinds of behaviours from bullies (Cappadocia et al., 2012). That theory makes sense, and fits with the patterns seen among non-autistic teenagers, for whom having at least one best friend acts as a protective factor against being bullied. Lots of the people we talked to had been bullied, with knock-on effects on how they felt about trying to make friends in general. Andrew and Krysia talked about this:

> My early teen years were devoid of friendships because I often got into fights with bullies. With the exception of one or two good friends I was a bit of a loner. I did not feel the sense of security required to form friendships as easily as neurotypical people often did.
>
> *(Andrew James Sanchez, 27, non-binary)*

> No one really wanted me as a friend back then. People just kept me as a token smart person, "oh Krysia's coming, she'll do x, y, and z. I'll copy her homework." I was excluded a lot from friendship groups who found it funny to pick on me, to bully me, and that sort of stuff has never left me.
>
> *(Krysia, 30)*

Bullying does tend to reduce over time – older autistic adolescents are bullied less than younger ones, and by the time they reach college age, bullying has dropped off significantly (DeNigris et al., 2018). This is the case whether the autistic teenager is in special or mainstream education. It might be that as everyone grows up and matures, non-autistic peers become more accepting of autistic young people and their differences, so they pick on them less. Equally, it seems likely that as they get older, autistic young people become more confident in themselves and their identity, and so are more difficult targets for bullies. Having been chronically bullied when younger seems to maybe even increase this identification with autism as a positive aspect of identity (DeNigris et al., 2018). Autistic teenagers also seem to make more solid friendships as they get older, which has the added benefit of the protective effect we mentioned in the last paragraph.

Being bullied can obviously have a major negative impact on a teenager's ability to attend or engage with school – whether they are autistic or not. Many autistic teenagers struggle to know how to cope with being bullied, often refusing to tell school staff for fear of making it worse (not unusual for any teenager) and then using a range of emotional outlets at home, with varying success. Many autistic students adopt school refusal as a way of avoiding their bullies altogether, which is understandable, but this has significant consequences for them in the long term (Bitsika & Sharpley, 2014). School avoidance is an issue amongst autistic children and adolescents of all ages, but if this coincides with major exams then it could be highly risky.

In terms of mental health, we also know that being bullied has really negative effects on people. Being bullied is associated with greater anxiety, depression, and worse long-term well-being, even into adulthood (Sigurdson et al., 2015). This is also the case for autistic teenagers – being a victim of bullying is linked to worse depression and anxiety, often severe (Chou et al., 2020). Sarah talked about this when she was a teenager:

> There was even more bullying at this point from boys and I was still struggling with my mental health, which made me not as great of a friend.
>
> *(Sarah O, autistic woman)*

Being socially anxious, though, also increases the chance of an autistic teenager being bullied, even if you allow for gender and age-based differences (Liu et al., 2021). This may be because young people who are socially anxious stand out as easier targets for bullies, because they react more to the early forms of being bullied, which encourages the bully to continue and escalate due to getting the reaction they want, or because they have fewer friends to defend them as we mentioned before. This last point has some evidence behind it – autistic teenagers who had more conflict in their best-friendships were more likely to be bullied (Zeedyk et al., 2014), which implies that having someone who is reliably on your side can help discourage bullies. When an autistic young person has a solid friendship to call on for support, the bully is effectively taking on two (or more) people, which is a much less appealing prospect than picking on a single, socially awkward teenager. Understanding the ways in which autistic teenagers can be protected from bullying, or at least from the worst of its effects, is really important – being bullied has recently been shown to significantly contribute to an increased risk of suicidality in autistic adolescents, especially autistic girls (Holden et al., 2020). The impact of peer relationships, both good and bad, on teenagers' mental health is well-known and well researched, but these more recent studies into the ways this affects autistic teenagers in particular show just how central these experiences can be.

66 Big school

Conflict within a person's friendships can also have a major impact on how people feel about themselves, how they manage relationships long term, and their mental health. This has been less researched but came up a lot among the autistic people we talked to for the book:

> It still reflects to this day that I don't cope very well with conflict, shouting or confrontation when people get enraged and angry. And this has sadly translated into adulthood as one of my friendships did break down as a result of constant argument.
>
> *(Jack)*

> Conflict has been the foundation of all my relationships, mastered mostly by doubtful sceptic minds.
>
> *(Imane, 15, autistic girl)*

> I get really freaked by accusations of conflict because I've been taught to be a people pleaser. It really jars me, as still to this current age I don't say everything I think about that person to that person because it can burn a lot of bridges. I really avoid it but if I do have to I will deal with it in a logical rather than an emotional response, which then makes me seem cold.
>
> *(Sarah O, autistic woman)*

Mental health, friendships, and camouflaging

Our friendships have an impact on our mental health no matter what age you are or what your neurotype is – same as being bullied does. For autistic adolescents, having friends and being less lonely is associated with being less anxious, especially socially anxious, probably because knowing you have a good friend helps boost your confidence in social situations (Schiltz et al., 2021). Unsurprisingly, having positive friendships and peer experiences is associated with reduced depression symptoms in autistic teenagers, while more negative experiences (such as being bullied) are linked to more depression symptoms (O'Connor et al., 2022). Interestingly, this same study found that for autistic teenage girls, having better friendships was associated with higher anxiety. While the study couldn't test which came first, the anxiety or the friendships, there are a couple of reasons this might be. First, it could be that autistic girls who have higher anxiety spend more time observing the friendship behaviours of other teenagers, and ruminating on friendships, and therefore learn what is expected of their peers more than those who have lower anxiety, which means that they are able to make more friends and have more positive experiences. On the other hand, it might be that autistic girls make friends, but then become anxious about being able to maintain those friendships, and worry about doing something wrong or losing the friend, and so even though they have good experiences, they are anxious about them. It may well be that, actually, it is a combination of both things, or that one aspect reinforces the other to build anxiety overall. This kind of anxiety about friendships can drive autistic adolescents (and adults) to engage in camouflaging or masking, to try to maintain the relationships they care about.

This means that an important context for understanding how mental health is impacted by friendship experiences is knowing about camouflaging, and how it is used in friendships.

Camouflaging, also called masking, is the name for when autistic people work to hide or suppress their natural autistic reactions when they are interacting with other people. This creates a mismatch between their internal 'state' of being autistic, and their external 'presentation' of their autistic self (Lai et al., 2017). Camouflaging has been talked about among the autism community for a long time, but has only recently become a focus of research. Autistic people often say that they mask so much that they struggle to know who they really are underneath it, or that it feels as though their whole life involves masking (Miller et al., 2021). It has been shown that autistic women tend to camouflage more than autistic men, autistic gender diverse individuals camouflage more than cisgender people, and those who are diagnosed in adulthood tend to camouflage more than those who were diagnosed as children (McQuald et al., 2021). Now that researchers are looking into masking among autistic people, they have realised that it has all-encompassing effects (as autistic people already knew). It is exhausting (Hull et al., 2017), and it has been shown to be linked to worse mental health in adults (Cage & Troxell-Whiteman, 2019; Hull et al., 2021), to increased suicidality (Beck et al., 2020; Cassidy et al., 2018), to difficulties with building a strong identity and sense of self (Cage & Troxell-Whitman, 2020) . . . and to have a role in friendships.

Several of our contributors talked about masking in social situations, and how their relationships changed if they didn't use the mask people were used to them having:

> I either had to pretend not to be me in order to appease them and not to annoy them or else be my natural self and be deeply irritating.
>
> *(anonymous, 62, autistic woman)*

It is important to note that some autistic people feel that masking is not all bad. It helps them get through difficult situations, it reduces the discrimination they face in interactions, and it can help in accessing social spaces (Bradley et al., 2021). It becomes toxic when it feels like it is essential all the time, in every setting, and with every person one comes into contact with – basically, when it becomes compulsory or compulsive, and when the autistic person doesn't have any safe spaces in which to drop the mask and be their authentic selves. Obviously, it would be better if there were more of these safe spaces for all autistic people, and hopefully one day we will get there. For now, though, the advice is often to try to find ways to use masking strategically, to your benefit, and to find those places and people where you do not need the mask to give themselves a break, which can help minimise or avoid the negative outcomes mentioned previously.

68 Big school

Camouflaging is measured, in most research, using something called the Camouflaging Autism Traits Questionnaire (CAT-Q, Hull et al., 2019). This is a 25-question measure which asks about a variety of different camouflaging behaviours, with higher scores meaning that someone does more camouflaging. It breaks it down into three types: compensation, where someone camouflages to compensate for difficulties in social situations; masking, where someone is trying to hide their autistic characteristics or appear non-autistic; and assimilation, where someone is employing strategies to try to fit in with the people around them. (You can take the test online for free on about a dozen different websites if you are interested!) It was designed with autistic adults, and initially tested with a large group (in the hundreds) of both autistic and non-autistic people to make sure it was measuring what it wanted to measure and that it was accurately capturing the differences between neurotypes. These people were aged between 16 and 82, which is an impressive spread, but means that the CAT-Q might not be as appropriate or accurate with children or younger teenagers, which is relevant to the research we are about to discuss.

(As a side note– Felicity is part of a team, led by Dr Laura Hull who developed the CAT-Q, to make a version which is suitable for younger people. This process will take at least a couple of years though, so though it will come out eventually, you won't hear about it or see it being used in research for a little while yet.)

We do know something about camouflaging and masking for autistic adolescents though, especially autistic girls. Because masking is higher in autistic women than men, this is one of the few areas where autistic teenage girls have been the focus of research above and beyond the studies which look at autistic boys – a very rare reversal in the literature. Most autistic adolescents do not necessarily *want* to be masking – they would rather have a reputation for being unique and different, and to be accepted for who they are than trying or pretending to be 'cool' (Cage et al., 2016). However, finding this acceptance amongst their peers, especially in early adolescence, is often very difficult, and so most autistic teenagers camouflage to some degree.

Autistic girls have been shown to camouflage more than autistic boys, at levels which are stable across adolescence (Jorgenson et al., 2020). This study found that non-autistic teenagers also engage in masking (rather than all aspects of camouflaging) and sometimes say they do this at higher rates than autistic teens – though this is partly because there is a significant increase in masking behaviours from early to late adolescence, especially for non-autistic girls. Linking back to the research described earlier – loneliness predicts how much camouflaging an autistic teenager does, in that those who are more lonely tend to camouflage more (Milner et al., 2022). This is probably because teenagers who are lonely are trying harder to make friends, so they can stop being lonely, and so they will work harder to hide their autistic traits to try to fit in with the non-autistic teenagers around them and be accepted socially. That makes it sound like this is a simple strategy, but it absolutely isn't. Autistic young people tend to develop different masks or camouflaging strategies for different social contexts, to help them fit in with different groups of people. That is hard work, and can lead to inconsistencies in how they manage their masks, and how successful these are (or aren't). We said earlier that camouflaging is exhausting, and that is because it requires a lot of conscious effort and energy to do it consistently and effectively. It makes sense, then, that research has shown that autistic teenagers who have more difficulties with executive function – planning ability, cognitive control, flexibility in thinking – do less camouflaging, because it is that much more difficult for their brains to maintain the mask alongside everything else they are doing and processing (Hull et al., 2020). We know that being able to drop the mask and be your authentic self is linked to better mental health for autistic adults, and the same is true for teenagers (Chapman, 2020). This makes sense – being accepted and valued as you are is a deeply validating experience for anyone.

Being accepted for yourself also helps you make friendships which you feel are genuine, rather than being based on someone you are pretending to be. Doing this, especially when younger, is something lots of people talked to us about:

> [I] have masked so heavily in any given social situation and just really forcing me to adapt my own social behaviour to how I'm meant to be . . . I became much more guarded as a person and more of a social chameleon than I would have been.
>
> *(Sarah O, autistic woman)*

This might be part of the reason that autistic girls who report having more friends are also more anxious – if they think that those people are friends with their 'masked' personality, rather than their true self, they will be worried that if they let the mask slip then they will lose their friends. Talking to autistic teenage girls, this seems to be the case – several studies have found that they are conscious of using masking and camouflaging to try to fit in with their peers, to make friends, and then to maintain those friendships (Cook et al., 2017; Halsall et al., 2021). Again, our contributors had experienced this personally:

> I would put on the mask and be sociable and I would maintain it for a certain period of time and then it would all fall apart because I couldn't keep it up. When the mask would slip then it's really disconcerting to be on the receiving end of that and what I noticed repeatedly was that relationships would break down as soon as the mask would slip. That used to seem at the time to me to be confirmation that if I ever showed my true self I would be forever rejected. Now in hindsight I can look back with a bit more perspective and understand just how disconcerting it would be to be on the receiving end of that and how difficult it would be to negotiate that in a developing friendship and how it's just easier to step away and not continue.
>
> *(anonymous, 54, autistic woman)*

Some of our contributors talked about the fact that even from being a teenager, finding friends with whom they could drop the mask and be more authentic was crucial. That didn't mean that they necessarily totally ignored how their natural

70 Big school

behaviours might appear or impact others, but that they felt much more comfortable being themselves with these genuine friends:

> I won't stim so much or I won't go off on an exposition of my favourite topic. I am still conscious of reining it in, but I'm not masking like I would be with others.
>
> *(anonymous, male)*

> I did become much more interested in developing friendships from my mid-teens and I did manage to find a group of friends that I genuinely felt comfortable with.
>
> *(anonymous, 54, autistic woman)*

Masking is often used in friendships, but it isn't really the answer for most autistic people. Autistic girls who camouflage are still targeted for bullying and have difficulties within their friendships, some of which come from the fact that some of their friends don't know they are autistic, and therefore maintaining the friendship and the mask at the same time can be overwhelming. Some of the things autistic girls talk about masking to try to help them make and keep non-autistic friends (and autistic friends or friends with other conditions) include their special interests, especially if they think these will be seen as immature, for example children's cartoons or games. It is reasonable to assume that autistic teenagers of all genders do this sort of thing, but there are very few qualitative studies which have tried to explore gender differences in masking, or the ways these relate to friendships.

There is some research into how the friendships of autistic teenagers differ by gender, though, which we discuss in the next section.

Gender differences in friendships

In non-autistic teenagers, there are some well-known and widely recognised gender differences in what friendships look like or how they are 'done'. In terms of how friendship groups develop, girls tend to have a smaller number of close friends – often forming pairs, trios, or quartets, plus a wider group of acquaintances. In contrast, boys tend to have a larger group of more equal friends, who they consider similarly close and important to them. Girls tend to spend more time talking to their friends, whereas boys focus on activities with theirs – something which is true from adolescence to adulthood. Female friendships tend to be more supportive and less competitive than male friendships, possibly because of the greater emotional sharing and bonding which comes through that greater focus on talking. Girls tend to be more jealous about their friendships, being more hostile to girls outside their friendship group and more protective of the friends they have, because they have fewer friends who they are closer to and therefore losing those friendships is potentially much more upsetting. Many of these patterns of gender difference are seen in autistic adolescent friendships too.

The topic of gender differences in autistic teenagers' friendships has only had research attention in the last decade or so, at most. With the lack of diagnosis which affected many autistic girls for many years, it isn't surprising that this is the case, but the good news is that the research is making up the difference relatively quickly. Autistic girls currently are the focus of a lot of interest, as the uniqueness of their experiences is being recognised – and the ways in which their support needs differ from autistic boys, because of the gender-based differences in social expectations they face from their peers.

Autistic girls tend to have better social skills than autistic boys the same age, especially in terms of their vocabulary and language use – something which is obviously really important for making friends with non-autistic girls who focus on building relationships through talking. It seems that those skills pay off, too – autistic girls are fairly consistently found to have higher-quality best-friendships than autistic boys, in that those friendships are closer and more supportive (Head et al., 2014). Felicity's PhD work is one of the main sets of studies which show this – for autistic girls with and without learning difficulties. Autistic girls have more social motivation (meaning that they are more interested in having friends) than autistic boys, and care more about engaging with and keeping the friendships they have. They talk about their friends more positively, as being more important to them, as spending more time together . . . essentially, as 'more' on every aspect of friendship which is measured by the common tools (Sedgewick et al., 2016; Sedgewick et al., 2018). The friendships of autistic girls were actually very similar to those of non-autistic girls, both on the statistical tests and in how they talked about their friends. Importantly, this was different to autistic boys, who rated their friendships as lower quality than all other groups, and who talked about their friends differently in interviews than any other group, including non-autistic boys. This is another piece of evidence against the Extreme Male Brain Theory of autism, which would predict that autistic girls should have worse friendships than non-autistic girls, and should have friendships which are quantitatively and qualitatively similar to those of autistic boys – because it essentially says that autism overrides gender.

Autistic girls do tend to have smaller numbers of friends than non-autistic girls, sticking to one or two very close, intense friendships, rather than three or four, and lacking the larger group of acquaintances which is typical for their non-autistic peers (Sedgewick et al., 2018). This is partly because they find it difficult to maintain the level of emotional engagement expected by non-autistic friends with more than a couple of people, and would rather have those one or two genuinely good friendships than exhaust themselves trying to build and maintain more. This can be because of the challenges of socialising with non-autistic people which come with being autistic – and most of the other people an autistic person meets will be non-autistic, and therefore most of their friends will be. The other part of it is that autistic girls tend to be more on the periphery of large groups, and so it is natural to make a smaller number of friends when most teenage girls around you socialise in groups:

> I was on the periphery of one or two friendship groups, but not really in the thick of anything and never really friends with girls in a way that was authentic. I just like physically remember like being physically on the edge.
>
> *(Sarah O, autistic woman)*

72 Big school

Also, autistic teenage girls without learning difficulties generally have a mature understanding of friendships and friendship expectations, in line with the attitudes of their non-autistic peers (Vine Foggo & Webster, 2017). This means they have similar anxieties when starting a new friendship, for example worrying about what the other person thinks of you; they have a sense of the difference between best friends and casual acquaintances, even though they tend not to spend as much effort on maintaining those casual relationships; and they are upset if they lose a friend through conflict or due to moving – all the things we would expect of any teenage girl (Ryan et al., 2020). Being aware of the differences between them and non-autistic peers is also common, as Louise talked about:

> Part of my problems at high school were because I did have a degree of social understanding. So I was keen to latch onto the popular groups because I wanted that social safety, but I couldn't.
>
> *(Louise, autistic woman)*

This is, we think, the key message from a lot of the work on gender differences in autistic adolescents' friendships – they exist! Autistic girls have to navigate a social world which has different expectations and challenges for girls than boys, and their gender is not negated by their neurotype.

One of the key gender differences we see in autistic adolescents is in their experiences of conflict with friends, and of being bullied. We looked at the general (mostly male) research in the 'negative peer experiences' section earlier in the chapter, but there is some evidence that this differs for autistic girls. Autistic girls are more likely to experience what is called relational aggression, and boys to experience overt aggression – which is also the case for non-autistic teenagers. Overt aggression is the stereotype of bullying, things like being physically picked on, being chased, having lunches stolen, and openly being called unpleasant names, for example. Relational aggression is more subtle, and fits in with the stereotypical 'mean girl' behaviour which we tend to associate with teenage girls. This can include things like spreading rumours, gossiping, stealing friends or preventing friendships, eye-rolling, and using sarcasm as a way of putting others down in front of people. This kind of aggression is mostly used by girls, and autistic girls seem to be the victims of it much more than non-autistic girls are – especially online (Cappadocia et al., 2012). Sarah and Eleanor both talked about their experiences of this:

> I always felt that there was something artificial when things went right, but I think that's also like the response to having a fair amount of mate crime where you know how girls twist things when they say to you things like they're not saying something nice, they're saying it to make you feel bad to show off in front of their friends.
>
> *(Sarah O, autistic woman)*

They would ride in the car with my mum and I to school and would be constantly diminishing me. For example, when we had a mock test I would still be studying in the car and still couldn't remember all the definitions. They would say "how stupid that you can't remember that" and stuff like that. And my mum thought that because I didn't react to it that I didn't care what they were saying, but they hurt me so much. And at the same time whenever someone in my class was mean to me, they would stand up for me. So I felt as if I was their thing to protect, but at the same time, they would just cut me apart. It made me feel like a charity project. Nobody was allowed to hurt me apart from them.

(Eleanor, autistic woman)

They also find it more difficult to recognise and respond to this type of behaviour, because it relies on that range of subtle social skills which are more complex and challenging for autistic people, and because lots of these behaviours can be 'spun' to seem less aggressive than they are. It is also the case that relational aggression can come from people who claim to be your friends. For autistic girls, who are more likely to have concrete and rigid ideas about who is and is not their friend, it can be confusing if someone in that category does something upsetting, and they may choose to ignore it rather than risk losing the friendship (Sedgewick et al., 2019). It seems that being the victim of bullying also has a bigger impact on the mental health of autistic girls than boys, particularly driving anxiety (Greenlee et al., 2020) and potentially contributing to self-harm behaviours, as autistic girls seek some form of physical release for the emotional distress they feel when being bullied or having arguments with friends (Sedgewick et al., 2018). It may be that the additional pressures autistic girls feel regarding their friendships contributes to the higher levels of mental health issues we see in this group, and this is something Eleanor talked about:

I thought I was just not interesting. People do not want to be with me. I'm stupid. Nobody likes me so why am I even trying? So I think that's when I stopped trying to be friends with somebody else. Before that I would always keep trying. So I quit being social, which is weird, since I'm not a quitter. I remember holding my pocket knife after a fight with my parents, looking at it and thinking: well I know how to end this, I know how to slice my vein. Shouldn't I do it and then everyone will be rid of me and I won't be a burden to anybody anymore. But I didn't do it, because I didn't want my family to feel guilty over me taking my own life.

(Eleanor, autistic woman)

Fear of social isolation is a real concern for many autistic girls. Because they have higher levels of social motivation, they are often more sensitive to peer rejection or neglect than many autistic boys. It has been shown that autistic girls may be more likely to be subject to this neglect than autistic boys – when classes groups are asked to nominate who they would or would not want to work with or play with, autistic boys tend to be actively rejected (named as someone to avoid) whereas autistic girls tend to be forgotten (not named at all) (Dean et al., 2016).

74 Big school

The exception to this is when the autistic girl has a close non-autistic friend, and then we see her being included via that friend, who acts as a sort of gateway to social inclusion. It has been shown that anti-stigma programs which specifically talk about autistic girls, rather than autism in general or autistic boys, can be effective in improving the social inclusion of autistic girls and how their peers behave towards them (Ranson & Byrne, 2014), but this was only a pilot and does not seem to have been systematically replicated on a larger scale, which is a shame. There is a lot of potential for such interventions to help transform the social lives of autistic girls, and their experiences of being accepted for who they are – which we know improves mental health, self-esteem, and lifelong outcomes.

Online friendships of autistic adolescents

The internet has been transformative for all of us, in so many ways. Autistic adolescents are no different, and the internet now plays a significant role in their friendships. Autistic teenagers, like non-autistic teenagers, are more likely to use social media to keep in touch with friends they have made (or at least people they know) in real life, rather than making entirely new connections online. Online interactions are usually used to reinforce or undermine offline relationships, becoming another tool in shifting social hierarchies and relationships – liking your friends posts to 'show' your connection to each other, or leaving a mean comment on someone's picture which you know other people in your class will see, for example. What is important to remember is that just because this is happening online does not mean that it is any less 'real' – these actions have offline impacts, and online relationships can be just as emotionally close and supportive as those made through in-person contact.

Aspects of social media can work well for autistic people, including teenagers – there are fewer social cues to decode, and there is the ability to take your time in working out what to say or do, for example. These things can make it easier to chat or interact with people, which can reduce the anxiety many autistic teenagers feel around friendships. Research has shown that autistic teenagers who use social media had strong friendships, and while this pattern was less strong in those with the highest levels of anxiety, overall it seemed to improve their friendships (van Schalkwyk et al., 2017). This reduction in anxiety may also be because autistic teenagers do less masking online, though girls still mask more than boys just as we see in offline situations (Jedrzejewska & Dewey, 2022). When asked why this was, teenagers talked about feeling like they could be more themselves online, and that they felt freer and more confident communicating in that format, which boosted their confidence.

The multi-modal options for communication in online contexts help autistic teenagers as well – even in games with voice chat options, for example, it is very normal to use written messages which can help with keeping track of the conversation (Stone et al., 2018). This doesn't mean the games always went smoothly –

the same team found that autistic teenagers tended to dominate their peers when creating things in Minecraft, for example, and that they often got into arguments about their plans in the game (Stone et al., 2019). Despite this potential for disagreements in virtual gaming environments, when autistic adolescents and young adults talk about what they get out of this kind of online gaming, they highlight things like learning social skills, greater emotional awareness, and building friendships through shared goals and supporting each other (Gallup & Serianni, 2017). As with anything, the effects and experiences of online socialising are varied, but there can definitely be benefits.

These benefits go against many of the concerns around autistic children and young people potentially having problematic, compulsive, or addictive technology usage. There is some indication that autistic young people do use the internet, video games, and technology, in general, more than non-autistic people the same age (MacMullin et al., 2016) – but this study only asked parents for their views of their child's technology use, and didn't try to ask what the young people were getting out of it. There have been many papers published which reflect a general sense of 'this must be a problem' about autistic young people engaging with technology – either because of fears of inappropriate use, of it causing a loss of in-person social skills, or their potential vulnerability to exploitation. Fears about exploitation online were important for some of the people we talked to:

> I didn't even have Facebook or any other social media until I went to university at the age of 19. I was 18 when I got Twitter and in some ways was good, as when you get social media at a young age I would be more vulnerable to certain exploitation. I enjoy social media now – Twitter and Instagram. I don't feel as though I missed out when I was younger with that.
>
> *(Jack)*

While this can be an issue, and we will discuss it in Chapter 9: Toxic, it isn't inevitable, and many autistic young people get far more benefit than harm from being online. In fact, although autistic adolescents can be vulnerable to cyberbullying or to online social exclusion, research is starting to suggest that they may actually be more risk averse on social media than their non-autistic peers (Rocheleau & Chiasson, 2022). This is important, and suggests that with gentle and age-appropriate conversations about online safety, autistic young people may be well-placed to take advantage of the social opportunities the internet offers.

Friendships during COVID

The big challenge which has recently faced autistic teenagers and their friends is the COVID-19 pandemic. In the UK, and around the world, people were put into 'lockdowns', where we were all told we should minimise going outside our homes, we couldn't socialise in person, and even once we could, there were significant restrictions on where, what, and for how long. The research into how the

76 Big school

COVID-19 pandemic tends to merge children, adolescents, and adults together – this was, understandably, research done at speed and trying to understand as many people's experiences as possible, as fast as possible, to generate recommendations for support. That is a noble goal, obviously, but means that this section of the book is also going to be a summary of the reported impact on autistic people of all ages at once.

Some autistic people reported that, initially, the lockdowns were almost good for their mental health in some ways – social anxiety in particular tended to drop, as the social expectations placed on them obviously dropped hugely (Bundy et al., 2022; Scott & Sedgewick, 2021). Despite this positive finding, though, the majority of the impact of lockdowns and restrictions on autistic people was bad. One of the overarching findings is that during the pandemic, autistic people's anxiety levels were significantly higher (even considering the relatively high starting point) and tended to stay this way even as restrictions started to lift for children (Panda et al., 2021; Toseeb & Asbury, 2022). Anxiety about COVID itself was often a major driver of this increased anxiety, plus the uncertainty of what was happening with the virus and the frequent changes to the rules around what was and was not allowed.

Although the initial reduction in social demands was a positive thing for many autistic people, the longer-term enforced social isolation was very difficult for most children, young people, and adults. They talked about desperately missing seeing friends, and even missing the more casual social interactions, such as at shop checkouts, which annoyed or overwhelmed them in normal times (Pellicano et al., 2022). This study was carried out in Australia, but Felicity has a piece of research which is not yet published where she asked autistic girls and women in the UK about how their friendships had been affected by lockdowns. Similarly to participants in other studies, they talked about how not needing to go to school or work had initially been a welcome relief from social and sensory pressures. Some participants also really enjoyed the shift to online socialising, such as structured online activities, being able to chat from the comfort of their own homes, and the move towards more use of texting and social media to keep in touch, as this was more regular than relying on meeting up in person. This, in particular, was something autistic girls and women wanted to keep in their friendships going forwards after lockdowns, as they felt it allowed them to engage on a more equal footing with their non-autistic friends. On the other hand, almost everyone talked about how much they missed seeing people in person, and felt that they had lost out on important time – especially teenagers, who were very aware of missing time at school, educationally and socially, and were worried about the impact this would have on them long term.

A couple of our participants talked about how during the pandemic their socialising had changed, and that some of this had been good in terms of them feeling more confident to ask to see friends in ways which work for them:

> A lot of friendships have turned into primarily not face to face now, but it's hard to differentiate the pandemic out of it. I've found that communicating

by text or WhatsApp is generally a good way and I think that I've also become much better in realising that I suck in group situations. I get overwhelmed, anxious, and I give an automatic response and go along with whatever everyone else is doing and I actually need to say "no", I need a two to one or one to one or be coordinating it slightly differently to going out with a group of ten people to the cinema.

(Krysia, 30)

We obviously can't know the long-term effects of COVID-19 or the lockdowns yet – as we write, it is only a few months since the restrictions were lifted in the UK. In terms of long COVID, mental health, child development, or adolescent development, we simply do not know and cannot easily guess how everything is going to pan out. The 'COVID generation' have been through something which hasn't hit the world in a century, and experienced this pandemic in a very different way to any previous time in history. How that affects all of us is going to be a focus of investigation for researchers in basically every discipline for decades.

Chapter conclusion

In this chapter, we looked at how friendships change in adolescence, becoming more complex and demanding at the same time as they become more important in terms of influencing behaviour and mental health. This process is true for autistic teenagers as well as non-autistic teenagers, and we see differences in friendships by gender in the same way too. More research is needed into the friendships of non-binary and trans autistic teens, who are navigating that social complexity alongside their emerging gender identity and how to present that to the world around them. It is likely that these young people are experiencing additional challenges, additional stigma, and hopefully additional joys which we do not currently have insight into. Of course, the other aspect of human relationships which becomes relevant in adolescence is romance and sexuality, which is the topic of the next chapter.

References

Bauminger, N., & Kasari, C. (2000). Loneliness and friendship in high-functioning children with autism. *Child Development, 71*(2), 447–456. https://doi.org/10.1111/1467-8624.00156

Bauminger, N., Shulman, C., & Agam, G. (2003). Peer interaction and loneliness in high-functioning children with autism. *Journal of Autism and Developmental Disorders, 33*(5), 489–507. https://doi.org/10.1023/A:1025827427901

Bauminger, N., Solomon, M., Aviezer, A., Heung, K., Brown, J., & Rogers, S. J. (2008). Friendship in high-functioning children with autism spectrum disorder: Mixed and non-mixed dyads. *Journal of Autism and Developmental Disorders, 38*(7), 1211–1229. https://doi.org/10.1007/S10803-007-0501-2/TABLES/3

Beck, J. S., Lundwall, R. A., Gabrielsen, T., Cox, J. C., & South, M. (2020). Looking good but feeling bad: "Camouflaging" behaviors and mental health in women with autistic traits. *Autism, 24*(4), 809–821. https://doi.org/10.1177/1362361320912147

78 Big school

Bitsika, V., & Sharpley, C. F. (2014). Understanding, experiences, and reactions to bullying experiences in boys with an autism spectrum disorder. *Journal of Developmental and Physical Disabilities*, *26*(6), 747–761. https://doi.org/10.1007/S10882-014-9393-1/TABLES/4

Bottema-Beutel, K., Malloy, C., Cuda, J., Kim, S. Y., & MacEvoy, J. P. (2019). Friendship expectations may be similar for mental age-matched children with autism spectrum disorder and typically developing children. *Journal of Autism and Developmental Disorders*, *49*(10), 4346–4354. https://doi.org/10.1007/S10803-019-04141-7/TABLES/6

Bradley, L., Shaw, R., Baron-Cohen, S., & Cassidy, S. (2021). Autistic adults' experiences of camouflaging and its perceived impact on mental health. *Autism in Adulthood*, *3*(4), 320–329. https://doi.org/10.1089/AUT.2020.0071/ASSET/IMAGES/LARGE/ AUT.2020.0071_FIGURE1.JPEG

Bukowski, W. M., & Sippola, L. K. (2005). Friendship and development: Putting the most human relationship in its place. *New Directions for Child and Adolescent Development*, *2005*(109), 91–98. https://doi.org/10.1002/cd.141

Bundy, R., Mandy, W., Crane, L., Belcher, H., Bourne, L., Brede, J., Hull, L., Brinkert, J., & Cook, J. (2022). The impact of early stages of COVID-19 on the mental health of autistic adults in the United Kingdom: A longitudinal mixed-methods study. *26*(7), 1765–1782 https://doi.org/10.1177/13623613211065543

Cage, E., Bird, G., & Pellicano, L. (2016). I am who i am: Reputation concerns in adolescents on the autism spectrum. *Research in Autism Spectrum Disorders*, *25*, 12–23. https:// doi.org/10.1016/j.rasd.2016.01.010

Cage, E., & Troxell-Whitman, Z. (2019). Understanding the reasons, Contexts and costs of camouflaging for autistic adults. *Journal of Autism and Developmental Disorders*, *49*(5), 1899–1911. https://doi.org/10.1007/S10803-018-03878-X/TABLES/5

Cage, E., & Troxell-Whitman, Z. (2020). Understanding the relationships between autistic identity, Disclosure, and camouflaging. *Autism in Adulthood*, *2*(4), 334–338. https://doi. org/10.1089/AUT.2020.0016

Cappadocia, M. C., Weiss, J. A., & Pepler, D. (2012). Bullying experiences among children and youth with autism spectrum disorders. *Journal of Autism and Developmental Disorders*, *42*(2), 266–277. https://doi.org/10.1007/s10803-011-1241-x

Cassidy, S., Bradley, L., Shaw, R., & Baron-Cohen, S. (2018). Risk markers for suicidality in autistic adults. *Molecular Autism*, *9*(1). https://doi.org/10.1186/s13229-018-0226-4

Chamberlain, B., Kasari, C., & Rotheram-Fuller, E. (2007). Involvement or isolation? The social networks of children with autism in regular classrooms. *Journal of Autism and Developmental Disorders*, *37*(2), 230–242. https://doi.org/10.1007/S10803-006-0164-4/FIGURES/2

Chapman, L. (2020). Don't treat autistic people like they're a problem, because we're not!: An exploration of what underpins the relationship between masking and mental health for autistic teenagers. (Doctoral Thesis). London: University College London.

Chou, W. J., Wang, P. W., Hsiao, R. C., Hu, H. F., & Yen, C. F. (2020). Role of school bullying involvement in depression, anxiety, Suicidality, and low self-esteem among adolescents with high-functioning autism spectrum disorder. *Frontiers in Psychiatry*, *11*(9). https://doi.org/10.3389/FPSYT.2020.00009/BIBTEX

Cook, A., Ogden, J., & Winstone, N. (2018). Friendship motivations, Challenges and the role of masking for girls with autism in contrasting school settings. *European Journal of Special Needs Education*, *33*(3). https://doi.org/10.1080/08856257.2017.1312797

Cresswell, L., Hinch, R., & Cage, E. (2019). The experiences of peer relationships amongst autistic adolescents: A systematic review of the qualitative evidence. *Research in Autism Spectrum Disorders*, *61*, 45–60. https://doi.org/10.1016/J.RASD.2019.01.003

Crompton, C. J., Hallett, S., Axbey, H., McAuliffe, C., & Cebula, K. (2022). Someone like-minded in a big place: Autistic young adult's attitudes towards autistic peer support in mainstream education. *Autism*. https://doi.org/10.1177/13623613221081189

Daniel, L. S., & Billingsley, B. S. (2010). What boys with an autism spectrum disorder say about establishing and maintaining friendships. *Focus on Autism and Other Developmental Disabilities*, *25*(4), 220–229. https://doi.org/10.1177/1088357610378290

Dean, M., Kasari, C., Shih, W., Frankel, F., Whitney, R., Landa, R., . . . & Harwood, R. (2014). The peer relationships of girls with ASD at school: comparison to boys and girls with and without ASD. *Journal of Child Psychology and Psychiatry*, *55*(11), 1218–1225.

DeNigris, D., Brooks, P. J., Obeid, R., Alarcon, M., Shane-Simpson, C., & Gillespie-Lynch, K. (2018). Bullying and identity development: Insights from autistic and non-autistic college students. *Journal of Autism and Developmental Disorders*, *48*(3), 666–678. https://doi.org/10.1007/S10803-017-3383-Y/TABLES/3

Dovgan, K. N., & Mazurek, M. O. (2019). Relations among activity participation, friendship, and internalizing problems in children with autism spectrum disorder. *Autism*, *23*(3), 750–758. https://doi.org/10.1177/1362361318775541

Finke, E. H. (2022). The kind of friend i think i am: Perceptions of autistic and non-autistic young adults. *Journal of Autism and Developmental Disorders*, 1–18. https://doi.org/10.1007/S10803-022-05573-4/TABLES/9

Finke, E. H., McCarthy, J. H., & Sarver, N. A. (2019). Self-perception of friendship style: Young adults with and without autism spectrum disorder. *Autism & Developmental Language Impairments*, *4*, 239694151985539. https://doi.org/10.1177/2396941519855390

Gallup, J., & Serianni, B. (2017). Developing friendships and an awareness of emotions using video games. *Education and Training in Autism and Developmental Disabilities*, *52*(2), 120–131. www.jstor.org/stable/26420384?casa_token=O1vBgsPFHzQAAAAA%3AkK0k-6C5zROFh69jb2LsSaKhapdYKV9QMAfDUPhuslOo3UbpqiORf52suc5XtZzmcSHf8H4dUKaR1Z_eoolHRwUR_yRyHjwcEamsOvPPf8EbtkVI-XQ&seq=1

Greenlee, J. L., Winter, M. A., & Marcovici, I. A. (2020). Brief report: Gender differences in experiences of peer victimization among adolescents with autism spectrum disorder. *Journal of Autism and Developmental Disorders*, *50*(10), 3790–3799. https://doi.org/10.1007/S10803-020-04437-Z/TABLES/4

Halsall, J., Clarke, C., & Crane, L. (2021). Camouflaging by adolescent autistic girls who attend both mainstream and specialist resource classes: Perspectives of girls, their mothers and their educators. *Autism*, *25*(7), 2074–2086. https://doi.org/10.1177/13623613211012819

Head, A. M., McGillivray, J. A., & Stokes, M. A. (2014). Gender differences in emotionality and sociability in children with autism spectrum disorders. *Molecular Autism*, *5*(1), 19. https://doi.org/10.1186/2040-2392-5-19

Hebron, J., & Humphrey, N. (2014). Exposure to bullying among students with autism spectrum conditions: A multi-informant analysis of risk and protective factors. *Autism*, *18*(6), 618–630. https://doi.org/10.1177/1362361313495965

Holden, R., Mueller, J., McGowan, J., Sanyal, J., Kikoler, M., Simonoff, E., Velupillai, S., & Downs, J. (2020). Investigating bullying as a predictor of suicidality in a clinical sample of adolescents with autism spectrum disorder. *Autism Research*, *13*(6), 988–997. https://doi.org/10.1002/AUR.2292

Hull, L., Lai, M. C., Baron-Cohen, S., Allison, C., Smith, P., Petrides, K. V., & Mandy, W. (2020). Gender differences in self-reported camouflaging in autistic and non-autistic adults. *Autism*, *24*(2), 352–363. https://doi.org/10.1177/1362361319864804

Hull, L., Levy, L., Lai, M. C., Petrides, K. V., Baron-Cohen, S., Allison, C., Smith, P., & Mandy, W. (2021). Is social camouflaging associated with anxiety and depression in autistic adults? *Molecular Autism*, *12*(1), 13. https://doi.org/10.1186/s13229-021-00421-1

Hull, L., Mandy, W., Lai, M.-C., Baron-Cohen, S., Allison, C., Smith, P., & Petrides, K. V. (2019). Development and validation of the camouflaging autistic traits questionnaire (CAT-Q). *Journal of Autism and Developmental Disorders*, *49*(3), 819–833. https://doi.org/10.1007/s10803-018-3792-6

Hull, L., Petrides, K. V., Allison, C., Smith, P., Baron-Cohen, S., Lai, M.-C., & Mandy, W. (2017). Putting on my best normal: Social camouflaging in adults with autism spectrum conditions. *Journal of Autism and Developmental Disorders*, *47*(8), 2519–2534. https://doi.org/10.1007/s10803-017-3166-5

Jedrzejewska, A., & Dewey, J. (2022). Camouflaging in autistic and non-autistic adolescents in the modern context of social media. *Journal of Autism and Developmental Disorders*, *52*(2), 630–646. https://doi.org/10.1007/S10803-021-04953-6/FIGURES/1

Jorgenson, C., Lewis, T., Rose, C., & Kanne, S. (2020). Social camouflaging in autistic and neurotypical adolescents: A pilot study of differences by sex and diagnosis. *Journal of Autism and Developmental Disorders*, *50*(12), 4344–4355. https://doi.org/10.1007/S10803-020-04491-7/FIGURES/2

Kloosterman, P. H., Kelley, E. A., Craig, W. M., Parker, J. D. A., & Javier, C. (2013). Types and experiences of bullying in adolescents with an autism spectrum disorder. *Research in Autism Spectrum Disorders*, *7*(7), 824–832. https://doi.org/10.1016/J.RASD.2013.02.013

Lai, M. C., Lombardo, M. V., Ruigrok, A. N., Chakrabarti, B., Auyeung, B., Szatmari, P., ... & MRC AIMS Consortium. (2017). Quantifying and exploring camouflaging in men and women with autism. *Autism*, *21*(6), 690–702.

Liu, T. L., Hsiao, R. C., Chou, W. J., & Yen, C. F. (2021). Social anxiety in victimization and perpetration of cyberbullying and traditional bullying in adolescents with autism spectrum disorder and attention-deficit/hyperactivity disorder. *International Journal of Environmental Research and Public Health 2021*, *18*(11), 5728. https://doi.org/10.3390/IJERPH18115728

Locke, J., Ishijima, E. H., Kasari, C., & London, N. (2010). Loneliness, friendship quality and the social networks of adolescents with high-functioning autism in an inclusive school setting. *Journal of Research in Special Educational Needs*, *10*(2), 74–81. https://doi.org/10.1111/j.1471-3802.2010.01148.x

Macmullin, J. A., Lunsky, Y., & Weiss, J. A. (2016). Plugged in: Electronics use in youth and young adults with autism spectrum disorder. *Autism*, *20*(1), 45–54. https://doi.org/10.1177/1362361314566047

Miller, D., Rees, J., & Pearson, A. (2021). Masking is life: Experiences of masking in autistic and nonautistic adults. *Autism in Adulthood*, *3*(4), 330–338. https://doi.org/10.1089/AUT.2020.0083

Milner, V., Mandy, W., Happé, F., & Colvert, E. (2022). Sex differences in predictors and outcomes of camouflaging: Comparing diagnosed autistic, high autistic trait and low autistic trait young adults. *Autism*, 136236132210982. https://doi.org/10.1177/13623613221098240

Munkhagen, E. K., Torske, T., Gjevik, E., Nærland, T., Pripp, A. H., & Diseth, T. H. (2019). Individual characteristics of students with autism spectrum disorders and school refusal behavior. *Autism*, *23*(2), 413–423. https://doi.org/10.1177/1362361317748619

O'Connor, R. A. G., van den Bedem, N., Blijd-Hoogewys, E. M. A., Stockmann, L., & Rieffe, C. (2022). Friendship quality among autistic and non-autistic (pre-) adolescents: Protective or risk factor for mental health? *Autism*, *26*(8), 2041–2051. https://doi.org/10.1177/13623613211073448

O'Hagan, S., Bond, C., & Hebron, J. (2022). Autistic girls and emotionally based school avoidance: Supportive factors for successful re-engagement in mainstream high school. *International Journal of Inclusive Education*, 1–17. https://doi.org/10.1080/13603116.2022.2049378

Ochi, M., Kawabe, K., Ochi, S., Miyama, T., Horiuchi, F., & Ueno, S. I. (2020). School refusal and bullying in children with autism spectrum disorder. *Child and Adolescent Psychiatry and Mental Health*, *14*(1), 1–7. https://doi.org/10.1186/S13034-020-00325-7/TABLES/3

Orsmond, G. I., & Kuo, H.-Y. (2011). The daily lives of adolescents with an autism spectrum disorder. *Autism*, *15*(5), 579–599. https://doi.org/10.1177/1362361310386503

Panda, P. K., Gupta, J., Chowdhury, S. R., Kumar, R., Meena, A. K., Madaan, P., . . . & Gulati, S. (2021). Psychological and behavioral impact of lockdown and quarantine measures for COVID-19 pandemic on children, adolescents and caregivers: a systematic review and meta-analysis. *Journal of tropical pediatrics*, *67*(1), fmaa122.

Park, I., Gong, J., Lyons, G. L., Hirota, T., Takahashi, M., Kim, B., Lee, S. Y., Kim, Y. S., Lee, J., & Leventhal, B. L. (2020). Prevalence of and factors associated with school bullying in students with autism spectrum disorder: A cross-cultural meta-analysis. *Yonsei Medical Journal*, *61*(11), 909. https://doi.org/10.3349/YMJ.2020.61.11.909

Parks, S. (2021). *Social learning among autistic young adult tabletop role players: A grounded theory study – Proquest*. Minneapolis: Capella University. www.proquest.com/docview/260840 1303?fromopenview=true&pq-origsite=gscholar

Pellicano, E., Brett, S., den Houting, J., Heyworth, M., Magiati, I., Steward, R., Urbanowicz, A., & Stears, M. (2022). COVID-19, Social isolation and the mental health of autistic people and their families: A qualitative study. *Autism*, *26*(4), 914–927. https://doi.org/10.1177/13623613211035936

Petrina, N., Carter, M., Stephenson, J., & Sweller, N. (2016). Perceived friendship quality of children with autism spectrum disorder as compared to their peers in mixed and non-mixed dyads. *Journal of Autism and Developmental Disorders*, *46*(4), 1334–1343. https://doi.org/10.1007/S10803-015-2673-5/TABLES/5

Płatos, M., & Pisula, E. (2021). Friendship understanding in males and females on the autism spectrum and their typically developing peers. *Research in Autism Spectrum Disorders*, *81*, 101716. https://doi.org/10.1016/J.RASD.2020.101716

Poulin, F., & Chan, A. (2010). Friendship stability and change in childhood and adolescence. *Developmental Review*, *30*(3), 257–272. https://doi.org/10.1016/J.DR.2009.01.001

Ranson, N. J., & Byrne, M. K. (2014). Promoting peer acceptance of females with higher-functioning autism in a mainstream education setting: A replication and extension of the effects of an autism anti-stigma program. *Journal of Autism and Developmental Disorders*, *44*(11), 2778–2796. https://doi.org/10.1007/S10803-014-2139-1/TABLES/2

Rocheleau, J. N., & Chiasson, S. (2022). Privacy and safety on social networking sites: Autistic and non-autistic teenagers attitudes and behaviors. *ACM Transactions on Computer-Human Interaction (TOCHI)*, *29*(1), 1–39. https://doi.org/10.1145/3469859

Rowley, E., Chandler, S., Baird, G., Simonoff, E., Pickles, A., Loucas, T., & Charman, T. (2012). The experience of friendship, Victimization and bullying in children with an autism spectrum disorder: Associations with child characteristics and school placement. *Research in Autism Spectrum Disorders*, *6*(3), 1126–1134. https://doi.org/10.1016/J.RASD.2012.03.004

Ryan, C., Coughlan, M., Maher, J., Vicario, P., & Garvey, A. (2020). Perceptions of friendship among girls with autism spectrum disorders. *European Journal of Special Needs Education*, *36*(3), 393–407. https://doi.org/10.1080/08856257.2020.1755930

Schiltz, H. K., McVey, A. J., Dolan Wozniak, B., Haendel, A. D., Stanley, R., Arias, A., Gordon, N., & Van Hecke, A. V. (2021). The role of loneliness as a mediator between autism features and mental health among autistic young adults. *Autism*, *25*(2), 545–555. https://doi.org/10.1177/1362361320967789

Scott, M., & Sedgewick, F. (2021). I have more control over my life: A qualitative exploration of challenges, opportunities, and support needs among autistic university students. *Autism & Developmental Language Impairments*, *6*. https://doi.org/10.1177/23969415211010419

Sedgewick, F., Hill, V., & Pellicano, E. (2018). Parent perspectives on autistic girls friendships and futures. *Autism & Developmental Language Impairments*, 3, 239694151879449. https://doi.org/10.1177/2396941518794497

Sedgewick, F., Hill, V., & Pellicano, E. (2019). It's different for girls: Gender differences in the friendships and conflict of autistic and neurotypical adolescents. *Autism*, 23(5). https://doi.org/10.1177/1362361318794930

Sedgewick, F., Hill, V., Yates, R., Pickering, L., & Pellicano, E. (2016). Gender differences in the social motivation and friendship experiences of autistic and non-autistic adolescents. *Journal of Autism and Developmental Disorders*, 46(4), 1297–1306. https://doi.org/10.1007/s10803-015-2669-1

Sigurdson, J. F., Undheim, A. M., Wallander, J. L., Lydersen, S., & Sund, A. M. (2015). The long-term effects of being bullied or a bully in adolescence on externalizing and internalizing mental health problems in adulthood. *Child and Adolescent Psychiatry and Mental Health*, 9(1), 1–13. https://doi.org/10.1186/S13034-015-0075-2/TABLES/7

Sosnowy, C., Silverman, C., Shattuck, P., & Garfield, T. (2019). Setbacks and successes: How young adults on the autism spectrum seek friendship. *Autism in Adulthood*, 1(1), 44–51. https://doi.org/10.1089/AUT.2018.0009

Sproston, K., Sedgewick, F., & Crane, L. (2017). Autistic girls and school exclusion: Perspectives of students and their parents. *Autism & Developmental Language Impairments*, 2, 239694151770617. https://doi.org/10.1177/2396941517706172

Stone, B. G., Mills, K. A., & Saggers, B. (2018). Online multiplayer games for the social interactions of children with autism spectrum disorder: A resource for inclusive education. *International Journal of Inclusive Education*, 23(2), 209–228. https://doi.org/10.1080/13603116.2018.1426051

Stone, B. G., Mills, K. A., & Saggers, B. (2019). Multiplayer games: Multimodal features that support friendships of students with autism spectrum disorder. *Australasian Journal of Special and Inclusive Education*, 43(2), 69–82. https://doi.org/10.1017/JSI.2019.6

Toseeb, U., & Asbury, D. K. (2022). A longitudinal study of the mental health of autistic children and adolescents and their parents during COVID-19: Part 1, quantitative findings. *Autism*, https://doi.org/10.31234/OSF.IO/HJYGT

van Roekel, E., Scholte, R. H. J., & Didden, R. (2010). Bullying among adolescents with autism spectrum disorders: Prevalence and perception. *Journal of Autism and Developmental Disorders*, 40(1), 63–73. https://doi.org/10.1007/s10803-009-0832-2

van Schalkwyk, G. I., Marin, C. E., Ortiz, M., Rolison, M., Qayyum, Z., McPartland, J. C., Lebowitz, E. R., Volkmar, F. R., & Silverman, W. K. (2017). Social media use, friendship quality, and the moderating role of anxiety in adolescents with autism spectrum disorder. *Journal of Autism and Developmental Disorders*, 47(9), 2805–2813. https://doi.org/10.1007/S10803-017-3201-6/FIGURES/1

Vine Foggo, R. S., & Webster, A. A. (2017). Understanding the social experiences of adolescent females on the autism spectrum. *Research in Autism Spectrum Disorders*, 35, 74–85. https://doi.org/10.1016/J.RASD.2016.11.006

Zeedyk, S. M., Rodriguez, G., Tipton, L. A., Baker, B. L., & Blacher, J. (2014). Bullying of youth with autism spectrum disorder, intellectual disability, or typical development: Victim and parent perspectives. *Research in Autism Spectrum Disorders*, 8(9), 1173–1183. https://doi.org/10.1016/J.RASD.2014.06.001

4

TEENAGE DREAMS

Adolescent dating

There is another type of relationship that emerges during adolescence, alongside the changes to everyone's friendships – that is, romantic relationships.

Dating

As puberty kicks in (a bit more on that follows), most people start to have sexual feelings, either for people of the opposite gender, the same gender, or both. This is a perfectly normal and natural process, for autistic teenagers as well as non-autistic teenagers. Historically, along with all the assumptions about autistic people not having friendships, it was assumed that they generally did not have romantic relationships at all. These are more complex than friendships in many ways, rely on an additional range of social skills, and are generally more difficult for anyone – especially the early forays into dating, as most of us can remember! So, what do we know about the beginnings of these relationships for autistic young people?

Puberty

Puberty is the backdrop to the development of romantic and sexual relationships for most people – either with others or with solo sexual exploration. It seems that autistic children may hit puberty slightly earlier than their non-autistic peers, especially autistic girls, whose periods start at a younger age than non-autistic girls (Corbett et al., 2020). In some studies, the average age for starting menstruation is as young as 11 for autistic girls, compared to nearly 13 for non-autistic girls (Eriksen, 2016). As you can imagine, puberty is a difficult enough time without being the first person you know to go through it, which is often the experience for autistic adolescents.

DOI: 10.4324/9781003044536-5

84 Teenage dreams

Puberty also hits at a time when lots of other things are going on, and the changes to your body, your relationships, and the academic expectations of this time can be overwhelming and have a negative impact on people's mental health:

> Your self-esteem is at a teetering point where you are going through massive body, hormonal and mind changes and being told that you have got to figure out your life for the rest of your life and then also the fact that there's so many ways that communication is being taken that you don't know. I messed up a lot of friendships because I didn't understand the social rules of what a 15- to 18-year-old was meant to be doing.
>
> *(Sarah O, autistic woman)*

Parents express a lot of concerns about their autistic children going through puberty, as this is a time when social relationships change and become much more complex alongside the demands of the physical process – social expectations from peers ramp up, and the emergence of dating adds an extra layer to school politics. This can be difficult for autistic teenagers to understand, of all genders, in ways we described in Chapter 3: Big School. 'Getting it wrong' in the eyes of their peers can leave autistic adolescents vulnerable to social exclusion, to being bullied, or to being exploited, all things their parents are very aware of. For parents of autistic daughters, they have additional worries around the changes that puberty brings – especially around periods, which we talk about in more detail later on – and around the potential sexual vulnerability of their daughters, who may be naive to the intentions of those around them (Sedgewick et al., 2018). Going through puberty brings changes to the parent-child relationship, whether the adolescent is autistic or not. This is something which has again been talked about with mothers of autistic daughters (Navot et al., 2017). This study found that mothers were initially very excited to know that they were having a girl, often expecting to easily build close relationships similar to those they had with their own mothers and sisters. They then had a process of adjustment when they realised that their daughter was different in some way, and working out what their mother-daughter relationship would look like – which shifted in adolescence towards having a connection which felt more based on shared experience and logic than mythical innate bonding.

Periods and PCOS

Getting your period for the first time, and managing your periods from then on, is a huge part of puberty for any girl (or person who menstruates – we will generally use 'girl' for ease of writing). It is associated with lots of changes, both in a girl's body and in how she organises her life. There are the obvious things like bleeding, period pain, sensitive or swollen breasts, and bloating – all of which can be unsettling to an autistic young woman who is used to her body being one way, and who is having to adapt to it doing something new. Sarah talked in her piece about how difficult her periods were, and how they affected her whole puberty and adolescence experience. There is also the executive function side of having periods – needing to track your cycle, work out what kind of period products suit you, and then make sure you carry them when you need them, and in the right quantity. There's actually quite a lot of planning and prediction involved, and it happens (roughly) every month.

There have been several studies looking at experiences around autistic menstruation and menses (the scientific word for getting your first period). Most of these have been hands-off surveys of medical records, like the one about autistic girls getting their period around 11, or interviews with parents about their views on their daughters going through that process. One paper which interviewed parents about their adolescent autistic daughters (who did not have learning difficulties) found that some felt that their daughters really struggled to manage their periods – especially at school, where difficulties with interoception could mean that they did not realise when they needed to change their tampons or sanitary pads (Mademtzi et al., 2018). The few days before a period starts tend to be a time when people are more emotional, usually more sad or more irritated by things, and this appears to be the case for autistic people too (Upadhyay & Vishwakarma, 2019). A study of autistic girls on the days before their periods, in addition to these emotional changes, found that elements of their autistic traits also intensified in this time – their sensory sensitivities became much more sensitive, they found it harder to cope with changes to their routines or plans, and they found socialising more difficult – something which is very important for adolescents trying to make and maintain those more complicated relationships we mentioned.

In contrast to lots of aspects of puberty and adolescence, there has been some research specifically into the experiences of autistic girls with learning disabilities around their periods (Cummins et al., 2020). The study involved interviewing parents and teachers, rather than the girls themselves, but the results suggested that puberty was actually more positive than parents were worried it was going to be for their daughters. While there was lots of individual variation in their experiences, parents felt that their girls had generally handled menstruation and bodily changes well, and that the thing which had really helped was emphasising dignity in managing periods, rather than treating it as something dirty or to be embarrassed about. This isn't exactly surprising, but it is good to know that this is how many families approach the topic with their daughters.

For some people, their periods come with even more challenges than the ones laid out earlier. Polycystic ovary syndrome (PCOS) is a hormonal imbalance issue which results in cysts growing on the ovaries, which can be intensely painful, lead to very heavy bleeding and anaemia, is associated with weight gain, and can affect fertility in adulthood. There is some evidence that mothers of autistic children are slightly more likely to have PCOS, and also that autistic women themselves are more likely to have PCOS (Cherskov et al., 2018; Odaydi & Puri, 2008). Which, long term, potentially implies that autistic women are more likely to have autistic children through the PCOS association along with the known genetic components of autism. What this means in the immediate present for autistic girls, though, is

86 Teenage dreams

that they are more likely to experience very painful and very heavy periods, which are difficult for anyone to go through and try to manage – especially people who have interoceptive and executive functioning challenges. So offer some extra sympathy to anyone autistic you know who is on their period, because they are likely to be having a rough time!

Sexual behaviours and exploration

The other thing which happens in puberty is that young people start to have sexual urges, and do things to explore those. Usually those experiments start solo, with self-stimulatory behaviours (otherwise known as masturbation!). This is perfectly normal for any, and every, adolescent, and it is not something that needs to be seen as a problem behaviour.

However, historically, masturbation and other sexual behaviours have been seen as something which calls for intervention in autistic young people – often because those who have learning difficulties engage in them inappropriately, such as in public or in front of other people. Wanting to teach someone about when it is and isn't a good idea to pleasure oneself is sensible, both for their own safety (so they aren't seen as sexually available by people who might want to take advantage of them, and to protect them from prosecution for public indecency) and to avoid discomfort for other people (witnessing someone in these kinds of behaviours without your consent can be distressing). There are lots of studies out there looking at this kind of intervention with autistic boys with learning difficulties, using a variety of methods from social stories to hormonal interventions like testosterone suppressants (Realmuto & Ruble, 1999). It has been pointed out, though, that the cause of a lot of inappropriate sexual behaviour by autistic young people is a lack of suitable sex education (Beddows & Brooks, 2016). After all, if you haven't been taught not to do something, or to do it in private, you don't know that is a social rule. And it isn't something people tend to talk about until it has already become a problem – most of us are a bit embarrassed discussing sex, let alone masturbation.

This is an issue in the sexual development of all autistic young people, not just those with learning difficulties. In the UK, and the US, we generally aren't great at teaching about sex and relationships to our young people full stop – teenagers in the UK score relatively low on sexual health questionnaires, and this knowledge gap is linked to more risk-taking behaviours around sexual relationships (Coleman & Testa, 2008). This is despite the fact that comprehensive and holistic sex and relationships education (SRE) has been shown to be associated with lower rates of sexually transmitted infections, lower rates of early or unwanted pregnancy, and better sexual well-being for young people of all genders and sexual orientations. If this is the picture for non-autistic young people, who are more likely to have picked up the social expectations around sexual behaviour, and who are potentially more able to seek out alternative, informal forms of information about sex and relationships, we can imagine how difficult this is for autistic teens.

This is especially the case because the research we have about SRE for autistic young people tends to show that they get less than their non-autistic peers, rather than more (or more detailed/deliberate SRE, which is likely to be helpful) (Hancock et al., 2017). Current SRE often focusses on the biology of puberty and reproduction, rather than talking about things like consent, unhealthy/healthy relationships, and the fact that these things can be pleasurable (especially for girls). Studies have shown that this can leave autistic young people confused, and without the information to understand what is happening or to keep themselves safe (Hannah & Stagg, 2016). It is also the case that autistic young people need to have conversations during SRE about how being autistic can impact sexual experiences – things like sensory overwhelm, for example.

Parents tend to think that they should be the ones to teach their autistic children about sex and relationships (Mackin et al., 2016), usually because they think they are best placed to know how to tailor the information to be accessible for their child. There can, however, be a tendency for parents to infantilise their autistic children, especially around the topic of sexual development, and to therefore assume that they need less information than they actually do – or that they need none at all. Parents tend to assume that their autistic children will not be interested in having sexual relationships (Sedgewick et al., 2018), or that they will lack the skills to make and maintain these kinds of connections if they are interested (Holmes et al., 2016). In fact, parental concerns about their autistic child becoming sexually aware or active can hamper their safe development, and it has been argued that instead of avoiding the topic, parents should help their children understand the social aspects of sexual and romantic relationships so that they are provided with the skills and knowledge to work out what they want for themselves. When parents do talk to their autistic teens about sex and relationships, they often focus on covering the basics rather than more nuanced topics or complex aspects of sexual health (Holmes et al., 2019), which can mean that young people are left to try to find information for themselves – if they are even aware of the gaps in their knowledge. Some of our contributors had this experience:

> I had a really really poor relationship with my parents when it came to talking about things like periods or sex and bodily autonomy, relationships with other people or social ones. The only advice I got from my mother about sex was "if a boy tells you he wants to have sex you need to say no and get out of the situation as quickly as you can". What use is that to a 20-year-old?"
>
> *(anonymous, 48, trans man)*

This attitude comes from the "not interested in sex" myth (Bennett et al., 2018), which came out of things like the Theory of Mind and other outdated models of autism – and which has now been thoroughly debunked. Some of the evidence that many autistic people are interested in, and do have, sexual relationships will be discussed in the next few sections. However, lots of parents also simply don't feel like they have the information or skills to talk to their children about these kinds

88 Teenage dreams

of experiences effectively: one parent summed it up as "I'm not sure we're ready for this" in a study looking at how parents try to support healthy sexuality (Nichols & Blakeley-Smith, 2009). This is especially the case for discussing the idea of sexual vulnerability, exploitation, and abuse (Kenny et al., 2021), despite the fact that this is something lots of parents are really worried about for their children. It is one of the most common 'concerns for the future' mentioned in any set of interviews with parents, especially parents of autistic girls, but there are not that many resources out there to help with this. What we would recommend is looking at the work of Carly Jones, an autistic woman who campaigns about improving autistic girls' safety. You can find out more about her and the things she does in the Recommended Reading List at the end of the book.

Romantic relationships

So how do romantic relationships get started?

In the 1960s, a researcher came up with a model for the stages from childhood friendships to adult couples (Dunphy, 1963). According to him, children start with small groups of same-sex friends, and these groups start to mix and interact more in early adolescence – think 12 or 13 years old. After this, mixed sex groups start to form, small at first, and eventually the whole group becomes mixed by late adolescence – roughly the end of high school. From there, in early adulthood, this large mixed group disperses into couples who go off and form their own nuclear families.

Now, this model clearly reflects a very specific view of relationship patterns, one rooted in the idea of small-town, middle-class, white America, where people married their childhood sweethearts in their early twenties and often never left the area they both grew up in. It assumes zero, or minimal, migration – not even the kind of migration which comes with moving away to university for a few years. That is no longer the standard for most people, at least not in the UK, where about half of young people go to university. Of those who don't, it is still far more normal for people to leave the areas they grew up in than it was in the 1960s, especially when looking for a job. The advent of online dating also means that people now often end up finding a partner from much further away than in previous generations, and one or both move in order to start their life together. This is a social world which those 1960s researchers couldn't have imagined!

Saying that, the core elements of the model aren't wrong. Children mostly have same-sex friendships when they are younger, they form mixed groups in their teenage years, and they start to date in their later teens. It's just that now, they don't tend to go straight from those first relationships into lifelong pairings (not that people did that in the 1960s as much as nostalgia would have us believe either . . . divorce is common among people who get married young). And lots of the ways that those first relationships make you feel haven't changed. The fact that love songs and poetry from the 17th century, or the 7th, or the 5th century BCE, when translated, are just as meaningful today, and when they were written is testament to that.

Teenage dreams **89**

A few years after Dunphy, an academic called Knapp came up with a model of the stages individual relationships go through, rather than an overall model of how they emerge within group dynamics. Knapp had ten stages of relationship development and dissolution, which fall into four phases. Not every relationship will go through every phase or stage, and there isn't a right or wrong speed to go through them either – they are more outlines of the processes that we see in relationships rather than a prescription.

1   Phase of coming together

1.1 *Initiation* – first meetings, first impressions, and starting communication with each other

1.2 *Experimentation* – starting to tell each other things about yourselves, to work out whether you are interested in this maybe becoming something more (small talk is common in this stage!)

1.3 *Intensifying* – working out whether and how much you like each other, and the start of building an attachment to the other person. This is when communication tends to get more frequent, things like pet names and inside jokes develop, and physical touch and other marks of affection tend to increase. It is in this stage where the couple are most likely to take the relationship public, telling friends and family about it.

2   Phase of coming together and relational maintenance

2.1 *Integration* – this is the first part of a relationship shifting to be long term, where the two people combine lots of aspects of their lives as individuals to build a life as an exclusive couple. This can include living together, having a shared friend group, and shared hobbies – alongside public displays of 'togetherness' such as being in profile pictures together on social media.

2.2 *Bonding* – this is the 'formalising' or 'bedding in' stage, where all of the behaviours from integration become long term and formally publicly acknowledged – for example, getting married. Relationships in this phase are considered truly intimate and fully bonded.

Of course, not all relationships stay together in that bonded state, just as not all relationships will reach that point. Knapp also has a two-phase/five-stage model of what relationships breaking down could look like – something we will talk about at different points in this book just as much as building relationships in the first place.

3   Phase of coming apart and relational maintenance

3.1 *Differentiating* – this is the first stage of a couple distancing themselves from each other, where they start to focus on the differences between them rather than the things they have in common (as in the coming together stages). It is important to note that this happening in a relationship does

90 Teenage dreams

not automatically mean that two people will break up – it is normal to have differences, and this can be part of a very healthy relationship. The key thing is how you manage those differences and negotiate differing needs.

3.2 *Circumscribing* – in this stage, a couple starts communicating less, and notably less about things which might cause conflict, even if talking about those exact things is what could help the relationship become stronger.

4 Phase of coming apart

4.1 *Stagnation* – this stage rather speaks for itself. It is the point in a relationship, usually a long-term established relationship, where the habits and patterns two people developed together become done by rote rather than because they are enjoyable. This can lead to one or both partners feeling trapped, and like the relationship has lost many of its positive qualities.

4.2 *Avoidance* – at this point, the partners start to avoid each other both physically and emotionally. That can be through choosing to be in the home at different times, or by ignoring each other when they are in the same space, or distancing through saying you don't want to do things together or even talk to each other. Each person begins to focus more on themselves, their wants, and imagining the things they want going forwards without their partner.

4.3 *Termination* – the final stage in the model is when the people involved call an end to the relationship, for whatever reason. Termination can be gradual or sudden, and can occur for any reason which seems valid to one or both of the partners. It comes with changes to public behaviour which signal to other people that the relationship is over, such as divorce, removing wedding rings, or separating aspects of the shared life which has been built.

This model is pretty comprehensive, when you look at it! It is also much more adaptable to changing social norms around relationships than the first model we told you about, because it is talking about categories of behaviour rather than specifics. Having someone in your profile picture would have been an alien concept when the model was created in the 1970s, but makes perfect sense when it is slotted into the context of that structure. That doesn't mean this is the one true model or anything, but we think it is a useful one and helps with thinking about many types of relationships we talk about in this book. It can definitely be seen in the emergence of romantic connections between teenagers, which we talk about next.

Teenage dating

Over half of young people have had some kind of romantic relationship by the age of 15. Our early romantic experiences help our social and emotional development, giving people the chance to learn about new types of intimacy, manage new expectations and priorities, and even learn advanced conflict management skills.

As they tend to be more invested in romantic relationships than friendships, teenagers have a higher stake in resolving conflicts that arise with their partners, and it has been shown that those who have even short-term relationships can develop better conflict resolution skills (Shulman et al., 2008). This is an important skill as adolescents move into adulthood, where they are likely to face more and more complex conflict situations, for example at work, and therefore need these skills. On the other hand, those who start dating earliest have more of a tendency towards what are called externalising behaviours – emotional difficulties, substance use, and potentially involvement in violent activities, especially if their partner is older (Connolly et al., 2013). This does not mean that having your first boyfriend or girlfriend at 11 instead of 13 (or whatever age) is a recipe for developing problem behaviours – just that there is an association, because dating can often come with exposure to a set of options which are generally intended for those who are older, and that is hard to handle for a still-developing brain.

Romantic relationships also have a major impact on well-being for adolescents. Having romantic relationships, even if they don't all go 'well', has been shown to have a positive impact on well-being for adolescents, possibly because it is a self-esteem boost to know that someone finds you attractive and interesting enough to date (Gomez-Lopez et al., 2019). Equally, those who have bad experiences, or simply who have had breakups which they find difficult to navigate, are more likely to show signs of poor mental health, especially depression, self-harm, and suicidality (Price et al., 2016). It does seem that young people are relatively good at seeking help for relationship-related mental health issues though, which is promising.

The variety of romantic experiences people have in their adolescence and early adulthood – dating, casual encounters, medium-term relationships – all help them learn about their preferences in a partner, the types of behaviours they do and do not like or value, and about how to maintain healthy boundaries (Jamison & Sanner, 2021). This all helps to put people into a better position to look for, build, and maintain a stable and supportive long-term relationship as they get older. It may not always feel like it (it definitely didn't for either of us!), but those painful encounters when you are younger are all helping you to learn something.

As many of us know from high school, more popular teenagers tend to date earlier, and more people, than others. Research into this phenomenon has shown that it is those adolescents who have more cross-gender friendships and who are more popular with opposite gender peers who tend to start dating earlier (Savickaite et al., 2019). Teenagers who are more socially anxious tend to have a more difficult time with their romantic relationships. That sounds like an obvious statement, but this seems to be as much because they have more difficulty with their friendships in general, which act as a kind of 'practice run' for romantic relationships. Considering that we know autistic people are more likely to have high levels of social anxiety, and to have fewer friendships, the implication of this work for autistic teenagers is that they may find their early romantic relationships that much more difficult than non-anxious and non-autistic peers do.

92 Teenage dreams

This is especially the case because some teenagers use 'dating' as a way to bully autistic young people, tricking them or asking them out as a joke to humiliate them. This was typical of the early 'romantic' experiences of some of our interviewees, and had a significant negative impact on their self-esteem and sense of themselves as sexual beings:

> There's a whole lot around 'ask her out on a dare'. It's an incredibly thinly veiled cruel thing to do. I experienced quite a lot of this from age 11 onwards, which feels far too young to have all that kind of traumatic experience around crushes and being asked out because it amounts to nothing and I'm just a useless eunuch of a person. Your body is being sexualised while simultaneously being desexualized.
>
> *(Sarah O, autistic woman)*

The other inevitable aspect of dating is, of course, the break up. The end of even a casual relationship can be significant for someone, especially if they were hopeful of it becoming a long-term thing or if it comes in a string of rejections and failed relationships. There is a joke that saying to someone "we can still be friends" when you break up is like saying "your dog died but you can keep it". That seems a little extreme to us, but there are factors which make it easier or harder to maintain a friendship once the romantic element of a relationship comes to an end. If there were high levels of satisfaction in the relationship aside from the factor which ended the romance, and high levels of friendship, then the friendship is more likely to continue. On the other hand, if other friends or family members are not supportive of the friendship continuing, if one or both people rapidly move into a new romantic relationship, or the relationship came to an end through neglect ('ghosting'), then a friendship is much less likely (Busboom et al., 2002). Navigating the politics of a breakup, at the same time as going through the emotional upset, can be challenging for any young person, and is likely even more so for autistic adolescents, though we have no studies on this kind of experience yet.

Going through a breakup is associated with a period of increased distress and worse mental health, especially for girls and women, and having higher levels of depressive symptoms contributes to it being harder to recover from that breakup (Shulman et al., 2017). Experiencing extreme distress around breakups can also impact someone when they are in a relationship, as it can lead to feeling anxious (anticipating the distress over what feels like the inevitable breakup) – and the behaviours people use to try to manage that can actually, counterproductively, increase the chances of someone leaving you. In adolescence, the main reasons for relationship breakup can be put into five categories: affiliation – how well you get on; intimacy – both physical and in terms of communication; autonomy – the desire to do things independently or explore options away from your partner; infidelity – cheating is rarely a recipe for relationship success; and status – having a similar position in the social hierarchy is often especially important for teenagers, so couples where there is a mismatch are more likely to break up

(Bravo et al., 2017). Feeling unsupported and less attracted to your partner are also key predictors of relationship breakup (Lantagne et al., 2017) – though that probably isn't specific to adolescents!

Technology and dating

Just as with friendships, the world of dating has been transformed by the advent of the internet, especially social media. Technology is ubiquitous – not only is it always with us via the smartphones in our pockets, but it is essential to navigating modern life. Teenagers today exist as much online as offline, and this applies to their romantic relationships as much as anything else.

Among adults, around half of relationships now start online, through specific dating apps or through encounters on social media like Twitter and Instagram. That number is generally still lower for teenagers, who are most likely to meet their partners at school or through in-person activities. It is actually still relatively rare for teenagers to say that they make friends purely online, although this is a bit different for boys who make friends around the world through online gaming. Also, LGBTQ adolescents are more likely to find a partner online than heterosexual adolescents, although overall they still tend to do this in their day-to-day offline activities (Korchmaros et al., 2015). Adolescents generally use their social media as an add-on for their offline relationships, rather than for making new friendships or relationships.

This can be seen in the fact that the most common uses for social media in adolescent friendships are public displays of affection – liking and commenting on posts, for example; monitoring your partner – by watching who they interact with or where and what they are posting; and communicating with your partner – usually through private messages. Teenagers who engage in more cyber-monitoring of their significant other tend to have lower self-esteem (Langlais et al., 2018), which makes sense as it is likely that teenagers who struggle with low self-esteem will be more anxious about the relationship. It may be that autistic teenagers are therefore more likely to engage in this kind of monitoring behaviour, as we know that they tend to be more anxious, but this can cause conflict within a relationship if it is excessive – and it can turn into cyberstalking, which we discuss in Chapter 9: Toxic. In terms of building relationships, even young adolescents use technology to help them – electronic messaging can be a more private way of approaching a potential partner, without the risk of a public rejection (Christopher et al., 2015). This is important for those who may be more socially awkward or who are approaching someone outside their usual social circle, as most often adolescent relationships are played out in front of the whole friendship group or class context, adding pressure to what is already a fairly anxiety-inducing process.

Sexting – sending or receiving explicit messages and images – is also fairly common for teenagers, and is increasingly seen as a normal part of a modern relationship. It is most commonly used as a bonding activity, where both people

94 Teenage dreams

build intimacy through sharing these materials as well as displaying trust in their partner by sending them. Autistic teenagers may be more likely to be manipulated or pressured into sharing these kinds of messages and images, as they are more likely to struggle to get into a relationship in the first place and therefore may be more willing to do things to maintain it. They also are likely to have fewer close friends with whom they can check whether different behaviours are normal – or simply whether it is a good idea to do something their partner has asked of them. There is more discussion of sexting in the chapter on adult romantic relationships (Chapter 6: Well, Hello There), but essentially we know very little about autistic experiences with this side of relationships, despite the general acknowledgement that it is an aspect of modern dating which everyone has to navigate at some point.

Sarah on puberty and dating

My periods started early at about age 12, but there was little communication, preparation, or support from my mother. I remember being in excruciating agony with them and being prescribed what looked like horse pills to ease the pain. I developed breasts and pubic hair a long time before my peers and the humiliation of having to endure mandatory communal showers after PE still makes me feel sick now. I would try anything to get out of doing PE because this was so awful and embarrassing, and tried to get my mother to write me letters that would excuse me from this, but to no avail. Some of the girls in the changing room were incredibly cruel. I was laughed at, teased, and isolated, and there was no escape.

I had older boyfriends and a mix of longer- and shorter-term romantic and sexual relationships from my early teens. I looked older than I was, with large breasts, which some boys seemed to like, and I really wanted to be liked. I enjoyed the attention, but didn't have the social awareness that would have informed me if someone was interested in me or if they were predatory. I was lucky with Danny, who was my first proper boyfriend. He was four years older than me and was a gentle soul and we were together for a year or so. I'm guessing that he was in part an emotional replacement for my father who wasn't present in my life at the time, but he was kind, and spending time with him took me away from my family difficulties. Other boyfriends were shorter term and probably so in part because I was a clingy and intense girlfriend. If anyone showed me a bit of attention I would fall hard and fast for them and was devastated when they broke up with me. I didn't have any sense of the fun of getting to know someone or hanging out, which was also reflected in my lack of close friendships, and I became far too romantically serious at far too young an age, far too often.

I also became chameleon-like when being with a boyfriend and his friends. I could be charming, funny, bitchy, or nasty as the mood of the group dictated, but I was never myself. I didn't know how to be, but was so desperate for love, attention, and acceptance that I didn't know any other way to behave. Of course, I know now that I was an autistic teenage girl who was masking like a pro, but at the time I was confused and operating in survival mode and as a result of trauma. I developed such a reputation that my name was plastered on the underpass on the way to school, but I never felt as if I was the word that was written describing me. I wanted to be loved, but had no idea of what could healthily achieve that goal. I people pleased, behaving in ways that I thought that boys and men wanted and didn't put any of my needs first. I didn't even know that I had any or that they were even of any importance. I was there to serve males, not myself.

Teenage dating did not help my self-esteem much as I was sometimes rejected by boyfriends because of my physical appearance. There was one brief relationship that ended because although he thought I had killer cheekbones, he didn't like the fact that I was overweight and so he finished with me. This sort of rejection only added to my desperation and unhappiness and I became pathetically grateful for any attention that was shown to me. I think this resulted in me staying in at least one relationship far longer than I should have done. I ignored his playing around because I was just grateful that I had someone and it took far too long for me to summon up the smidgeon of self-respect that I possessed to dump him.

There are other factors that influenced my dating and sexual behaviour as a teenager and beyond, but I will discuss this in the chapter on toxic relationships. Overall, my experience of adolescent dating wasn't a happy one and was a painful reflection of the unhealthy attachment styles that I had developed since my childhood and lack of friendships in my teenage years. Meeting my first husband when I was in my late teens was probably the apotheosis of this. He was a friend of a friend and we got together and became engaged while I was in my last year of high school. It was ridiculously young, but we were both from difficult backgrounds and I think that we clung to each other to escape from the people who had caused us harm. We married after my first year at university, which was in no doubt influenced by my residual extreme religiosity and expectations from the 'cult'. The relationship lasted for six, often difficult, years together, before divorcing due to my infidelity. We have both moved on to better relationships with ourselves and with other partners since then, and I wish him well.

Autism and teenage dating

Despite the lack of sex education we talked about earlier, autistic teenagers are still dating and having sexual experiences. Getting into these relationships can be tricky, even for those who want them, because people tend to signal romantic interest in fairly subtle ways – which one of our contributors talked about:

> I was oblivious to guys showing an interest in me. So I would have had a sense of failure and I thought that I was unattractive and nobody would have been interested, but actually I would have missed the signs and not have had a clue if anyone showed an interest in a socially appropriate way.
>
> *(anonymous, 54, autistic woman)*

Autistic teens generally have fewer romantic relationships than their non-autistic peers, and their first sexual experiences tend to be a few years later, but they are having them (Mehzabin & Stokes, 2011). Autistic boys without learning difficulties develop their sexual behaviours and interests in the same way, and at the same rate, as their non-autistic peers (Dewinter et al., 2015), and there is no reason to suppose this would be different for autistic girls.

Parents tend not to be aware of, or at least underestimate, their autistic child's level of sexual experience, either solo or with a partner (Dewinter et al., 2016). This throws some of the aforementioned findings on things like sexual behaviour or knowledge into doubt, as the majority of studies rely on parent or teacher report rather than asking young people themselves. This isn't totally unexpected – and isn't automatically a problem. After all, most parents of non-autistic teenagers don't know everything they do either, especially around dating and sexual behaviours. It would probably be more unusual for a parent to know exactly what their teenager has or hasn't done at every point! Having that independence and autonomy in emerging relationships is important in the development of any young person, as long as it is done safely. It has been shown that parents of autistic teenagers tend to assume that their child is more comfortable confiding in them about these topics than they actually are, and also that autistic teens are accessing forms of information their parents don't know about (Teti et al., 2019). These are usually online, and mostly porn – something which, again, isn't unusual for parents to be unaware of.

Autistic teenage boys and men report having higher levels of sexual desire, and more frequent masturbation than autistic girls and women. They also tend to say that they are more satisfied with the sexual experiences they have had than their female peers (Pecora et al., 2016). A similar amount of autistic and non-autistic boys say they have masturbated to orgasm by the age of 16, but autistic boys are much less likely to have experience with a partner at this age. For given behaviours with partners, there were no real differences between the groups in terms of when they first tried things, though slightly fewer autistic boys said that they enjoyed their first time having sex, and they were a bit more likely to regret the specific experience – possibly because they were more likely to have been surprised by it happening, for example it was not a planned encounter but a progression during a normal make-out session (Dewinter et al., 2016). This study talked to autistic boys at the age of 16 and then again at 20, and the majority of the more advanced sexual interactions had happened between those ages for all participants, regardless of neurotype. A similar study has yet to be done with autistic girls as they grow up, but it would be interesting to see not only what sexual experience they have and when, but how they feel about it. We know that early experiences in any type of relationship have an impact long term, so understanding how first sexual explorations go on to affect autistic people is really important for their lifelong well-being.

One of the things our contributors raised was the difficulty of knowing what was considered 'proper' behaviour in a relationship. There is often an expectation of some kind of sexual contact with your partner, but what and when is 'right' is a difficult balancing act to manage:

> Social norms for me, especially the sexual side of it, what has taken my peers maybe 6, 8, 10, 12 weeks to get to, I was doing it in one or two weeks. Not understanding why the person didn't want to see me anymore, because that's all tied up with patriarchal norms as well. Don't date the girl that's a slag or take her home to your mother. How do you know you're one if nobody tells you? If it's not explained to you so that you understand. I didn't know any better.
>
> *(anonymous, 48, trans man)*

> I had a lot of sexual experiences in college. In my head it was kind of like, "let's try anything".
>
> *(anonymous, 47, autistic male)*

When asked what they would look for in an ideal partner, a group of autistic boys and girls (mostly boys) said that they would want someone who was loyal, and who was accepting of them being autistic. They generally did want relationships, and some had good experiences, but as for many people regardless of neurotype, the reality did not always live up to the ideal scenarios in their heads for those who had dated. Instead, several of the young people had experiences of being cheated on, being used in some way, or simply having high levels of conflict and low levels of contact in their relationships, which they found confusing and stressful (Cheak-Zamora et al., 2019). Finding a partner in the first place has been noted as a specific challenge for autistic young people (once again, the studies focus on boys generally), as is negotiating being part of a couple once you are in the relationship (Dewinter et al., 2017). When interviewed, the young men in this study who had sexual experiences with a partner felt that it was difficult to know what the other person was genuinely enjoying or interested in, and several found it hard to adapt their needs to work with the needs of their partner – although they tried to do so. On a linked point, one of our interviewees talked about the fact that what they really wanted was the romantic side of the relationship, rather than the sexual activity which many teenagers focus on:

98 Teenage dreams

> I was a lot less interested in sexual romantic relationships then people my age, as I had virtually no sex drive. I did however, seek out romantic relationships more than my peers. I wanted to experience dating, and cuddling with a partner who loved me.
>
> *(Andrew James Sanchez, 27, non-binary)*

Social and communication skills are what are most studied in relation to autistic people's romantic relationships generally, but one review looked at what factors are associated with successful romantic experiences (Yew et al., 2021). This showed that finding someone who likes you as much as you like them, your partner being supportive of your autistic identity, and your partner helping to meet your needs emotionally and practically, are all associated with better relationships. Looking at that list, all you would do to make a how-to guide for good partnerships in general is remove the word 'autistic' from in front of 'autistic identity'. Hopefully by this point in the book, we have emphasised this message enough, but here we go again – autistic people can have relationships just as good as those of non-autistic people, and they don't need anything which is wildly unusual – just acceptance and support from people who value them as they are.

Autism and non-heterosexuality

Nearly all of the research discussed in this chapter so far has, implicitly, been looking at the experiences of heterosexual teenagers. However, autistic people are far more likely to be non-heterosexual than non-autistic people (George & Stokes, 2018). Your sexuality is a lifelong thing, and so we need to acknowledge that autistic teens are therefore also more likely to be non-heterosexual than their peers. Autistic teenage girls are several times more likely to say that they are bisexual than their non-autistic peers, for example (May et al., 2017). This has consequences in many ways – for the kind of sex and relationship education they need, for their early romantic and sexual experiences, and for their development as individuals.

Somewhere between roughly 5% and 30% of autistic people will identify as non-heterosexual or gender diverse in some way, depending on which studies you look at (Dewinter et al., 2017; Sedgewick et al., 2020). It is worth noting that being asexual is included in those statistics, because that is a valid sexual identity where someone feels little or no desire for sexual and/or romantic relationships. Autistic people are more likely to be asexual than non-autistic people, with men being four times more likely and women twice as likely (George & Stokes, 2017). Autistic people are also more likely to be lesbian, gay, or bisexual, as we said – there are various theories for why this might be, from increased exposure to certain hormones in the womb to a lower level of investment in social norms around attraction, meaning that they are more open to same-sex relationships. Regardless of the theories for why someone may have the sexuality they do (which frankly, does not interest us much), it is interesting to hear the stories of some of our contributors about how they explored and worked out their sexuality:

Teenage dreams **99**

> I slept with a few women. I found that it wasn't really my thing even though it was very biologically practical it was not something that I wanted to pursue. Then I started experimenting with guys, gender fluid people, and so on. I eventually settled with men and right now I identify as gender fluid gay. I do use he/him pronouns and I do feel that I've never been much of a manly man or a womanly woman. I kind of like somewhere in the middle so I think that gender fluid would be more appropriate.
>
> *(anonymous, 47, autistic male)*

Gender dysphoria is much more common among autistic people of all ages than it is in non-autistic people (George & Stokes, 2016), which is part of why autistic young people are 'over-represented' in gender clinics (in the opinions of some commentators). It has been argued by those same commentators that if someone is autistic, then they cannot properly know their own gender, and so should not be given gender-affirming care – we believe this is false, and harmful. Accessing gender-affirming care in most parts of the world is a very long and difficult process, and the longer young people go without support, the worse their mental health and well-being. We should never be advocating for damaging people, but instead should be finding ways for them to explore their identity in a supportive way. We aren't going to go into the arguments about this in detail here, because that would be a whole book of its own. There is growing research about the experiences of autistic people who are gender diverse though, which highlights that autistic girls are more likely to experience gender-body incongruence than autistic boys, and that autistic children who feel this dysphoria have worse mental health and higher levels of suicidality (Corbett et al., 2022). It can be difficult for autistic children and young people to explain these feelings though:

> I remember having discussions with my family with my mother in particular about 8/9/10 saying things like, "but would it not just be easier if nobody had a gender" and then "wouldn't it be easier if we could just hang our bits onto ourselves in the morning". As a child trying to describe how I felt, but I couldn't say anything about how I felt because I didn't have the descriptive language to do that.
>
> *(anonymous, 48, trans man)*

Autistic people tend to feel happier in themselves as they move towards a social identity and presentation which aligns with how they identify, although they still worry about moving through life with two stigmatised identities – being autistic and being trans (Coleman-Smith et al., 2019). There isn't enough research on the relationship experiences of trans and gender-diverse autistic people for a full section here (yet) – hopefully there will be by the time we write a second edition.

The fact that autistic people are more likely than non-autistic people to be gay, lesbian, or bisexual has only been recognised recently in research, and although it has been known for a long time in the community, open discussions about this fact

100 Teenage dreams

are also relatively recent. For a long time, people who were not heterosexual had to hide their sexuality for fear of stigma and prejudice from society and the people around them – and lots of people still face these attitudes. Homophobia has not gone away, even though it is reducing with each generation, and with the increased visibility of LGBTQ people in public life.

Indeed, autistic LGBTQ people may face additional stigmatisation as being part of a 'multiple minority', where they have minority status both in terms of neurotype and sexual identity. While recent research suggests that they do not report experiencing more frequent discrimination in practice, they are much more concerned about facing everyday prejudice from those they encounter, and are more aware of how their autism, gender, and sexuality intersect to build their identity (Khudiakova & Chasteen, 2022). This is in line with the Multiple Minority Stress Theory, which was first developed looking at the mental health of gay men in America. It argues that people with minority identities on some axis – race, gender, sexuality, religion – experience more stress in their lives, and that this negatively impacts their mental health. For those who have multiple minority identities – being black and female, or gay and Muslim, for example – this effect is multiplied, with corresponding impacts on mental health and general life outcomes. Autistic people are also a minority in terms of neurotype, and we have discussed the ways in which we know their mental health is worse, as the theory would predict – something which has been explored academically by Monique Botha (Botha & Frost, 2018). It is reasonable to assume that autistic LGBTQ people will face additional stigma and stress on top of that which comes with being autistic and straight, and there are indications that autistic gender-diverse people do have worse mental health (Sedgewick et al., 2020), which would support this theory. More work is needed (as ever) to understand the experiences of autistic LGBTQ people, as they form such a large part of this community and may be uniquely vulnerable in many ways.

Regardless of the fact that many LGBTQ people could not be open about their love lives for a long time, there have been studies of how sexuality develops as an identity since the 1970s, in response to the cultural shift of the 1960s towards being more liberal about sex and sexuality. One of these earliest models was developed by an academic named Cass, working with gay men, who published their identity model in 1979. This model had six stages, from *identity confusion* (thinking "Could I be gay?") through *identity comparison*, *tolerance* and *acceptance*, to *identity pride* and *identity synthesis* (when being gay feels like one part of an overall identity rather than the dominant feature). All of this is very much inwards facing – it is all about how someone feels or thinks about their sexuality. Fifteen years later, another academic developed a model of how people embody their sexuality – effectively looking at the different stages of 'coming out' as gay (again, he only worked with gay men in the US). This also had six stages – something about the number six seems to appeal to academics building models! He felt that homosexual identity started with *exiting heterosexuality*, similar to *identity confusion* from Cass. He then argued that the rest of Cass' stages, though, could be collapsed into one – *developing a personal LGBTQ identity*. From there, he argued that people developed a *social LGBTQ identity* (coming out to friends or in social spaces), had a process of *becoming an LGBTQ offspring* (coming out to your parents and family), developing *LGBTQ intimacy* (having sexual relationships with same-sex people), and he saw the final stage as *entering the LGBTQ community*. Obviously common sense tells us that people often do not go through these stages in the order laid out here – coming out to family, for example, can often be the last step for someone rather than one of the earliest.

Those models were both developed with non-autistic gay men. We don't know if they work for lesbians, bisexuals, or people who are realising that their gender identity is other than the one they were assigned at birth. We definitely don't know whether they work for autistic people. There is no obvious reason to assume that they don't apply at all, but it is important to spend time talking to autistic people to understand their experiences.

We also don't know anything, formally, about the early love lives of autistic teens who aren't heterosexual, though we have a bit of information about autistic adults' experiences on this front, discussed in Chapter 6: Well, Hello There. Based on what we know about heterosexual autistic adolescents, they probably have fewer relationships and sexual experiences than their non-autistic peers, and start these a bit later. Gay, lesbian, and bisexual autistic teens definitely exist, and definitely have relationships. Andrew again summed up the challenges autistic LGTBQIA+ teenagers face when they said:

> You are made to walk a tightrope between showing your authentic self and acting in accordance with bizarre neurotypical courtship procedures enforced by the gender binary that I as a bisexual, non-binary person of colour found meaningless. Those I would date however were mostly neurotypical and so if you show your authentic and unmasked autistic self too early you risk being called 'weird' and because the 'weird and quirky' autistic stereotype was reserved for white Americans and I was a lovely brown colour from my mixed heritage, my autistic traits were not treated as something endearing but as something worth ditching me or breaking up with me over.
>
> *(Andrew James Sanchez, 27, non-binary)*

There has been just one study into the SRE needs of autistic LGBTQ teenagers, which found that there are no systematic programmes out there. The researchers did suggest, though, that in addition to the general need for concrete and specific SRE for autistic young people, and discussions about how being autistic impacts your sexual experiences, it is important to discuss how to navigate disclosure of their sexual orientation safely and appropriately, and how to handle the range of responses they may face (Herrick & Datti, 2022). The issues of education about healthy and safe relationships are just as important for them as for heterosexual teenagers, and parents need to find ways to talk about this with them.

Chapter conclusion

Overall, a lot happens in the teenage years! On top of the changes to the social world and friendships, a whole new realm of desire and demands opens up as autistic adolescents reach puberty. These have different rules, come with different behaviours, and are often emotionally intense in new, confusing, and difficult to manage ways. There isn't yet a huge amount of research about autistic people's experiences in the early stages of their romantic and sexual lives, other than that we know autistic people feel desire, act on it, and have romantic relationships. That should feel obvious, and it is, but in the context of the long history of autism research, it hasn't been. Old models and theories put blinkers on the eyes of researchers, who missed the relationships of real life autistic people in front of them because they didn't fit with what they expected to see. We are starting to learn more about these relationships, and the ways they impact autistic young people across their lives, but we're not all the way there yet.

References

Beddows, N., & Brooks, R. (2016). Inappropriate sexual behaviour in adolescents with autism spectrum disorder: What education is recommended and why. *Early Intervention in Psychiatry*, *10*(4), 282–289. https://doi.org/10.1111/EIP.12265

Bennett, M., Webster, A. A., Goodall, E., & Rowland, S. (2018). Intimacy and romance across the autism spectrum: Unpacking the not interested in sex myth. *Life on the Autism Spectrum*, 195–211. https://doi.org/10.1007/978-981-13-3359-0_10

Botha, M., & Frost, D. M. (2018). Extending the minority stress model to understand mental health problems experienced by the autistic population. *Society and Mental Health*, *10*(1), 20–34. https://doi.org/10.1177/2156869318804297

Bravo, V., Connolly, J., & McIsaac, C. (2017). Why did it end? Breakup reasons of youth of different gender, Dating stages, and ages. *Emerging Adulthood*, *5*(4), 230–240. https://doi.org/10.1177/2167696817700261

Busboom, A. L., Collins, D. M., Givertz, M. D., & Levin, L. A. (2002). Can we still be friends? Resources and barriers to friendship quality after romantic relationship dissolution. *Personal Relationships*, *9*(2), 215–223. https://doi.org/10.1111/1475-6811.00014

Cheak-Zamora, N. C., Teti, M., Maurer-Batjer, A., O'Connor, K. V., & Randolph, J. K. (2019). Sexual and relationship interest, knowledge, and experiences among adolescents and young adults with autism spectrum disorder. *Archives of Sexual Behavior*, *48*(8), 2605–2615. https://doi.org/10.1007/S10508-019-1445-2/TABLES/1

Cherskov, A., Pohl, A., Allison, C., Zhang, H., Payne, R. A., & Baron-Cohen, S. (2018). Polycystic ovary syndrome and autism: A test of the prenatal sex steroid theory. *Translational Psychiatry*, *8*(1), 1–10. https://doi.org/10.1038/s41398-018-0186-7

Christopher, F. S., McKenney, S. J., & Poulsen, F. O. (2015). Early adolescents crushing: Pursuing romantic interest on a social stage. *Journal of Social and Personal Relationships*, *33*(4), 515–533. https://doi.org/10.1177/0265407515583169

Coleman, L. M., & Testa, A. (2008). Sexual health knowledge, attitudes and behaviours: variations among a religiously diverse sample of young people in London, UK. *Ethnicity and Health*, *13*(1), 55–72.

Coleman-Smith, R. S., Smith, R., Milne, E., & Thompson, A. R. (2020). Conflict versus congruence: A qualitative study exploring the experience of gender dysphoria for adults with autism spectrum disorder. *Journal of Autism and Developmental Disorders*, *50*(8), 2643–2657. https://doi.org/10.1007/S10803-019-04296-3/FIGURES/1

Connolly, J., Nguyen, H. N. T., Pepler, D., Craig, W., & Jiang, D. (2013). Developmental trajectories of romantic stages and associations with problem behaviours during adolescence. *Journal of Adolescence*, *36*(6), 1013–1024. https://doi.org/10.1016/J.ADOLESCENCE.2013.08.006

Corbett, B. A., Muscatello, R. A., Klemencic, M. E., West, M., Kim, A., & Strang, J. F. (2022). Greater gender diversity among autistic children by self-report and parent-report. *Autism*, 136236132210853. https://doi.org/10.1177/13623613221085337

Corbett, B. A., Vandekar, S., Muscatello, R. A., & Tanguturi, Y. (2020). Pubertal timing during early adolescence: Advanced pubertal onset in females with autism spectrum disorder. *Autism Research*, *13*(12), 2202–2215. https://doi.org/10.1002/AUR.2406

Cummins, C., Pellicano, E., & Crane, L. (2020). Supporting minimally verbal autistic girls with intellectual disabilities through puberty: Perspectives of parents and educators. *Journal of Autism and Developmental Disorders*, *50*(7), 2439–2448. https://doi.org/10.1007/S10803-018-3782-8/FIGURES/1

Dewinter, J, De Graaf, H., & Begeer, S. (2017). Sexual orientation, Gender identity, and romantic relationships in adolescents and adults with autism spectrum disorder. *Journal of Autism and Developmental Disorders*, *47*(9), 2927–2934. https://doi.org/10.1007/s10803-017-3199-9

Dewinter, J., Van Parys, H., Vermeiren, R., & Nieuwenhuizen, V. C. (2016). Adolescent boys with an autism spectrum disorder and their experience of sexuality: An interpretative phenomenological analysis. *Autism*, *21*(1), 75–82. https://doi.org/10.1177/1362361315627134

Dewinter, J., Vermeiren, R., Vanwesenbeeck, I., Lobbestael, J., & Van Nieuwenhuizen, C. (2015). Sexuality in adolescent boys with autism spectrum disorder: Self-reported behaviours and attitudes. *Journal of Autism and Developmental Disorders*, *45*(3), 731–741. https://doi.org/10.1007/s10803-014-2226-3

Dunphy, D. C. (1963). The social structure of urban adolescent peer groups. *Sociometry*, *26*(2), 230. https://doi.org/10.2307/2785909

Eriksen, W. (2016). Facing puberty: Exploring the onset, symptoms and experience of menses in females with autism spectrum disorder. Publicly accessible penn dissertations. https://repository.upenn.edu/edissertations/2270

George, R., & Stokes, M. A. (2016). Gender is not on my agenda: Gender dysphoria and autism spectrum disorder. In *Psychiatric Symptoms and Comorbidities in Autism Spectrum Disorder*. New York: Springer International Publishing, pp. 139–150. https://doi.org/10.1007/978-3-319-29695-1_10

George, R., & Stokes, M. A. (2017). Sexual orientation in autism spectrum disorder. *Autism Research*, *11*(1), 133–141. https://doi.org/10.1002/aur.1892

George, R., & Stokes, M. A. (2018). Sexual orientation in autism spectrum disorder. *Autism Research*, *11*(1), 133–141.

Gómez-López, M., Viejo, C., & Ortega-Ruiz, R. (2019). Well-being and romantic relationships: A systematic review in adolescence and emerging adulthood. *International Journal of Environmental Research and Public Health 2019*, *16*(13), 2415. https://doi.org/10.3390/IJERPH16132415

Hancock, G. I. P., Stokes, M. A., & Mesibov, G. B. (2017). Socio-sexual functioning in autism spectrum disorder: A systematic review and meta-analyses of existing literature. *Autism Research*, *10*(11), 1823–1833. https://doi.org/10.1002/AUR.1831

Hannah, L. A., & Stagg, S. D. (2016). Experiences of sex education and sexual awareness in young adults with autism spectrum disorder. *Journal of Autism and Developmental Disorders, 46*(12), 3678–3687. https://doi.org/10.1007/S10803-016-2906-2/TABLES/2

Herrick, S. J., & Datti, P. A. (2022). Autism spectrum disorder and sexual minority identity: Sex education implications. *American Journal of Sexuality Education, 17*(2), 257–276, https://doi.org/10.1080/15546128.2021.2002225

Holmes, Laura G., Himle, M. B., & Strassberg, D. S. (2016). Parental romantic expectations and parent-child sexuality communication in autism spectrum disorders. *Autism, 20*(6), 687–699. https://doi.org/10.1177/1362361315602371

Holmes, Laura G., Strassberg, D. S., & Himle, M. B. (2019). Family sexuality communication for adolescent girls on the autism spectrum. *Journal of Autism and Developmental Disorders, 49*(6), 2403–2416. https://doi.org/10.1007/S10803-019-03904-6/TABLES/4

Jamison, T. B., & Sanner, C. M. (2021). Relationship form and function: Exploring meaning-making in young adults romantic histories. *Personal Relationships, 28*(4), 840–859. https://doi.org/10.1111/PERE.12400

Kenny, M. C., Crocco, C., & Long, H. (2021). Parents plans to communicate about sexuality and child sexual abuse with their children with autism spectrum disorder. *Sexuality and Disability, 39*(2), 357–375. https://doi.org/10.1007/S11195-020-09636-1/TABLES/4

Khudiakova, V., & Chasteen, A. L. (n.d.). *The experiences of stigmatization and discrimination in autistic people of different genders and sexualities.* June 2, 2022. www.researchgate.net/publication/360826507

Korchmaros, J. D., Ybarra, M. L., & Mitchell, K. J. (2015). Adolescent online romantic relationship initiation: Differences by sexual and gender identification. *Journal of Adolescence, 40*, 54–64. https://doi.org/10.1016/J.ADOLESCENCE.2015.01.004

Langlais, M. R., Seidman, G., & Bruxvoort, K. M. (2018). Adolescent romantic relationship – Oriented facebook behaviors: Implications for self-esteem. *Youth and Society, 52*(4), 661–683. https://doi.org/10.1177/0044118X18760647

Lantagne, A., Furman, W., & Novak, J. (2017). Stay or leave: Predictors of relationship dissolution in emerging adulthood. *Developmental Psychology, 5*(4), 241–250. https://doi.org/10.1177/2167696817699750

Mackin, M. L., Loew, N., Gonzalez, A., Tykol, H., & Christensen, T. (2016). Parent perceptions of sexual education needs for their children with autism. *Journal of Pediatric Nursing, 31*(6), 608–618. https://doi.org/10.1016/J.PEDN.2016.07.003

Mademtzi, M., Singh, P., Shic, F., & Koenig, K. (2018). Challenges of females with autism: A parental perspective. *Journal of Autism and Developmental Disorders, 48*(4), 1301–1310. https://doi.org/10.1007/S10803-017-3341-8/TABLES/2

May, T., Pang, K. C., & Williams, K. (2017). Brief report: Sexual attraction and relationships in adolescents with autism. *Journal of Autism and Developmental Disorders, 47*(6), 1910–1916. https://doi.org/10.1007/S10803-017-3092-6/TABLES/2

Mehzabin, P., & Stokes, M. A. (2011). Self-assessed sexuality in young adults with high-functioning autism. *Research in Autism Spectrum Disorders, 5*(1), 614–621. https://doi.org/10.1016/j.rasd.2010.07.006

Navot, N., Jorgenson, A. G., & Webb, S. J. (2017). Maternal experience raising girls with autism spectrum disorder: A qualitative study. *Child: Care, Health and Development, 43*(4), 536–545. https://doi.org/10.1111/CCH.12470

Nichols, S., & Blakeley-Smith, A. (2009). I'm not sure we're ready for this . . .: Working with families toward facilitating healthy sexuality for individuals with autism spectrum disorders. *Social Work in Mental Health, 8*(1), 72–91. https://doi.org/10.1080/15332980902932383

Obaydi, H., & Puri, B. K. (2008). Prevalence of premenstrual syndrome in autism: A prospective observer-rated study. *Journal of International Medical Research, 36*(2), 268–272. https://doi.org/10.1177/147323000803600208

Pecora, L. A., Mesibov, G. B., & Stokes, M. A. (2016). Sexuality in high-functioning autism: A systematic review and meta-analysis. *Journal of Autism and Developmental Disorders, 46*(11), 3519–3556. https://doi.org/10.1007/S10803-016-2892-4/TABLES/2

Price, M., Hides, L., Cockshaw, W., Staneva, A. A., & Stoyanov, S. R. (2016). Young love: Romantic concerns and associated mental health issues among adolescent help-seekers. *Behavioral sciences 2016, 6*(2), 9. https://doi.org/10.3390/BS6020009

Realmuto, G. M., & Ruble, L. A. (1999). Sexual behaviors in autism: Problems of definition and management. *Journal of Autism and Developmental Disorders, 29*(2), 121–127. https://doi.org/10.1023/A:1023088526314

Savickaitė, R., Dijkstra, J. K., Kreager, D., Ivanova, K., & Veenstra, R. (2019). Friendships, Perceived popularity, and Adolescent romantic relationship debut. *The Journal of Early Adolescence, 40*(3), 377–399. https://doi.org/10.1177/0272431619847530

Sedgewick, F., Hill, V., & Pellicano, E. (2018). Parent perspectives on autistic girls' friendships and futures. *Autism & Developmental Language Impairments, 3*, 239694151879449. https://doi.org/10.1177/2396941518794497

Sedgewick, F., Leppanen, J., & Tchanturia, K. (2020). Gender differences in mental health prevalence in autism. *Advances in Autism, 7*(3), 208–224. https://doi.org/10.1108/AIA-01-2020-0007

Shulman, S., Mayes, L. C., Cohen, T. H., Swain, J. E., & Leckman, J. F. (2008). Romantic attraction and conflict negotiation among late adolescent and early adult romantic couples. *Journal of Adolescence, 31*(6), 729–745. https://doi.org/10.1016/J.ADOLESCENCE.2008.02.002

Shulman, S., Seiffge-Krenke, I., Scharf, M., Lev-Ari, L., & Levy, G. (2017). Adolescent depressive symptoms and breakup distress during early emerging adulthood: Associations with the quality of romantic interactions. *Emerging Adulthood, 5*(4), 251–258. https://doi.org/10.1177/2167696817698900

Teti, M., Cheak-Zamora, N., Bauerband, L. A., & Maurer-Batjer, A. (2019). A qualitative comparison of caregiver and youth with autism perceptions of sexuality and relationship experiences. *Journal of Developmental and Behavioral Pediatrics, 40*(1), 12–19. https://doi.org/10.1097/DBP.0000000000000620

Upadhyay, S., & Vishwakarma, A. (2019). Effect of premenstrual period on symptoms of autism. *The International Journal of Indian Psychology, 7*(2). https://d1wqtxts1xzle7.cloudfront.net/64164613/18.01.084.20190702-with-cover-page-v2.pdf?Expires=1653602909&Signature=d2QoirprpvvE7kwerSSE2i3Vl0HlK2YUXuHMxkOfyskfhfEguW809q9TrFbGrPmK6peZ0PMZ6zm1S126mQOW~Qoms8xcKDKo3C7entxE2IulNDHKLpQVzxTRz-MuFsLTuXTtV3tWisKb4y4Owqsf7yjgyvkJnNWjHLrvMZjsXJ2rDm5MRUulUndarLVNrWnJsVXTb6xL7L7G8mGWyhL7liByvpdUYn4VKlfcrrlhbUSeyIxa2XrDBqL1tH1vNf9YoOXC4~8RLleruVQ9f5MflCuA8BFXtFozz8Rf-pwuiFdbDZwAAKLJop2tp10XE5e6x9ry3F1K4DEmDpVh54tCEw__&Key-Pair-Id=APKAJLOHF5GGSLRBV4ZA

Yew, R. Y., Samuel, P., Hooley, M., Mesibov, G. B., & Stokes, M. A. (2021). A systematic review of romantic relationship initiation and maintenance factors in autism. *Personal Relationships, 28*(4), 777–802. https://doi.org/10.1111/PERE.12397

5

WITH A LITTLE HELP FROM MY FRIENDS

Adult friendships and finding community

We talked a lot in the earlier chapters about how important friends are for children and teenagers – but they are hugely important for adults too! Sometimes we keep our friends from childhood throughout the rest of our lives, sometimes we don't, and sometimes we make the best friends of our lives as adults. This chapter looks at some of the work around adult friendships, the impact they have, and what we know about adult friendships for autistic people. We're also thinking about community connections – not all our friendships are one-on-one or small groups of close-knit people, after all. So this chapter is split into clear sections, and before each one Sarah has written about her own experience of these relationships, which are so important in her life – the same way they are for many, many people.

Sarah on adult friendships

I haven't kept in touch with anyone I went to school with, which isn't surprising, as I don't recall having many positive friendship experiences until I went to university, where for the first time in my life, I met people with whom I really connected, and 32 years later, are still close to. The sort of friendships that don't seem to need a lot of regular attention; that after many months of non-contact, are picked up from the place where they were left, with no diminishment of relational quality. There is an unwritten understanding that all of our lives are different and busy, and there is no rancour following months of silence. This is the perfect arrangement for me as my autistic wiring means that I tend to focus intently and solely on one thing at a time, which can result in everything else that my brain sees as peripheral being neglected. I constantly forget birthdays, have an utter

DOI: 10.4324/9781003044536-6

dread of writing Christmas cards, and am spectacularly bad at keeping in touch, but none of that seems to matter with my uni mates. We accept and like each other for who we are and always have. We were a bunch of misfits who were more than a little unusual and we gravitated towards each other. I did not know I was autistic then and it is not my place to suggest that some my friends are possibly neurodivergent, but I do know that some of us came from different places and experiences of difficulty prior to university and we found each other. There is the quality of unconditional love about these friendships and after experiencing a difficult younger life, with little in the way of being cherished or considered good enough, they are precious and hugely important to me.

I went to a university in a small town which because it didn't have much going on in terms of an exciting nightlife, meant that my group of friends and I made our own entertainment and formed our own societies. We had our own Dr Who society, which generally involved watching vintage tapes of our favourite pre-Eccleston Doctors, wobbly scenery and unconvincing monsters, but the most unique university community for me was Burgess Productions. I don't to this day know how Gavin got us to dress up as Star Trek or James Bond characters and act out cheesy scripts in a disused quarry, but he did and we had a lot of fun making these truly magnificent mini-films. We even held our own film awards ceremonies, called the Braftas and had our own stage names. Mine was Marlene Deeptrench, which is probably best forgotten, but I recall winning best supporting actress at some point, which, in all likelihood was actually an award for being the person most easily cajoled into wearing some ridiculous pointy ears and a blonde wig!

Although it was a relief to finally have met people who I really clicked with, I was still undiagnosed and my mental health was still poor. I developed severe anxiety attacks, became too scared to eat, and dropped three stones in a couple of months. It was the first time in my life when I had been a smaller size, but it wasn't healthy at all. Mental health provision in the early 1990s wasn't great, but the university did allow me to take my exams in a small group so that did help with the overwhelm. I was masking constantly and couldn't cope with the late night noise and drunkenness that accompanied university life. Having a vomit phobia didn't help, and I was fearful that I was a fraud and that my friends, as supportive and lovely as they were, would at some point find me out and reject me. I didn't have the confidence to be entirely honest about my fears and had no idea what I needed in a friendship, but, even so, these were far better times than I had ever experienced before.

Over the years I have met close friends through work, some of whom are neurodivergent, others not. I do seem to gravitate towards younger people as I often find my peers to be a bit dull, unless they are artistic or cynically interesting like Adam and Ricky, cake-loving anti-peoplers like Rebecca, or counter-cultural reflectives like Cath. I had been diagnosed for a couple of years when I began working on the Nespresso campaign and met a lot of people who were also misfits in society, most of whom were younger than me. There were a lot of LGBTQ folk and some who have since discovered that they too are neurodivergent, so it is no surprise that we got on. Being happily married, I mercifully missed out on the frequent office relationship dramas, but this group of friends were the most diverse I have ever met and my life has been far richer for having known them. I learned a huge amount about LGBTQ lives and experiences and enjoyed going out for karaoke nights at the now sadly defunct Proud Bar in Old Market and marching in the Bristol Pride march with them. Answering the phone to entitled coffee crack heads who couldn't work out how to switch on a kettle when their beloved coffee machine was broken was a challenging job, but the friends I made there more than made up for it. Similarly, my job as an HCA at an endoscopy clinic could in many ways be described as shitty, but the bottom-related banter and friendships that I made there with Hannah, the Lucys, Heidi, and Kelly got us through some difficult shifts, and although we are all doing different things now, we are still in touch and meet up as often as we can.

I have developed many good friendships with people who are autistic, and we socialise in a variety of ways – some are online, others are face to face, and one friendship in particular is based around a mutual love of the band Muse. For one friend and I, seeing Muse live is the best passionate interest, and, to date, we have seen them twice together in London. For both of us the sensory experience of the lights, music, and crowd is extraordinarily uplifting and neither of us can quite work out how this can be, as in other contexts, large groups of people or noise can be overwhelming for both of us. I think she explains it really well when she says, "It's like I become a different person at gigs and I experience music really intensely" and adds that "I can get lost in the music and find that it is easier to handle than a lot of more everyday environments."

I agree and never feel more alive than when I am at a live music event, but I do find it difficult to navigate music or theatre venues. I can become very anxious or overwhelmed if I don't have support so it's great to go to gigs together as we can look out for each other and make sure each other's autistic needs are being met. We meet up in the queue and put the autistic world to rights for a couple of hours while waiting for the doors to open as well as planning where we are going to position ourselves in the venue.

It's really important that both of us feel comfortable with where we are standing. I also have to factor in the following day as a rest day in order to recuperate and my friend agrees: "gigs of that size are a lot to take in and I know I'm usually writing off the next day." We make the necessary accommodations for each other so that our "autistic friendship is a safe space not just to be open about our needs and struggles, but also to revel in the joy together."

Sarah's writing emphasises something most of us know – our friendships continue to be important in adulthood! Our friends are sources of fun, laughter, support, and comfort. They give us people to talk to about our lives and our problems, something which is invaluable regardless of whether you have a romantic partner or not.

That social support has tangible effects on our health and well-being, just as it does in childhood and adolescence. Non-autistic adults who have good friends and social networks have lower levels of depression, better quality of life, and even have better physical health into old age (Antonucci & Akiyama, 1987). There are conversations to be had about whether having friends keeps you healthy, or healthier people have friends – and the types of activities you do with those friends plays a role in this, because going for long walks is different for your functional health than sitting eating cake, obviously (Everard et al., 2000). Having a same-sex best friend to confide in is associated with less depression and higher life satisfaction for women (though less so for men, who tend to confide in their wives or no one) (Antonucci et al., 2010). Being part of a diverse network of friends and family who you can turn to for social support is linked to lower levels of depression in older adults, and having friends but no family is better for your mental health than having family but no friends (Fiori et al., 2006). During the COVID-19 pandemic, people who were part of strong neighbourhood networks had lower levels of loneliness and depression, especially if they also had some form of contact with friends regularly (Gan & Best, 2021). There are many more research studies we could discuss which show the myriad benefits of friendship for adults, but these give a flavour – and show that in a crisis, your friends matter as much as anyone else.

Autistic adults' friendships

Once again, we start this section by saying that this is the same for autistic adults as it is for non-autistic adults. Also, once again, we will point out that there isn't a huge amount of research out there about autistic adult's friendships. Early research done with people diagnosed in the 1960s, 70s, 80s, and 90s – before the shift to recognising the broader autism spectrum – suggested that most autistic adults would not have friends, or at least not what the researchers considered to be 'good' friends (Howlin et al., 2000). We talked earlier about how having friends in adulthood is

110 With a little help from my friends

good for the mental health of non-autistic adults, and the same is true for autistic adults – something which we are sure will shock no one reading this book. Having friends predicts better self-esteem, lower depression, lower levels of anxiety, and increased life satisfaction (Mazurek, 2014). Even this study, though, said that autistic people tended to have few friends and high levels of loneliness.

These studies painted a picture of isolation for autistic people in adulthood, their social connections limited almost entirely to family and to people they met at structured activities, and without deep or meaningful independent friendships and relationships. Other work, which included autistic adults without learning difficulties, found that even then, they scored much lower than non-autistic adults on something called the Friendship Questionnaire (Baron-Cohen & Wheelwright, 2003). This questionnaire asks people things like whether they have a best friend, and what they talk to their friends about, and they have to pick one of three options which describes them best. The answers are given different amounts of points, with higher scores suggesting that they have more or better friendships. In this original study introducing the measure, autistic men and women scored very similarly (although there were only 17 women to 51 men involved, so this should be taken with a grain of salt), which is the opposite to what we see in non-autistic people, where women consistently score higher on friendship measures.

Luckily, our knowledge has moved on from that point! As the diagnostic criteria expanded to allow recognition of autistic people who did not have co-occurring learning difficulties, and made the option of an adulthood diagnosis possible, we have started to gain more understanding of the range of people's experiences with friends once they leave school.

While there are still some autistic people who struggle to make and maintain friendships in adulthood, or who feel that they do not have anyone they would consider a 'best friend', this seems to be the minority. A couple of years ago, Felicity carried out a big online study with nearly 1000 people (532 autistic, 417 non-autistic), where among other things she asked them about their general friendships – using the Friendship Questionnaire (FQ) created by Simon Baron-Cohen mentioned earlier – and their best friendship or the person they had the closest relationship with – using the Unidimensional Relationship Closeness Scale (Sedgewick et al., 2019). Eight hundred seventy-five people said they had a best friend, someone they were dating, a live-in partner, or a spouse (470 autistic people, 405 non-autistic people). Of those, 227 of the 470 autistic people said their closest relationship was a best friend or someone they were dating, and 181 non-autistic people said the same. The questionnaire has the built in assumption that a live-in partner or spouse will also be your best friend, but the scores we expect for long-term romantic couples are a bit different, which is why the groups got split up that way. So, while autistic people were slightly less likely to say they have these types of relationships, it was definitely still the majority!

One of the most interesting findings from this research was that while the FQ scores in this much larger sample were in line with some of the findings from the original paper – autistic people scored lower than non-autistic people – when scores were broken down by gender the findings differed. With a much larger and more representative sample of non-male participants, it turned out that autistic non-binary people and autistic women scored much more highly than autistic men, which mirrors the gender differences seen in non-autistic people (although autistic and non-autistic non-binary people scored very similarly actually). This challenges many of the early narratives about autistic adults' friendships – they do have them, and the gender differences that are almost taken for granted in non-autistic people also apply for a lot of autistic people.

The other thing that was measured in this large-scale study of adult best-friendships was the closeness of people's specific nominated relationship. Although one group talked about their long-term partners, which we will discuss in the next chapter, the others specifically rated their best friend or someone they had been dating for a shorter time – most, their best friends. Here again, autistic people scored lower than non-autistic people did, saying that they were less likely to consider their best friend when making a big life decision, for example. Autistic women and non-binary people scored very similarly, and higher than autistic men, so again the gender differences were in line with non-autistic people. This was the first time anyone had tried to look at the best-friendships of autistic people in a large-scale quantified way, rather than smaller interview-based studies. And what it shows us is, once again, that so many long-standing assumptions based on historic autism research are false. Baron-Cohen and Wheelwright used the first FQ paper as evidence for Baron-Cohen's Extreme Male Brain theory, arguing that their results showed that autistic women were essentially the same as autistic men in terms of their social relationships. We talked earlier about many ways that theory has been debunked, but this study adds to that evidence base.

We know that for most people, their childhood and teenage friendship experiences can be used to predict their adult relationships, both romantic and not. Those earlier friendships act as models for your friendships as you move into adulthood, and the patterns people establish earlier can often be carried on later in life as well – both good and bad. This has been seen with autistic women, who talk about the things they struggled with as teenagers still being difficult as adults (Sedgewick et al., 2018). One common example given was struggling to understand the politics in female friendship groups, which transferred to confusion over the politics of groups of mums at the school gates, or in the office. Being seen as someone who 'gets these things wrong' can have wide-ranging impacts on other areas of your life, and is something which autistic women have talked about in other studies as negatively affecting their careers (Webster & Garvis, 2017). These sorts of social skills are never formally taught, and people are generally expected to just 'pick them up' as they mature, but for autistic people this can be very difficult. This leads to misunderstandings and misinterpretations of meaning or intention across the lifespan (Camus et al., 2022) – in line with the Double Empathy Theory.

Not everything stays the same from being a teenager to being an adult, obviously. Conflict management and resolution is one of the skills which many autistic women in particular talk about developing as they got older (Sedgewick et al.,

112 With a little help from my friends

2018). Although many had very all-or-nothing views on arguments when they were younger, just as autistic teenage girls report currently, in adulthood they instead had a more nuanced take on these disagreements. And, even if they felt that the other person had been in the wrong, they had more flexibility and experience in looking at it from the other person's point of view. They used that to work to find solutions which worked for them and their friends, which enabled them to hold on to more of the friendships they valued. Equally, some women felt that they had developed a stronger sense of self and their own needs, and so they were able to walk away from friendships which were harmful without the guilt they would have previously felt – which is also an important skill in life.

A study which tried to look at parts of why autistic adults can find it more difficult to make and maintain friendships, especially with non-autistic people, also took the Double Empathy Theory as their framework. They looked at the preferred friendship behaviours and the friendship 'congruence' (how much they agree on what their friendship is like) of autistic and non-autistic young adults (Finke, 2022). The results showed that autistic people tended to focus more on functional communication than non-autistic people, who focussed on social communication – the difference between calling to make plans and calling to chat, for example. Also, autistic people tended to say they were better at coming up with practical solutions than discussing feelings with their friends, and thought that their friends liked them because they were fun more than because they were someone who offered emotional support. When it came to thinking about arguments with friends, as in the preceding paragraph, autistic people were more likely to consider ending a friendship altogether after an argument – in fact, none of the non-autistic group picked this response option, whereas 17% of autistic people did. A lot of autistic people have talked in other studies about actively trying to avoid conflict with their friends, and masking to do so – especially autistic girls (Vine Foggo & Webster, 2017). It may be that they do this precisely because they feel that if there is a conflict, at least some of the time, the most likely outcome is a loss of that friendship altogether. Everyone in Finke's study reported being similar to their friends in terms of personality, interests, and preferences for things like meeting up – many of the key elements in any friendship. However, some of those other differences we have described add up to potentially large discrepancies in what autistic and non-autistic people expect in a friendship, and this mismatch may lead to challenges.

One study which has specifically looked at the differences in the friendships autistic adults have with other autistic people and with non-autistic people comes from the team in Edinburgh who carried out the Diverse Intelligences project testing the Double Empathy Theory (Crompton et al., 2020). This work, using in-depth interviews with 12 autistic adults, found that there can be cross-neurotype difficulties in understanding each other, even when both parties have the best of intentions, and that this means socialising with non-autistic people can be more effortful and tiring than socialising with autistic people. Some people also talked about how it could be useful to have a non-autistic person with them in group situations as well though, because they could act as a 'translator' and help them understand what was going on. In contrast, most participants said they found spending time with other autistic people easier, because everyone had more similar behaviours and expectations, or were more used to being explicit about these sorts of things, rather than guessing at unwritten or unspoken social rules. This is something lots of the people we talked to for the book mentioned, even if they didn't know at the time that this was who they connected with best:

> Not until I became friends with a group of misfits and oddballs mid to late secondary school and I just gelled with them. In hindsight, the only people I genuinely connected with were probably neurodivergent.
>
> *(anonymous, 54, autistic woman)*

> The friendship groups I have now have a mix of people who are autistic, otherwise neurodivergent . . . the friends since I had from primary school, it's clear that although I was identified as autistic quite young a lot of them are autistic or ADHD as well and are only just finding out.
>
> *(Krysia, 30)*

> My friends today are mostly neurodivergent, sharing my trials, homing my thoughts meaningfully.
>
> *(Imane, 15, autistic girl)*

> It's like talking to drunk people or dolphins. It's like NT people are on a very different wavelength to what I am. Autistic people might turn to each other or find each other, even by accident. When you find people you can really connect with, you can understand what you say and think it is always appreciated and you can build stronger relationships.
>
> *(anonymous, 47, autistic male)*

This doesn't mean every autistic–autistic interaction is automatically straightforward and harmonious (more on this in Chapter 9: Toxic) – people's sensory needs can clash, and the honesty which many autistic people are proud of can be just as blunt and hurtful for other autistic people as it is non-autistic people, if it is used in an insensitive way. Many of the participants in the aforementioned study talked about feeling like they were in the minority, both in terms of understanding social rules and in terms of being listened to when activities were being planned. This meant that some social situations were inaccessible for them, increasing their sense of being left out or not being able to 'keep up' in group situations, which often form a significant part of non-autistic socialising.

The final theme the researchers identified from what people told them in this study was around a sense of belonging. Participants consistently talked about feeling like they belonged in majority-autistic social groups, that they were better understood, and that they were more able to be themselves, and therefore make more genuine friendships. A study looking at why it might be easier for autistic people to

114 With a little help from my friends

make friends with each other identified two key factors – autistic people tended to be more generous in assuming they had common ground, which reduced conflicts, and they had less need for coordination in terms of things like timing of speech in conversations (Heasman & Gillespie, 2018). It has also been found that autistic people tend to rely less on traditional markers of rapport in conversation to guide the level of rapport they actually experience, another way in which autistic and non-autistic people differ in how they build relationships with each other (Rifai et al., 2022). This means that some of the key ways in which autistic–non-autistic communication can be disrupted had less of an impact on autistic–autistic communication, leaving both parties happier with the interaction. These are relevant points regardless of how old an autistic person is, but is something lots of people in lots of studies discuss as happening for the first time once they leave school.

For many autistic adults, they remember university as the first time they were able to make genuine friends – something Sarah wrote about as well. There is something about moving away from the people who have known you all through school which allows people to often be more authentically themselves; exactly what Andrew talked about:

> I made new friends as I went to college. I was out from under the sheltering and overbearing nature of parents who had covered up any trail that might lead me to my late diagnosis as an autistic person. Because of this I got to learn who I was and who I wanted to be without the interference of familial and cultural expectations to exist and act in a way that would be seen as normal by neurotypical elders, parents, and siblings within Black and Latino families.
>
> *(Andrew James Sanchez, 27, non-binary)*

That opens up the opportunity to make much more authentic friendships, because you aren't trying to hide who you are and so can connect better. That is certainly what lots of autistic people currently at university, or who have been to university, tell us. For example, they talk about how since they came to university they have made better friends through their hobbies and interests than they previously had at school, because they aren't friendships based on forced proximity but on real shared passions and fun (Scott & Sedgewick, 2021). This was something people we talked to mentioned as well:

> I found the same sort of dynamic with my new group of friends at university that I met through having shared interests.
>
> *(anonymous, 54, autistic woman)*

These students found that their university friends were much more willing to learn about autism, and much more supportive of their needs, than their school friends had been. Their university friends did not make a big deal of their differences and actively tried to help them avoid things like sensory triggers or to manage anxiety – and this normalisation of autistic behaviours has been shown to be central to good adult friendships in other studies too (Sosnowy et al., 2019). For some participants in these studies, these were the first friends they felt truly comfortable with, and building these relationships had a positive impact on their self-esteem, their mental health, and their ability to engage with their courses as well.

That doesn't mean that everyone has an easy time socially at university, or immediately makes the best friends they'll ever have. The social aspects of being at university can still be very challenging – it is all happening on a much larger scale than at school; you are living with other people the same age in close quarters, usually for the first time; and you need to work out the differences between lectures, seminars, labs, clubs, and all the other settings involved in university life in terms of the social norms and expectations. In the face of all that, it also isn't guaranteed that everyone you come into contact with will know much about autism, or be understanding when you explain. Although levels of autism stigma are often lower amongst university students and staff, it definitely still exists. This can lead to autistic students feeling misunderstood and isolated, which has a negative impact on their mental health (Gurbuz et al., 2019). These social challenges at university can significantly contribute to wanting to withdraw from higher education, even for students who are easily capable of the academic side of university life (Cage et al., 2020). This is understandable – worries about the social world of being at university is one of the biggest concerns for autistic young people who are about to start their time in higher education, along with the academic demands and the practical side of living away from home (Lambe et al., 2019). For some students, the first year especially is socially challenging, and finding their place and their people at university is hard work, leaving them dissatisfied, although those who found an autism or neurodiversity society to join had a better time (Goddard & Cook, 2021). But a lot of autistic students find that the increased chances to meet people who are interested in the same things as them, either through their course or through societies, gives them the opportunity to make friends in a way that didn't exist in the smaller social world of high school. It makes sense, then, that more of them find better friends than before – and that should be hopeful for anyone who is about to go to uni.

Long-term friendships are more common between people who are similar in some way. This does not have to just be a shared neurotype or shared interest, it can be a shared experience of being 'different' on some measure. Lots of our contributors talked about how their most important friendships were with people who also had experience of being outsiders, either because they were drawn to them or because these were the people who were more accepting of their own differences:

> Most of these longer-term friendships are with people who would categorise themselves as either introverts or outsiders in some way. The geeks and freaks basically. There is a certain cohesion in the way they think and the way I think.
>
> *(anonymous, male)*

> Sometimes the ones who were most welcoming and kinder and nicer . . . The people that I ended up having putative friendships with were either really

clever like me or outcasts. The unattractive kids, the kids that didn't fit in for one reason or another or the kids who were not that clever, but basically had a good heart and were probably used to being put down by other people.

(Louise, autistic woman)

Being part of social networks and being involved in social communities in different ways is how anyone makes friends, regardless of neurotype. This is how you meet people, find the ones you get on with and have fun with, and move from acquaintances to friends. For autistic adults, in addition to making friends at work, in your area, and through hobbies, they often meet friends through autism support services, and make more friends online than non-autistic people do (Chan et al., 2022). Just as the online world is important for autistic teenagers in their friendships and relationships, the same is true for autistic adults.

Autistic adults' online friendships

We highlighted some of the research into autistic people's use of the internet and social media in their relationships in Chapter 3: Big School and Chapter 4: Teenage Dreams, where we focussed on adolescents. You can also find another section looking at online dating for adults in Chapter 6: Well, Hello There. Here, though, we are specifically interested in what we know about how autistic people use technology to make and maintain their friendships – and we have a bit about finding online communities later on as well. Autistic people spend more time online than non-autistic people in general, even when allowing for the fact that autistic adults are more likely to be unemployed and therefore have more free time in which to do so (van der Aa et al., 2016). They are more likely to use the internet to meet new people than non-autistic people (Gillespie-Lynch et al., 2014), and this often intersects with self-advocacy work around being autistic:

I now also have really good deep meaningful friendships within my neurodivergent network.

(anonymous, 54, autistic woman)

I have a number of people I talk regularly online to sometimes by video or most often by text. I don't have anybody that I go out with anywhere and I feel happier this way.

(anonymous)

A lot of my friendships are quite text based, phone based. It's not so much meeting up and physically doing things but it's about support and being there when we both need it and it's often not in a physical face to face sense although we've often met face to face, a lot of it takes place in an online or kind of other communication way. Generally they're the ones I find that work.

(Krysia, 30)

One of the main ways which autistic people talk about online friendships is using the internet, especially Facebook, Twitter, and blog sites, to find other autistic people to talk to and be friends with. Finding people who you know will understand at least some aspects of your life in ways non-autistic people can't is an important element in building strong bonds (Bargiela et al., 2016). Most autistic people use social networking sites like Facebook and Twitter, and most start using them intending to foster and support their friendships – which works, because autistic adults who use these sites are more likely to have close friends, and those friendships tend to be better (Mazurek, 2013). Although this is an older study in the context of social media – several apps which are now ubiquitous didn't exist in 2013, like TikTok for example – the numbers of people on social networking sites has only increased in that time, so the findings are still relevant. Autistic adults who use social media tend to be happier, particularly those who predominantly use Facebook rather than Twitter (Ward et al., 2018). This might be because of the different natures of these two platforms, with Facebook being more about connecting with people through shared interest groups, which often have moderators and rules about interactions, compared to Twitter where everyone's posts are open to everyone else, and the tone tends to be more political. Either way, social media and the friendships made through it can be seen as supporting positive well-being and quality of life for autistic people.

Alongside finding other autistic people online, one of the main ways in which online friendships have been investigated in autism research is online gaming (almost always in boys and men), particularly multiplayer games. Autistic boys and men who game online have more friends than those who don't game, and gaming is associated with feeling less lonely generally. They don't necessarily make best friends through online gaming, but there is still a lot of value in the friendships (Sundberg, 2018). Autistic adults also talk about how video games act as a stress relief outlet – and although they can become a time sink, the social connections built through gaming are one of the best parts of what the games offer (Mazurek et al., 2015). In contrast to many non-autistic male gamers, many autistic adults talked about actively disliking games with lots of violent or sexual content, especially because these sorts of games were more likely to have other users who were aggressive or unpleasant, which spoiled their enjoyment of the social nature of the game.

There are still rules and norms for how to use social media effectively, and these are unwritten and untaught just as much as the hidden social rules of in-person interaction. Especially as new platforms emerge, and as the population using each one shifts over time, this can be complicated for anyone to navigate but especially autistic people. There is some evidence that this is the case – university students with higher levels of autistic traits tended to find it harder to work out appropriate behaviours or 'online manners', and this when combined with lower levels of using social media was linked to higher loneliness (Suzuki et al., 2021). This might be because their peers interact with them less online in reaction to them 'getting it wrong' in terms of what is considered good online behaviour – and it can be easier to ignore someone online because there are not the same pressures to acknowledge each other or interact

118 With a little help from my friends

as there are even in casual offline encounters. Communicating online can exacerbate difficulties with things like trusting people too easily or disclosing too much personal information too early – both for autistic and non-autistic people – because it both feels more impersonal and more intimate than getting to know each other in person. It can also be easier to fall into inflexible thinking and to avoid taking other perspectives into account, because algorithms tend to push users towards more of the same, and usually more extreme versions of whatever they already tend to engage with. This can cause problems for some autistic people in maintaining relationships online, because they may be more likely to fall into having rigid views which push other people away (Burke et al., 2010). This is obviously not always or even often the case, but can be how online behaviours and relationships develop for some autistic people.

The other thing which can be difficult about socialising online is the chance of being a victim of cyberbullying or online harassment. We mentioned negative social interactions in online gaming earlier, and the risks of trusting people more easily online, which can leave autistic people vulnerable to manipulation and exploitation. Outside of those situations, which have not been fully studied, there are very few pieces of research into cyberbullying of autistic adults. What has been done shows that those who use social media more are more likely to get this kind of negative engagement on their posts or sent to them directly (Triantafyllopoulou et al., 2021). This makes sense, because the more active users are, then the more people their posts end up in front of, which increases the chances of their content being found by trolls and people who will send these kinds of unpleasant messages. Some people report being targeted specifically with ableist abuse because they are open about being autistic online, which is often difficult to make the sites take seriously or take action over.

There is plenty of evidence for the internet being important in autistic people's friendships, unsurprisingly, just some of which we have described here. There are lots of reasons why this might be, but one of the big ones is that internet-mediated relationships largely rely on written communication. When asked about how they preferred to communicate in different situations, most autistic people said first and foremost that they hated using the phone – but then that they strongly preferred using electronic written communication for most things. This could be email or instant messaging or social media, but generally they found that it worked better for them because it gave them more time to process what was said and work out their response; that it meant they had a record of exactly what had been said, which was helpful; and that they could use things like emojis to help make sure that they were giving exactly the meaning and impression that they wanted to (Howard & Sedgewick, 2021). For being in touch with friends and family, face-to-face communication was the top preference, which makes sense, but if this wasn't possible then written communication in the form of texting and instant messaging was the next best option for most people. They allow for rapid and regular communication with people you are close to, while still having the processing time and other benefits which are useful in so many other contexts. This clarity, the chance to interact with people from around the world, and the opportunity to connect with people from the comfort of your own home, without navigating the sensory challenges of many other settings, may be why the autism community has really flourished online, which we will talk about more later in the chapter.

Diagnosis and relationships

A thread running through the preceding sections is about the authenticity of connection that makes friendships better in adulthood for a lot of autistic people. One element of that, as we saw in the discussion from university students, is making friends who know and accept you as autistic, and who support you within the friendship as an autistic person.

What about if you don't know you're autistic? Or at least, don't know for a long while?

The rates of autism diagnoses have exploded in the last 20 years, and this increase has been greatest amongst adults (Russell et al., 2022). Getting a diagnosis in adulthood is often described as a sense of relief, of finding an explanation for 'what is going on', and an ability to reflect on the challenges you have had in life without the sense of guilt or blame which many people have felt for so long. Some people have called this process of realisation 'biographical illumination' (Tan, 2018), where the newly diagnosed person suddenly sees their life to date in a new light.

This greater understanding of yourself has a huge impact on relationships for a lot of late diagnosed autistic people, including on their friendships. Autistic women, for example, have talked about how it felt like it gave them 'permission' to be open about the things they needed from other people to make a friendship manageable, like changing the contexts in which they met up to work for their sensory needs (Sedgewick et al., 2019). It can bring increased patience with and insight into a range of behaviours that autistic people have, for them and their friends, and this can improve the friendship. Seeking that acceptance from other people is a key theme in many autistic adults' experiences around getting a diagnosis, and if it is forthcoming it makes the rest of the process much easier for them (Harmens et al., 2022). It isn't always an easy thing to work through getting a diagnosis with the important people in your life – some can use it as a basis to patronise or infantilise the newly diagnosed person, for example, based on the stereotypes they hold about what it means to be autistic. Negotiating these relationships in light of the diagnosis, though, is often talked about as a key part of building a new identity as an autistic person (Leedham et al., 2020). This can lead to a new sense of confidence in choosing friendships and relationships which are beneficial and where the autistic person is listened to and valued, and in finding new ways to feel a sense of belonging. It also helps the people in the autist's life to understand some of the things that have happened in the relationship, and potentially to heal old hurts:

> With my son it's been easier, as when he got his autism diagnosis he felt that it enabled him to understand me better and almost forgive me for some of the stuff that happened in a way that he hadn't felt able to before.
>
> *(anonymous, 62, autistic woman)*

It is worth noting that all of the studies cited in the paragraph were done with autistic women. Women are more likely to get a late diagnosis than men, in general, largely due to the greater chance of them being missed in childhood

120 With a little help from my friends

or getting alternative mental health diagnoses (Gould, 2017). There are late-diagnosed men out there, though, and increasing numbers of late-diagnosed non-binary and trans people too. We need more research which looks into their experiences of this process and how it affects their relationships. While many of the themes are likely to be the same, or similar, there are also probably some things which are specific to having a non-female gender. Men, for example, may find that getting a diagnosis impacts their sense of masculinity and how they are expected to perform socially in different settings, such as relieving the pressure to be 'one of the boys' – but we don't know. Equally, we don't know how being told you are autistic may complicate the relationship experiences of gender diverse individuals who already face additional stigmas and complexities on this front. Considering the large proportion of autistic people who this applies to, this is a big gap in our knowledge.

Sarah, like thousands of autistic adults out there in the world, didn't have a label for the challenges she experienced for the majority of her life. When she did find out, it changed . . . not everything, but quite a lot of things. These are her reflections on the personal side of what is behind the research we have just discussed.

Sarah on late diagnosis, self-discovery, and relationships

For the majority of my life I didn't know who I was. I had no connection with my true self, and the choices I made about so many aspects of my life were dominated by the needs, expectations, and demands of others. I had no idea what I wanted or needed but in the ten years since my late autism diagnosis, I have learned a lot about what being authentically autistic means for me. This has had an enormous impact both on the quality of my life, my relationship with myself and with others. It hasn't been a rediscovery of the me that has been buried, it is a revelation of who I am for the first time. This hasn't been a linear, nor an immediate process. I was so disconnected from my core autistic self, and the amount of baggage that had accumulated during the years of confusion and survival meant that my diagnosis at age 42 wasn't the epiphany that might have been expected. Some of the dots were joined, but my well-disguised distress and poor mental health wasn't suddenly alleviated because I now had this piece of paper telling me that I had Asperger's syndrome.

If anything, at the time, it felt like a setback and further proof that I was 'wrong'. Even though I did experience a degree of relief when I was diagnosed, as it did give me some answers, being given an autism label also meant that there was something pathologically wrong with me and that I was even more broken than I had already thought. I had seen how negatively my nephew's autism diagnosis had been received by some family members and I didn't want to be judged similarly, as being autistic would only add to the deeply ingrained message that I was not good enough or acceptable. I also didn't present like the stereotypically autistic males in the family and I think that because I was empathic, assumed the role of peacemaker between disparate factions and hated trainspotting, I thought that my difficulties were rooted in poor mental health, not neurodivergence. Of course I now know better, but my internally ableist self wanted none of it. So although I was offered post-diagnostic support, I didn't think that I needed it, as in my head I was functioning because I had a job, husband, child, and friends. The fact that there was a screamingly obvious reason why I had been operating in survival mode for four decades, somehow at the time eluded me.

What I did do is try to address some of my difficulties through CBT sessions and talking therapy. My long-established emetophobia had flared again and was affecting my ability to leave the house and left me in a permanent state of dread. This affected all of my relationships, particularly as I avoided social arrangements around eating or made excuses to leave early because of the terror that I might be sick in public. I was offered a course of NHS CBT sessions, but, if anything, this made the problem worse. I was told by the therapist that my phobia had developed because of my faulty thinking and that my coping strategy of carrying anti-emetics at all times and eating 'safe' foods was, I was told, only adding to the problem and that in order to recover I had to ditch these supports and change my cognitive patterns. This coupled with the therapist's aloofness and apparent disinterest in me as a person left me feeling even more broken and at fault. The appointments were paused after only two sessions due to my mother's death, as it wasn't deemed appropriate to continue while I was bereaved, but when I re-contacted the GP surgery at a later date, it transpired that I had been signed off and the service was no longer available to me, so that was that.

I also tried person-centred counselling with a local charity, but struggled to answer questions about how certain situations made me feel, even though I knew I experienced strong emotions, and ended up being overly compliant and responding in ways that I thought the counsellor wanted. I didn't seek any other help; I was in debt and my series of low-paid jobs meant that there was no spare cash even for concession therapy, and as I had been told by my GP that I wasn't mentally ill enough for NHS support, I gave up on that as well. I didn't feel as though I was left with any choices other than to keep taking the Prozac and to focus on supporting my son through his GCSEs and A Levels. It was more important to me that he was healthy, whole, and knew that he was loved, irrespective of the grades he achieved, so I put my autism diagnosis to one side. In hindsight, this wasn't the healthiest of paths for me, but I was driven by a desire to be a better parent than mine had been, and although I was stuck in a place of not being able to identify my needs or even that my needs mattered for a further four years, I don't regret it, as he has become a well-rounded and confident adult who has a good sense of who he is and what is important to him.

So what changed and how did I find myself? An empty nest, in all honesty. My son was enjoying his gap year and I finally turned my attention from focussing on parenting to learning about autism and what it meant for me. I started reading everything I could find on the subject and quickly learned that I wasn't deficient or broken and that the majority of my difficulties were due to stigma, being disabled socially, and the stress of masking for so many years. A chance meeting with an autism specialist counsellor at a conference led to me having what I can only describe as life-changing and probably life-saving counselling. Right from the start, Deborah Wortman believed and understood my experiences, and the following years of sessions have been a constant revelation about the validity and wonder of my neurodivergent brain wiring. I cannot stress the pivotal importance of being believed, being helped to know and believe my truth, and begin the move from denial to acceptance with a strange, new self-belief that I mattered. Of course, my husband has always believed me – he is consistently my best cheerleader, partner, and friend, but I needed professional help away from my most important relationship in order to keep it safe.

It was Deborah who recognised my ADHD, complex PTSD, and the debilitating effect of having had ME/CFS for 20 years, but feeling constantly fraudulent. It was Deborah who suggested that Sertraline, which anecdotally seems to be an effective support for autistic people who have co-occurring anxiety, may be more helpful than the Prozac that I had been on for nearly two decades, and it turned out to be game-changing for me. The anxiety and depression that had dominated for so long felt more manageable, and although I suspect that I will need this as a life-long medication, I take it without shame as I know the positive impact it has on my quality of life and relationships.

With Deborah's help I was making progress, but it was the space and time for reflection during the pandemic when the penny finally dropped that I was genuinely chronically mentally and physically ill. I was initially told by my GP to shield, as my asthma was considered severe enough in the early months of 2019 to put me in the extremely vulnerable category, particularly when coupled with the debilitating effect that my ME/CFS had on my ability to cope with and recover from viruses. This shocked me, as I was gearing up to be redeployed to one of the newly built Nightingale hospitals to support the COVID effort as a healthcare assistant. I was still massively in denial about the reality of my health and it wasn't until a few months later, when the horrendous effects of menopause were kicking in, coupled with a massive ME/CFS flare following a series of stressful family events, that I finally realised that I had to take Deborah's advice and be signed off on what turned out to be long-term sick leave, occupational health, and being disabled out of my job. With Deborah's support, I also successfully applied for PIP after having resisted for so long, as my internally ableised self didn't think I deserved it, even though I can now see that I had been struggling too much for too long. The process was ghastly and inhuman, but I was granted it and it has been invaluable for helping with my day-to-day life.

In the past few months I have been diagnosed with ADHD, prescribed stimulant medication that makes a huge difference to my ability to focus and function, and have recently completed an initial series of EMDR sessions for CPTSD, which felt like witchcraft at the time, but seems to have been a promising start on the road to recovery. There is still a lot of unpacking and healing to do on top of maintaining the improvements that I have made, and I am currently working on my long-term self-harm behaviours and eating disorders, and learning to pace my ME/CFS. Developing an understanding that I matter, that my needs are important, and that I am not a fraud has been an incredible journey. I now feel no shame in being disabled and different, nor in advocating for myself and asking for the supports and accommodations that I need to thrive.

It will come as no surprise then that my voyage of self-discovery has also had a positive effect on the quality of my other relationships. Ten years post diagnosis, I feel more closely connected to and congruent with friendships than I have at any point in the previous 40. Now that I know myself better and understand what it is that I need, I can be completely honest about whether an occasion is going to work for me or suggest tweaks that make allowances for my social, sensory, or energy differences. On the way to one such recent occasion, Lucy and Blythe's wedding, Lucy L and Hannah both made the point that they don't see me as being their autistic friend, but rather that I am their friend who just happens to be autistic. My particular brain wiring doesn't have any kind of negative connotation for them and they like me for who I am. They have also seen me change over the six years since we first met, from someone who was a chronic people pleaser to someone who is honest about the difficulties I experience, unapologetic about who I am, and unafraid to say what I need. Not only have they witnessed this change, they are also partly responsible for this newfound feistiness and confidence.

124 With a little help from my friends

Getting a diagnosis isn't always a cure-all for the difficulties someone is having, obviously. Knowing you are autistic does not stop your sensory experiences being overwhelming, or mean that people suddenly communicate in ways which make sense to you. Working with a neurodiverse team at the University of York, Felicity has just submitted a paper where we looked at the well-being of autistic women at different points along the diagnostic process – before formal diagnosis, shortly after diagnosis, and several years after. What we found was that there is an improvement in well-being around the time of diagnosis, as people get the explanations they have been looking for, but that for some autistic women their well-being then gets worse a few years later – precisely because their problems persist. This is something one of our interviewees talked about:

> The closest I came to suicide was after my diagnosis, which was unexpected as once I had it I thought I would be home and dry because I would understand. It turned out that this was just the start. The difficult thing now is that the same situations occur, I know why, but I still can't prevent them from happening because it's not all in my control. There are still people who react to me in very toxic ways because they pick up that difference about me and I'm still struggling with that kind of situation and then there's the kind of hopelessness that comes out of thinking that I've done everything that I can. I've discovered that I'm autistic, I'm having psychotherapy, I've got insight, I understand the theory and mechanics of it. I can't avoid these microaggressions and I can't get myself into a place where I am safe from these really unpleasant, really damaging situations.
>
> *(anonymous, 62, autistic woman)*

Equally, some people we talked to who had a later diagnosis actually thought that this had been a good thing, because if they had been diagnosed when they were younger they would have faced more stigma than they did:

> I don't think having an autism dx at that point would have added anything extra to that other than stigma and misunderstanding from teachers, who at that point I know they didn't understand ADHD so they wouldn't have got autism either.
>
> *(Sarah O, autistic woman)*

> If I'd gone into adulthood with this dx I'm not sure I would have done what I've done. I can wear the label now and it's not going to inhibit me, where I'm not sure whether wearing the label 20 years ago would have been. That's both in terms of the perceptions of others, but also in the way in which we might perform according to our own personal expectations.
>
> *(anonymous, male)*

Finding communities and feelings of belonging

Stigmatising attitudes towards autistic people is an important piece of context to remember for all the relationships and social interactions we have talked about throughout the book. Finding spaces which do not have this stigma is one of the best things to do for quality of life and mental health, and what we talk about next.

Finding communities and feelings of belonging

At several points in the previous sections of this chapter, we have mentioned that we are going to think about communities and the role these play in autistic adults' social lives. This is the place where we do that, as promised.

Most research about autistic adults' connectedness to communities was focussed on the experiences of adults in supported living situations, and looked at how embedded they were in their local areas and local networks. This usually found that they were only minimally involved in the community around them, unless they were directly supported to take part in things like group activities by their carers (Gray et al., 2014). These studies rarely prioritised looking at what the autistic adults themselves thought about the activities they were taken to or the people they were being expected to socialise with, instead asking those same carers about the frequency or type of activity. It may be, then, that a lack of engagement with community in these studies comes from the fact that the autistic people weren't actually interested in being part of those groups – people all like different things, and there is no reason to expect that carers automatically always find things that the person they are looking after is into. Equally, the research did not really look at whether these communities were genuinely accepting and supportive of the autistic people who were trying to join them, which could also make it harder for someone to feel part of the group.

Despite these challenges, in many social spaces and groups, many autistic people have always managed to find some communities where they feel safe, supported, and happy. We speculated earlier about whether people who sought out a religious life in the mediaeval period may have had high levels of autistic traits, as these close-knit communities with clear rules and behavioural expectations may have appealed to autistic people. Equally, academia has often been looked on as a refuge for those who struggle with social skills and who are deeply passionate about specific topics – the 'ivory towers' of the 18th, 19th, and 20th centuries were probably also communities with higher-than-average concentrations of autistic men (it is only from the late 1800s that women were allowed into universities, and only generally so from the mid-1900s). These are just two examples of communities across time which have been potentially autism-friendly, and there are equally lots of spaces which are positive for autistic people today – Sarah's piece coming up tells us about just some of the ones which she has found and benefited from being part of.

Autistic people also, obviously, make their own communities – both in person and online. The widely recognised first autistic-run community was formally started in 1992, in the form of Autism Network International, which sent out

126 With a little help from my friends

newsletters and articles written by autistic people. Out of this network came a collection of in-person retreats and conferences run by and for autistic people all over the world, including AutScape in the UK and AutSpace in the US. Now, there are a plethora of autism-led initiatives, support groups, and interest groups through which autistic people can find welcoming communities. We highly recommend the book *Autistic Community and the Neurodiversity Movement*, by Steven Kapp, an autistic researcher, if you are interested in learning more about this history and how autistic people have driven the neurodiversity movement forwards from the beginning. There is still demand for more of autistic-friendly and autistic-led spaces, of course, and some autistic people are still likely to find that there is nothing in their local area because much of this work happens online, but the picture is better than it was and improving all the time. Tejas, one of our non-speaking contributors, talked about the value of autistic and neurodivergent people building truly inclusive spaces:

> [It is] rewarding on so many levels to be building a trusted community of neurotypicals and neurodivergent. The best rewarding relationships are with friends, it isn't about romance, it is about loving the same things that you do and having respect for your neuroidentity.
>
> *(Tejas, 24, male)*

Sarah's experience of community and belonging

As I have aged and particularly in the last few years since I have been exploring my neurodiversity, community has become increasingly important to me and plays a big part in my well-being. Growing up outside of the party was a lonely experience, but finding the tribes in adulthood where I can be vulnerable and real has resulted in a definite shift from isolation towards feeling a sense of communal belonging. Being a part of a supportive community is generally thought to be an essential component for well-being, regardless of neurotype, but for people who are marginalised from and stigmatised by society, it is even more important to find safe and nurturing spaces in which to heal, share, and belong.

I began by exploring various autism groups on social media armed with a utopian ideal that because I was autistic, I would have an instant connection with every other autistic person on Facebook and I would discover fluffy and united autistic friendship communities. It was going to be a marvellous discovery of like-minded autists, who agreed on everything and would be a safe haven from the nasty neurotypical world. Well, of course, it didn't turn out to be like that. Some groups felt too big or overwhelming and others seemed to be riven with factions or did not feel like safe spaces to discuss anything, let alone autism-related things. This came as a disappointing surprise to me as I naively thought that I would instantly connect with my tribe. It may well be that the many years of desperately wanting to fit in, copying others to do so, and hiding behind my neurotypical mask did not equip me to interrelate with other people who were more authentically autistic. Unlearning my social ableism and beginning to unmask has become as much a part of the process of developing community relationships as it has with my friendships and family.

I've also learned that the common denominator of being autistic does not mean that everyone in a social media group will like each other, hold other things in common, or even treat each other kindly. There have been occasions where I have had to take a break from or leave groups because of unpleasant interactions, and it was a painful, but necessary, lesson to learn that autistic people, like every other neurotype, are complex, have different ideas and opinions, and that sometimes cause upset when communicating them. It was incredibly naive of me to think that an online autistic community was going to be perfect. I'm not, and I know that I have handed out my fair share of snark in my several thousand tweets to date, so why would I expect other autistic people to be angelic communicators? I have come to realise that autistic communities are full of severely traumatised people and, although it can be hard to be on the receiving end of someone else's pain and projection, I understand this more now and try to respond or push back in a more informed way.

It is absolutely true, as the marvellous Sara Gibbs tweets that,

> *when two autistic people are on a wavelength, the communication tends to be wonderful, nuanced, stimulating, supportive & without incident, https://twitter.com/Sara_Rose_G/status/1508843 930074468352 March 29th 5.30 pm 2022*

And since I have been exploring online autism communities I have found some wonderful groups on social media that fit this description, but for me, it is Sara's insightful phrase, "on a wavelength" that sums it up. The FB groups that I feel at home in now are safe and supportive and a good fit for me, but it took a while for me to recognise that kinship will not automatically happen just because of a shared particular neurotype. Being on the same wavelength also really matters and finding the right community connections has very much been a process of discovering my particular tribe within the larger autistic one and also with non-neurotype specific groups.

Of course I won't be naming the closed Facebook groups that I am part of, but a public one that I can mention is the YouBelong group, which I discovered during lockdown. It was set up by Laura Neale in early 2019 when she discovered that like her, there were many chronically ill and disabled Christians who needed an accessible and welcoming community to belong to. It is a diverse group, with many different experiences, but what unites us is our faith and the questions that chronic illness and/or disability raise within that context and our experiences of being marginalised because of that and what being chronically ill and/or disabled means to us. We share and support each other and 'get it' in ways other people never could, nor indeed, sadly ever try to.

I've also been part of a local church for over 25 years and attend, off and on, with my husband. There are times when I can't engage in a physical church community because of sensory or social overwhelm, but I have found St Matthews to be loving, accepting, and open to inclusion, difference, and improving disability access. It is a special place for me as Kyle and I were married there and I have developed some lovely friendships, particularly with people who are also misfits or who aren't afraid to think radically or counterculturally. The Vicar Ian Tomkins describes the ethos that underpins the relational nature of St Matthews when he says that, "What binds our church family together is unconditional love, grace and servanthood. We want to be a community that serves our wider diverse community" (3 March 2022), which is a good fit with my strong sense of social justice and a desire to make things better for marginalised people. I can be myself in this place and feel a sense of belonging that I hadn't experienced from faith groups earlier in my life.

Two of my favourite pastimes are singing and music, and joining the Autistic Adult Choir has been a discovery of not just a singing group set up for autistic people but also a place where autistic well-being and support are central to the ethos of the organisation. Jill Bradford, the Autistic Adult Choir's co-founder and leader set it up seven years ago, along with Henry Tillman, because she saw a need for meaningful social and community activities for autistic adults. As well as feeling drawn to working with autistic people, she wanted to provide a supportive musical outlet for autistic adults who may have had traumatic experiences being in music groups before and stopped playing or singing because of it. Jill did face negativity about her plans from others, but following consultation with autistic friends she started the group with five people and it has grown from there. Jill has achieved this by basing all of her choir decisions on the diverse needs of the group and creating an atmosphere of trust and belonging.

TAAC regularly performs at a variety of venues including private engagements, charity events, carol services, schools, as well as sporting and festival events. The shift to Zoom during the pandemic helped to deepen relationships as during the online sessions we would present talks about our intense interests or musical tastes and it was a great way to learn more about each other on a personal level. Not only is there an incredible amount of talent and musical knowledge in the choir, there is fun, friendship and a sense of family. I never feel the need to disguise my autistic self and quickly came to realise what Jill means when she describes TAAC being a 'mask-free zone'.

Jill is also careful to make sure that the different needs of the choir are accommodated for and that if she feels that a planned singing event is not supportive of that at any stage then she pulls the choir out. Her priority is not for the show to go on regardless, but for the welfare of the choir members which refreshingly flies in the face of the prevalent social attitude that autistic people are expected to fit in around the needs of others or the environment in which they are placed.

For Jill the choir is much more than a singing group. She feels like,

> *The choir is part of my family and I feel closer to the choir than to a lot of people. I feel like we've been on a journey together and have shared experiences that only we know and can relate to. To be given the chance to do this and be trusted with their well-being is a huge responsibility and it is my priority.*

The final group of people that are an important part of my life is the RockFit community. Based in Plymouth, this brainchild of Hannah Hawkey exploded online during the pandemic, which really suited me as I could enjoy exercise at home without the social and sensory overwhelm that tends to put me off attending physical classes. The online classes are accompanied by a Facebook RockFit UK community, Transformations group and events such as the brilliant recent Download Festival Flash-mob, all of which are choreographed and administered by Hannah and her team. Similarly to Jill at TAAC, Hannah's priority is to put strong boundaries in place to protect her community. If an event isn't going to work or be safe for her Rockfitters then it isn't happening. The welfare of her tribe is Hannah's primary concern and the show will not go on if that is compromised.

For me, RockFit combines a revisiting of the music I loved as a teenager, but had not listened to for years out of misplaced guilt and an ongoing discovery of the decades of banging tunes that I have missed out on. I do feel

130 With a little help from my friends

as though I am playing catch up, but discovering Rammstein and Download Festival aged 52 is definitely better late than never. Release of trauma and difficult emotions through listening to metal are well documented and I find that lyrics on tracks like Korn's Twisted Transistor are intimate, insightful and healing.

https://psychcentral.com/health/benefits-of-listening-to-metal-music

Metalheads may look scary, but I have found this community to be empathic, kind, and on the whole generous in sharing their musical recommendations. An impromptu RockFit UK Facebook live posting during the recent extraordinary Eurovision song contest wasn't just a shared existential confusion of the UK actually doing well for a change, it was a shared love of music and humanity.

I even feel accepted as a Christian in the group, which I'll admit I wasn't expecting. Past indoctrination of the Satanic Panic of the 1980s in relation to all things rock-related had become rooted in me and when I tentatively revealed my faith in the online group I was expecting immediate rejection. Not a bit of it. There are even Vicar's wives who are members! Hannah describes the ethos of RockFit as being one of "Zero judgement, zero pressure, no pretence, inclusiveness, acceptance, encouragement and a combination of music and community pulling together," and that creating it was not just about not liking the music in more mainstream fitness classes, it was about making something where she felt she belonged and represented others like herself who need authenticity. She adds,

> *I have a love of misfits and rejects. All of us have been the round peg in the square hole; outcasts in so many places and in so many parts of our lives and it's nice to find a place that accepts us for who we are. The ethos of the metal and rock gig community is that if somebody is down, you pick them up again, and this isn't just in a physical mosh pit, but in the online RockFit community too. Someone will post that they are having a hard time and then there will be 50 encouraging answers, so it's a mental pick up too. It's unique.*

I can certainly vouch for this as I have posted about my disabilities, neurodivergence, and chronic illness on the online group and have received nothing but support and understanding. RockFit draws in so many diverse people who are neurodivergent, disabled, LGBTQ, or experiencing poor mental health, and some have openly said that this community has kept them alive. It is extraordinarily powerful to have disclosure of vulnerability and feelings of being an outsider lifted up in this way and it is no surprise

> *that people on the periphery do seem to favour particular genres of music like metal or rock. There is a collective sense of alternative thinking, creativity, and unconventionality, which is why an autistic person like me feels so at home in the RockFit community. I occasionally (ME/CFS allowing) do some exercise as well!*
>
> *All of these communities may at first glance seem quite disparate, but threads of genuine inclusion, kindness, acceptance, and a celebration of difference weave through them all. They are safe places for me to be my authentically autistic self and instead of feeling as though I am still outside of the party desperate to be invited in, I am now happy to inhabit the periphery and find my voice with my friends on the fringes.*

Most of the communities Sarah talks about here, which are so important in her life, are offline, rather than online, and this is probably the case for many autistic adults. A recent systematic review, combining the results of 58 studies, showed that autistic people are involved in a wide range of communities both offline and online, independently and with support (Cameron et al., 2022). This involvement had a positive impact on mental health and well-being, and was valuable for all the adults included. Community participation is important for all autistic adults, as we've said, and another recent paper looked at levels of involvement and satisfaction with that involvement among a large sample of autistic adults, with and without learning difficulties, in the US (Shea et al., 2021). This showed that autistic adults with learning difficulties reported being involved in fewer community activities than those without, but that they also felt this was less important to their well-being overall. Autistic adults with higher incomes were happier with their level and variety of community activities, which makes sense as they had more resources with which to pursue their interests. People living alone tended to say they felt their community involvement was further from what they would want in an ideal world, probably because when living alone other forms of social interaction become your main way of spending time with people, so it is easier to feel lonely at least some of the time.

Church communities are one of the few settings which have had more than just one study – although the research is still far from extensive. There have been studies which make specific recommendations for how churches can be more inclusive of autistic people, referring back to scripture as a model for welcoming those who are different (Burnett, 2020). This paper focussed on how pastoral carers in the church should support autistic adults to be their "lovely, God-given selves" (p. 214) and should look for the strengths and gifts autistic people bring to the church, including in leadership roles. While some autistic Christians in this study talked about the bad practice they had experienced – such as being patronised, or being told that they need prayer to 'cure' them – the majority said that relatively easy supports allowed them to be involved fully in the life of their church. This is important, because

132 With a little help from my friends

worship experiences can be difficult for autistic people to access, even though they deeply value being part of the community:

> One of the really big things that has come out is that from [online] church they miss being with other people but then people find [physical church] really inaccessible, so the barriers are the lack of access and the access is physical, psychological, sensory, everything under the sun.
>
> *(Krysia, 30, talking about experiences of online church during COVID)*

This mix of experiences and attitudes seems typical of how autistic people are included in and perceived by churchgoers (Waldock & Forrester-Jones, 2020). Interviewing 21 adults who went to church regularly, it was revealed that there was a highly varied collection of views – some people were very positive about autistic people in the church, often linked to having a more neurodiversity-informed view of autism. Others were more negative and displayed ableist views about what autistic people were and were not capable of in their community, often linked to seeing autism as a disorder rather than as a difference. The church practices reported by all these participants varied as much as their attitudes – most people were aware of what might be barriers to being part of the church community, but some were unsure how to address these, or to what extent it was even possible. Saying that, several people gave examples of specific ways their church had worked to include autistic congregation members, both adults and children, such as giving information about the service or activities in advance, and allowing them to follow their own preferences around contributing to things. This shows how we should take each local community on its own merits – there is no singular 'church response to autistic people' in the same way as there is no unified school or university or workplace response to autistic people. Talking to us about her work, Krysia said:

> Another thing I've found especially with the majority non-autistic groups I've run from religious groups is that there is a massive divide between what people theoretically think inclusion and belonging are and when we provide them with a vignette they go and say something completely different like 'that person's weird, that person's a stroppy teenager, they just need to be included, ooh I'll go and make eye contact with them.' I'm thinking . . . 'that's nothing . . . how have you moved so far from the conversation we had where you were saying that everyone is valued?'
>
> *(Krysia, 30)*

This emphasises how important it is for communities to not just 'talk the talk' on inclusion, but also 'walk the walk' – being genuinely accepting and supportive of neurodivergent members, not just saying they are. As we have seen with so many relationships in the book, true acceptance is the key to good relationships for autistic people.

Community, autistic identity, and well-being

Just as with making autistic friends online, finding and becoming part of autistic communities online is a really important experience for many autistic people. These groups help autistic people to see their personal difficulties as part of a political struggle for equality and justice (Botha & Gillespie-Lynch, 2022). This is often felt to be a process of 'reclaiming' an autistic identity, seeing autistic behaviours as natural and normal, and finding agency in navigating the world on their terms (Parsloe, 2015). It helps autistic people to understand themselves as different, rather than 'broken' or 'deficient', as so many cultural narratives paint them out to be, and often gives them access to a strengths-based, positive account of being autistic for the first time. Research has shown that autistic people who feel more strongly connected to this positive autism framing through community involvement tend to have higher self-esteem and feel stronger identification with other autistic people (Cooper et al., 2021). Being part of the community also helps you to understand why other relationships can have gone wrong, something else Krysia talked about in her research:

> What I found with autistic people is that a positive identity, knowing you're autistic and understanding the exclusion through the lens of the double empathy problem seems to be quite massive in terms of how people understand it through the times when it hasn't gone right.
>
> *(Krysia, 30)*

What this means is that being part of an active, positive online autism community can be part of a positive cycle – joining the community helps you feel better about being autistic, feeling better about being autistic improves your self-esteem, and improved self-esteem helps keep the community positive for the newly diagnosed people joining it, who then also get the benefits.

This is in direct contrast to how many autistic people experience communities and lack of belonging in the wider world, where they represent a minority identity (just as someone can be of a minority ethnicity, or sexuality, they can be of a minority neurotype). People with any type of minority identity tend to have more stressful lives, because of systematic and specific barriers, stigma, and the pressure to conceal this identity or to fit in with the majority – something called, very originally, Minority Stress Theory. It has been shown that this theory can help to understand some of the reasons behind the higher rates of mental health problems we see in autistic people (Botha & Frost, 2018). Most autistic adults report having experienced discrimination in the wider community at some point, which definitely contributes to anxiety, depression, and feelings of exclusion (Jones et al., 2022), and this just emphasises how important it is to have supportive communities where autistic people can be themselves.

In fact, the strength of online communities such as Twitter in supporting autistic people has been recognised widely, both anecdotally and in research. The way these spaces operate has been held up as a model for creating better offline communities for autistic people (Saha & Agarwal, 2016). For example, the way knowledge about autism and developments in understanding autistic people is collated and shared through these networks is often much more egalitarian and accessible than in traditional or formal structures, meaning that more people can make use of this information faster.

134 With a little help from my friends

Alongside this spread of knowledge, the biggest factor which seems to link autistic community involvement and well-being is the sense of belonging and authenticity people gain from it, sometimes for the first time. Feeling like you are part of something bigger, that you are seen for who you really are and accepted without question, is affirming in basically every way.

> When you have spent a long time being made to feel like the weird one because you see things differently to other people or you engage with a situation differently to other people and to have a situation where someone actually affirms that or backs it up like our interactions on Twitter. When someone says that insight has been really helpful for me it's deeply meaningful.
>
> *(anonymous, male)*

> In terms of community being beneficial I think for me for autistic people in terms of positive community when there is that likemindedness it seems to work.
>
> *(Krysia, 30)*

The potential for offline autistic-led spaces to create this sense of belonging has been talked about for years – it is one of the reasons why these events were set up so many decades ago now (Milton & Sims, 2016). Being able to be open about your true self and embrace your autistic identity has been shown to have an important effect on mental health (improving it) and masking behaviours (reducing them), and feeling more confident to disclose that you are autistic in other contexts as well (Cage & Troxell-Whitman, 2020; Seers & Hogg, 2022). A different study by some of the same researchers found that autism community connectedness did not predict lower masking behaviours in another sample of autistic people (Cage et al., 2021), but that it was directly related to better well-being, the same as in the other research. There are a number of reasons this may be – those people who are more involved in the autism community may be more aware of the discrimination autistic people can face, and so may be more likely to mask outside the community safe space to try to avoid this for themselves. Also, autistic people are not a monolith – intersectionality between different aspects of identity means that disclosing your diagnosis or stopping masking carries different consequences for some people than others. People who have multiple minority identities, such as being autistic and black, or female, or LGBTQ, may face greater risks for disclosing and therefore be less likely to do so in order to keep themselves safe. This doesn't negate the mental health benefits of being part of an online autism community, but instead is a reflection of the fact that the offline world has not yet caught up in terms of autism acceptance.

Chapter conclusion

The threads of inclusion, kindness, and acceptance which Sarah closed her reflections on community with are a good summary of the themes of this chapter. Friendships are not always easy for autistic people, and can often be outright difficult. Not everyone has good friendships as a child, or even as a teenager, and that makes it harder to know how to find those kinds of connections as you become an adult. Equally, though, lots of autistic people do have friends early in life, as we have seen in other chapters, and this is the same for autistic adults. In fact, the move into adulthood, with the much greater freedom to socialise in ways and spaces which work for you, can lead to much better friendships than previously. The Double Empathy Theory and the evidence for it which we have discussed have shown that autistic people can and do have excellent friendships with each other, with more instinctive and smoother communication than they have with non-autistic people. That doesn't mean that good friendships with non-autistic people are impossible, obviously. They very much are, and lots of the studies and contributors in this chapter also show that (as do we!). When autistic adults find people who accept them for who they are, who actively seek to include them – whether that is in a one-to-one friendship, an online space, or an in-person community – then beautiful friendships can flourish regardless of neurotype.

References

Antonucci, T. C., & Akiyama, H. (1987). Social networks in adult life and a preliminary examination of the convoy model. *Journal of Gerontology*, *42*(5), 519–527. https://doi.org/10.1093/geronj/42.5.519

Antonucci, T. C., Lansford, J. E., & Akiyama, H. (2010). Impact of positive and negative aspects of marital relationships and friendships on well-being of older adults. *Applied Developmental Science*, *5*(2), 68–75. https://doi.org/10.1207/S1532480XADS0502_2

Bargiela, S., Steward, R., & Mandy, W. (2016). The experiences of late-diagnosed women with autism spectrum conditions: An investigation of the female autism phenotype. *Journal of Autism and Developmental Disorders*, *46*(10), 3281–3294. https://doi.org/10.1007/s10803-016-2872-8

Baron-Cohen, S., & Wheelwright, S. (2003). The friendship questionnaire: An investigation of adults with asperger syndrome or high-functioning autism, and normal sex differences. *Journal of Autism and Developmental Disorders*, *33*(5), 509–517. https://doi.org/10.1023/A:1025879411971

Botha, M., & Frost, D. M. (2018). Extending the minority stress model to understand mental health problems experienced by the autistic population. *Society and Mental Health*, *10*(1), 20–34. https://doi.org/10.1177/2156869318804297

Botha, M., & Gillespie-Lynch, K. (2022). Come as you are: Examining autistic identity development and the neurodiversity movement through an intersectional lens. *Human Development*, *66*(2), 93–112. https://doi.org/10.1159/000524123

Burke, M., Kraut, R., & Williams, D. (2010). Social use of computer-mediated communication by adults on the autism spectrum. *Proceedings of the 2010 ACM Conference on Computer Supported Cooperative Work – CSCW'10*, 425. https://doi.org/10.1145/1718918.1718991

Burnett, E. R. (2020). Different not less: Pastoral care of autistic adults within christian churches. *Practical Theology*, *14*(3), 211–223. https://doi.org/10.1080/1756073X.2020.1850402

Cage, E., Cranney, R., & Botha, M. (2021). Brief report: Does autistic community connectedness moderate the relationship between masking and wellbeing? *Autism in Adulthood*, *4*(3), 247–253. https://doi.org/10.31234/OSF.IO/P6BT5

Cage, E., De Andres, M., & Mahoney, P. (2020). Understanding the factors that affect university completion for autistic people. *Research in Autism Spectrum Disorders*, *72*, 101519. https://doi.org/10.1016/J.RASD.2020.101519

136 With a little help from my friends

Cage, E., & Troxell-Whitman, Z. (2020). Understanding the relationships between autistic identity, disclosure, and camouflaging. *Autism in Adulthood, 2*(4), 334–338. https://doi.org/10.1089/AUT.2020.0016

Cameron, L. A., Borland, R. L., Tonge, B. J., & Gray, K. M. (2022). Community participation in adults with autism: A systematic review. *Journal of Applied Research in Intellectual Disabilities, 35*(2), 421–447. https://doi.org/10.1111/JAR.12970

Camus, L., Macmillan, K., Rajendran, G., & Stewart, M. (2022). *I too, need to belong: Autistic adults perspectives on misunderstandings and well-being.* https://doi.org/10.31234/OSF.IO/5MYSH

Chan, D. V., Doran, J. D., & Galobardi, O. D. (2022). Beyond friendship: The spectrum of social participation of autistic adults. *Journal of Autism and Developmental Disorders,* 1–14. https://doi.org/10.1007/S10803-022-05441-1/FIGURES/1

Cooper, R., Cooper, K., Russell, A. J., & Smith, L. G. E. (2021). I'm proud to be a little bit different: The effects of autistic individuals perceptions of autism and autism social identity on their collective self-esteem. *Journal of Autism and Developmental Disorders, 51*(2), 704–714. https://doi.org/10.1007/S10803-020-04575-4/FIGURES/1

Crompton, C. J., Ropar, D., Evans-Williams, C. V. M., Flynn, E. G., & Fletcher-Watson, S. (2020). Autistic peer-to-peer information transfer is highly effective. *Autism, 24*(7), 1704–1712. https://doi.org/10.1177/1362361320919286

Everard, K. M., Lach, H. W., Fisher, E. B., & Baum, M. C. (2000). Relationship of activity and social support to the functional health of older adults. *The Journals of Gerontology: Series B, 55*(4), S208–S212. https://doi.org/10.1093/GERONB/55.4.S208

Finke, E. H. (2022). The kind of friend i think i am: Perceptions of autistic and non-autistic young adults. *Journal of Autism and Developmental Disorders,* 1–18. https://doi.org/10.1007/S10803-022-05573-4/TABLES/9

Fiori, K. L., Antonucci, T. C., & Cortina, K. S. (2006). Social network typologies and mental health among older adults. *The Journals of Gerontology: Series B, 61*(1), P25–P32. https://doi.org/10.1093/GERONB/61.1.P25

Gan, D. R. Y., Best, J. R., Hennessy, C., & Douglas, E. (2021). Prior social contact and mental health trajectories during COVID-19: Neighborhood friendship protects vulnerable older adults. *International Journal of Environmental Research and Public Health 2021, 18*(19), 9999. https://doi.org/10.3390/IJERPH18199999

Gillespie-Lynch, K., Kapp, S. K., Shane-Simpson, C., Smith, D. S., & Hutman, T. (2014). Intersections between the autism spectrum and the internet: Perceived benefits and preferred functions of computer-mediated communication. *Intellectual and Developmental Disabilities, 52*(6), 456–469. https://doi.org/10.1352/1934-9556-52.6.456

Goddard, H., & Cook, A. (2021). I spent most of freshers in my room – A qualitative study of the social experiences of university students on the autistic spectrum. *Journal of Autism and Developmental Disorders 2021, 52*(6), 2701–2716. https://doi.org/10.1007/S10803-021-05125-2

Gould, J. (2017). Towards understanding the under-recognition of girls and women on the autism spectrum. *Autism, 21*(6). https://doi.org/10.1177/1362361317706174

Gray, K. M., Keating, C. M., Taffe, J. R., Brereton, A. V., Einfeld, S. L., Reardon, T. C., & Tonge, B. J. (2014). Adult outcomes in autism: Community inclusion and living skills. *Journal of Autism and Developmental Disorders, 44*(12), 3006–3015. https://doi.org/10.1007/S10803-014-2159-X/TABLES/5

Gurbuz, E., Hanley, M., & Riby, D. M. (2019). University students with autism: The social and academic experiences of university in the UK. *Journal of Autism and Developmental Disorders, 49*(2), 617–631. https://doi.org/10.1007/s10803-018-3741-4

Harmens, M., Sedgewick, F., & Hobson, H. (2022). The quest for acceptance: A blog-based study of autistic women's experiences and well-being during autism identification and diagnosis. *Autism in Adulthood*, *4*(1), 42–51. https://doi.org/10.1089/AUT.2021.0016

Heasman, B., & Gillespie, A. (2018). Perspective-taking is two-sided: Misunderstandings between people with Asperger's syndrome and their family members. *Autism*, *22*(6). https://doi.org/10.1177/1362361317708287

Howard, P. L., & Sedgewick, F. (2021). Anything but the phone: Communication mode preferences in the autism community. *Autism*, *25*(8), 2265–2278. https://doi.org/10.1177/13623613211014995/ASSET/IMAGES/LARGE/10.1177_1362361321 1014995-FIG2.JPEG

Howlin, P. (2000). Outcome in adult life for more able individuals with autism or asperger syndrome. *Autism*, *4*(1), 63–83. https://doi.org/10.1177/1362361300004001005

Jones, S. C., Gordon, C. S., Akram, M., Murphy, N., & Sharkie, F. (2022). Inclusion, Exclusion and isolation of autistic people: Community attitudes and autistic people's experiences. *Journal of Autism and Developmental Disorders*, *52*(3), 1131–1142. https://doi.org/10.1007/S10803-021-04998-7/TABLES/3

Lambe, S., Russell, A., Butler, C., Fletcher, S., Ashwin, C., & Brosnan, M. (2019). Autism and the transition to university from the student perspective. *Autism*, *23*(6), 1531–1541. https://doi.org/10.1177/1362361318803935

Leedham, A., Thompson, A. R., Smith, R., & Freeth, M. (2020). I was exhausted trying to figure it out: The experiences of females receiving an autism diagnosis in middle to late adulthood. *Autism*, *24*(1), 135–146. https://doi.org/10.1177/1362361319853442

Mazurek, M. O. (2013). Social media use among adults with autism spectrum disorders. *Computers in Human Behavior*, *29*(4), 1709–1714. https://doi.org/10.1016/J.CHB.2013.02.004

Mazurek, M. O. (2014). Loneliness, friendship, and well-being in adults with autism spectrum disorders. *Autism*, *18*(3), 223–232. https://doi.org/10.1177/1362361312474121

Mazurek, M. O., Engelhardt, C. R., & Clark, K. E. (2015). Video games from the perspective of adults with autism spectrum disorder. *Computers in Human Behavior*, *51*, 122–130. https://doi.org/10.1016/J.CHB.2015.04.062

Milton, D., & Sims, T. (2016). How is a sense of well-being and belonging constructed in the accounts of autistic adults? *Disability and Society*, *31*(4). https://doi.org/10.1080/09 687599.2016.1186529

Parsloe, S. M. (2015). Discourses of disability, Narratives of community: Reclaiming an utistic identity online. *Journal of Applied Communication Research*, *43*(3), 336–356. https://doi.org/10.1080/00909882.2015.1052829

Rifai, O. M., Fletcher-Watson, S., Jiménez-Sánchez, L., & Crompton, C. J. (2022). Investigating markers of rapport in autistic and nonautistic interactions. *Autism in Adulthood*, *4*(1), 3–11. https://doi.org/10.1089/AUT.2021.0017/ASSET/IMAGES/LARGE/AUT.2021.0017_FIGURE2.JPEG

Russell, G., Stapley, S., Newlove-Delgado, T., Salmon, A., White, R., Warren, F., Pearson, A., & Ford, T. (2022). Time trends in autism diagnosis over 20 years: A UK population-based cohort study. *Journal of Child Psychology and Psychiatry*, *63*(6), 674–682. https://doi.org/10.1111/JCPP.13505

Saha, A., & Agarwal, N. (2016). Modeling social support in autism community on social media. *Network Modeling Analysis in Health Informatics and Bioinformatics*, *5*(1), 1–14. https://doi.org/10.1007/S13721-016-0115-8/TABLES/5

Scott, M., & Sedgewick, F. (2021). I have more control over my life: A qualitative exploration of challenges, opportunities, and support needs among autistic university students. *Autism and Developmental Language Impairments*, *6*. https://doi.org/10.1177/23969415211010419

Sedgewick, F., Crane, L., Hill, V., & Pellicano, E. (2018). Friends and lovers: The relationships of autistic and neurotypical women. *Autism in Adulthood*, *1*(2), 112–123. https://doi.org/10.1089/aut.2018.0028

Sedgewick, F., Hill, V., & Pellicano, E. (2019). It's different for girls: Gender differences in the friendships and conflict of autistic and neurotypical adolescents. *Autism*, *23*(5). https://doi.org/10.1177/1362361318794930

Sedgewick, F., Leppanen, J., & Tchanturia, K. (2019). The friendship questionnaire, autism, and gender differences: A study revisited. *Molecular Autism*, *10*(1), 1–12. https://doi.org/10.1186/s13229-019-0295-z

Seers, K., & Hogg, R. (2022). "Fake it 'till you make it": Authenticity and wellbeing in late diagnosed autistic women. *Feminism & Psychology*, 09593535221101455.

Shea, L. L., Verstreate, K., Nonnemacher, S., Song, W., & Salzer, M. S. (2021). Self-reported community participation experiences and preferences of autistic adults. *Autism*, *25*(5), 1295–1306. https://doi.org/10.1177/1362361320987682

Sosnowy, C., Silverman, C., Shattuck, P., & Garfield, T. (2019). Setbacks and successes: How young adults on the autism spectrum seek friendship. *Autism in Adulthood*, *1*(1), 44–51. https://doi.org/10.1089/aut.2018.0009

Sundberg, M. (2018). Online gaming, loneliness and friendships among adolescents and adults with ASD. *Computers in Human Behavior*, *79*, 105–110. https://doi.org/10.1016/J.CHB.2017.10.020

Suzuki, K., Oi, Y., & Inagaki, M. (2021). The relationships among autism spectrum disorder traits, loneliness, and social networking service use in college students. *Journal of Autism and Developmental Disorders*, *51*(6), 2047–2056. https://doi.org/10.1007/S10803-020-04701-2/FIGURES/2

Tan, C. D. (2018). I'm a normal autistic person, not an abnormal neurotypical: Autism spectrum disorder diagnosis as biographical illumination. *Social Science & Medicine*, *197*, 161–167. https://doi.org/10.1016/J.SOCSCIMED.2017.12.008

Triantafyllopoulou, P., Clark-Hughes, C., & Langdon, P. E. (2021). Social media and cyberbullying in autistic adults. *Journal of Autism and Developmental Disorders*, 1–9. https://doi.org/10.1007/S10803-021-05361-6/TABLES/4

Van Der Aa, C., Pollmann, M. M. H., Plaat, A., & Van Der Gaag, R. J. (2016). Computer-mediated communication in adults with high-functioning autism spectrum disorders and controls. *Research in Autism Spectrum Disorders*, *23*, 15–27. https://doi.org/10.1016/J.RASD.2015.11.007

Vine Foggo, R. S., & Webster, A. A. (2017). Understanding the social experiences of adolescent females on the autism spectrum. *Research in Autism Spectrum Disorders*, *35*, 74–85. https://doi.org/10.1016/J.RASD.2016.11.006

Waldock, K. E., & Forrester-Jones, R. (2020). An exploratory study of attitudes toward autism amongst church-going christians in the south east of england, United Kingdom. *Journal of Disability and Religion*, *24*(4), 349–370. https://doi.org/10.1080/23312521.2020.1776667

Ward, D., & Webster, A. (2018). Understanding the lived experiences of university students with autism spectrum disorder (ASD): A phenomenological study. *International Journal of Disability, Development and Education*, *65*(4), 373–392. https://doi.org/10.1080/1034912X.2017.1403573

Webster, A. A., & Garvis, S. (2017). The importance of critical life moments: An explorative study of successful women with autism spectrum disorder. *Autism*, *21*(6), 670–677. https://doi.org/10.1177/1362361316677719

6

WELL, HELLO THERE

Sexual and romantic relationships in adulthood

Friends and community are not the only relationships we make and maintain in adulthood. They are actually, often, not what people think of when you say 'adult relationships'. Romantic, or sexual, relationships, are usually what we jump to when thinking about adult relationships. As with much else in this book after the age of about 11, not a huge amount is known about autistic people's romantic relationships – and a lot of what is known about their sexual relationships is sad. Autistic people face high rates of victimisation and intimate partner violence, a phenomenon which is only just beginning to be publicly explored and talked about. That is the focus of Chapter 9: Toxic. This chapter is going to focus on what we know about the better sides of their relationship experiences, along with things like looking at the ends of relationships, and how this compares to what we know about non-autistic people.

What little work there was on sexual and romantic experiences of autistic adults mainly came from looking at autistic people in residential care and their self-stimulatory behaviours – usually from the perspective of trying to stop them having any. One of the few longitudinal pieces of work which looked at autistic adults' relationships came from Patricia Howlin, who was the first person to do this kind of work. She and her team first saw a group of autistic children in the 1980s, when they were roughly seven years old, then saw them again 20 years later (Howlin et al., 2004). What the team found was that the majority of the autistic adults still lived with their families rather than independently, and they did not have romantic partners or families of their own. Working with a different set of autistic people – also over 20 years – Howlin and her team found that 77% of the 60 adults had nothing they defined as friendships, and 83% had no romantic relationships to date (Howlin et al., 2013). This set the tone for expectations for autistic people in relation to romantic relationships, that is, none. Our contributors were aware of this stereotype, and openly discussed how their own lives contradicted it:

DOI: 10.4324/9781003044536-7

140 Well, hello there

> It's a stereotypical thing that autistic people can't have long romantic relationships.
>
> Relationships have been very difficult for me to handle. The beginnings of them, the middle of them, the ends of them. They've been messy, they've caused hurt for other people. It's hurt me, but the one thing I can say is that it hasn't been devoid of romantic relationships. It's been packed full with them. That's the kind of stereotype that makes someone like me think that they couldn't be autistic.
>
> *(both quotes from anonymous, 62, autistic woman)*

Many of the adults in the early studies, though, were people with co-occurring learning difficulties or other disabilities, and the reporting on their relationships was done via a standardised questionnaire by their parents or carers. When we look at studies where autistic people speak for themselves about their experiences, and when we listen to autistic people without co-occurring learning difficulties or who received their diagnosis in adulthood, a different picture appears.

Autism and attachment in adulthood

Earlier in the book (in Chapter 1: First Steps) we talked a lot about attachment – what it is, the different types, and how research has found that early attachment styles are carried into adulthood and impact adult romantic relationships for non-autistic people. We also promised that we would look at what is known about attachment and adult relationships for autistic people, and that moment has come.

There have not been as many studies into this as we would like – considering how important attachment has been considered for non-autistic people, it is remiss of earlier researchers not to have carried their investigations through the lifespan for autistic people as well. There have been some, however, and we can have a look at their findings before reflecting on how these link with what our contributors have told us about the influence of their early lives on their later relationships.

One such study used the Adult Attachment Interview with 20 autistic adults to assess their attachment style and their ability to tell the story of their attachment experiences over their lifetimes. They found that a similar proportion of autistic adults were classed as securely attached as you would expect in other 'clinical populations' (this means groups with other developmental or mental health diagnoses). The study also showed that autistic people's narratives came across as more disorganised and less reflective than control participants, but that some of this was due to differences in general communication style (Taylor et al., 2008).

Another study did what is very common in psychology research – got a load of (presumed) neurotypical undergraduates to do some questionnaires and then looked at the relationships between autistic traits and something else. This is called looking at the Broad Autism Phenotype (BAP) and is often done as a way of giving an indication of what patterns we might expect to see in autistic people – it is much harder to collect data from large numbers of clinically diagnosed autistic people, so this is often a useful way of judging what direction to go in next. It does mean that results need to be treated with caution though, as obviously young adults with varying levels of autistic traits are not exactly the same as those who meet clinical thresholds (as much as the gatekeeping around who gets a diagnosis is itself problematic, this difference is probably still one to keep in mind!). So, this piece of research asked just over 300 university students about their autistic traits and their attachment styles. It found that the more autistic traits someone had, the more likely they were to have an avoidant attachment style. Also, those participants who said they had more communication difficulties had lower levels of emotional closeness with their partner, although there was no connection between autistic traits and anxiety about the relationship (Gallitto & Leth-Steensen, 2015). In a more recent study on similar lines, 263 18- to 25-year-old undergraduates completed questionnaires covering autism traits, their attachment, and their satisfaction with their current romantic relationship. What they found was that those with higher BAP scores tended to have lower relationship satisfaction, largely because they were more likely to have insecure attachment and associated relationship anxiety (Beffel et al., 2021). This chimes with what the childhood literature says – that autistic people can and do have secure attachments, but that they are more likely to have insecure attachments than those who are not autistic or who have higher levels of autistic traits. It adds further evidence to the idea that early attachment styles and relationship experiences can and do carry on into adulthood and influence how young adults experience their romantic relationships – including those who are autistic.

Romantic relationship formation

The models of relationship formation (and break down) which we talked about in Chapter 4: Teenage Dreams apply to adult relationships as much as teenage ones. They were actually developed for adults, but it makes sense for the way we have organised this book to have told you about them before now. Adults go through the same processes and stages in making, maintaining, and leaving relationships as adolescents do. This means that adolescent experience with romantic relationships is useful for adults, because it acts as 'practising' for your adult love life, learning the skills and norms which help you to be successful.

Around half of adult romantic relationships now start online in some way, and as far as we know there are no significant differences in that number for autistic and non-autistic people (though no one has checked). When relationships start online, it can look a little bit different to the offline process we talked about earlier. The steps are the same – noticing each other, initiating contact, and developing mutual interest – but the actions involved are different. Rather than noticing each other in a bar, it can be liking each other's Instagram pictures. Instead of making a comment about the weather in a coffee shop queue, it is replying to a tweet. And in place of swapping numbers, following and following back is the first stage in establishing a mutual online relationship, which then deepens through getting to know each via

142 Well, hello there

chatting in the DMs (direct messages, which are private rather than public posts – for anyone who isn't aware). Of course, there are billions of people active online around the world, which means that one's chances of having a random interaction which leads to a person noticing someone they are interested in are that much higher than in real life – but we still tend to live in 'bubbles' online, just as much as we live in a certain neighbourhood or city offline, and this limits the number of people a person actually encounters.

It has been suggested that there are three 'types' of ways relationships begin online – *naturally forming* (where people meet through a shared interest or activity, such as gaming or being part of a fandom); *networked relationships* (where you both know someone in common and therefore see each other's interactions with that person); and *targeted relationships* (those which come from specific dating sites) (McKenna, 2008). Although this research predates the creation of dating apps like Tinder, those three categories still basically make sense of the ways people meet and find romantic relationships online. The other way in which social media is widely used in relationship formation, or at least in the early stages of a relationship, is to research a potential partner – looking at their profile to see what kinds of things they post, what they like, what activities they are into – to help in deciding whether to pursue a relationship with them. Considering how much of our lives many people put online, this is actually a very sensible strategy, but it can also become unhealthy in terms of trying to constantly check up on what a partner is doing through their posts, leading to jealousy (Van Ouystel et al., 2016). The ways in which technology plays a role in dating changes over the course of a relationship, something we will talk about throughout this chapter.

Research which has looked at how autistic adults go about relationship formation is relatively uniform in participants saying that they find this difficult – many feel they don't know how to do this at all, or that they have learned only through making multiple mistakes. They also talk about struggling to read the subtle social signals other people send to try to indicate that they are either interested or not interested, which is crucial in knowing when your advances are unwelcome or when someone is flirting with you (Mogavero & Hsu, 2020). This is true for both men and women, with autistic women talking about lacking a 'map' of how dating is supposed to go, and therefore not doing it because it is hard work (Kock et al., 2019). Difficulties in early relationship formation have also been linked to the lack of appropriate sex education for autistic people (Penwell & Eleanor, 2015). As sex education usually does not cover topics like how to start relationships, autistic people are often trying to do this complex set of social interactions without much guidance – hence the reliance on trial and error. Many of our autistic contributors talked about starting relationships being hard, for example:

> I had started to learn about this . . . he would express interest in different ways and if I hadn't been looking for it I wouldn't have noticed.
>
> *(anonymous, 54, autistic woman)*

knowing when someone is interested in me. I've had difficulty in expressing when I am interested in them too. I've had problems expressing myself within a relationship.

(anonymous, 48, trans man)

These difficulties with starting relationships in the face-to-face world lead many autistic adults (and non-autistic adults!) to online dating to try to find a partner. Of the autistic people surveyed, just over half of those who were looking for or who had looked for relationships had used online dating (Roth & Gillis, 2015). Most people who had tried online dating found it easier than trying to approach people in real life, because it enabled them to share important information up front, and it allowed them to avoid unpleasant sensory environments. Nearly half had a long-term relationship with someone they met this way – although it is worth noting that this was a very small sample, and people who were successful are probably more willing to share their experiences than someone who wasn't. Regardless of success, though, many participants worried about the safety of online dating, particularly about the other person lying about who they are or being manipulated by someone who exploits their lack of social skill to take advantage of them.

Adult autistic sexual experiences

Sex is an important part of most adult romantic relationships – it helps build attachments, and couples who have a satisfactory sex life tend to say their relationship is higher quality (Birnbaum & Reis, 2019). As we discussed in the chapter on adolescent sexual and romantic relationships (Chapter 4), autistic people remain less likely to have romantic relationships in adulthood, and in early adulthood their relationships tend to end sooner than those of non-autistic people around the same age (Hancock et al., 2020). However, those who had better peer relationships and friendships tended to have more positive romantic relationships overall, regardless of their neurotype. In fact, one study has found that being neurodivergent (specifically being autistic or having ADHD) is associated with showing more passionate love in a relationship, and certainly not with showing less (Soares et al., 2021). This just serves to emphasise the fact that we should not make assumptions about autistic people's capacity for romantic and sexual relationships – including the fact that they can look more positive and successful when people find the opportunity and the right partner, on all fronts.

Autistic women, generally, report less sexual interest than autistic men – as in they are less motivated to pursue or engage in sexual activity, and feel sexual attraction to other people less frequently (Pecora et al., 2019). This is similar to non-autistic women compared to non-autistic men, as they also tend to say they are less sexually motivated or interested – although we have to be aware of the element of social desirability bias there may be in these answers. Society expects women to be less sexual, and punishes women who are openly sexual or talk about enjoying sex – so

144 Well, hello there

women may be likely to under-report the amount of sexual motivation and desire they actually feel. That question aside, despite the lower levels of sexual interest they feel, autistic women report having more sexual experience than autistic men – often unwanted, regretted, or in the form of unwelcome advances. Autistic women in the study were also more likely to have these negative experiences than non-autistic women, suggesting that they are more likely to have experienced victimisation and abuse than either autistic men or non-autistic women. We discuss negative relationship experiences in Chapter 9: Toxic, and sadly there is a lot of evidence from both the research and our contributors' lived experience which supports that conclusion.

It is also the case that for some autistic people, the model of casual dating which is dominant in society, particularly for young people, does not appeal. These relationships are often short term, carry an expectation of being casual, and are portrayed as susceptible to being changeable rather than deep and meaningful, which is both difficult to manage emotionally and not necessarily all that compatible with some autistic profiles, such as a preference for sameness and for predictable relationships:

> There was no meaningful model of the non-serious relationship in my mind.
>
> *(anonymous, male)*

> I always went into every relationship thinking it would be long term. I couldn't imagine being with someone who's family I didn't get on with. Shorter-term relationships I didn't have a clue about.
>
> *(anonymous, 48, trans man)*

Some other autistic people we talked to said that actually, casual relationships were better for them. When the other person was not looking for a deep emotional connection, it was easier for them to manage their own emotions and meant that they could deal with their physical needs without social complications:

> I tended to link up with people who weren't free really or people who would have been bouncing in and out of other relationships. Looking back I think it meant that I didn't really have to interact.
>
> *(anonymous, 19, autistic woman)*

> Encounters and casual sex it really doesn't count as relationships as it's very transactional. I like you, you like me, let's go have coitus. So there is no further bonding after."
>
> *(anonymous, 47, autistic male)*

> I like the idea of being able to have sex without all the other stuff that goes along with it. Years ago I would have had that sense of wanting to fill the void at times and I couldn't have imagined getting to the point where I am totally comfortable alone and I don't have that desire at all. The autism dx has allowed that freedom.
>
> *(anonymous, 54, autistic woman)*

Most of this research has been conducted with all or majority-heterosexual participants. When talking to LGBTQ autistic adults about their experiences with sex (not in the X-rated sense!) one of the main things they emphasise is that it is even more complicated for them than for heterosexual people. We discussed the ways in which becoming comfortable and secure in a minority sexuality identity is a process in Chapter 4: Teenage Dreams, but as well as that challenge, it can be difficult for autistic LGBTQ people to find people who understand them, and for them to recognise their sexual needs and desires and then communicate these to a partner (Lewis et al., 2021). They often feel 'othered' within the LGBTQ community, with people questioning or rejecting their diagnosis, or rejecting them because of their diagnosis.

Just as for heterosexual autistic people, sensory sensitivities impacted their sexual encounters, with hypersensitivity to touch or smell often being overwhelming, and this could negatively impact their ability to communicate their wants and needs both in sexual situations and in the relationship more generally. This is in line with things some of our interviewees said:

> Going to clubs when you are seeing someone casually it's complex because it involves physical pain for me. Going to a restaurant is complicated because of the smells. Sex is complicated because of the smells.
>
> *(anonymous, 47, autistic male)*

LGBTQ relationships and relationship formation also comes with its own set of rules and norms, which participants in the Lewis study talked about finding difficult to work out – having struggled to understand the rules of heterosexual society for the majority of their lives, this was then a new set of norms on top, which was additionally challenging.

Moving to longer-term relationships

'Commitment' or 'committed' is considered a specific stage of a relationship by researchers, where both partners have agreed that this is a significant and often exclusive relationship which they intend to pursue long term. Most people see their partners in this way, though the timing can differ depending on individual and contextual differences. Looking at what happens once this commitment has been made, we see that generally people see their partners as their preferred 'safe haven' about four months later, which means that if they were upset, their partner is the person they would want to go and spend time with, for example. It can take more like two years for people to shift to their partner being their primary 'secure base' though – in attachment terms, the person who you rely on for emotional and practical support, both when exploring the world and when needing comfort and reassurance. Adults who have a more anxious attachment style tend to develop a sense of reliance on a partner as 'safe haven' faster than those who do not have an anxious attachment style. Securely attached adults tend to see their partners as their secure base sooner, and this is associated with being less likely to break up

146 Well, hello there

(Fagundes & Schindler, 2011). So, yet another way in which those early attachments and interactions pop up as being relevant years afterwards!

For adults today, moving into committed long-term relationships tends to happen later than it did in previous generations. This change is happening for a variety of reasons, including (but not limited to) extended time in education, increased female independence, normalisation of casual or shorter-term relationships with multiple people before commitment, and the economic challenges of establishing a life which looks like the 'traditional' picture of commitment (getting married, buying a house, having children). This leads to the actual lives of emerging adults (usually defined as between 18 and 30 years old) being a challenge to the theoretical models of relationship development we have discussed in other chapters. As it has become the norm for both partners to build careers, this adds a new challenge to becoming established in a shared life – the need to coordinate work commitments and options alongside working out what your life plans are and whether they agree (Shulman & Connolly, 2013). While these questions can often be what leads to a relationship breaking up, if a couple does work out mutually acceptable answers, that period of conflict resolution often becomes the groundwork for a long-term committed relationship – because both people have agreed that this is the life they want together.

The online factor doesn't go away after a relationship is formed, either. People are still just as online once they are in a couple, and this means that the internet and social media become part of the landscape of relationship maintenance. One of the main ways this happens is through public displays of affection – posting images together, or posts about how good the relationship is and how attached the couple are, as well as announcing your relationship status on Facebook – which is often seen as a significant moment. These kinds of public displays of affection, and the performance of the relationship for an online audience of family, friends, and broader connections, is associated with higher relationship satisfaction (Kwok & Westcott, 2020). It can be easy to assume that a couple who are very public about their relationship are 'trying to prove something' and that this signifies issues they are trying to hide or ignore, but the research says this isn't always the case. Men and LGBTQ people are more likely to display these kinds of public online investments in their relationships earlier on, either because they are trying to 'stake their claim' (more often heterosexual men) or because they are displaying joy in a new relationship (more often LGBTQ people) (Marcotte et al., 2021). This shows how we must be careful to look at differences in the motivations for behaviours which look the same on the surface – what is driving people to show their relationship online can be highly varied.

Cybersexuality is also an element of many modern relationships. This covers things like using technology to consume pornography (either alone or together) and sexting (sending or receiving explicit messages, images, or videos). Generally, doing these activities together or in ways which both people enjoy is associated with more relationship satisfaction, largely because this helps to meet both people's sexual needs. People who have anxious attachment styles, though, may feel like their partner expects sexting from them and therefore are more likely to do this regardless of their own opinions and desires, in an attempt to keep their partner (Weisskirch & Delevi, 2011). This is not the only risk associated with cybersexuality – the growing phenomenon of 'revenge porn',

Well, hello there **147**

where explicit images are posted by the partner or ex-partner of someone to punish them, often for a break up, is another. Digital messages and images are hard to entirely delete, and can easily be shared beyond the original recipient without consent. Autistic people are likely to be at risk for this kind of behaviour being perpetrated against them, as they may be more susceptible to being pressured into sending explicit material if they are told that this will 'save' a relationship they are in. But, as with many things, we don't know what autistic people's experiences with revenge porn are because the phenomenon is too recent for research to be published on it yet, if it is happening at all.

Your other relationships are still part of your life when you get into a committed romantic relationship, although they may well change. Couples tend to spend a lot of their time together or talking to each other, and lots of us will have experienced a friend being in touch less often when they have a partner, then wanting to spend more time with you when they are single again. This is called the 'social withdrawal hypothesis', and is well documented. It actually fluctuates a bit though – for those in longer-term relationships, they spend more time with their friends around the two-year mark than they did in the first few months, and more again once they have lived with their significant other for two years (Rozer et al., 2015). This makes sense, because the early days of a relationship are often the most intense, and so as you settle in with each other, people are more likely to reach back out to their friends.

We don't know whether autistic people do the social withdrawal process in the same way, but there are hints that this might be a bit different for them. For example, in interviews about their relationship experiences, some autistic women talked about their partner being a 'shortcut' to a social life (Sedgewick et al., 2019). The women were then able to socialise with the existing friendship group of their partner, rather than going through the difficult process of making their own friends – especially tricky in adulthood when it is harder to meet new people. This was often a successful strategy for them, as it meant that they only really needed to focus on maintaining the one romantic relationship rather than trying to work out the balance between multiple competing relationships. When this could be a problem, though, was when a romantic relationship ended – with the end of the partnership, they often also lost most or all of the friends they made through their partner, leaving them isolated.

Sarah on finding a good partner

Following separation from my first husband I had a couple of brief relationships that didn't go anywhere. I was burnt out and tired of all the emotional upheaval and resolved to steer clear of anything remotely romantic at least for a while. It came as a relief not to be looking for love or connection in this period of time and was the respite I needed to help me to recover some sort of equilibrium. I started trying out new things – going to opera performances and briefly revisiting tap dancing lessons being two of the more memorable experiences. I was then invited to a barn dance at Clifton High School by a friend and as the Pulp song goes, something changed.

148 Well, hello there

It was a great evening from the start. Lots of dancing, chatting, and generally having fun. The friend that I had gone with also knew other people there and that is when I was introduced to someone called Kyle. We immediately hit it off and spent almost the entire evening talking about literature, history, and music as well as just about avoiding treading on each other's toes whilst Dosey-Doeing. It was wonderful. Here was an intelligent, educated, and informed person who was genuinely interested in getting to know me and what I thought and liked, rather than staring at my chest and having an ulterior motive. It was quite a revelation and very much the tonic I needed. He was even handsome, with lovely dark hair and eyes, but it was his love of learning, gentle and respectful manner, and witty humour that really attracted me to him. It felt so different to anything I had experienced before and we arranged to meet up again for a meal and cinema visit.

Italian food and Sense and Sensibility was the perfect evening, although I may have banged on about Alan Rickman a bit too much. It felt like this could be the start of something special, but I didn't want my past failed relationships and the shame that hung over me from them to spoil what we could have together. After the film we went for drinks, and I will never know if this was a colossal overshare that was way too soon into whatever this was, but I told him that I was technically still married and that I had had more than a few difficult experiences growing up and that if this put him off, then I would understand.

Well reader, my past didn't deter him at all. It was me he liked – my personality, my brain, and the way I looked. Kyle thought that I was beautiful (and still does, although his glasses prescription has become stronger with age) and wanted to spend more time together. So we did, and to this day I have not met anyone who makes me feel as elevated and valued as Kyle does. He saw me as nobody else had ever done before and as we began to fall in love I also began to start liking myself a bit more.

We decided to go on holiday to Barcelona, and this was an exciting prospect as I had not flown before and we were both looking forward to exploring the Gaudi art and wandering down The Ramblas together. Unfortunately, our luggage went to Lisbon and when I went down with the most appalling food poisoning, I didn't have any spare underwear to change into. It is not the most romantic of things for your future husband to have to deposit what can only be described as a steaming pair of destroyed knickers in a bin outside the hotel, but needs must and it clearly didn't put him off as we started to make plans to get married and spend the rest of our lives together. I also met Kyle's parents and sister and was struck by the uncomplicated and loving welcome that I received from them as they brought me into their family.

My divorce had come through and our vicar Ray Brazier had no qualms about marrying us in church, which was incredibly important to us. He is one of the most gracious, real, and loving church leaders I have met and this act of kindness meant an awful lot to both of us. We got married just before Christmas, honeymooned in Paris, and then came back to Bristol to start our lives together, which 11 months later and before our first anniversary also included baby Rob.

I've written about parenting and some aspects of our little family later on in the book, but what I will say here is that meeting Kyle and having Rob were the two most pivotal points in my life. Their love helped me to experience a certain amount of healing from the past and for the first time in my life I felt secure. It wasn't a fluffy fairytale, as I found being a new mum hard, was struggling with anxiety and depression and after contracting chicken pox as an adult, developed ME/CFS which 20+ years later shows no sign of wanting to leave, but I was loved and was able to love in return.

I was, however, still undiagnosed, and when the ME/CFS was severe, needed to sleep and rest a lot, which did affect the dynamic of our relationship. There were times when I was overwhelmed or couldn't face going out or needed time to myself, which meant that Kyle sometimes went out with his friends by himself without me. Or there were other occasions when we had booked theatre tickets, but I felt too unwell to attend. I felt really guilty about this, which didn't help my mental health, but was always reassured by Kyle that this was absolutely fine. I've never doubted his love for me, but I do think that there were times in my thirties and forties when I was struggling with my physical and mental health that I relied on him too much and was rather codependent and passive. We loved each other through these difficult times and they weren't always hard, but our life together all these years later feels richer, less confusing, and has more hope and purpose now that I know who I am and have learned to value myself as Kyle always has.

Autistic long-term relationships

A large number of autistic people are in committed relationships, contrary to the early assumptions of what adulthood looked like for those on the spectrum. One study showed that about half of autistic adults without learning disabilities were in relationships, and most of these people lived with their partners – just as we would expect for non-autistic people (Dewinter et al., 2017). This research was much larger than most studies of autistic sexuality and relationships, with 675 autistic people taking part. That means that we can trust their findings as fairly

150 Well, hello there

representative of experience across the autistic population, as it is large enough to ensure that there are a variety of people included.

Another study which looked at the long-term romantic relationships of autistic people compared to non-autistic people was the one we mentioned in Chapter 5 by Felicity (see page 183). In contrast to the results for friendships and more casual relationships, when it came to people who lived with their partners or were married, there were no differences in scores between autistic and non-autistic people, or by gender (Sedgewick et al., 2018). This means that everyone who took part, regardless of neurotype, said that their partner was similarly important to them, their relationship was similarly close, and they were similarly satisfied with those relationships.

We've highlighted how intimacy, both physical and emotional, can be one of the key factors in having a successful long-term romantic relationship, and this is true for autistic people in a couple too. Good communication; sharing aspects of your lives; having similar interests, goals, and values; and having respect for the other person have all been shown to support building intimacy for both autistic and non-autistic people (Sala et al., 2020). The same study looked at what the barriers to intimacy were for both groups, and found that these were also mostly the same – arguments or conflict with your partner, and internal challenges such as poor mental health were the key things. Autistic people, though, had additional barriers they talked about in their relationships – such as feeling uncertain in the relationship and in communication. Some felt that they lacked experience compared to their partner, or desired partner, which made them feel insecure; others struggled to show when they were interested, or understand when someone was interested in them, which made it hard to start a relationship. This shows how, even when autistic people are in long-term relationships which are going well, there are elements which remain challenging and need ongoing work and understanding with their partner. For example, the way the autistic person may show they care might be different than expected:

> This whole process has helped [my wife] to understand that I am not 'being a bastard' and earlier she did wonder if that is what was going on. She does now say that she is so grateful that I am the way I am because other people are much more emotionally driven and are not as stable. She perceives me as a very stable person. At times she has perceived this as an uncaringness. Whereas recently she has recognised that my way of caring manifests in a different way than what she might want it to, but ultimately she values it so I'll do certain things for her or arrange things in a certain way to help her feel better in her circumstances. The love languages and love praxes may well be different for an autistic person.
>
> *(anonymous, autistic man)*

Any relationship, there are going to be arguments and it's learning to know when an argument is an argument or an argument that's turned into a meltdown. So we could both be riled up and we could both be trying to get our point across, but at some point I've had to learn that to recognise that it's not about the argument any more, that you're overwhelmed and there is no point in pushing this point any further until things have calmed down. We've both learned to walk away and take a little bit of space and come back to it when we're a bit calmer.

(Ella's non-autistic husband)

One of the things which autistic people talk about as helping them have better relationships is when they date another neurodivergent person, rather than a neurotypical person, or at least someone with neurodivergent straits (Strunz et al., 2017). This is because the two neurodivergent people have more inherent understanding of the ways in which they may interact with the world and each other differently to general social expectations, and have more patience for these differences. This is something our contributors talked about:

I think that what really gets to the heart of why there is a mismatch between autistic and NT relationships from the start is that there really isn't that level of understanding of what we need from a relationship, what our priorities are and when they are not met, on one or both sides, the reaction to it is very different.

(anonymous)

When I met my wife online we hit it off straight away. I would say that there are aspects of her which I'd say are very autistic. Like, she's very, very honest. She doesn't like lying. She doesn't like people who do lie. She'd very direct with me. She's quite blunt about things. She doesn't hide things and all that's been there right from the start.

(anonymous)

It is possible for autistic people to have happy and successful relationships with non-autistic and neurotypical people, obviously. Several of the people we talked to for this book were in deeply happy mixed-neurotype relationships:

Everything just seemed to fit. Not just the whole being with somebody or dating somebody that was really easy and I thought, "am I doing something wrong here? This is like too easy. It should be difficult or arguments, discussion and who wants to do what on a Friday night. It should be the point where I have to say I'll just put what I want on the back-burner, but none of that ever happened"

(anonymous, 48, trans man)

I just think you're quite a stable person and I feel that you've compensated for a lot of the executive functioning challenges that I have so when we first got together I found it very difficult to run a household budget or to plan meals or anything really that involves getting a task done. I was living very much moment to moment so you've helped me to learn how to do those things

152 Well, hello there

> . . . I mean neurotypicals, we shouldn't just look at their challenges, they also have some amazing strengths, right?
>
> *(Ella, autistic person)*

> I think that as far as strengths go, in every relationship, it's about how you complement each other. Obviously there are some things that I do that are strengths that you probably have gained from in the way that I have gained from your strengths. Working together as a team we seem to have done quite well all this time. And that side of your autism that means that life's a bit more exciting and a bit more satisfying and a bit more fulfilling probably balanced by my lack of wanting to do anything or go anywhere.
>
> *(Ella's non-autistic husband)*

> It was just like not holding up a relationship to conventional standards. I'm not a conventional person so why should I abide by convention. Being able to have those frank conversations about what this is like for me and the things that I enjoy doing. Being able to create that dialogue and keep it open. That is really important to me. Having someone who is open to listen to me and believe me and asking me about my experience rather than relying on what he has read in a book.
>
> *(Sarah O, autistic woman)*

Most long-term partnerships will be mixed-neurotype, just based on the statistics of how many people in the population are autistic. One study of newly wed Dutch couples looked at the impact of autistic traits (in either partner) on the relationship (Pollman et al., 2010). The participants did not have formal autism diagnoses, so some of the findings might not be totally applicable to autistic people, but it is the best we've got at this point. What they found was that men tended to report having more autistic traits than women, and that this was associated with lower relationship satisfaction for the men in the marriage – largely because these traits interfered with things like communication of their emotions (important in maintaining a relationship) and intimacy with their partner. However, overall both people in all the marriages were relatively satisfied with the relationship, and one person having more autistic traits did not predict the other person being less happy, which is promising.

There is another paper (which came out three weeks before this book was sent to the publishers, doing nothing good for Felicity's stress levels!) which looked at how the partners of autistic people talked about them in online support groups for people in neuro-mixed relationships (Lewis, 2022). It is worth noting, from the outset, that not all of the autistic partners discussed in the study had formal diagnoses – this is important. Through online interviews with over 160 non-autistic partners of diagnosed or presumed autistic people, five relationship profiles were developed:

Well, hello there **153**

- *Mutual partnership* – where they saw themselves and their autistic partner as equals, with mutual respect and effort
- *Companionship* – where they saw their autistic partner as a friend, but lacking deeper connection and intimacy, with autism being a limiting factor on the relationship
- *Caregiving* – where they saw their autistic partner as someone they had to care for, often in a similar way to a child, because autism was disabling
- *Detachment* – where they saw the relationship as irrevocably damaged by their partner's autistic traits, and withdrew from them
- *Discriminatory* – where they actively said and believed negative things about autism and autistic people, seeing autistic people as incapable of good relationships and equating being autistic to being abusive

There is a clear pattern there, from good, supportive, and accepting relationships at the top (mutual partnership) through to more negative views at the bottom, with 'discriminatory' partners as the extreme of that scale. Effectively, the more the non-autistic people had a pathologising view of autism, the more negative their attitudes towards their (possibly) autistic partner. People in mutual partnerships talked about sharing responsibilities, making efforts to understand each other, and appreciating the things their autistic partner brought to the relationship. They saw autism as a *difference* which should be valued. While acknowledging that there are times when needing to adapt to the needs of their autistic partner happened, they did not generally talk about resenting this, but about the ways in which both partners compromised to support each other. This is one of the hallmarks of a healthy long-term relationship, regardless of neurotype, and shows that these relationships can be and are successful for many people.

In contrast, those who fit the detachment and discriminatory profiles saw autism as a *disorder* felt that autistic people were automatically bad partners and that the autistic person was to blame for relationship difficulties.

Some of the ways the people in these profiles talked about their autistic or possibly autistic partners is frankly deeply upsetting – seeing autistic people in relationships as inherently abusive, for example. What is especially difficult about those participants is that they tended to be people whose partners did not actually have an autism diagnosis or self-diagnosis, and actually they reported that their partner disagreed with them that they were autistic. What this means is that these participants were in difficult relationships, and had gone online and found autism as a label which they thought explained what they were experiencing, then they were going out and perpetuating the idea that autistic people are 'dangerous' to be in relationships with based on their own assumptions, not evidence. They especially focussed on the feeling of being 'tricked' into a relationship on the assumption that their partner was neurotypical, and on social isolation as a result of their partner being 'autistic' and not wanting to socialise with other people the same way they did.

154 Well, hello there

Our participants talked about previous relationships where their exes would have fallen into the detachment or discriminatory profiles, and how these had been damaging to them, for example:

> An ex-partner of mine was the first person who worked out that I was autistic. She worked with a number of young men who had an Aspergers diagnosis and she kept on saying how much they reminded her of me, but she used it against me. She kept on going on to me that I should see a therapist and do some CBT because then you'll realise that it's not the world that hates you, it's you that hates the world.
>
> *(anonymous)*

The thing is that if that is how you think and feel about your partner – you are never going to improve that relationship. Seeing someone as broken, or interpreting everything they do as abusive, is a recipe for mutual unhappiness. The evidence from the mutual partnership groups shows that neuro-mixed relationships do not have to be that way, but there is clearly a long way to go in challenging stereotypes about autism and the way these are used by those without much knowledge to justify their own ideas about the world and their partners. For those people, who are so deeply unhappy and believe that it is to do with their partner's neurotype, we would suggest that the best response for both people is to end the relationship – so both can find other partners who love and appreciate them as they are.

When relationships end

Unless you are in the relatively small group of people who spend your whole life with your first high school partner, everyone goes through the end of a romantic relationship at some point. This can be your first heartbreak, which is usually especially intense – there is a reason all those pop songs talk about your first love and your first breakup! Or the end of a relationship where you have grown apart, or don't want the same thing, or you just realised that you really couldn't cope with their specific annoying habit for the next however-many years, or someone cheated, or your partner died, or, or, or . . . There are thousands of reasons relationships end. Probably nearly as many as there are relationships, really, as they are all unique.

The end of a committed romantic relationship is usually distressing for the person who has not initiated that breakup. It can be distressing even if the relationship is not committed; let's be honest! Women tend to report being more upset by breakups than men do, as do people who were broken-up-with rather than the person who ended the relationship, people where the breakup was unexpected, and those who have not found a new partner yet (Field et al., 2009). The process of going through and recovering from a breakup can be similar to grief, because you are effectively grieving that relationship loss, and it has been shown that some of the same principles apply. For example, people who have more 'internalising continuing bonds' with their ex-partner (wondering what they would think if they were here; wanting to contact them with news) feel more grief and breakup distress than those with fewer of these bonds (Valois et al., 2016). Autistic people may feel this more, as their partners are often central relationships with fewer other relationships to turn to.

Although the majority of research on breakup distress has focussed on women, because they tend to show more of it, men can also be traumatised by their partner leaving them – this can be felt to be a threat to their masculinity ('not being "man enough" for her to stay'), and this plus their emotional response can compound this challenge to their identity because patriarchal social norms teach men that they shouldn't feel sadness alongside the demand to be sexually active and dominant (Hartman, 2021). This 'male breakup trauma' may be worse for autistic men, who are likely to have found it more difficult to get into a relationship to begin with, to be highly invested in the relationship, and who may struggle to understand the reasons their partner has broken up with them. However, we don't know whether this is the case, as there is not yet research on the breakup experiences and responses of autistic men and boys.

Having someone to talk to about one's emotions following a breakup has been shown to help with recovering from that breakup, if a person can be open with their feelings and doesn't feel constrained to present the situation or feelings in a certain way (Harvey & Karpinski, 2016). Also being able to reflect on the good times with a past partner, having less concern about future relationships, and having other strong social relationships are all associated with less breakup distress and faster recovery (Gilbert & Sifers, 2011). Saying that, there are four patterns to recovery from a breakup – *resilience, fast recovery, slow recovery,* and *chronic distress* (Verhallen et al., 2021). Those who fall into the last two groups tend to show more depressive symptoms, and higher levels of rumination and neuroticism, meaning that they spend more time going over and over the breakup, and that they tend to be more emotionally reactive, especially to negative events like a breakup – so it has a bigger and longer lasting effect on their emotional state overall. Again, we can see ways in which this could interact with being autistic – autistic people can struggle to recognise and regulate their own emotions, and they are more likely to develop ruminative thoughts as part of their monotropic cognitive style, where their attention becomes hyperfocussed on specific things. Combined with the likelihood of more negative social experiences across the lifespan, autistic people may be more likely to be in the 'slow recovery' and 'chronic distress' groups, and breakups are therefore probably more difficult for them to process and move on from than for non-autistic people.

Technology once again has a role in the breakdown of a relationship, as much as in its formation and maintenance. While people are together they tend to build up a collection of 'digital assets' – photos, texts, videos, shared Netflix passwords . . . which together symbolise and memorialise their time together. When they break up, something has to be done with all that shared digital 'stuff', just as much as splitting a CD collection or working out who is keeping which plates. Equally, removing your ex-partner from your online presence and profiles is often a key step in

156 Well, hello there

a breakup, and refusing to engage with their posts can be a sign that a relationship is in the process of breaking down (LeFebvre et al., 2014). Deleting photos of you together, or message histories, are also common strategies in trying to get over an ex, and people who stay connected to their ex online tend to take longer to move on from the relationship. Research shows that women and LGBTQ people are more likely to carry out these 'disinvestment behaviours' after a breakup than heterosexual men (Marcotte et al., 2021) – and men may be more likely to continue monitoring their ex online after a breakup, with a higher risk of this developing into what is considered 'cyberstalking'.

This kind of behaviour is usually called 'unwanted pursuit' in the literature. People who are more likely to engage in these behaviours tend to be more anxious in their attachment style, to have been more invested in the relationship, and to have been more jealous within the relationship. Jealousy in the relationship, in particular, predicts aggression in the tactics used in the unwanted pursuit – so the more jealous someone was in the relationship, the more likely they are to be aggressive in their unwanted pursuit after a breakup (Tassy & Winstead, 2014). People who base more of their self-worth in being in a relationship also feel more distress when their relationships break down, because this undermines their sense of self, and tend to show more unwanted pursuit of their ex-partner, in an attempt to re-establish that part of their self-esteem and self-identity (Park et al., 2011). It is normal for most people who have been broken up with to engage in at least one unwanted pursuit behaviour (Langhinrichsen-Rohling et al., 2000) – sending texts, calling, or finding a way to talk to your ex. It is when these behaviours become frequent, aggressive, persistent, or distressing that this becomes a problem, and can lead to the involvement of the criminal justice system if it does not stop.

It's not all bad though – some people report going through a period of personal growth after a breakup, particularly women (despite their greater levels of distress initially). Especially if someone feels that their relationship broke down because of environmental factors – being long distance, wanting different things – rather than because of something one person actively did (like cheating), then personal growth and learning is a common outcome (Tashiro & Frazier, 2003). Learning what is and isn't manageable for you and taking those lessons into new relationships helps to improve people's relationship quality and satisfaction overall – back to that idea that we can learn from all our relationship experiences, even the difficult ones.

For autistic people, there is very little research on their experiences of romantic relationships ending. That isn't surprising, considering how little there is on autistic people's romantic lives in general. We included some ideas on what the patterns, similarities, and differences might be earlier, based on what we know about autism and autistic people from other types of research. But, once again, we want to call for research into these really important experiences in autistic people's lives – if there are things which are more difficult for autistic people about breakups, knowing what they are and how to help is important for supporting healthy social development of autistic young people and better well-being across the lifespan.

Several of our contributors discussed the ends of relationships they had been in, either why they thought they ended or how the endings affected them:

> I'd had a lot of relationships and all of them seemed to fall down on the not being able to talk about emotions or feelings. Me not understanding what the other person was trying to communicate to me and being very confused and them being very confused by me.
>
> *(anonymous, 62, autistic woman)*

> I think that the reason we broke up was again due to masking because I recognised that I was autistic and was dx when we were together and it was then that the mask started slipping. As I began to learn more about who I am without the mask and I started to let the mask slip in the relationship and despite the fact that he learned as much as he could about autism and said that he wanted me to be authentic, he preferred the mask.
>
> *(anonymous, 54, autistic woman)*

> We fell together and stayed together and had a child and stayed together probably longer than we should have, even though we split up, we have managed to remain lifelong friends. It would probably have ended sooner if we hadn't had our child and we eventually realised that we brought out the worst in each other.
>
> *(anonymous, 54, autistic woman)*

> You get married when you finish university and you work locally at the community hospital, and you get your angel wings and I was like, "no, I'm not doing that" so I had to split up with him and it was very difficult because I had never split up with anybody because people always left me up to that point.
>
> *(anonymous, 48, trans man)*

One of the most common ways marriages end now is through divorce. Divorce can be seen through the staged model of relationship breakdown we discussed in Chapter 4: Teenage Dreams – despite the variety of reasons people get divorced, or long-term relationships break up, they often still fit into that pattern. Couples who have a more 'dramatic' relationship (characterised by frequent fluctuations in how happy and committed they feel and with high levels of conflict) are more likely to divorce than those who have a more stable relationship with high levels of focus on each other's contentment (Ogolsky et al., 2016). Before people are married, men and women are equally likely to instigate a breakup (there is no research on non-binary people's likelihood), but women are more likely to request a divorce than men (Rosenfield, 2018). This is probably because women tend to be less happy in their marriages than men, due to the increased care burden that comes with gendered roles within a relationship. There is also the increased social acceptability around leaving a marriage which makes you unhappy now, whereas in previous generations divorce was either impossible or would make the partners, especially the woman, into social pariahs.

158 Well, hello there

Just as autistic people get married, some will get divorced, but there is no research published on these experiences. Instead, searching for 'autism divorce' results in a set of papers about parents of autistic children divorcing after their child is born or diagnosed – an incredibly important event in the life of that child, but not what we want to understand for autistic adults. There are a few studies of the experiences of wives of autistic men, which found that the longer they are married, the more crises these couples go through, and the more unhappy the wives became, because they felt that their autistic husbands were not handling situations or behaving in the marriage as they would want (Deguchi & Asakura, 2018). While most of the participants had remained married, this may be partly due to cultural factors, as it was carried out in Japan where divorce is still more rare than it is in most Western societies. This study didn't talk to the husbands themselves though, which means that we are missing the other side of the story – the autistic side of the story.

Several of the autistic people we talked to for the book had gone through divorce, and we have included some of their quotes here. For some people, the divorce had been a relatively amicable process, as discussed by one of our anonymous contributors. For others, it resulted in complete changes in every area of their lives. Another of our anonymous contributors' story is a good example of this:

Having married someone relatively quickly, her ex-partner died by suicide four weeks into her new marriage, which meant that she was dealing with significant grief and bereavement very early on in the relationship – a naturally fairly disruptive thing to go through. The combination of this, of someone at work telling her husband he looked like the ex who had died, and a clash between her autistic traits and his personality (such as being able to see how systems worked to fix the car, which he felt undermined his confidence and standing), meant that the marriage was deeply flawed. They had two children together and had some happy times, but her training as a lecturer was treated by him as her trying to leave, which became a self-fulfilling prophecy. When she did leave the marital home, our contributor did not take her children with her, which led to judgement from people around her, despite her thinking it was the right decision:

> A lot of people thought I should have taken the children with me but I was going to live with a strange man who I knew next to nothing about and also they would change schools, they had a nanny, who lived in the house, their grandparents lived just up the road. So if I had taken them with me they would have gone to a completely new city with a man they didn't know, no nanny, no grandparents, no Dad, no school. How would that have been sensible, but I got a lot of grief from other women saying that I would never abandon my children, whereas to me in the circumstances it was the best thing that I could do.

This meant that her relationships with her children were impacted, as were her relationships at work (the man she moved in with was from her organisation), and everything in her life changed. Despite this, it actually took several years for her

Well, hello there **159**

and her husband to divorce, and it only happened because he wanted to marry someone new. This story shows some of the extreme ways in which divorce can affect autistic people, compared to some other accounts in this book, and these experiences need to be properly understood.

Another study which looked at the experiences of the partners of autistic people, without talking to the autistic people involved, focussed on how they felt when their partner went through the diagnostic process (Lewis, 2017). Here they discussed the fact that they experienced unique challenges in their relationship before their partner was diagnosed, such as difficulties communicating about emotions, inflexible thinking, and a lack of sex and intimacy. As their partner started to explore whether they might be autistic, and go through the diagnostic process, many found this validating – the participants had often been the one to suggest that their partner was autistic in the first place. It also brought upset for them in realising that the things which were difficult were never going to change, because it was due to their partner's underlying neurotype rather than behaviour, which was actively decided on. Some, sadly, felt that they were in some way trapped in their marriages, either because they didn't believe in divorce or because they were worried that no one else would look after their partner if they left. Many participants talked about being conflicted about the ideas of both leaving and staying – they were worried about leaving, but also the idea of staying felt overwhelming, because it meant committing to potentially decades of additional 'work' in the relationship in ways which they had never expected to need to do. This is not to say that the partners were all planning to leave their autistic significant other – most were not – but for some people the confirmation of what life was always going to look like which came with the diagnosis was too much. These relationships were in crisis, and the divorce process would potentially be high in conflict and emotional distress for both partners who felt misunderstood and unsupported.

It does not have to be that way, even when a marriage is coming to an end due to irreconcilable differences based on neurotype. One person was happy for Sarah to write an account of their divorce for the book – an amicable divorce, where an autistic and non-autistic couple realised that their needs were no longer compatible, talked about it, and came to a decision which left them both happier, rather than being unhappy together for the sake of staying married.

> Some relationships come to a natural end and for one autistic/non autistic couple, this is what has happened recently. He had spent his whole life feeling as though he was weird but when he was diagnosed a few years ago aged 62, he found himself and understood why he had been feeling like this for so long. He had always been happy being in a couple with their autistic daughter and with minimal social contacts outside of this immediate family unit, or with being solitary as reflected by his choice of career of being a shepherd. But her needs had changed over the years and she didn't want to be responsible for his social support any more and she needed more varied social experiences, so they split amicably, are still fond friends and support their daughter between them.

160 Well, hello there

This shows how divorce does not have to be an adversarial process, including for autistic people. Understanding and respect between partners, even those who are breaking up, and making space for the autism-driven aspects of someone's needs, can lead to better outcomes for everyone involved.

The other way people lose their spouse is through death, sadly. We know very little about the grieving process for autistic people – more on this in Chapter 8: Getting Older – but common sense tells us that it is just as emotionally intense, just as difficult, and just as real as it is for non-autistic people. Following the loss of a spouse, most people go through mourning, including mourning their own identity as a partner, then through stages of changes in their identity to being an individual, and beginning to engage with the social world again. Those who are able to make some kind of meaning out of their experiences – creating a coherent narrative about what has happened or engaging with religion being common ways of doing this – tend to experience less complicated grief (Pan et al., 2018). Engaging with religion and rituals around death, for those who believe, has been shown to help with the grieving process for people of all sexualities, not just heterosexual people, although these studies generally do not include trans and non-binary people (Pentaris et al., 2022). Grief is very much a personal experience, and without a proper evidence base around grief for autistic people, we don't want to speculate too much. Instead, we are sharing the stories of some of our contributors about their own losses.

> ## From Sarah – the bereavement and grief of a wife and sister
>
> *My brother Doug died nearly five years ago following catastrophic multiple counts of gross medical negligence, aged 54. He went into hospital with a resolvable kidney injury and came out in a box, leaving our family shell-shocked, angry, and bewildered as to how such a strong, robust person could end up dying like this. Unbelievably, nearly five years later we are still waiting for the coroner's inquest, but this ongoing bureaucratic nightmare is not the focus of my reflection today. Instead, I want to briefly unpack my grief and the impact that Doug's untimely death has had on his widow and myself.*
>
> *Grieving is different for everyone irrespective of their neurotype. There may be 'stages of grief' for some, but my experience is of a non-linear overwhelming sadness that invades my mind when something that reminds me of him pops up. It could be an item about Hornby trains on 'Bargain Hunt' or when one of the many rock tunes that he loved plays on Spotify; the accompanying emotions still catch me out, but now I have become more used to the feelings of sadness, reflection, loss, and the sense of injustice that he was robbed of many years of life. The grief is the same, it's just that I have become more accustomed to the emotional overwhelm and I let*

it wash over me when it happens. My sister-in-law describes her own grief journey in a similar fashion. The enormity of her devastating loss has not been diminished by time, but slowly and tentatively, she has rebuilt her life around it. Her grief is still as raw and huge, but her life is now expanding.

I regret not understanding more fully about the difficulties Doug had experienced when he was alive. His kindness outweighed his gruffness but sometimes I found his behaviour towards me to be oppressive and felt rather bullied by him on occasion. I had no idea of how much he had struggled with anxiety throughout his life until after he had died, and I realised that it was no fun for him being the elder son with so much patriarchal expectation weighing heavily on him. He was clearly autistic, but undiagnosed until the day he died, and I wish that we could have had that conversation where he opened up about his mental health and asked for help. However, when he was on life support and had no opportunity, for once, to answer me back, I was able to tell him how much I loved him and to thank him for his kindness to me when nobody else in the family cared.

Doug hated his first name Alfred, always preferring to be called by his middle name, but of course, all the official documentation referred to him as Alfred Goddard, hence the title of my eulogy;

> **"My Brother Doug, not Alfred"**
> **Older brothers are an irritation. They are over-bearing, over-protective and interfering. They play their Prog Rock too loud while mocking your taste in music. Boyfriends had better watch out and too bad if you don't like to be tickled to death or dragged out for an afternoon of train-spotting.**
> **Older brothers make time. They play Monopoly with you, teach you card games, include you in their friendships and take you on bike rides or sailing.**
> **Older brothers are there for you when nobody else is. They give you a home when you are homeless, or a hug when others are cold. They cry quietly when a beloved guinea pig dies, to protect you from the hurt.**
> **My older brother should have had another thirty years to continue being a kind, obnoxious, annoyance not just to me, but to anyone who needed help. He should have had another thirty years to grow old with his wife and to become an even grumpier old man. He should have had another thirty years but doesn't because of medical arrogance and neglect.**
> **His name was Doug, not Alfred. He was my older brother and I miss him.**

162 Well, hello there

Doug's death revealed the festering and unresolved difficulties in my family with accusations and cruel behaviour creating a tsunami of relational consequences. Additional and unconnected revelations from other family members finally led me to the drastic, but necessary act of severing ties with some long-standing relations. This decision followed a period of time when I had been gradually finding myself and could see the reality of the years of generational and abusive poison more clearly. Putting these boundaries in place may sound extreme, but doing so has been incredibly liberating and healing for me. Other relationships however, particularly with Doug's widow Helen, have strengthened and been nurtured throughout this turbulent time.

Another person who has talked to us about their grief went through the traumatic experience of their husband dying by suicide. While they want to remain anonymous, they have agreed to share elements of what they have gone through. Sarah has written up their story to ensure that everyone involved cannot be identified.

The husband of my friend died by suicide a few years ago and this dreadful news came as a huge shock for everyone else, but not for the couple involved. Both were autistic, but undiagnosed officially, had grown into middle adulthood knowing that they were different, being told for years that they were weird or wrong by their families and both having chronic suicidal ideation and anxiety. His wife knew that it was only a matter of time, following many attempts and near-misses, that one day he would be successful and leave the life that had become too overwhelmingly difficult to keep navigating. She understood why he couldn't stay and although she wishes with every fibre of her being that he was still here with her, she knows that the circumstances that played into this final choice had made life so unbearable that he could not go on.

My friend has lost the only other person in her life who fully understood and completely loved her, her neurodivergence and saw her for who she truly is. She has lost her cheerleader and her best friend, but instead of being supported by her family, she has been accused of driving him to do what he did because she was caricatured from an early age as being 'difficult' and 'mentally unwell' and blamed for being different.

There are no words to describe this level of cruelty, but this is what stigma, prejudice and ignorance of how autistic people experience the world and communicate can lead to. Being misunderstood, ridiculed and shamed by early caregivers and siblings not only creates unhealthy attachment styles, it ostracises, isolates, and inhibits our ability to trust others with our truth. Death by suicide for autistic people is multiple times higher than the general population and accumulative trauma and gaslighting, I suspect, play a huge part in this awful phenomenon.

> *It is no wonder then, that neither my friend nor her husband ever shared who they were and the difficulties they experienced from a very early age with their families. Being vulnerable requires trust and being safe in the knowledge that what is shared is respected and held empathically and this was certainly not present in their familial relationships. They found and loved each other in their own cocoon, keeping each other alive for as long as they could. They haven't been honoured by the people who should have been there for them, but I hope that this account goes at least a little way to doing so.*

These two stories highlight the depth of loss autistic people feel when facing the death of a loved one. One of the problems with the focus on autism in childhood, among many, is that it means our research to date has ignored these kinds of life-changing experiences for autistic adults. There are ways in which we know the stigma autistic people face comes into effect around death and grieving which needs to be better understood, so that we can find ways to stop this additional hurt and harm to people going through the worst times of their lives.

What if you don't have, or want, romantic relationships?

Not everyone will have long-term, or short-term, romantic relationships. Building this kind of connection is often hard work, and may feel too difficult for some autistic (and some non-autistic) people, so they decide not to put themselves through it. Others are asexual, and have no interest in having sexual relationships, or aromantic, with no interest in romantic relationships – and people can be both, with no interest in these types of interactions at all. Autistic people are more likely to be asexual than non-autistic people are, and autistic women more likely again than autistic men. Asexual autistic women report being satisfied with their status and their sex lives, more than autistic women of other sexual orientations (Bush et al., 2021), which shows how finding a sex life which works for an individual supports well-being. Some of our contributors identified this way:

> At this stage of my life I would count myself as being aromantic. In previous relationships I don't think I've ever been in love . . . relationships started as friends and then we stayed together over the years, but if I were to examine my experience I don't think that I have ever experienced romantic love, which I'm fine with. A lot of the time I did find myself going through the motions of what was expected of a relationship.
>
> *(anonymous, 47, autistic male)*

> I wasn't interested in boys like the other girls. I actually got bullied because the girls said I was a lesbian since I would observe them trying to understand

164 Well, hello there

how I was supposed to behave. I was never sure who I was attracted to because I didn't know how you were supposed to feel. I was insecure about that. Boys would make me feel anxious and I didn't understand the girls' behaviour.

(Eleanor, autistic woman)

So, there is a portion of the autism community whose approach to this aspect of life is very different to what the majority of society, including autistic society, expects. Equally, there are autistic people who really want romantic and sexual relationships, but who struggle to make them or to find partners who accept their differences. What do we know about the experiences of these groups?

Well, once again – very little. Researchers are far less likely to investigate the absence of something (in this case, romantic relationships) than the presence of it. Especially because autistic people who did not have these kinds of relationships were what the theories all those researchers had been trained in predicted would be there if they looked. Theory of Mind, especially, led to the assumption that autistic people were not going to be able to form and maintain long-term romantic relationships successfully, because they would lack the skills and empathy to do so. That justified researchers not looking for people with those relationships, which reinforces the idea they don't exist . . . another cycle of ignorance which is only to the discredit of the researchers who did not talk to autistic people themselves.

We do know that more autistic adults with learning disabilities, or who are non-speaking, are single and have never had an intimate relationship than adults without learning disabilities and who use verbal communication, especially those who are in supported living situations. This is often because their opportunities for sexual and romantic relationships are controlled by their caregivers, and the attitudes the caregivers have towards the idea of them being sexually active. It has been shown that staff in many supported living contexts have broadly negative attitudes towards the people they care for having these relationships (Grieve et al., 2009). This often comes from a paternalistic assumption that they need other people to decide what is best for them, that is, the staff, because people who require support in their living arrangements cannot fully understand what is involved, and the potential consequences – and that they therefore cannot truly consent. There have been challenges to this view though, from a variety of perspectives, calling for education for staff on how to support the autonomy of the people they work with in this regard, and for ways to enhance capacity to consent (Dukes & McGuire, 2009). Doing this would mean that safe relationships are an option for those who want to pursue them, potentially improving their well-being and quality of life.

One of the people who contributed to this book, Tejas, is a non-speaking autistic man who reflected on the difficulties he has and the way he feels about not having intimate or romantic relationships:

The work to get autistics authentic relationships is not yet done. I am alone. I am lonely. Tired of working to better my life. I am 24, autistic, nonspeaking, worthy of delighting another in giving love and receiving love. . . . How can I have a relationship? My body is sensory, tuning into autistic nightmarish impulsive motor loops. . . . Try to charm a woman to wear your ring when you wear an ID bracelet because you cannot say your name or address. Try to charm a woman when you cannot say or share what you have in your head. . . . I love myself on a good working day. I hate myself on a bad working day.

(Tejas, 24, male)

Among autistic adults without learning disabilities, those without intimate relationship experience tend to be younger, male, and heterosexual – they tend to feel more anxiety around sex and the idea of partnered sex, and feel less desire and arousal overall (Byers et al., 2013). Despite this, though, these young men still had better sexual functioning than the autistic women in this study, who had more sexual anxiety, less partnered arousability and desire, less frequent solo sexual activity, and fewer positive thoughts about sex overall. This suggests that for some autistic people, not having sexual or romantic relationships may be something they actively choose – particularly autistic women – because if you aren't feeling much desire for it, why would you pursue it? This is something Jack described when reflecting on his teenage and early adulthood:

I didn't participate and didn't have those kind of intimate encounters. There's nothing I did that was shameful or embarrassing. Some might say that it's a rite of passage, but in my case I was in my own cloud and Dr Who or other special interest areas might be more my area of contentment.

(Jack)

Just as there are some non-autistic people who are not interested in having long-term relationships, autistic people need to have their autonomy in making that choice recognised. Being single doesn't have to be pathologised or assumed to come from a 'lack' in the autistic person; it can be a positive choice for individual well-being.

Chapter conclusion

Many autistic adults have romantic and sexual relationships – with different degrees of success at times, sure, but that is the normal experience! Non-autistic people also go through more or less positive relationships, which last different amounts of time; they also get broken up with when they wish they hadn't been, or flat out told someone they find attractive isn't interested in them. All of these things are part of the normal pattern of dating, romance, and sex, and while they can be difficult to understand or navigate for autistic people, that doesn't mean that these difficulties are in some way pathological, or that they mean autistic people cannot or do not take part. We have talked here about the positive side of romantic and sexual relationships for autistic people, the ways in which they work with their partners to

166 Well, hello there

build stable, loving, long-term relationships, and how these should not be denied to autistic people simply because of their diagnosis. The next chapter looks at the other relationships which develop and change in adulthood – the networks of our families, both the ones we are born into and the ones we build for ourselves.

References

Beffel, J. H., Cary, K. M., Nuttall, A. K., Chopik, W. J., & Maas, M. K. (2021). Associations between the broad autism phenotype, adult attachment, and relationship satisfaction among emerging adults. *Personality and Individual Differences, 168,* 110409. https://doi.org/10.1016/J.PAID.2020.110409

Birnbaum, G. E., & Reis, H. T. (2019). Evolved to be connected: The dynamics of attachment and sex over the course of romantic relationships. *Current Opinion in Psychology, 25,* 11–15. https://doi.org/10.1016/J.COPSYC.2018.02.005

Bush, H. H., Williams, L. W., & Mendes, E. (2021). Brief report: Asexuality and young women on the autism spectrum. *Journal of Autism and Developmental Disorders, 51*(2), 725–733. https://doi.org/10.1007/S10803-020-04565-6/TABLES/4

Byers, E. S., Nichols, S., & Voyer, S. D. (2013). Challenging stereotypes: Sexual functioning of single adults with high functioning autism spectrum disorder. *Journal of Autism and Developmental Disorders, 43*(11), 2617–2627. https://doi.org/10.1007/s10803-013-1813-z

Deguchi, N., Asakura, T., Deguchi, N., & Asakura, T. (2018). Qualitative study of wives of husbands with autism spectrum disorder: Subjective experience of wives from marriage to marital crisis. *Psychology, 9*(1), 14–33. https://doi.org/10.4236/PSYCH.2018.91002

Dewinter, J., De Graaf, H., & Begeer, S. (2017). Sexual orientation, Gender identity, and Romantic relationships in adolescents and adults with autism spectrum disorder. *Journal of Autism and Developmental Disorders, 47*(9), 2927–2934. https://doi.org/10.1007/s10803-017-3199-9

Dukes, E., & Mcguire, B. E. (2009). Enhancing capacity to make sexuality-related decisions in people with an intellectual disability. *Journal of Intellectual Disability Research, 53*(8), 727–734. https://doi.org/10.1111/J.1365-2788.2009.01186.X

Fagundes, C. P., & Schindler, I. (2012). Making of romantic attachment bonds: Longitudinal trajectories and implications for relationship stability. *Personal Relationships, 19*(4), 723–742. https://doi.org/10.1111/J.1475-6811.2011.01389.X

Field, T., Diego, M., Pelaez, M., Deeds, O., & Delgado, J. (2009). Breakup distress in university students. *Adolescence, 44*(176), 705–727. https://web.p.ebscohost.com/ehost/detail/detail?vid=0&sid=f9348b32-d081-475a-bffb-6e31202988ce%40redis&bdata=Jn NpdGU9ZWhvc3QtbGl2ZQ%3D%3D#AN=47715860&db=ehh

Gallitto, E., & Leth-Steensen, C. (2015). Autistic traits and adult attachment styles. *Personality and Individual Differences, 79,* 63–67. https://doi.org/10.1016/J.PAID.2015.01.032

Gilbert, S. P., & Sifers, S. K. (2011). Bouncing back from a breakup: Attachment, time perspective, mental health, and romantic loss. *Journal of College Student Psychotherapy, 25*(4), 295–310. https://doi.org/10.1080/87568225.2011.605693

Grieve, A., McLaren, S., Lindsay, W., & Culling, E. (2009). Staff attitudes towards the sexuality of people with learning disabilities: A comparison of different professional groups and residential facilities. *British Journal of Learning Disabilities, 37*(1), 76–84. https://doi.org/10.1111/J.1468-3156.2008.00528.X

Hancock, G., Stokes, M. A., & Mesibov, G. (2020). Differences in romantic relationship experiences for individuals with an autism spectrum disorder. *Sexuality and Disability, 38*(2), 231–245. https://doi.org/10.1007/S11195-019-09573-8/FIGURES/3

Hartman, T. (2021). Male breakup trauma. *Qualitative Psychology*, *8*(2), 255–263. https://doi.org/10.1037/QUP0000204

Harvey, A. B., & Karpinski, A. (2016). The impact of social constraints on adjustment following a romantic breakup. *Personal Relationships*, *23*(3), 396–408. https://doi.org/10.1111/PERE.12132

Howlin, P., Goode, S., Hutton, J., & Rutter, M. (2004). Adult outcome for children with autism. *Journal of Child Psychology and Psychiatry*, *45*(2), 212–229. https://doi.org/10.1111/j.1469-7610.2004.00215.x

Howlin, P., Moss, P., Savage, S., & Rutter, M. (2013). Social outcomes in mid- to later adulthood among individuals diagnosed with autism and average nonverbal IQ as children. *Journal of the American Academy of Child & Adolescent Psychiatry*, *52*(6), 572–581.e1. https://doi.org/10.1016/J.JAAC.2013.02.017

Kock, E., Strydom, A., O'brady, D., & Tantam, D. (2019). Autistic women's experience of intimate relationships: the impact of an adult diagnosis. *Advances in Autism*.

Kwok, I., & Wescott, A. B. (2020). Cyberintimacy: A scoping review of technology-mediated romance in the digital age. *Cyberpsychology, Behavior, and Social Networking*, *23*(10), 657–666. https://doi.org/10.1089/CYBER.2019.0764/ASSET/IMAGES/LARGE/CYBER.2019.0764_FIGURE2.JPEG

Langhinrichsen-Rohling, J., Palarea, R. E., Cohen, J., & Rohling, M. L. (2000). Breaking up is hard to do: Unwanted pursuit behaviors following the dissolution of a romantic relationship. *Violence and Victims*, *15*(1), 73–90. https://doi.org/10.1891/0886-6708.15.1.73

Lefebvre, L., Blackburn, K., & Brody, N. (2014). Navigating romantic relationships on facebook: Extending the relationship dissolution model to social networking environments. *Journal of Social and Personal Relationships*, *32*(1), 78–98. https://doi.org/10.1177/0265407514524848

Lewis, L. F. (2017). We will never be normal: The experience of discovering a partner has autism spectrum disorder. *Journal of Marital and Family Therapy*, *43*(4), 631–643. https://doi.org/10.1111/JMFT.12231

Lewis, L. F. (2022). Autism as a difference or a disorder? Exploring the views of individuals who use peer-led online support groups for autistic partners. *Autism*, 136236132210978. https://doi.org/10.1177/13623613221097850

Lewis, L. F., Ward, C., Jarvis, N., & Cawley, E. (2021). Straight sex is complicated enough: The lived experiences of autistics who are gay, lesbian, bisexual, asexual, or other sexual orientations. *Journal of Autism and Developmental Disorders*, *51*(7), 2324–2337. https://doi.org/10.1007/S10803-020-04696-W/TABLES/2

Marcotte, A. S., Gesselman, A. N., Reynolds, T. A., & Garcia, J. R. (2021). Young adults' romantic investment behaviors on social media. *Personal Relationships*, *28*(4), 822–839. https://doi.org/10.1111/PERE.12390

McKenna, K. Y. A. (2008). MySpace or your place: Relationship initiation and development in the wired and wireless world. *Handbook of Relationship Initiation*, 235–247.

Mogavero, M. C., & Hsu, K. H. (2020). Dating and courtship behaviors among those with autism spectrum disorder. *Sexuality and Disability*, *38*(2), 355–364. https://doi.org/10.1007/S11195-019-09565-8/TABLES/4

Ogolsky, B. G., Surra, C. A., & Monk, J. K. (2016). Pathways of commitment to wed: The development and dissolution of romantic relationships. *Journal of Marriage and Family*, *78*(2), 293–310. https://doi.org/10.1111/JOMF.12260

Pan, H., Cheung, C. K., & Hu, J. (2018). Intimacy and complicated grief among chinese elders having lost their spouses: Mediating role of meaning making. *Journal of Loss and Trauma*, *23*(3), 244–258. https://doi.org/10.1080/15325024.2018.1435367

168 Well, hello there

Park, L. E., Sanchez, D. T., & Brynildsen, K. (2011). Maladaptive responses to relationship dissolution: The role of relationship contingent self-worth. *Journal of Applied Social Psychology, 41*(7), 1749–1773. https://doi.org/10.1111/J.1559-1816.2011.00769.X

Pecora, L. A., Hancock, G. I., Mesibov, G. B., & Stokes, M. A. (2019). Characterising the sexuality and sexual experiences of autistic females. *Journal of Autism and Developmental Disorders, 49*(12), 4834–4846. https://doi.org/10.1007/S10803-019-04204-9/TABLES/3

Pentaris, P., Patlamazoglou, L., & Schaub, J. (2022). The role of faith in the experience of grief among sexually diverse individuals: A systematic review. *Psychology and Sexuality*, 1–17. https://doi.org/10.1080/19419899.2022.2057869

Penwell, B. J., & Eleanor, M.-T. (2015). Qualitative exploration of sexual experiences among adults on the autism spectrum: Implications for sex education. *Perspectives on Sexual and Reproductive Health, 47*(4), 171–179. https://doi.org/10.1363/47e5715

Pollmann, M. M. H., Finkenauer, C., & Begeer, S. (2010). Mediators of the link between autistic traits and relationship satisfaction in a non-clinical sample. *Journal of Autism and Developmental Disorders, 40*(4), 470–478. https://doi.org/10.1007/S10803-009-0888-Z/FIGURES/1

Rosenfeld, M. J. (2018). Who wants the breakup? Gender and breakup in heterosexual couples. *Social Networks and the Life Course*, 221–243. https://doi.org/10.1007/978-3-319-71544-5_11

Roth, M. E., & Gillis, J. M. (2015). Convenience with the click of a mouse: A survey of adults with autism spectrum disorder on online dating. *Sexuality and Disability, 33*(1), 133–150. https://doi.org/10.1007/S11195-014-9392-2/TABLES/2

Rözer, J. J., Mollenhorst, G., & Volker, B. (2015). Romantic relationship formation, maintenance and changes in personal networks. *Advances in Life Course Research, 23*, 86–97. https://doi.org/10.1016/J.ALCR.2014.12.001

Sala, G., Hooley, M., & Stokes, M. A. (2020). Romantic intimacy in autism: A qualitative analysis. *Journal of Autism and Developmental Disorders, 50*(11), 4133–4147. https://doi.org/10.1007/S10803-020-04377-8/TABLES/4

Sedgewick, F., Crane, L., Hill, V., & Pellicano, E. (2018). Friends and lovers: The relationships of autistic and neurotypical women. *Autism in Adulthood*, 150. https://doi.org/10.1089/aut.2018.0028

Sedgewick, F., Leppanen, J., & Tchanturia, K. (2019). The friendship questionnaire, autism, and gender differences: A study revisited. *Molecular Autism, 10*(1), 1–12. https://doi.org/10.1186/s13229-019-0295-z

Shulman, S., & Connolly, J. (2013). The challenge of romantic relationships in emerging adulthood: Reconceptualization of the field. *Emerging Adulthood, 1*(1), 27–39. https://doi.org/10.1177/2167696812467330

Soares, L. S., Alves, A. L. C., Costa, D. de S., Malloy-Diniz, L. F., Paula, J. J. de, Romano-Silva, M. A., & Miranda, D. M. de. (2021). Common venues in romantic relationships of adults with symptoms of autism and attention deficit/hyperactivity disorder. *Frontiers in Psychiatry, 12*, 958. https://doi.org/10.3389/FPSYT.2021.593150/BIBTEX

Strunz, S., Schermuck, C., Ballerstein, S., Ahlers, C. J., Dziobek, I., & Roepke, S. (2017). Romantic relationships and relationship satisfaction among adults with asperger syndrome and high-functioning autism. *Journal of Clinical Psychology, 73*(1), 113–125. https://doi.org/10.1002/JCLP.22319

Tashiro, T., & Frazier, P. (2003). I'll never be in a relationship like that again: Personal growth following romantic relationship breakups. *Personal Relationships, 10*(1), 113–128. https://doi.org/10.1111/1475-6811.00039

Tassy, F., & Winstead, B. (2014). Relationship and individual characteristics as predictors of unwanted pursuit. *Journal of Family Violence*, *29*(2), 187–195. https://doi.org/10.1007/S10896-013-9573-2/TABLES/3

Taylor, E. L., Target, M., & Charman, T. (2008). Attachment in adults with high-functioning autism. *Attachment and Human Development*, *10*(2), 143–163. https://doi.org/10.1080/14616730802113687

Valois, D. D., Novoa, D. C., & Davis, C. G. (2016). Since you've been gone: Coping with a relationship breakup. *Journal of Interpersonal Relations, Intergroup Relations and Identity*, *9*, 10–21.

Van Ouytsel, J., Van Gool, E., Walrave, M., Ponnet, K., & Peeters, E. (2016). Exploring the role of social networking sites within adolescent romantic relationships and dating experiences. *Computers in Human Behavior*, *55*, 76–86. https://doi.org/10.1016/J.CHB.2015.08.042

Verhallen, A. M., Alonso-Martínez, S., Renken, R. J., Marsman, J. B. C., & ter Horst, G. J. (2021). Depressive symptom trajectory following romantic relationship breakup and effects of rumination, Neuroticism and cognitive control. *Stress and Health*. https://doi.org/10.1002/SMI.3123

Weisskirch, R. S., & Delevi, R. (2011). Sexting and adult romantic attachment. *Computers in Human Behavior*, *27*(5), 1697–1701. https://doi.org/10.1016/J.CHB.2011.02.008

7

A FAMILY AFFAIR

Adult families

Thinking about adulthood, there is a set of key relationships which we haven't yet mentioned, and which also change significantly as people grow up and become adults – family relationships. They are where we started the book and are important to come back to. Family relationships are not fixed in amber at the point of an autistic person turning 18, or moving out, or whichever arbitrary point of your choice. People build their own families, relationships with older and younger siblings shift as all become more independent and mature, and our relationships with our parents can change significantly as they start to need care instead of providing it. As with the rest of the relationships we have discussed, as the autistic people we are interested in get older, the amount of research about their lives decreases, but we will sum up what we can in partnership with the insights from our contributors.

Parenting

Being a parent is a huge part of life for anyone it happens to. It is an intense relationship, with extreme emotions involved, and the highest level of dependency anyone else will ever show you. This means that it comes with a lot of pressure, and usually the absolute desire to do it 'right' and to do the best you can for your child or children. This is just as much the case for autistic people as non-autistic people, and we can give an overview of the research and share some thoughts from autistic people here.

DOI: 10.4324/9781003044536-8

Sarah's autobiographical experience – parenting and family life

Becoming a parent and having a family was not on my radar at all. I had been traumatised by my own parents and wider family and being the youngest sibling, had no experience of babies and so didn't really register the existence of small people. The day I found out that I was pregnant, having done a test in the loos at work, following a week of feeling a bit 'off', was the first time in my life that I had ever held a baby. One of the admin women who was on maternity leave was visiting the office and I was offered a cuddle with her offspring. It was a terrifying combination of paranoia that I was going to drop this precious bundle and a growing terror that in approximately eight months I was going to be given one of these myself. The fact that I had only been married for two months and had handed in my notice a week before finding out my happy news and therefore wouldn't be eligible for company maternity pay, only added to this anxiety.

I wasn't diagnosed until my son was fourteen, and it wasn't until five years later when I really started exploring what being autistic meant for me, so there were many years of confusion and difficulty alongside the joy of navigating parenthood. I really didn't like much of the hormonal and sensory experiences of pregnancy, although I loved being in a bath and watching the ripples of the water as Rob moved around inside me. Having emetophobia is no fun when feeling constantly nauseous and although I didn't actually vomit, the fear and discomfort of pregnancy-related interoception difficulties was exhausting and anxiety inducing.

I also had a bit of a panic when Kyle and I were in Brittany attending a friend's wedding. I went down with gastroenteritis and then started experiencing powerful contractions, which at six months is frankly, undesirable. The size of the syringe that the doctor, who spoke limited English, produced from his bag will be forever etched in my memory. He injected me with something that mercifully stopped the contractions while looking fiercely at my terrified expression exclaiming, "I am a doctor!" which wasn't entirely reassuring. I will be forever grateful for Kyle's ability to speak fluent French and although a post-Brexit dual passport may well have been a bonus for Rob, I was mightily relieved not to have given birth away from home.

There were no more dramas, my pregnancy was healthy, and Kyle and I were featured in a pregnancy magazine cooing about our impending happy event. The birth itself was for the most part surprisingly calm thanks to an epidural and Massive Attack playing in the background (cassette, not the actual band . . . although Grant from MA did have the pleasure of me telling him the tale of his musical presence at the birth as he brought his kids to a toddler group that I helped to run!) The last hour though, was more stressful when Rob's oxygen levels dropped and he had to be extracted first via forceps and when that was not successful, by ventouse. I must have vaguely given consent for student doctors to witness this as I remember the room being full of white coats and having a drug-induced chat with the lucky one of them tasked with stitching me up. Not very well, as it turned out.

I was a combination of exhausted, wired from the drugs, and anxious from a wave of nausea, but this was nothing compared to the overwhelming wave of love that washed over me as I held my boy for the first time. I was kept in for a few days as I was experiencing difficulties with breastfeeding and although I was completely in love with Rob, I was struggling with the sensory aspect of being in hospital and was constantly in tears. The first few weeks at home were stressful beyond imagining and although we had a very welcome visit from Kyle's parents and my brother, Doug, Kyle and I did all of the child care between us. I wasn't able to sleep between feeds, had no confidence in my ability to be a parent, and eventually was diagnosed with PND. I was an apparently functioning ball of anxiety and depression who had no idea of how to look after a helpless infant or communicate the extent to which I was struggling. Kyle was a hands-on Dad, loved us both, and supported me, but neither of us knew then that my mental health was deteriorating because my neurodivergent needs were not being met. I had learned from my absent mother, who showed no interest in supporting me as a new parent or meeting her newest grandchild, that women were ornamental and were expected to be cheerful and smiley, so that is what I did. I put on a happy fake smile and pushed through the sensory and social hell that was sleepless nights, breastfeeding and carer and baby groups.

I hated the feeling of obligation of going to groups and being thrown together with other people whose only common ground was that we had had babies all at the same time. The utter torture of feeling that I had to make shiny, happy, small talk when I was both sleep deprived and not giving a shit about the sorts of things that 'normal' new mothers talk about was a horror that I could well have done without, as was the overwhelming noise, busyness and god-awful baby smells. How anything so small can produce such copious foulness is beyond me. Having undiagnosed sensory sensitivities to the smell and texture of vomit and ripe bums was horrendous. The sheer effort that it took me to smile, look concerned and come out with supportive, clucking mum wisdom when what I really wanted to do is rock in the corner with my hands over my ears, was, looking back, beyond human endurance. My autistic masking 'super-power' (sarcasm!) however, made it possible as did finding another mum who was equally curmudgeonly, but less secret about it than I was and we have remained best friends to this day.

My son, though, was everything. The intensity of the love I had for him was completely overwhelming and from day one I made a conscious decision to bring him up very differently to how I was raised. He would know that he was loved, cherished and valued for who he was and I think that this mission and him became my long-term hyperfocus, my intense interest. I have no regrets about this and am assured by him that I didn't become a (s)mother and that his memories of growing up are good. He has become the quietly confident, secure-in-his-own-skin man that healthy and loving attachments produce, so hurrah for autistic passions and the right kind of perseverance!

As my son grew older I started a job, oddly enough as an LSA for an autistic child, at the local primary school that he also attended. To this day I find it bizarre that at the time I had no idea that I was also autistic, but I couldn't possibly be as I was female, chatty and amiable, with a profound dislike of all things to do with trains. That happens when your very obviously autistic brother drags your young self around freezing, boring stations for 'fun'.

I felt completely out of my depth and overwhelmed by the sights, sounds, and smells of the school environment. I also felt very cowed by some of the teaching staff, but the saving grace of the job was that it enabled me to avoid the social and political hell that was the PTA and parent support groups. As an employee of the school, I could get away with saying that to be involved would be a conflict of interests and so could avoid having to volunteer for whatever group was being set up. The truth, of course, was that I was autistic and too much peopling, even though some of the parents were lovely, was just too difficult.

When my son became a teenager and went to high school, the primary school-style social pressure diminished and as I was now a total embarrassment, the more hands-on parenting that accompanies younger children also changed. He was naturally doing more of his own thing with his mates and school involvement was only really parent's evenings and the occasional drinkies or meals with parents that I could just about deal with as long as they were on an infrequent basis. My mental health was just as bad and I had shocking social anxiety, but on these occasions I put on a 'brave' masked face and pushed through. I hated it, but because I believed that it was expected, I made myself put on the show, with a lipsticky smile and forced humour. My relationship with my son, however, was solid and loving and when we clashed, we quickly made up and I think we learned from each other. I learned to trust him and allow him to grow and myself to let go. Of course, none of this would have been possible without my husband's love and support and he was invaluable when my many insecurities frequently showed up along the way.

Becoming a parent helped me to appreciate my own parents' difficulties, although I will never fully understand their treatment of me growing up. They were both products of zipped up post-war sensibilities, and their own experiences of childhood had not been particularly happy or emotionally secure. I can see that my father's focus on education is rooted in his regret of not going to university like his favoured brother. He probably thought that he was doing his best for my brothers and I, but it was like we were all groomed for nothing else than higher education. Nothing else mattered. Not our hopes and interests and certainly not our mental health. I can also see that my mother was worn down by my father's behaviour and the development of various health problems that left her too exhausted to raise a troubled teenage daughter or show much interest in her grandson.

Apart from an initial outpouring of grief upon hearing of her death in 2012 my mother hasn't been in my thoughts as much as I thought she would be and I wonder if this is because I spent so much of my younger life grieving for the relationship that never was and the one that I desperately wanted. I don't know, but since learning what autism means to me I suspect that my mother was also autistic, but never knew. She was intelligent, but hid it with her own brand of people-pleasing and gender conformity and, in all probability, also learned to mask from an early age. So what I do feel is a sense of being posthumously closer to her tinged with the sadness that she, like so many past generations of undiagnosed women and AFAB folk, was never able to discover who she really was. Later diagnosed autistics like myself are often referred to as 'the lost generation', but I can't help but grieve for all the many lost generations throughout history who didn't have the privilege that I have now.

The years of not knowing that I was autistic didn't just affect my mental health and well-being but also, to an extent, my ability to enjoy being a parent. I had put my heart and soul into making sure that my son knew that he was loved, valued, and that he could always depend on his mum and dad, but because I was constantly on high alert, doing what I thought was expected of me socially, and ignoring my own needs, there wasn't much room for simple enjoyment and just being. So, if there are any parenting regrets, that would be it, but I do consider myself fortunate that the undiagnosed version of myself was still enough for my son to be healthy and happy and our relationship only gets stronger as I learn to be more authentically myself. Ten years post-diagnosis I am feeling more at peace with myself. I have a better sense of my own worth and autonomy and being secure in the knowledge that I am loved and valued by my boys has translated into increased relational happiness and enjoyment of all aspects of our lives as a family.

Rob has really noticed the positive change in me since he has left home, but cheekily adds that, "these may not be noticeable to the average person, as mum has always been a loud and lively person who has a lot to say". He continues by saying that, "Dad and I can see that by looking at her past and how her autism diagnosis affects her, Mum is becoming more like herself and living for herself more, which is great to see. I was surprised when Mum explained the deep anxiety and fear she would feel before going on holiday. These have always been positive memories for me, so hearing about how stressed out it made Mum was initially quite sad, but since having conversations with her about autistic masking I understand far more now. It has been challenging to hear about the tough times in Mum's life, but it's good to know that she also has positive memories too".

As Rob says, although I loved being with my boys, holidays used to be difficult for me, but now I can genuinely enjoy days out or time away knowing that it is absolutely fine to ask for any accommodations that I may need or spend time alone or rest without any need to mask or feel guilt. This has a positive knock on effect for Kyle and Rob as they now understand what I need to avoid the distress of meltdown, anxiety, and fear. Now I have a greater understanding of the times where I become very tired, anxious, impatient, or overwhelmed and I can ask for accommodations and supports which then means they happen less frequently. I can communicate about them more effectively and Kyle knows how to support me better. The overall effect is an enhanced mutual understanding, less self-blame for my differences, and more self-compassion.

Kyle has always been able to see me more clearly and from a more rounded perspective than I have, but now he has a greater understanding about the person that he fell in love with, what I experience on a day to day basis, and why I may react to something in a certain way. This has given him more of a peace of mind whereas in the decades before my diagnosis and self-discovery at times he felt confused or upset as he didn't know how to help me. Neither of us knew why I was struggling so much and this new knowledge brings him more patience, understanding, and hope for the future.

> *Kyle's view is that it is not autism that wrecks marriages, it is ignorance of the features and needs of an autistic person that can cause problems. He thinks that there is a responsibility on both the autistic person and their partner to educate themselves about autism in order to build and nurture mutual understanding. He has loved me through some very dark times and there are occasions when I have taken this for granted and others when I have felt misunderstood and lonely, and Kyle has felt anxious and unsure how to help me, but he feels that these times were bolstered with better ones and experiences which balanced out those unhappy periods. Kyle adds he thinks that I need to take a lot of credit for the way that even when I didn't have full knowledge of what was going on with me and was struggling, I was still loving and determined to nurture our little family and our marriage. He also offers a gentle reminder not to blame myself or my autism because I am still the same autistic person that he fell in love with all those years ago, it's just that now I have a diagnosis, we both understand each other better.*
>
> *Both Rob and Kyle are immensely proud of what I have achieved and the work that I am doing in autism research, debt awareness, and sexual violence support and can see the change in my confidence levels and self-belief. I do, on occasion, still catch myself thinking that if someone I love is showing signs of distress or emotion then it is because of something I have done and when I am low or exhausted or having a particularly bad ME/ CFS day I do need reassurance from Kyle, but I hold onto Rob's comment that he made after first noticing this change in me, "Mum, you're self-actualising!" with equal amounts of gratitude and pride. I have also been able to set in place strict relational boundaries with regard to family members whose behaviour and attitudes I have found to be damaging. I feel no guilt for doing so and am so much happier having people that I am related to, but find it impossible to have a healthy relationship with, at arm's length. My only regret is that I didn't do it sooner. To have arrived in this place aged 52 may have taken me many years, but I think it is infinitely better to be finally living my best life late, rather than never.*

Autistic pregnancy and childbirth

Parenting starts with pregnancy and childbirth. Well, in most cases – obviously adoption does not involve the parents themselves going through pregnancy, but someone did, so the previous statement isn't exactly wrong. Anyway . . .

Very little is known about the pregnancy and birthing experiences of autistic people. There are a few early career researchers leading the way on this. Sarah Hampton is one of the key authors in the field of autistic pregnancy and childbirth, so you're about to see her work cited a lot in the next few paragraphs.

One of the key findings that all the research into autistic pregnancy has in common are the difficulties people have around communicating with services (Rogers et al., 2017). While pregnant, there can be literally dozens of different health and social care professionals someone comes into contact with, from midwives to social workers to GPs to breastfeeding consultants. This means a large number of new relationships and social interactions someone needs to navigate, which often involve discussing things which are normally kept private about your health, your body, and your sex life. This can be awkward for anyone, but can be especially difficult for autistic people, who have often been told to 'stop oversharing' at different points in their lives.

Sensory issues are also a major part of pregnancy experiences – again, not just for autistic people, but perhaps more intensely so. This has also been picked up in multiple papers, which were included in a review of the topic (Samuel et al., 2022). They showed that this is something which comes up in every set of interviews with autistic women who have been or are currently pregnant, with things like changes to sensory sensitivities, new sensory sensitivities, and the impact of sensory overwhelm on their relationships and interactions with health professionals coming up consistently. For example, if your sensory sensitivity to lights and smells is intensified while you are pregnant, and you are in a brightly lit doctor's office which smells overwhelmingly of the chemicals they use to clean hospitals, it can make it that much more difficult to focus on the questions you are being asked and to give accurate answers. This can be important for the people checking on you and the baby, as they may miss signs of things to follow up on. Equally, being more sensitive to touch when most appointments will involve, at least, someone taking your blood pressure and touching your stomach in order to listen for the baby's heartbeat, can be very difficult for autistic women.

In the interviews, many autistic women talked about working hard to overcome these challenges for the sake of their baby, because they wanted to be sure that they were doing all the right things for the pregnancy to go well (Hampton et al., 2021). Autistic mothers are more likely to experience complications in pregnancy and childbirth – some of this is because many healthcare professionals lack knowledge about autism and how to support autistic people in pregnancy; some of it is because autistic mothers themselves say they are less sure of what is 'normal' or not, and so may not raise alarm as early as some non-autistic mothers. This can be seen in the lower satisfaction autistic people report with their pre-, birth-, and post-natal healthcare (Hampton et al., 2022); the higher rates of preterm birth, pre-eclampsia, and emergency C-sections among autistic people (McDonnell & DeLucia, 2021), and the calls for autism-specific learning for professionals supporting autistic people through pregnancy.

The greater likelihood of difficulties does not stop with the birth of a child – autistic mothers are more likely to experience post-natal depression than non-autistic mothers, for example (Pohl et al., 2020). Breastfeeding is often difficult, especially in terms of the sensory side of the process, despite autistic mothers doing significant research and being determined to do it if they possibly can (Grant et al., 2022). Autistic mothers tend to be more anxious in the first few weeks following the birth of their child, although this decreases by the time their child is six months old (Hampton et al., 2022). They also tend to find early motherhood a more isolating experience, with it

178 A family affair

being more difficult for them to find and rely on social support networks, or to access things like new mother groups. On top of these difficulties with relationships, many autistic mothers report facing stigma from people like healthcare visitors, who may be judgmental about their ability to be a good mother because they are autistic. Indeed, in one paper the participant said that "they thought I was an incompetent parent" (Rogers et al., 2017), an attitude which lots of autistic mothers worry about from professionals. Awareness of, and fears about, this kind of prejudice can lead to mothers trying to minimise when they are having problems, because they do not want to reinforce that image or give the impression that they cannot cope or are bad parents – but this means that they do not get support which can help them and their baby.

Autistic parenting

The (very) little research we have about autistic experiences of parenting actually suggests the opposite. Autistic parents of autistic children can be, and are, excellent parents, and may well be able to understand their children better than non-autistic parents would. Many of the papers which looked at pregnancy experiences also cover the first few months of motherhood, so you will see some of the same names popping up in this section. What we want to emphasise, along with the challenges described in lots of the research, is that most autistic people talk about being a parent as a really rewarding relationship and something which brings them genuine joy.

Lots of participants in studies about autistic parenting feel that actually, being autistic gives you an advantage as a parent. For example, attention to detail and being used to looking for cues in other people's non-verbal behaviour prepares them for working out what their baby needs and recognising different types of crying. Or sensory abilities being a strength, because your own sensitivities help you to guess what sensation might be upsetting them or what will soothe them. Equally, an autistic parent's preference for routines may help model this for their child, so that they settle into something more predictable and manageable earlier than lots of babies do (Hampton et al., 2021). Equally, the ability to hyperfocus and do deep research into being a good parent was talked about as a strength by our interviewees:

> Once you decided that you wanted to be a mother, that's what you wanted to do, and you became a mother and you focussed on being a mother, being the best mother you possibly could.
>
> *(Ella's non-autistic husband)*

> When the children were babies I was devoted to them, almost too devoted. I breast fed them, was very focussed on them, loved them when they were toddlers and we used to be doing art and out looking at stuff. They were very verbal and we used to make up songs. It was great, we had a lovely time together.
>
> *(anonymous, 62, autistic woman)*

This is in direct and stark contrast with many of the general societal narratives about autistic people, which suggest they are likely to be poor parents who are cold and aloof – something which autistic people are also challenging through their own writings (Fletcher-Randle, 2022). Autistic parents actually feel huge amounts of warmth and love for their children – which anyone sensible could have guessed, if they weren't approaching it from a point of prejudice!

Autistic parents (almost entirely mothers, in the research) talk about the fact that they have intense connections and love with their children, and that parenting is a joyful experience. Many mothers talked about feeling an instant bond with their child, while others said that this developed over time – something which is normal for all mothers. Being autistic themselves helped them to understand and better care for their autistic children, as they had insight into the things which their child was either struggling with or enjoying (Dugdale et al., 2021). Statistical research suggests that there may be no significant differences between autistic and non-autistic parents in terms of family and child outcomes (Adams et al., 2021). This doesn't capture some of the qualitative reports of autistic parenting though, which emphasise these strong connections and the potential for autistic children of autistic parents to grow up in autism-affirming spaces. We don't yet know what the long-term impact of that will be, but we have to assume it can only be positive.

One small way in which this neurodiversity-positive, or at least neurodiversity-aware, parenting by autistic parents has been explored in research is looking at how autistic parents talk about their autistic child's diagnosis with them, in comparison to how non-autistic parents approach the topic (Crane et al., 2021). Both sets of parents talked about how important they felt it was to be honest and open about the diagnosis, and to actively talk to their child about autism. What the autistic parents had that was different, though, was the ability to talk to their child about autism from the perspective of their own lived experience. They could, and did, talk to their child about the ways in which autism affected them, which they felt helped to build understanding and empathy with their children. They were also less concerned about disclosure having a negative effect on their child – probably because they were able to talk to them about the positives about being autistic, rather than relying on mostly negative information from professionals in the way many non-autistic parents might. The information non-autistic parents get when their child is diagnosed is slowly changing to be more positive (hopefully this book can be part of that shift!) but it is still not quite the same as hearing about it first-hand from an autistic parent.

The tricky parts of parenting

None of the preceding means that being an autistic parent is all easy, with innate understanding of everything your child thinks and feels, no tantrums, and no sleepless nights!

180 A family affair

One of the most common things anyone will say to a new parent, regardless of neurotype, gender, or often even how well they know each other, is "How bad are the nappies?" It usually comes with laughter, and mock disgust. And yes, nappies aren't the most fun part of having a baby (especially the early few, and then the ones when you move to solid food!) And for autistic parents, their sensory sensitivities may make handling these, and other, elements of having a baby or a small child more challenging (or a teenager, when it comes to it . . .). This is something which, again, autistic parents have talked about in research, in addition to the sensory challenges associated with being pregnant. There are also the auditory elements of having a baby – the crying, the loud toys, and the incredibly repetitive songs; or the fact that being a parent is a very tactile process, with lots of touch required by the baby and often still demanded from healthcare professionals, which can become overwhelming (Talcer et al., 2021).

The same paper highlights that the expectations of socialising in motherhood can also be difficult for autistic people, and that these demands increase as a child moves into nursery and school, rather than the opposite. Organising playdates and additional activities for the child often comes with associated socialising for the parent who takes them to these things. There is also the culture 'mums on the playground' and lots of small talk which builds slightly-more-than-casual friendships between parents. This can be really important as a way of building up a network for informal social support and childcare help, such as finding a couple of people who you can ask to wait with your child if you are running late after school. But it also is a lot of effort and can require intense masking, which is exhausting – on top of being exhausted from everything else in life.

There is also the fact that not every autistic person has the same needs or sensory sensitivities, even parents and children. This can mean that what an autistic child finds sensorily pleasurable may be horrid for their autistic parent, or the other way around. Unfortunately for parents, as the adults in the situation, they are the ones who are expected to adjust for their child, which can be difficult and may risk their own overwhelm. Equally, it is very difficult to take time alone away from a child in order to recover from the demands of parenting (Hampton et al., 2021). That isn't unique to autistic parents, of course, but it can be especially challenging for people who are used to needing solo decompression time to maintain their well-being.

The pressures of parenting only increased during the COVID-19 pandemic, which affected the globe starting in March 2020. Lots of studies were carried out with non-autistic parents which showed that their stress levels increased (Chu et al., 2021). This was especially true for mothers who took on the majority of responsibility for additional childcare and homeschooling, often on top of the move to working from home themselves and the existential dread of a then-poorly understood disease (Almeida et al., 2020). There has been one paper published looking at the experiences of parenting during the pandemic for autistic parents (Heyworth et al., 2022). This work was carried out in Australia, and involved talking to 35 autistic parents – 33 mothers, one father, and one non-binary parent – about their family life during lockdown. Many said that they felt their connection to their child/ren had grown stronger during lockdown, due to all the time spent together, and that the early stages of the lockdowns were actually something of a relief from the demands of everyday life for everyone in the family. After the initial period of enjoying time together without those pressures, though, life became much more difficult for autistic parents, whose mental health suffered. Autistic parents reported knowing that they needed help, but that they struggled to reach out to their usual informal support networks – partly because they were aware of how stressed their autistic friends also were. Without this informal support, autistic parents wanted to seek out more formal support, but this was non-existent, leaving them feeling as though they had been forgotten by their government and policymakers.

Parenting and getting your own diagnosis

It is actually very common for parenting to lead to recognising that the parent themselves is autistic. This is especially the case for mothers, who are more likely to have gone undiagnosed previously due to the stereotypes about autism being a 'male thing'. Instead, as they begin to spot and investigate the difficulties their child is having, and come to the conclusion that their child is autistic, they realise that they also had, or have, some of the same behaviours, and may also be autistic. This pattern has been seen in several studies looking at women's experiences of getting a diagnosis in adulthood (Harmens et al., 2022; Zener, 2019). It may also be the case for fathers, but this hasn't been explored in the literature, and because men generally share less of their lives online, there are also fewer examples of first-person blogs or tweets about this.

The increased personal understanding that comes with getting an autism diagnosis, at any point in your life, can be invaluable to people. For autistic parents of autistic children, it can provide massive insights into how and why you find it easier to understand your child than many of the other adults in their lives do. Even when the first autism diagnosis in the family comes when everyone is older, it has the potential to help explain past difficulties, or to provide a direction through which to understand current challenges:

> Getting our autism dx was helpful. My daughter didn't want to get an autism assessment, but I remember saying to her if she had stuff hanging around for her that she needed to talk through with somebody . . . she's never spoken to me about how she feels about all that. She's very closed down about it. I've never felt able to broach the subject with her.
>
> *(anonymous, 62, autistic woman)*

This is why it is important to raise children in families that understand and accept neurodivergence – it gives autistic (and other neurodivergent) children the chance to grow up in spaces which are empowering, supportive, and which

182 A family affair

build positive self-identity. In doing so, parents are setting them up for greater success throughout their lives than if they have been told that their way of experiencing and interacting with the world is somehow 'wrong'. For any parents of neurodivergent children, we highly recommend looking at the LEANS materials (links in the Recommended Reading List) to help with this. Running the whole programme in your living room might not be the answer, but thinking about the materials and the questions they raise is a good starting point for having those conversations.

Autistic fatherhood

It is worth noting, briefly, that the majority of work on autism and parenting is done with mothers – both mothers of autistic children and autistic mothers themselves, which can also be one and the same person. This is common in parenting research unless the researchers specifically set out to do work with fathers, and especially so in work around SEN. The general social trend for men to earn more than women means that when a child is born, mothers tend to be the ones who take on more of the childcare, and this means that they are the ones who respond to research requests about child rearing. When a child has a form of SEN, it is common for parents to become advocates on their behalf, and this happens for autistic children too. This is where the stereotype of the 'autism warrior mum' comes from – needing to fight for your child to be recognised and diagnosed, for appropriate support at school, for access to activities . . . and again, this tends to fall to mothers more than fathers.

The studies we have talked about, and most of our contributors who talked about parenting, were coming from the perspective of being mothers. There is, to date, no research we could find on the experiences of autistic fathers, although we know that there are likely to be lots of them out there. Autism tends to run in families, and studies looking at autistic traits in immediate relatives of autistic children (parents and siblings) have shown that parents of autistic children tend to have higher rates of autism traits – implying that some may be undiagnosed autistic people (De la Marche et al., 2012; Rubenstein & Chawla, 2018). The work which is out there at the moment is all about non-autistic fathers' experiences of parenting autistic children, particularly autistic sons. That's great, but means that we are missing insights from a group of people who are key in the lives of most autistic children. It also means that we know nothing about what it feels like to be an autistic father – which is just as transformational an experience as being an autistic mother, even if it doesn't come with the same biological processes.

Sarah has written some reflections on what she knows about how her brother Doug experienced being an autistic father. While this isn't the same, it is useful to at least start thinking about what it might mean for autistic men to be fathers – especially the ways in which, like autistic mothers, they can excel in the role.

Sarah's reflections on autistic fatherhood

My late brother Doug was an autistic father to two boys, one of whom is also autistic. He was a parent who supported his kids with their interests by becoming involved in them too. When the boys started developing an interest in swimming, Doug would volunteer and trained to be a life-saver so that he could spend time with them both, doing something that they loved. His character and interests were more aligned to those of his older son, and both attended the same university in Leicester, but he loved them equally and fully supported his younger son when he needed help during times of emotional and mental difficulty. Doug was fiercely protective of his family and he needed to be as when his eldest was diagnosed with autism and ADHD, they were harshly judged by our father and other family members, who considered the root of their difficulties to be down to bad parenting and behaviour. Like me, Doug chose to be a very different parent to the ones we had. Of course, neither of us were perfect parents, and any child-parent relationship fluctuates, but Doug chose to be a supportive and hands-on father in a way that was largely opposite to what he had experienced growing up.

Sibling relationships over time

Just as we mentioned in the Early Family Relationships chapter, siblings are important people in the lives of those who have them, and that generally doesn't change as people grow into adults. Your siblings are still among the people who have known you longest, and in many cases, among the people who know you best, and they have insights into the way you were brought up and how they shaped you into who you are today which can be invaluable. While there can be all sorts of pressures on siblings in adulthood which affect the relationship, adult siblings are more likely to garner support from each other in the face of family challenges than they are to become distant. Obviously, this does not mean that those who do become distant are somehow wrong or lacking – we are not making that value judgement – because family is often complicated and this can be the right thing for people's well-being.

As children move into adolescence from childhood, they tend to spend less time together, and each sibling becomes more like their friends than their brother or sister – their main identity and behavioural influence shifts to being their peers, whose opinions teenagers care about intensely, rather than their family, who we (generally) assume will stick around and like us regardless. This reduced time together does not automatically mean that siblings stop being important to each other, but ageing and adolescence brings in new factors. While sisters tend to rate their relationship as staying emotionally close in adolescence, brothers become more competitive with

184 A family affair

each other – just as they become more competitive with peers during this period. Interestingly, in late childhood and early adolescence opposite-gender siblings tend to say that they are the least close, but this changes as both children get older they get closer and closer with age (Kim et al., 2006). As each child becomes more secure in their own identity, likes, dislikes, and behaviours, it tends to be easier for them to feel that they are not in competition and therefore they can build strong bonds to carry them into adulthood.

A lot of the research into non-autistic sibling relationships in adulthood happened in the 1980s and 1990s, so although we have tried to reference more recent work, some of it is pretty old. What the research has found though, largely, is what is called "U shaped curve" to sibling relationships over the lifespan. What this means is that things like proximity, contact, help, and closeness tend to be high when people are young, decrease significantly in early adulthood, levels are maintained in middle adulthood, then start to increase again into older adulthood (White, 2001). Interestingly, although most people report talking to their siblings much less in adulthood – essentially once the elder sibling moves out of the home – there seems to be a shift towards more meaningful conversations when they do happen, so overall closeness ratings do not decline in the same way for sibling pairs born more recently, possibly because of the increase in communicative technologies available to them (Hamwey et al., 2018; Milevsky, 2019).

Unsurprisingly, adult siblings who are emotionally and geographically closer see or talk to each other more often than those who are more distant in both senses – a similar pattern to what we see in adult friendships (Lee et al., 1990). This is because a lot of sibling relationships in adulthood move to being more like chosen friends than we see in childhood and adolescence, because each person is living independently and has more choice in whether they have an active relationship, or any relationship at all.

Another factor which influences the long-term closeness of siblings in adulthood is gender. In the West, women are generally the 'kin-keepers' within a family, that is, they are the ones who maintain family relationships as older generations pass on – the ones who sent birthday and holiday cards, who organise family get-togethers, and who remember the names and jobs of all the cousins and their partners. This tends to result in sister–sister siblings being closer and more helpful to each other than brothers or mixed siblings (Connidis & Campbell, 1995). However, one study in Taiwan found the opposite, that brother–brother dyads tend to be the most helpful for each other (Lu, 2007). Cultural differences in family migration patterns and kinship norms are important, both at the macro (Taiwan vs UK) and micro (family to family) level – but across all contexts, getting on with your sibling better predicts more contact and more help.

This doesn't mean that adult sibling relationships are all sunshine and rainbows however. Many adult siblings do not have close and helpful relationships, and some effectively – or actively – cut off communication. Difficult or non-existent adult sibling relationships have been explored in the context of the LGBTQ community (which many autistic people are part of, as discussed in Chapter 4: Teenage

Dreams). Sibling relationships for this group – and probably any group where there are major identity differences between siblings – fell into three categories. First was *solidary*, where the relationship was strong and warm; second was *conflictual*, where the relationship existed but was difficult in some way; and third was *tangential*, where the sibling bond was not really present any more, either because the sibling did not accept their identity or because they had both built lives independent of each other and lost their connection (Reczek et al., 2022).

Each of these categories of relationships with siblings, or at least family members in general, can be seen in our contributors' conversations with us. Warm relationships which fall into the *solidary* category:

> I'm friends with my sister. She's six and a half years younger than me. She's not autistic, but we get on, but we don't get on being in close confinement. The friendship I have with her is quite different to a lot of the friendships I have with people the same age as her, because she's not autistic, I think.
>
> *(Krysia, 30)*

But also ones which fall into *conflictual* and *tangential*, suggesting that having a neuro-minority identity can lead to sibling conflict in a similar way to having a minority sexual identity. For example:

> I've gone for years without speaking to either of my brothers and it's not because there is anything bad between us it's just none of us is particularly attuned to meet or keep up contact.
>
> *(anonymous, male)*

> My brother is neurotypical and you will never have come across a more nasty or cruel little shit in your life. He literally takes delight in hurting people.
>
> *(anonymous)*

Between autistic and non-autistic adult siblings, the relationship is often defined by mixed feelings – just as we discussed for childhood sibling relationships. The factors which contribute to these mixed feelings are similar to those from childhood as well – teenage siblings report warmer and closer relationships when the autistic sibling displays fewer behavioural symptoms and outbursts, something which continues into adulthood relationships too. Equally, the more supportive parents are within the family, the better the sibling relationship is reported to be (Orsmond et al., 2009). This is possibly because more engaged and supportive parents reduce the 'parentification' of the non-autistic sibling, allowing them to have a more 'normal' sibling relationship.

A large-scale population survey from the United States asked the siblings of autistic adults and the siblings of adults with Down's syndrome about their sibling relationship and their own health and depression. What it found was that for both groups, the level of contact between the siblings decreased with age, especially once the neurodivergent sibling was over 45. It also found that the siblings of autistic

186 A family affair

adults felt that they were less close and had a less warm relationship with their sibling than did the siblings of those with Down's syndrome – although the key mediating factor in this was how 'good at' maintaining friendships their neurodivergent sibling was (Hodapp & Urbano, 2007). This suggests that what matters most is the reciprocity in a sibling relationship, rather than something about either brother or sister as an individual – perfectly in line with the predictions which arise from the Double Empathy Theory about how autistic and non-autistic people interact.

What has been highlighted as important to autistic/non-autistic sibling relationships as well as these two-way interactions are the attitudes non-autistic siblings have towards autism, autistic people, and their autistic sibling specifically. The more positive the attitudes held by the non-autistic sibling, the more support they gave to their autistic adult sibling, as well as rating their own life satisfaction more highly, with lower levels of stress and depression (Tomeny et al., 2017). This may be because those who feel more positively towards a sibling they are helping find giving this support less burdensome, and therefore are happier with their life including this supportive role. Interestingly, an earlier study had shown that non-autistic sisters of autistic girls and women had the most positive attitudes and warmth towards their autistic sisters, whereas non-autistic men had the least positive attitudes and feelings about their autistic sisters (with attitudes towards autistic brothers falling in the middle). Non-autistic adult siblings were also more likely to spend time in shared activities with their autistic brother or sister if the autistic person was younger than them (Orsmond et al., 2009) – possibly because in this dynamic the older sibling has always been aware of and able to account for their autistic sibling's needs in a way that younger siblings tend not to do for their older brothers and sisters. Indeed, when interviewed about having an autistic sibling, non-autistic siblings specifically talk about the ways in which they adapt their behaviours and expectations to account for and support and include their autistic brother or sister (Angell et al., 2012), and by adulthood these siblings have a lifetime of practice at how to do this effectively to maintain a warmer and more involved sibling relationship.

A 2007 review paper on the relationships of autistic/non-autistic siblings over the lifespan found that the research up to that date suggested positive and negative aspects to the sibling relationship in childhood, but that adult sibling relationships were characterised by a lack of closeness and some resentment of caring responsibilities among non-autistic siblings (Davys et al., 2011; Orsmond & Seltzer, 2007). This may arise from the 'parentification' of the non-autistic sibling from early in life, assuming caring responsibilities in childhood to try to help their parents and reduce the challenges of looking after an autistic child which can then continue into adulthood (Egan & Walsh, 2001). This can result in the non-autistic sibling having positive outcomes, such as being more mature and feeling positive about their ability to help care for their sibling (Cridland et al., 2015), but there can also be feelings of guilt when the non-autistic sibling leaves home to start their independent lives (Tozer et al., 2013). The social support the non-autistic sibling receives broadly moderates the distress which parentification causes them; those adult siblings who recalled getting a lot of social support, and whose parentification focussed on caring for their sibling, reported much less distress than those who had low levels of support and whose parentification focussed on caring for their parents (while their parents cared for their sibling) (Tomeny et al., 2016). The less distress the adult non-autistic siblings felt around their caring role for their autistic brother or sister, partially because of that social support, the more positive and warm they felt towards their sibling and the better their relationship overall. Understandably, this leads to complex and mixed feelings within the sibling relationship, on both sides, which explains the different findings from different studies on the topic.

Parental relationships in adulthood

The other relationships which do not stay the same as we age are those with our parents. The increased independence, and the building of new relationships and families which do not have them at the centre, shifts the tone. Generally, this results in more equality between adult children and their parents. These changes start in adolescence, as children demand and are slowly given more freedom, until in adulthood, most parents recognise that their children are their equals – although there can be a lot of conflict and negotiation along the way! There are three generally recognised ways in which adult child–parent relationships develop. The first is *normative*, where that independence process happens relatively smoothly, with a warm, positive, and relatively equal relationship being the outcome. The second is *increasingly negative*, where over time the adult child and their parent/s become more and more hostile towards each other, with a relationship defined by aggression and unpleasant interactions. The third is *distancing*, in which case as children become adults, they have reduced interactions with their parents – either consciously or through broader circumstances – and neither party works to maintain a close relationship for whatever reason (Sieffge et al., 2010). There are obviously a huge range of factors which go into deciding which of these patterns any individual and their parents end up in, but things like warm and responsive parenting in childhood are more likely to result in the normative pattern, whereas highly authoritative or controlling parenting may be more likely to result in either increasingly negative or even distancing relationships. Adult children have the option of ceasing communication with parents who are disapproving, manipulative, or abusive, and many choose this path rather than maintain painful relationships once they have the autonomy to do so.

Ageing parents of autistic children

There is another side to parenting which gets talked about a lot in the world of autism, though less so by autistic people – the phenomenon of parents of autistic children (and adults) who are getting older themselves. It is, of course, normal and natural for parents to age – time happens that way to everyone, except maybe Doctor Who and Doc from Back to the Future. The thing is, for parents of autistic people with a high level of need, that process can feel especially difficult. This is because they

188 A family affair

are aware of the fact that they are going to become less able to look after a child who depends on them long past the point at which children usually become independent.

Parents of autistic children with high levels of support need are understandably concerned about what will happen to their children in the part of their future where the parents are not around. Many autistic children will never live 'independently' in the way society normally thinks about independent adulthood, and this can lead parents to want to make decisions far in advance, while being aware of the fact that they can't actually predict exactly what support their child will need in five, ten, twenty, or forty years' time (Marsack-Topolewski & Graves, 2020). Parents often feel that there is a lack of structure to what they can expect for their child's future, with not much clarity about what their child will be able to access once they are gone.

One of the major sources of reassurance parents talk about consistently in the research is their social networks. Friends, family, and support groups make a huge difference to their well-being and therefore their ability to look after their children, often more so than formal services do (Hines et al., 2013). It isn't all easy and positive, obviously. Some parents experience social exclusion because of the care needs and practical demands of looking after their child, which can mean they aren't able to attend social events, or because of the stigmatisation they and their child face from people in their networks (Marsack & Perry, 2018). Despite this, many parents talk about the joy and pride that comes with being the parent of an adult autistic child, seeing their growth and enjoying the times they spend together – and how this, along with the connections they have, gives them hope for the future as well.

Parental care

The other way in which parental relationships change significantly over time is the shift from the parents being *carers* to *cared for*. This is a very normal part of the ageing process within a family dynamic, but that does not necessarily make it emotionally easier for anyone involved. For the parent, finding themselves in need of help can be disturbing, undermining a long-held identity as the person who looks after other people and who sorts things out for themselves. This can make it hard for them to even admit to needing help, or lead to them being irritated when they are forced to accept it. Equally, for the adult child, this role reversal can feel just as discomforting, as they are faced with the reality of their parents ageing and the implications of their mortality that come with it. Alongside these existential aspects of parental care, the practicalities of looking after parents, often at the same time as caring for not only yourself but partners, children, and pets.

Daughters are more likely to take on this caring role than sons, especially when mothers are the ones who need care. This is hardly surprising, considering the gendered nature of care work overall, both inside and outside the home. How this caring role goes over time is hugely impacted by the wider family relationships, as the more supported daughters feel in their caring role, the better their relationship with the parent they are caring for as well as their own mental health being better. Sibling relationships can be important in this scenario, as these are the people who would naturally be expected to share parental care (as they are equally related to the parent needing care, in most cases). It has been shown, though, that characteristics of family dynamics from decades earlier have significant impacts on parental care. For example, when childhood sibling relationships were warm and supportive, adult siblings are better at agreeing on care for their ageing parents, for example what kind of care is needed and how to share responsibility. When childhood relationships were more negative, or there was a lot of parental favouritism, the result was a much more difficult and argumentative process in making care decisions (Woolley & Grief, 2021). This is just one more example of the ways in which early relationships have sometimes unexpected consequences even decades later – and why we need to think about building positive relationships of all kinds for autistic children and young people from as early as possible.

Autism, ageing parent relationships, and parental care

There are precisely zero papers published about autistic experiences of parental relationships or parental care as the parents of autistic people become elderly. As in many other sections where there is a lack of research evidence, we can make some educated guesses about how this can affect autistic people – and some of our contributors were able to share their own experiences. For some, caring for ageing or unwell parents was the first time they felt able to build a genuine relationship with them. For example:

> Part of the reason I moved back to London wasn't just to look after him, but to get to know him a bit better. He led an interesting life, but I felt I learned more about it from his 70th birthday celebrations and then his funeral than I ever learned from him. Every now and then some fascinating snippet from his life would come up.
>
> *(Fergus, 44, autistic adult)*

> I had a very stormy relationship with my mother growing up and yet she was very unwell for a couple of years before she died and I feel absolutely privileged that I was able to care for her in her last few years and we were lucky enough to be able to really heal the relationship from the past.
>
> *(anonymous, 54, autistic woman)*

The positive sides of being able to care for an ageing or terminally ill parent were raised by several of those who had gone through this experience, as in the preceding quote. There is value in being able to make the most of the time you know you have left with someone, and in being able to support them to do what they want to with that time, which transcends neurotype:

> It was frustrating that I couldn't get up to see her as much as I'd liked when she was still in good health. A bit less than a year after she moved we learned that she had pancreatic cancer. . . . I was able to get compassionate leave and was there for most of her last few months and it was enough

190 A family affair

time for Dinah to say goodbye to everyone basically and spend a bit of time with many of the people that she was close to. A lot of people came to visit and she made it down to London for a last visit there. She got to see Monotropism taking hold and there was new research regularly being published that mentioned Monotropism. She felt like she got to see her life's work realised.

(Fergus, 44, autistic adult)

The practical challenges of coordinating care for a parent are likely a bit more difficult for autistic people who have difficulties with executive functioning, as this is a central aspect of organising support. Fergus specifically mentioned this in the context of caring for his mother, Dinah Murray (the brilliant woman who created the Monotropism theory):

In a lot of ways we're very alike, including various ways in which I wish that we weren't, like a total inability to deal with any paperwork.

(Fergus, 44, autistic adult)

It may also be that the requirement to make multiple phone calls to organise healthcare, or communicate with residential settings (often not the most technologically advanced institutions) can be anxiety inducing. The rollercoaster of caring for an elderly or unwell parent can be overwhelming, which is hard to process for anyone but especially autistic people who need extra time to work through their emotions. There are myriad other ways caring for ageing parents is complicated for autistic people, and we need more work to understand these experiences and support people through this potentially complicated and difficult time.

Equally, the ways in which parents developed over time into their later years caused some deep reflections for many of our contributors. For some, this meant re-evaluating their own lives and seeking help with their mental health or seeking an autism diagnosis:

I didn't want to turn into my mother. My mother in her late seventies early eighties has become excessively anxious, lacking in confidence, very, very afraid of everything. When she answered the phone it was with panic and fear and I didn't want to be like that so I wanted to get to the root of what was causing me so much anxiety.

(anonymous, 62, autistic woman)

For others, it led to reconsidering their family history and being able to identify patterns of autistic behaviour between the generations, which explained things about the way they had been brought up:

As I look back down through the family, autism absolutely runs down the female line. In hindsight we had a shared experience of being autistic. We both understood and expected some very unconventional behaviour in the family and from each other.

(anonymous, 54, autistic woman)

In my mind, my parents are both autistic and would be assessed as autistic. My mother told me about her childhood and her best friend was a rabbit. She would invite friends' round and then say, "let's read our books", like I did. Then there's the attraction between her and my dad could have been because they were velcroing on to each other.

(anonymous, 62, autistic woman)

These kinds of reflections are important for autistic adults, as they help to contextualise your own life experiences and what may have been the root cause of many difficult or traumatic events. Having this kind of explanatory power can help to mitigate some of the associated pain, just as getting an autism diagnosis can help to explain some of the things a person goes through and give them insights into themselves.

Parental death

Sadly, after the period of caring for elderly parents, there is the inevitability of them dying. This, obviously, has a huge impact on anyone who experiences it, with associated grief and an ongoing sense of loss which often changes over time, but does not really go away.

The majority of research into experiences of, and responses to, parental death look at the impact of a parent dying when someone is a child or teenager. Unsurprisingly, the studies find that this is almost always a traumatic experience for the young person, with negative impacts on their emotional and personal development, and it is associated with worse mental health, worse educational achievement, and poorer relationships well into adulthood.

Luckily, the majority of us do not lose a parent this young, and it is much more common for our parents to be with us into our middle and older adulthood. This means that people tend to have built other support networks who can help them to navigate their grief and the simple practicalities associated with a death, such as funeral arrangements. Indeed, it has been shown that generally, the older someone is when their parent dies (being middle aged vs being an adolescent or young adult, for example), then the less negative the impact is on them. Equally, being married or having a strong group of friends and family relationships also mitigates some of the negative impact (Hayslip et al., 2015). That doesn't mean there is no negative impact, obviously, but that it tends to be easier to cope with overall.

As with many of the relationships and experiences we have talked about in this book, there is also a gendered aspect to going through parental loss. Men tend to be more affected by the loss of their fathers, and women more by the loss of their mothers – and men tend to show more physical symptoms in reaction to this loss than women do (Marks et al., 2007). Alcohol consumption tends to increase following

192 A family affair

parental death, particularly for men. This is a common coping response to all kinds of difficult situations across the (adult) lifespan – although not necessarily a healthy one, if done in excess and for a long time – so it shouldn't be surprising to see that in the literature. There may be a particular risk around alcohol and drinking for autistic adults in the time period following parental death though, as the 'numbing' effect of being tipsy or drunk may feel like it is helping to avoid processing difficult emotions, and therefore it may be more likely for excessive drinking to be maintained longer-term than for non-autistic people. We'll emphasise that this is just our speculation though, and there have been no studies on this – there are very few studies on autistic people's experiences with alcohol full stop, if we're honest!

Talking about parental ageing, and thinking about what that means logically, Rose reflected that:

> I suspect that I'm going to have some difficulty when my parents die because there is a lot of unfinished business there. Bereavement has never been easy for me to deal with at all. Not my dog, my ex, even someone I knew well at work who died unexpectedly in his twenties, it always is a phenomenally difficult thing for me to handle so I'm wondering how that's going to be.
>
> *(anonymous, 62, autistic woman)*

Humans are not generally good at dealing with death – often because the death of someone close to us reminds us that we, personally, are also not immortal, which is an uncomfortable thought. For autistic people, the death of a parent not only brings those kinds of existential reflections, but is a significant and irreversible change to the make-up of their social world. For most of us, our parents are the people who have known us the longest, who are our most stable relationship, and are the ones who understand us incredibly well. Losing that is deeply emotionally upsetting, and can be disruptive to the patterns of our lives – both of which are things which autistic people can struggle to cope with. Unfortunately, we have no 'evidence' as to whether that is the case from research, but the following excerpt from 'Heavy Weather' by Fergus Murray, reflects on his grief of losing his mother, Dinah, last year.

> It's just over a year since we learned my mum probably had pancreatic cancer, and more than seven months since it killed her. She lived a good life, and died a pretty good death as far as that goes, but a death is a death, and the death of a beloved parent is perhaps the hardest kind. I miss her a lot. So it goes.

When it comes to research about autistic experiences of parental death, there is also nothing. Instead, when you type 'autism parent grief' into Google Scholar, what you get back is thousands of search results focussed on parents who feel 'grief' when they find out that their child is autistic (plus a handful about supporting autistic children through grief). That is both very sad, and not what we are trying to write about, but is worth noting as a phenomenon. Parents are obviously allowed

A family affair **193**

to feel whatever comes naturally, and to take time processing those emotions, but for anyone reading this who is going through that at the moment – please remember that your child is still here, and very much not dead, and there is lots of joy among the challenges that you are currently facing or are anticipating facing. Please join some support groups, either in your local area or online, and find some of the more positive information that is out there, and ways to support you and your child to have the best and happiest times together that you can.

Parental death and sibling relationships

The loss of either parent, or both parents, has a significant impact on overall family dynamics, and often kicks off a period of major change and reorganisation of relationships for those still living. Just as with parental care, where siblings often share responsibilities, after parental death siblings are generally the ones left to support each other, and whose relationship continues.

Because the sibling relationship is the one which persists, there has been more research into the impact of parental death on siblings. A very recent study found that the loss of the first parent, regardless of whether it was a mother or father, led to an 'intensification' of siblings' relationships with each other and with their surviving parent – they had more frequent contacts and became emotionally closer (Hank, 2021). This is in line with earlier (though still fairly recent) research, where nearly 70 people in middle adulthood who lost a parent were interviewed about what this had done to their sibling relationships (Greif & Woolley, 2015). In this study, it was clear that for those siblings who had a relationship which was already at least neutral or vaguely positive, they tended to become closer after parental death, with a feeling of it being 'just us now'. However, for those who had a more difficult prior relationship with their sibling/s, or where settling things after the parent died was contentious, for example over the will, parental death could make their relationship worse or mean that they had now lost the one thing still keeping them in contact.

Unsurprisingly, there is no research specifically on what parental death does to sibling relationships in adulthood when one or more of the siblings are autistic. This is, once again, an important area of people's life-long relationships which we simply know nothing about, and because of the lower average life expectancy for autistic people (which we discuss in detail in the next chapter), there are relatively few autistic adults available to share their first-hand experiences. Hopefully, that will change over time, both with improved healthcare for autistic people meaning that more autistic adults live into old age, and with greater recognition of the importance of understanding these experiences through research.

Chapter conclusion

Families are complicated, and that complexity does not go away as everyone grows up and becomes adults. It shifts and changes, and there tend to be more options for how a family is 'formatted', as such, but family is still there and usually still of

194 A family affair

central importance to people's lives. This is a part of life where so much happens, which impacts people in so many ways, and yet relatively little is still known. We know it sounds like a stuck record, but we really need more people to share their experiences, and for more researchers to focus on these parts of autistic people's lives, in order to build support and understanding with something which, after all, covers most of the lifespan and some of our most impactful connections.

References

Adams, D., Stainsby, M., & Paynter, J. (2021). Autistic mothers of autistic children: A preliminary study in an under-researched area. *Autism in Adulthood*, *3*(4), 339–346. https://doi.org/10.1089/AUT.2020.0078

Almeida, M., Shrestha, A. D., Stojanac, D., & Miller, L. J. (2020). The impact of the COVID-19 pandemic on women's mental health. *Archives of Women's Mental Health*, *23*(6), 741–748. https://doi.org/10.1007/S00737-020-01092-2

Angell, M. E., Meadan, H., & Stoner, J. B. (2012). Experiences of siblings of individuals with autism spectrum disorders. *Autism Research and Treatment*, 1–11. https://doi.org/10.1155/2012/949586

Chu, K. A., Schwartz, C., Towner, E., Kasparian, N. A., & Callaghan, B. (2021). Parenting under pressure: A mixed-methods investigation of the impact of COVID-19 on family life. *Journal of Affective Disorders Reports*, *5*, 100161. https://doi.org/10.1016/J.JADR.2021.100161

Connidis, I. A., & Campbell, L. D. (1995). Closeness, confiding, and contact among siblings in middle and late adulthood. *Journal of Family Issues*, *16*(6), 722–745. https://doi.org/10.1177/019251395016006003

Crane, L., Lui, L. M., Davies, J., & Pellicano, E. (2021). Autistic parents' views and experiences of talking about autism with their autistic children. *Autism*, *25*(4), 1161–1167. https://doi.org/10.1177/1362361320981317

Cridland, E. K., Jones, S. C., Stoyles, G., Caputi, P., & Magee, C. A. (2015). Families living with autism spectrum disorder, *Focus on Autism and Other Developmental Disabilities*, *31*(3), 196–207. https://doi.org/10.1177/1088357615583466

Davys, D., Mitchell, D., & Haigh, C. (2011). Adult sibling experience, roles, relationships and future concerns – A review of the literature in learning disabilities. *Journal of Clinical Nursing*, *20*(19–20), 2837–2853. https://doi.org/10.1111/J.1365-2702.2010.03530.X

De La Marche, W., Noens, I., Luts, J., Scholte, E., Van Huffel, S., & Steyaert, J. (2012). Quantitative autism traits in first degree relatives: Evidence for the broader autism phenotype in fathers, but not in mothers and siblings. *Autism*, *16*(3), 247–260. https://doi.org/10.1177/1362361311421776

Dugdale, A. S., Thompson, A. R., Leedham, A., Beail, N., & Freeth, M. (2021). Intense connection and love: The experiences of autistic mothers. *Autism*, *25*(7), 1973–1984. https://doi.org/10.1177/13623613211005987

Egan, J., & Walsh, P. N. (2012). Sources of stress among adult siblings of irish people with intellectual disability. *New Pub: Psychological Society of Ireland*, *22*(1), 28–38. https://doi.org/10.1080/03033910.2001.10558261

Fletcher-Randle, J. E. (2022). Where are all the autistic parents? A thematic analysis of autistic parenting discourse within the narrative of parenting and autism in online media. *Studies in Social Justice*, *16*(2), 389–406. https://doi.org/10.26522/SSJ.V16I2.2701

Grant, A., Jones, S., Williams, K., Leigh, J., & Brown, A. (2022). Autistic women's views and experiences of infant feeding: A systematic review of qualitative evidence. *Autism*, https://doi.org/10.1177/13623613221089374

Greif, G., & Woolley, M. (2015). Adult sibling relationships. In *Adult Sibling Relationships.* Columbia University Press.

Hampton, S., Allison, C., Baron-Cohen, S., & Holt, R. (2022). Autistic people's perinatal experiences II: A survey of childbirth and postnatal experiences. *Journal of Autism and Developmental Disorders,* 1–15. https://doi.org/10.1007/S10803-022-05484-4/TABLES/6

Hampton, S., Man, J., Allison, C., Aydin, E., Baron-Cohen, S., & Holt, R. (2021). A qualitative exploration of autistic mothers' experiences II: Childbirth and postnatal experiences. *Autism : The International Journal of Research and Practice,* 13623613211043700. https://doi.org/10.1177/13623613211043701

Hamwey, M. K., Rolan, E. P., Jensen, A. C., & Whiteman, S. D. (2018). Absence makes the heart grow fonder: A qualitative examination of sibling relationships during emerging adulthood. *Journal of Social and Personal Relationships, 36*(8), 2487–2506. https://doi.org/10.1177/0265407518789514

Hank, K. (2021). Linked in life and death: A note on the effect of parental death on sibling relations in young and middle adulthood. *Journal of Family Issues, 42*(11), 2679–2690. https://doi.org/10.1177/0192513X20985566

Harmens, M., Sedgewick, F., & Hobson, H. (2022). The quest for acceptance: A blog-based study of autistic women's experiences and well-being during autism identification and diagnosis. *Autism in Adulthood, 4*(1), 42–51. https://doi.org/10.1089/AUT.2021.0016

Hayslip, B., Pruett, J. H., & Caballero, D. M. (2015). The "how" and "when" of parental loss in adulthood: Effects on grief and adjustment. *Omega (United States), 71*(1), 3–18. https://doi.org/10.1177/0030222814568274

Heyworth, M., Brett, S., Houting, J. den, Magiati, I., Steward, R., Urbanowicz, A., Stears, M., & Pellicano, E. (2022). I'm the family ringmaster and juggler: Autistic parents experiences of parenting during the COVID-19 pandemic. https://doi.org/10.1089/AUT.2021.0097

Hines, M., Balandin, S., & Togher, L. (2014). The stories of older parents of adult sons and daughters with autism: A balancing act. *Journal of Applied Research in Intellectual Disabilities, 27*(2), 163–173. https://doi.org/10.1111/JAR.12063

Hodapp, R. M., & Urbano, R. C. (2007). Adult siblings of individuals with down syndrome versus with autism: Findings from a large-scale US survey. *Journal of Intellectual Disability Research, 51*(12), 1018–1029. https://doi.org/10.1111/J.1365-2788.2007.00994.X

Kim, J. Y., McHale, S. M., Osgood, D. W., & Crouter, A. C. (2006). Longitudinal course and family correlates of sibling relationships from childhood through adolescence. *Child Development, 77*(6), 1746–1761. https://doi.org/10.1111/J.1467-8624.2006.00971.X

Lee, T. R., Mancini, J. A., & Maxwell, J. W. (1990). Sibling relationships in adulthood: Contact patterns and motivations. *Journal of Marriage and the Family, 52*(2), 431. https://doi.org/10.2307/353037

Lu, P. C. (2007). Sibling relationships in adulthood and old age: A case study of taiwan. *Current Sociology, 55*(4), 621–637. https://doi.org/10.1177/0011392107077646

Marks, N. F., Jun, H., & Song, J. (2007). Death of parents and adult psychological and physical well-being: A prospective U.S. National Study. *Journal of Family Issues, 28*(12), 1611–1638. https://doi.org/10.1177/0192513X07302728

Marsack, C. N., & Perry, T. E. (2018). Aging in place in every community: Social exclusion experiences of parents of adult children with autism spectrum disorder. *Research on Aging, 40*(6), 535–557. https://doi.org/10.1177/0164027517717044

Marsack, C. N., & Wilson, K. P. (2020). Coping strategies used by aging parental caregivers of adults with autism spectrum disorder. *Families in Society, 102*(1), 119–132. https://doi.org/10.1177/1044389420913121

McDonnell, C. G., & Delucia, E. A. (2021). Pregnancy and parenthood among autistic adults: Implications for advancing maternal health and parental well-being. *Autism in Adulthood, 3*(1), 100–115. https://doi.org/10.1089/AUT.2020.0046

196 A family affair

Milevsky, A. (2019). Sibling dynamics in adulthood: A qualitative analysis. *Marriage and Family Review*, *56*(2), 91–108. https://doi.org/10.1080/01494929.2019.1655127

Orsmond, G. I., Kuo, H. Y., & Seltzer, M. M. (2009). Siblings of individuals with an autism spectrum disorder: Sibling relationships and wellbeing in adolescence and adulthood. *Autism*, *13*(1), 59–80. https://doi.org/10.1177/1362361308097119

Orsmond, G. I., & Seltzer, M. M. (2007). Siblings of individuals with autism spectrum disorders across the life course. *Mental Retardation and Developmental Disabilities Research Reviews*, *13*(4), 313–320. https://doi.org/10.1002/MRDD.20171

Pohl, A. L., Crockford, S. K., Blakemore, M., Allison, C., & Baron-Cohen, S. (2020). A comparative study of autistic and non-autistic women's experience of motherhood. *Molecular Autism*, *11*(1), 1–12. https://doi.org/10.1186/S13229-019-0304-2/TABLES/10

Reczek, R., Stacey, L., & Dunston, C. (2022). Friend, foe, or forget 'em?: The quality of LGBTQ adult sibling relationships. *Journal of Marriage and Family*, *84*(2), 415–437. https://doi.org/10.1111/JOMF.12821

Rogers, C., Lepherd, L., Ganguly, R., & Jacob-Rogers, S. (2017). Perinatal issues for women with high functioning autism spectrum disorder. *Women and Birth*, *30*(2), 89–95. https://doi.org/10.1016/J.WOMBI.2016.09.009

Rubenstein, E., & Chawla, D. (2018). Broader autism phenotype in parents of children with autism: A systematic review of percentage estimates. *Journal of Child and Family Studies*, *27*(6), 1705–1720. https://doi.org/10.1007/S10826-018-1026-3/FIGURES/2

Samuel, P., Yew, R. Y., Hooley, M., Hickey, M., & Stokes, M. A. (2022). Sensory challenges experienced by autistic women during pregnancy and childbirth: A systematic review. *Archives of Gynecology and Obstetrics*, *305*(2), 299–311. https://doi.org/10.1007/S00404-021-06109-4/TABLES/2

Seiffge-Krenke, I., Overbeek, G., & Vermulst, A. (2010). Parent – child relationship trajectories during adolescence: Longitudinal associations with romantic outcomes in emerging adulthood. *Journal of Adolescence*, *33*(1), 159–171. https://doi.org/10.1016/J.ADOLESCENCE.2009.04.001

Talcer, M. C., Duffy, O., & Pedlow, K. (2021). A qualitative exploration into the sensory experiences of autistic mothers. *Journal of Autism and Developmental Disorders*, 1–16. https://doi.org/10.1007/S10803-021-05188-1/FIGURES/1

Tomeny, T. S., Barry, T. D., & Fair, E. C. (2016). Parentification of adult siblings of individuals with autism spectrum disorder: Distress, sibling relationship attitudes, and the role of social support. *Journal of Intellectual & Developmental Disability*, *42*(4), 320–331. https://doi.org/10.3109/13668250.2016.1248376

Tomeny, T. S., Ellis, B. M., Rankin, J. A., & Barry, T. D. (2017). Sibling relationship quality and psychosocial outcomes among adult siblings of individuals with autism spectrum disorder and individuals with intellectual disability without autism. *Research in Developmental Disabilities*, *62*, 104–114. https://doi.org/10.1016/J.RIDD.2017.01.008

Tozer, R., Atkin, K., & Wenham, A. (2013). Continuity, commitment and context: Adult siblings of people with autism plus learning disability. *Health & Social Care in the Community*, *21*(5), 480–488. https://doi.org/10.1111/HSC.12034

White, L. (2001). Sibling relationships over the life course: A panel analysis. *Journal of Marriage and Family*, *63*(2), 555–568. https://doi.org/10.1111/J.1741-3737.2001.00555.X

Woolley, M. E., & Greif, G. L. (2021). Adult sibling relationships in the United States: Mostly close, occasionally contentious, and caring for ageing parents. *Brothers and Sisters*, 205–221. https://doi.org/10.1007/978-3-030-55985-4_12

Zener, D. (2019). Journey to diagnosis for women with autism. *Advances in Autism*, *5*(1), 2–13. https://doi.org/10.1108/AIA-10-2018-0041/FULL/PDF

8

GETTING OLDER

Older adulthood

Of all the autistic people in the world, autistic elderly people (often referred to online as autistic elders) are among the least researched, least listened to, and the least understood.

There have been calls from the autism community for proper, methodical, meaningful research into autism and ageing since 2015, when a powerful editorial was published in the journal *Autism* by Cos Michael, an autistic campaigner (Michael, 2016). In that piece, Cos wrote about the fears and anxieties of autistic people and their families as they age, facing elderly care which not only does not support them, but often does not even consider or acknowledge that autistic people exist in their settings. The challenges associated with non-autistic ageing all apply to autistic people as well – physical health issues, increasing frailty, decreasing independence, a reliance on others for daily living care, difficulty understanding and accessing new technologies which become essential to navigating the world around you, isolation. . . . Currently, we know very little about how autistic people experience these aspects of growing older.

But we also know very little about what happens to people's autism as they age either. Autism is a lifelong neurodevelopmental disorder – and there is no reason to assume that it is in some way 'fixed' and static after the age of 18, or 25, or 40, or 60. The thing is, nobody has yet studied what happens to autistic traits, sensory sensitivities, or much else when autistic people get older. For someone who has been confident and comfortable in the routines of their working life, what does retirement do to your sense of self and your ability to get through the day? For someone who develops cancer, or dementia, or other illnesses common in older age, what are the experiences of treatment or care like? How does being autistic change those experiences? If you have had one set of familiar sensory sensitivities your whole adult life, do these change with age (as taste buds may do for non-autistic people)? And if they do, again, what does that do to someone's

DOI: 10.4324/9781003044536-9

198 Getting older

understanding of their interactions with the world? There are so many questions without answers about autism and ageing.

The historical bias towards research with autistic children understandably excluded people over the age of 18, which older people definitely are. As this childhood bias has started to be rectified in recent years, there has been an explosion of research into the experiences of autistic adolescents, emerging adults, and adults – but the majority of participants are still under the age of 50. Indeed, only 2% of all autism research includes people over the age of 55, and most of those studies are not focussing on the specific experiences of older people, they simply don't exclude them.

Now many of you will be thinking "Hang on you two! 55? Older people? Don't be ridiculous!" And it is true, at 55 most people are still looking forward to another decade of work, and a couple of decades of life at least. Hardly old-aged.

Unfortunately, this is not always the case for autistic people. The average life expectancy for an autistic person, according to the latest high-quality population-level data, is **54**.

Take that in for a second.

As things stand, the average autistic person can expect to live to just 54 years old. Thirty years less than non-autistic people.

That's no age. That's people not seeing their grandchildren born, not seeing their own children hit their thirties, not getting even close to retirement and spending more time with family or on their hobbies. It's decades of lost joy, and fun, and experiences, and connections, for a community that makes up roughly 1% of the global population.

It's heartbreaking.

So why is the average life expectancy so low?

The 54-years-old statistic encompasses all the autistic people in the (Swedish) population (Hirvikoski et al., 2016). This means that it includes those who have other conditions which are likely to reduce life expectancy, such as epilepsy, which was a common form of early death in the report – but this doesn't change the overall picture, because we know that epilepsy is a commonly co-occurring condition for autistic people, and this life expectancy is lower than for non-autistic people with epilepsy. This implies that there is something happening whereby autistic people are potentially getting less, or less effective, epilepsy treatment, leading to more and earlier deaths from complications associated with epileptic fits. A recent paper from a team of autistic researchers and healthcare professionals suggests why this may be. The team collected data from over 500 autistic adults (including those over 55, with the oldest participant being 73) about their experiences of primary healthcare, such as interactions with a GP. What came out of the study was that autistic people face a plethora of barriers to accessing healthcare – from difficulty working out whether they even needed to get an appointment for their issue, to difficulties with using the phone to book appointments (something also seen in Felicity's work on communication mode preferences of autistic people – Howard & Sedgewick, 2021), to delaying making an appointment because they felt misunderstood by healthcare professionals and therefore anxious about seeing them. Sensory issues due to the set-up of healthcare spaces were common, and these further impacted on autistic adult's ability to communicate their needs.

Alongside issues around planning, organising, and being able to predict (or not) how an appointment would go, many of the participants felt that they faced stigma from healthcare professionals and administrative staff, such as negative reactions to stimming, and this further made seeking help difficult (Doherty et al., 2022). These barriers to healthcare add up, and the paper also reported on the adverse consequences for autistic people on this front. Around two-thirds of all participants reported that they had gone without treatment for both physical and mental health conditions because of these barriers. Nearly half had not attended appointments where they had been referred on to a specialist to help them with their condition, and they were half as likely to take part in regular screening programmes such as cervical, breast, or prostate cancer screenings. It goes without saying that this means autistic people are potentially at higher risk of having cancers and other illnesses going unnoticed until they are more advanced, and indeed all of the barriers autistic people reported were associated with health outcomes which were worse than if those barriers had not been in place, including needing more intensive or invasive treatment once they did seek help. Multiply that effect across a whole population, especially one which is known to face more physical and mental health issues than the general population, and you start to see why life expectancy is lower. You can also see, however, that this is a reversible effect – if primary healthcare was made more accessible for autistic people, then they would be more likely to and effective in seeking help, and would receive treatment earlier, improving both their quality and quantity of life.

The other important side of the average life expectancy statistic which needs mentioning is that a higher-than-expected number of autistic people die by suicide, many of them before that average age. Mathematically, that brings the average life expectancy down. Outside the dry realm of numbers, this is another catastrophe of struggle and despair, grieving families, and lives which have been missed out on. A recent eye-opening review of over 1300 coroner's reports in cases of suicide found that nearly 11% of cases showed evidence of autism (either a diagnosis, or based on clinical or family reports), significantly higher than the 1.1% of the UK population who are autistic (Cassidy et al., 2022). What this means is that autistic people are about ten times more likely to complete suicide than we would expect if they were doing so at the rate we would expect for their prevalence in the population – a shocking statistic.

The risk of suicidal behaviours is much higher for autistic people without learning difficulties, and higher for autistic women than for autistic men (Hirvikoski et al., 2020). This is the opposite pattern to the non-autistic population, where men are more likely to complete suicide than women. Indeed, autistic women may be as many as 14 times more likely to complete suicide than non-autistic women,

200 Getting older

and seven times more likely than autistic men. In light of the existing bias against considering autism in girls and women generally, any professional supporting those who have attempted suicide or have suicidal ideation should also now be looking at including autism screenings in their evaluations, in order to fully understand the patient. Studies have shown that up to two-thirds of autistic people experience suicidal ideation at some point in their lives, and around one-third will make a suicide attempt (Hedley & Uljarevic, 2018), with more autistic people experiencing suicidal ideation than had depression – again, different to the non-autistic population (Cassidy & Rodgers, 2017). One very recent study specifically looked at self-harm and suicidality in older people (average age in the sample was 62) (Stewart et al., 2022). What it found was that adults with high levels of autistic traits were between five and six times more likely than people with low levels of autistic traits to self-harm, to experience suicidal ideation, and to have engaged in suicidal self-harm. This difference was true even when controlled for depression levels in the participants – so regardless of depression, high-trait people were still many times more likely to self-harm or be suicidal.

If that paragraph feels like one shocking, devastating statistic after another, that is because it is. It is only incredibly recently that we have started to really talk about and seek to understand suicide amongst autistic adults, and once we did it became apparent that the picture is much worse than anyone had previously suspected. We have included quotes elsewhere from interviewees who have experienced suicidal ideation, both as teenagers and adults, showing just how common this issue is. And often, those suicidal feelings are driven, or at least influenced by, the social experiences autistic people are having – a long way from the old picture of autistic people as lacking interest in, understanding of, or opinions on, their interactions and relationships with other people.

The good news is that there are people trying to find ways to improve the picture around autistic suicidality, designing better suicidality screening measures, tailored support for autistic people, and creating better ways of understanding autistic experiences which lead people to that point.

These factors all combine to create that 54-year life expectancy statistic. And while an average life expectancy is not the same as an absolute life expectancy – autistic people do not automatically drop dead on their 55th birthday – it has a significant impact on what we do, or even can, know about autism and ageing. If a significant proportion of the population aren't reaching what is considered old age, then obviously we cannot study what happens as autistic people become elderly in the same way as we can look at their childhood or adolescent experiences.

This phenomenon is called 'survivorship bias'. It means that we assume things based on the people who 'get through', rather than based on everyone who didn't. A famous example of this is the air force in World War II, who were looking to strengthen their planes and make them more likely to survive dogfights and make it home, crew safe and sound. Initially, they made a map of all the planes which made it home and looked at where they had been hit by bullets – largely tailfins, wings, and the cockpit. The engineers therefore suggested reinforcing these areas, adding

Getting older **201**

armour, so that they would be stronger as they were obviously the areas most often being hit. There is a brilliant diagram you can find on the internet, if you are interested. A statistician called Abraham Wald, however, pointed out that actually what they needed to do was reinforce the areas with no damage at all – planes which had been hit on those areas (engines, fuel tanks, the central part of the tail) had not made it back at all. In this way, the planes that survived their encounters with the enemy had originally biased the engineers' thinking, just as it may be that our understanding of autism in older people may be biased by only being able to study those who survive to those ages.

That does not mean it is not still incredibly important to do better at understanding those people though! Of course it is, especially when, as pointed out earlier, we know so little about them, their needs, and their experiences. It just means that throughout this chapter, we acknowledge that we can only share what we know about things from those who are with us, and we recognise that there are many people whose stories and insights are lost.

Sarah on getting older

In all honesty I am amazed to still be here, writing at age 52 and pondering about my hopes, dreams, and fears for the future. A lot of people who know me may be surprised to read this, but is only in the last couple of years that my chronic suicidal ideation has begun to diminish and is being replaced by a desire to live life to the full. As I have said elsewhere in this book though, better late than never, as in the autistic community, there are far too many people who don't make it through to older age. Felicity has written about the appalling statistics and research findings, so I won't dwell on them here, but as the average autistic age of death at 54 looms ever closer, I am determined to make the next two years count. Hopefully I will have more years than that, but my brother didn't and there are no guarantees.

Helen is sadly more aware than most that the odds are stacked against autistic people. Before Doug's untimely death, ironically at 54, she was encouraging him to pursue an autism diagnosis because she believed that accessing healthcare as he aged would have been easier if he had an official diagnosis to help him advocate for any accommodations that he needed in a medical setting. I agree and as I age I have found that having a good understanding of what supports and accommodations I need from medical teams and the ability to advocate for myself, or take people with me who can speak for me on a non-speaking day, has helped tremendously with recent procedures and appointments. I am also starting to see better responses from health professionals who generally do respectfully act on the information I give them, but of course, this varies across the country and neurodiversity awareness and training is patchy. Waiting lists, however, are so appallingly long, that even if I did not have the privilege of a diagnosis, I would still self-advocate for my differences because it would give me the best chance of being treated humanely and not be further traumatised by the experience. Anecdotally, complex PTSD seems to be the norm for far too many autistic folk and I have no wish to add to mine by having terrible experiences with medical professionals as I age.

I have jokingly said that if Kyle, who is ten years older than me, dies first, I'll finally be able to get a cat as he is allergic to them. True love eh? Sacrificing my love of kitties for my beloved. The reality though, is that I will, in all likelihood, be the first to go or won't be as long-lived as Kyle, as in the words of Indiana Jones, "It's not the years honey, it's the mile-age". Too many years of living in survival mode, running on cortisol and other stress hormones, and not paying enough attention to self-care will, no doubt, have taken their toll. I only really began to look after myself better since I have had therapy and was walloped by menopause and I guess adding on the years of chronic mental and physical illness to that would logically wipe off at least a few years. But it is what it is and will be what it will be. One of the many reasons why I love Julian of Norwich is that her famous phrase, "All Shall Be Well" helps me to philosophically and grate-fully reflect on how, against the odds, I have survived life thus far and gives me hope that I will survive at least a little longer.

So, as this #AutisticElder (hopefully) ages I am aware that I am doing so feeling far better equipped for the future than I did when I was younger. I know who I am, am unapologetic about it and unafraid to ask for what I need. Whether or not I will always get what I need is another matter entirely, but having the self-knowledge and sense of autonomy I have now gives me the confidence to negotiate that I didn't have before. I am also privileged because at this stage of my life I am not vulnerably housed and have the love and support of my network of friends, communities, and close family members. Isolation is far too common for autistic people throughout their entire lifespan and ageing without a sense of belonging, purpose, or practical help would be a frightening prospect for me.

I have had conversations with friends about the future and ideas rang-ing from shared houses to supportive communities are being considered as serious options. I really quite like the idea of living in an autistic community of tiny houses or dwellings made from converted shipping containers but I think that, if by that time I was by myself, the driving factor would be to do anything to avoid being in residential care. I've worked as a support worker with autistic adults who had additional mental health conditions and there is no way that I would want to get old in that kind of setting.

There simply is not enough community-approved research-based training or understanding about what autistic people need or adequate resources provided for a good ageing autistic life at present and I would avoid it like the plague. Speaking of which, the government's shocking response towards vulnerable, elderly, and disabled people during the pandemic and particularly those in residential care only serves to add to my feelings on this subject. Ageing autistic communities organised by the #actuallyautistic community may well then be the way forward. Who's with me cat-loving comrades?!

I do, however, have hopes and dreams other than not dying alone and uncared for. Of course, I want to enjoy the fabulous people in my life for as long as I can, but I also do have 'late-starter' ambitions. I want to learn the skills to do a masters and a PhD and to build on my involvement at SARSAS, supporting neurodivergent and disabled survivors of domestic and sexual violence. I may even complete my counselling training as, God knows, we need as many trained neurodivergent therapists as we can get. I also want to continue singing, dancing, and going to as much theatre, live music, and festivals for as long as possible and continue learning how to be, to breathe, and to appreciate the things in my life that give me #actuallyautistic joy.

Like cake. Eating lots of cake.

Autism, ageing, and relationships

The majority of research that has been conducted focussing on older autistic adults has focussed, for understandable reasons, on things like their health and the ageing process, and a very few studies into things like their needs in supported-living situations. This means that there is very little research directly into how autistic people's relationships change as they become older, but we have done our best to summarise what there is, and to look at how our contributors talk about their own experiences of ageing and relationships.

We know, for example, that autistic people continue to have worse mental health than their non-autistic counterparts into old age, although these are lower than they are for autistic people earlier in life – especially social anxiety (Lever & Guerts, 2016). Alongside poor mental health, older autistic adults report lower subjective quality of life than older non-autistic adults, and more problems with experiencing high levels of loneliness and having fewer social supports (Wallace et al., 2016). In contrast, autistic adults between the ages of 40 and 83 (so mostly in the older adult category, we will forgive the researchers a little slippage from the general definition!) who felt they had good social support networks had better physical and psychological quality of life, even after controlling for differences in things like economic resources and depression diagnoses (Charlton et al., 2022).

204 Getting older

Many single autistic people are particularly concerned about what their live will look like as they age, and what that lack of a partner might mean:

> I would be nervous about the idea of growing infirm and alone, but at the same time, I couldn't imagine sharing my space with another human being. I'm too self-contained.
>
> *(anonymous, 54, autistic woman)*

Loneliness, and its opposite, social connectedness, are known to be linked to quality of life and overall life satisfaction for non-autistic people (if you are more lonely, you tend to have worse quality of life; if you have lots of social connections then you tend to have better quality of life). Therefore it makes sense that the same is true for autistic people – as long as you aren't some of those traditional autism researchers who believe in the old theories we outlined in Chapter 1, and that autistic people aren't interested in having relationships and get no benefit from them.

The preceding work largely focusses on social connectedness or loneliness in the context of them being contributing factors to mental health or quality of life, rather than looking at social experiences as important and valuable aspects of people's lives in their own right, or how they interact with aspects of life other than health. This may be because the effects on social interactions are often seen as a side effect of what the researchers are primarily interested in, and so they do not make it into the published reports. Equally, there is a massive – and justifiable – push to understand and improve mental health for the whole population, so it makes sense that this has also been a major focus for autism research, and that this ends up framing how social relationship information is seen and treated when it is collected. Research doesn't happen without funding, funding follows government or institutional priorities, and therefore research follows those same priorities.

An example of social experiences being included in work because they were highlighted as important by the autistic people themselves can be seen in a qualitative paper looking at the experiences of older autistic adults who received their diagnoses just a few years earlier (Hickey et al., 2018). The researchers set out to explore what it was like for people to find out they are definitely autistic in middle and late adulthood, and what this did to their understanding of themselves and their relationships with other people. They interviewed 13 autistic adults who were over 50 (the oldest person was 71), and one of the main themes which they identified from the outset was a 'longing for connection'. A lot of the autistic adults talked about struggling to make connections with other people throughout their lives, and the fact that they had attributed this to intrinsic differences between them and others, which they then worked to reduce or hide in order to try to make it easier for people to be around them and to try to build relationships. All the adults talked about having felt lonely and isolated at different ages of their lives, but that getting a diagnosis started to make a change to their relationships. Knowing that they were autistic gave them the ability to ask for adjustments or understanding from the people around them which they previously hadn't felt able to do, something which is a common experience for many people who get a diagnosis in adulthood. They used this new knowledge about themselves to give themselves space to engage with people and groups in ways which worked for them, such as focussing on their shared interest rather than trying to force a friendship, or finding autism support groups where they could talk to other autistic people who they felt were on the same wavelength. The participants also talked about feeling differently about relationships as they got older – "as I've got old, I've found that I want to do less and less . . . see less people" (p. 6 Hickey et al., 2018).

This is important because it shows the ways in which autistic people's desire for relationships changes over time, alongside the more traditional research interest in how their social skills may increase or decrease with age. Thinking about the subjective and qualitative experiences older autistic people have in terms of socialising is moving back towards the principles of participatory, community-led autism research, which puts the priorities and interests of autistic people ahead of those of non-autistic academics. That is something we both believe researchers should be aiming to do, and especially want to emphasise is important among older autistic people who have generally been so ignored.

Menopause and relationships

One area where older autistic adults experiences of social relationships has been incidentally explored rather better than we might expect is around autistic menopause. By 'better than we might expect', there are still only four published papers . . . but compared to a lot of areas of older people's lives, that is positively oodles of research evidence! It obviously isn't actually a huge amount, nor can it tell us much about the variety of experiences autistic people who go through menopause have. The one study which looked at differences in menopausal experiences from a statistical perspective showed that autistic women experienced more menopausal symptoms and more depression, but did not look at social relationships or impacts (Groenman et al., 2021). It may, however, hint at part of why autistic women are so likely to have high suicidality rates, if mental and physical health are taking a significant hit at this generally very difficult time of life. It is presently unknown as to whether there is any connection between increased mortality in autistic people and heightened suicidality around menopause, but research in this area could be important in helping professionals support autistic people to live longer, happier lives, through menopause and beyond. As stated by one researcher in this field,

> It would be extremely important for future research to establish how suicide risk changes throughout the lifetime of autistic people, paying particular attention to known 'biopsychosocial points', such as puberty and menopause, when neurobiological influences are believed to put extra strain on the individual.
>
> *(Dr Rachel Moseley, personal communication)*

The other three of the four studies on menopause are all small-scale and interview- or focus-group based, so we don't have any information on a broad scale about what experiences might be common, for example. Despite this, the insights from these studies are incredibly valuable.

Menopause work in autism is being led, undoubtedly, by Dr Rachel Moseley. She published the first work on the topic – in just 2020 – and is still the top author in the field. The first paper reported on an online focus group with seven autistic people assigned female at birth, including Sarah. The themes which came out of that discussion were (1) a lack of knowledge and understanding about menopause and the symptoms and processes associated with it; (2) cracking the mask and adaptive functioning, that is, the ways in which menopause disrupted existing coping strategies and finding new ways to manage; and (3) finding support to help navigate the challenges of menopause, and in life after menopause. Importantly, the participants felt that menopause intensified existing challenges associated with being autistic, as well as introducing new difficulties, especially cognitive, emotional, and sensory challenges, which then impacted on social relationships (Moseley et al., 2020). Among non-autistic women, it is common for menopause to have a negative effect on relationships, as hormonal mood swings, irritability, and difficulty managing physical symptoms lead to more arguments or less patience with people around them. The same was true for autistic people assigned female at birth, some of whom worried that the changes in things like their reaction to physical touch from partners might be a sign that they were no longer in love with their partners, for example. In another study published later the same year, Dr Moseley interviewed 17 autistic people assigned female at birth who had experienced or were experiencing menopause. The themes from those interviews were, unsurprisingly, similar to those from the focus group just outlined. Adding to the reflections on the impact of menopause on social relationships from the previous study, participants talked about how they found it harder to maintain masking behaviours they had built up beforehand, and that this, combined with things like menopausal 'brain fog', negatively impacted their interactions with other people. They also struggled to explain the changes and things they were going through to their partners, family, and friends, making things even more difficult (Moseley et al., 2021).

As a contrasting point, several participants talked about how going through menopause made their interactions with people in the wider world easier in some ways. They felt that it reduced the pressures to be 'sexy' or 'put together', as is often expected of women. While many autistic people have talked about feeling invisible as a bad thing, for these participants it was a blessing because it gave them an excuse to drop behaviours which they did not find personally valuable or which were difficult for them. Using menopause as a way to subvert or ignore societal expectations of women, especially older women, also came out from some of the participants in another study, where they talked about things like surprising younger people with piercings and increasing their own sense of well-being through accepting people assigned at birth, menopause can be freeing, even if it is a tumultuous process to go through in many ways.

Several of our contributors who were assigned female at birth have also experienced or are experiencing menopause, and some of them talked about the impact it has or had on their relationships. For example, one of our anonymous autistic women in her fifties talked about the fact that pre-menopause she had a relatively long-standing and mutually beneficial friends-with-benefits situation. After going through menopause, however, she no longer wanted anything to do with that person, and the idea of having sex had become actively unpleasant. This kind of change is not uncommon for women, as their hormones are very different and libido can drop significantly. For autistic women, then, menopause may change the types of relationships they want to have, although little is known about this.

Sarah on menopause

Menopause changed everything for me. I naively thought that I would be more prepared for the onset of menopause-related anxiety and depression as I had experienced many years of living with both conditions. They had become my normal and in my head I was 'sort of' functioning, but the reality was that I was already ground down by long-term ME/CFS and poor mental health, as reflected in my frequent need to take time off work, so when menopause hit, it tipped me over the edge. My already poor sleep patterns developed into chronic insomnia, and my anxiety went through the roof. The ADHD that my therapist had already recognised became very apparent and my previously poor working memory and ME/CFS brain fog became even worse. I went from 'just about hanging on by my fingertips' to utterly broken. I lost all ability to mask, and felt as though I was becoming demonstratively more autistic. I developed regular periods of time when I could not speak, needed to visibly stim, and spend a lot of time in solitude. My sensory profile became more intense. My intolerance to heat became debilitating and I really struggled with bright light, needing curtains to be closed during the day. I was even more emotionally all over the place and my chronic suicidal ideation became more intrusive. I could not function and it all became too much, particularly when my ME/CFS flared following a period of personal family distress; I ended up on long-term sick leave and eventually had to retire early from my job due to ill health.

The Fawcett Society's report on Menopause in the Workplace (Andrew Bazeley, Catherine Marren and Alex Shepherd (April 2022 p. 7) states that,

> *Disabled women are affected more by menopause symptoms. 22% said that had left a job due to menopause symptoms, compared to 9% of non-disabled women.*

I'm not surprised that the figure for disabled women is so high, but then again, I am so used to seeing shocking figures for lifespan outcomes for disability and autism that I've become desensitised to the relentless inequality.

Also weary. Very, very weary. My cynical self is, however, encouraged by the recent rise in visible discussion and destigmatising around menopause and was myself invited to the 2021 Autistica Conference to speak about my autistic experience of it. I am also delighted that there is currently a new participatory autism menopause study underway entitled "Bridging the Silos" that is partnering UK and Canadian academic expertise and lived experience including Community Research Associates Rose Matthews and Christine Jenkins.

During this time, my husband is being his usual loving and supportive self. He's read up on menopause literature, listens when I talk about it, and gives me space when I need it. I need to rest a lot and he supports me by taking over the majority of the day-to-day running of the house and food shopping. I count myself lucky to have this level of support and understanding and also for the timing when menopause intensified eve-rything else for me. My increasing need for solitude and rest coincided with the pandemic and lockdowns so relationship maintenance was either restricted to occasional socially distanced walks when I could and Zoom calls, both of which I could plan for and ration what little energy I had.

I am now further along the menopause path and have managed to put in place supports that have made a real difference to my day-to-day life. On top of my husband's consistent care, I am taking Oestrogen only HRT (I have a Mirena coil, which releases progesterone) in gel and cream form and am very careful to eat well, exercise gently as and when my ME/CFS allows it, and build in regular rest periods during the day. I am also still taking Sertraline and now ADHD stimulants, which have been utterly game-changing. Learning to self-care and pace myself after a lifetime of not doing so is an ongoing challenge, but I owe it to myself to do this work (and it is essential work) and learn about what I need in order to thrive, not just survive.

Part of this, for me, has been to learn to focus on the friendships and loved ones in my life who are nurturing, supportive, and fun to be around and to reassess my relationship with those who aren't. I have found that by doing this I have become far less of a people pleaser and also that the quality of my relationships has become richer. Talking and writing about my vulnerabilities and difficulties during this time has led to a feeling of more honesty and congruence across all of my relationships, including that with myself. I am embracing the pleasure of having a coffee with a friend followed by a guilt-free nap; attending theatre performances and gigs with support and rest periods built in afterwards, and allowing myself to be nurtured by my creative interests like singing and sewing. And yes . . . there have been tattoos and a nose piercing!

Learning to set relational boundaries has been an important part of navigating this part of the lifespan and is a much-needed addition to my self-care tool kit. I will always need accommodations and support as when (please God!) I am through menopause and hopefully these symptoms settle down, my disabilities won't have magically disappeared. The lessons learned, however, will put me in a good place to take care of autistic me as I age.

Elderly care and relationships

Another aspect of getting older where relationships and interpersonal interactions can be very important, and is (yet again) under-researched, is elderly care. We have talked earlier in this chapter about the loneliness which many autistic elders experience, and the isolation. What happens when you are struggling to live independently though? Most elderly people in this situation move into a group living situation, with varying levels of practical support, from minimal intervention (think having your own flat in a block designated as being for people over 55, which may have a meal delivery service option and some group social events put on for those who are interested) to the all-encompassing, where paid support workers may be doing everything from feeding someone to helping bathe and toilet them. In this scenario, which is more common for those who have complex or severe medical and care needs such as dementia and Parkinson's, staff often make decisions for that individual about things like their social lives, putting people in a room together to watch one television, listen to one type of music, or play a predetermined game like Scrabble or dominoes.

These different types and levels of care, then, clearly come with highly varied levels of independence and autonomy, over every aspect of life, including socialising. For non-autistic people, a lack of control over what happens in your day or your life is associated with lots of frustration, worse mental health, and sometimes a sense of helplessness. There is no reason to assume that this would be any different for autistic elderly people, and indeed several reasons to predict that it may be even more difficult for this group.

Think about the diagnostic criteria we told you about in the Introduction. Difficulties with executive function and a strong preference for sameness and predictability could, in theory, work quite well for someone in residential care, because the pattern of individual days often does not vary all that much, and there is often ample notice for any events that are put on. On the other hand, the lack of control residents have over their days, their meals, and even what is on the television in communal areas (or the volume it is on at) could trigger the intolerance of uncertainty which often underlies anxiety for autistic people. This could lead to intense anxiety about each day for an autistic person, which we know can be difficult to communicate to the people around them, leading to frustration, outbursts, and

210 Getting older

what is labelled as 'challenging behaviour' as they seek to avoid whatever it is that causes the anxiety. In children this is often interpreted as tantrums or attention seeking or being naughty. How is it perceived in elderly people? How do staff try to manage these behaviours? Especially if they do not know someone is autistic, because many older people will not currently have a formal diagnosis, is this seen as a 'difficult' resident, who is to be avoided, or who needs extra medication to keep them calm?

It isn't just executive function and anxiety which might be challenging in residential care. The social side of living in an elderly care setting also cannot be ignored – especially in a book about relationships. The immediate thing that might jump to mind are the other residents. Care homes range from very small, with just a handful of people, to the really quite large, with dozens of residents, and the degree of interaction they have with each other can vary significantly as well. In some places, people are given a lot of choice over how much time they spend with others, and how they do that – choice which is central to building natural and more positive friendships through the kind of interactions you want to seek out. In others . . . not so much. Sometimes, the people living in these settings are essentially made to go to communal 'social' spaces – often a take on a living room with lots of individual chairs in a circle facing a TV, maybe some board games and small tables. This kind of forced socialising, regardless of whether you are in the mood to be around other people or not, could be deeply distressing for an autistic elderly person, especially if something about the room doesn't work for their sensory sensitivities. This approach to filling the time of residents (usually in settings where people require higher levels of personal or medical care) can also mean that autistic elderly people aren't given the time alone they need to recover from being around people, or to enjoy things like their interests which can help to improve well-being and joy in life. Though, to try to also look for a positive perspective, it may be that if an autistic person finds someone who shares an interest, or who they get on well with, in their residential setting, then they have easy and regular access to that person and can build a friendship supported by the environment both people are in.

There are also potential social challenges for an autistic person in residential care when it comes to the staff. Firstly, these are people who are often involved in very personal aspects of your daily life, aspects which you have spent a lifetime handling, privately, for yourself. The change to needing help with these kinds of tasks is difficult for anyone, but possibly even more so for autistic people who can be fiercely independent and struggle with change. Help with tasks like washing, toileting, and dressing can feel like an invasion of personal space, even when done sensitively and with good intentions – and sadly, not all staff will be as gentle or as respectful as we would hope, as they are under pressure to see more residents than they really can in the time allotted them, and all for far less pay than they deserve for what is a physically and emotionally demanding job. This can lead to things like reactions to sensory or emotional discomfort being ignored or dismissed, which is obviously not likely to build a positive relationship between the autistic person and whoever is doing it. These conditions also lead to another issue – high turnover of staff in care settings. We know that this is common across the UK, and indeed anywhere in the world that such things are tracked and reported on. There is always a demand for more staff in the social care sector, but working conditions are often not good, and so people move frequently in search of something a bit better. For autistic care home residents, this means that they may have new support staff every few months. They have to try to get to know new faces, new names, new social expectations, predict new moods and attitudes, adapt to new ways of doing the things asked of them. This, for people who can find social interaction exhausting, sounds pretty horrid, right? Especially if you put the effort in to get to know the staff who work with you, and start to feel like you have a friendship, only for them to go away, this must be incredibly difficult. If you don't like them, maybe them going away isn't such a bad thing, but you also can't predict who you will get next – an additional source of anxiety.

There is no research into whether the ideas we layed out previously are how autistic people experience residential care, or whether something entirely different is going on. Only two papers have been published thinking about this issue, alongside the editorials we mentioned earlier from Cos Michael, and she is an author on both. One reports on the insights from three roundtable discussions about the issue of residential care for older autistic adults, where experts from a range of disciplines got together with older autistic adults to work out what the priorities are for future research in this area and for practitioners to think about when trying to improve their support offer (Crompton et al., 2020a). The outcomes of those discussions were the creation of a Top Ten priorities for research, including:

- Managing transitions into residential care
- Autism training for residential care staff
- Recognising and respecting autistic differences, and understanding autistic well-being
- Supporting physical health
- The sensory environment and sensory processing
- Design principles (of the residential environment)
- Creating community and belonging
- Autonomy and choice
- Advocacy
- Evaluating care quality

Increased knowledge and more sensitive practice in these areas would lead to significant improvements in the lives of older autistic people living in residential care.

The second paper from this team reports on the development of a tool to start evaluating whether residential care is working for autistic people – in line with the final bullet point in the preceding list. With autistic adults and a range of experts, they created the Autistic Satisfaction with Care Holistic Interview (Crompton et al., 2020b). This is a tool specifically for researchers or practitioners to use with autistic people in residential care to assess whether multiple different aspects of their living situation are positive for them or not. Areas covered include – importantly from our perspective – their relationships and social time with others, alongside things like the environment, the available activities, and their health and well-being. Although this tool is free to use and openly available online, so far it has not been used in any published research, which suggests that there is a huge opportunity for anyone who is passionate about this topic and who wants to make it the focus of their career for a while!

Chapter conclusion

Overall then, as with non-autistic people, the elderly have generally been ignored in autism research. But, the little bits of evidence we do have suggest that this is another period of major transitions for autistic people, with important implications for their relationships, well-being, and quality of life – and one which deserves to be better understood going forwards.

References

Cassidy, S., Au-Yeung, S., Robertson, A., Cogger-Ward, H., Richards, G., Allison, C., Bradley, L., Kenny, R., O'Connor, R., Mosse, D., Rodgers, J., & Baron-Cohen, S. (2022). Autism and autistic traits in those who died by suicide in England. *The British Journal of Psychiatry*, 1–9. https://doi.org/10.1192/BJP.2022.21

Cassidy, S., & Rodgers, J. (2017). Understanding and prevention of suicide in autism. *The Lancet Psychiatry*, 4(6), e11. https://doi.org/10.1016/S2215-0366(17)30162-1

Charlton, R. A., McQuaid, G. A., & Wallace, G. L. (2022). Social support and links to quality of life among middle-aged and older autistic adults. *Autism*, 136236132210819. https://doi.org/10.1177/13623613221081917

Crompton, C. J., Michael, C., Dawson, M., & Fletcher-Watson, S. (2020a). Residential care for older autistic adults: Insights from three multiexpert summits. *Autism in Adulthood*, 2(2), 121–127. https://doi.org/10.1089/AUT.2019.0080

Crompton, C. J., Michael, C., & Fletcher-Watson, S. (2020b). Co-creating the autistic satisfaction with care holistic interview to examine the experiences of older autistic adults in residential care. *Autism in Adulthood*, 2(1), 77–86. https://doi.org/10.1089/AUT.2019.0033

Doherty, M., Neilson, S., O'Sullivan, J., Carravallah, L., Johnson, M., Cullen, W., & Shaw, S. C. K. (2022). Barriers to healthcare and self-reported adverse outcomes for autistic adults: A cross-sectional study. *BMJ Open*, 12(2), e056904. https://doi.org/10.1136/BMJOPEN-2021-056904

Groenman, A. P., Torenvliet, C., Radhoe, T. A., Agelink van Rentergem, J. A., & Geurts, H. M. (2021). Menstruation and menopause in autistic adults: Periods of importance? *Autism* https://doi.org/10.1177/13623613211059721

Hedley, D., & Uljarević, M. (2018). Systematic review of suicide in autism spectrum disorder: Current trends and implications. *Current Developmental Disorders Reports*, 5(1), 65–76. https://doi.org/10.1007/S40474-018-0133-6/TABLES/1

Hickey, A., Crabtree, J., & Stott, J. (2018). Suddenly the first fifty years of my life made sense: Experiences of older people with autism. *Autism*, 22(3), 357–367. https://doi.org/10.1177/1362361316680914

Hirvikoski, T., Boman, M., Chen, Q., D'Onofrio, B. M., Mittendorfer-Rutz, E., Lichtenstein, P., Bölte, S., & Larsson, H. (2020). Individual risk and familial liability for suicide attempt and suicide in autism: A population-based study. *Psychological Medicine*, *50*(9), 1463–1474. https://doi.org/10.1017/S0033291719001405

Hirvikoski, T., Mittendorfer-Rutz, E., Boman, M., Larsson, H., Lichtenstein, P., & Bölte, S. (2016). Premature mortality in autism spectrum disorder. *British Journal of Psychiatry*, *208*(3). https://doi.org/10.1192/bjp.bp.114.160192

Howard, P. L., & Sedgewick, F. (2021). Anything but the phone: Communication mode preferences in the autism community. *Autism*, *25*(8), 2265–2278. https://doi.org/10.1177/13623613211014995/ASSET/IMAGES/LARGE/10.1177_13623613211014995-FIG2.JPEG

Lever, A. G., & Geurts, H. M. (2016). Psychiatric co-occurring symptoms and disorders in young, Middle-aged, and older adults with autism spectrum disorder. *Journal of Autism and Developmental Disorders*, *46*(6), 1916–1930. https://doi.org/10.1007/S10803-016-2722-8/TABLES/7

Michael, C. (2016). Why we need research about autism and ageing. *Autism*, *20*(5), 515–516. https://doi.org/10.1177/1362361316647224

Moseley, R. L., Druce, T., & Turner-Cobb, J. M. (2020). When my autism broke: A qualitative study spotlighting autistic voices on menopause. *Autism*, *24*(6), 1423–1437. https://doi.org/10.1177/1362361319901184

Moseley, R. L., Druce, T., & Turner-Cobb, J. M. (2021). Autism research is all about the blokes and the kids: Autistic women breaking the silence on menopause. *British Journal of Health Psychology*, *26*(3), 709–726. https://doi.org/10.1111/BJHP.12477

Stewart, G. R., Corbett, A., Ballard, C., Creese, B., Aarsland, D., Hampshire, A., Charlton, R. A., & Happé, F. (2022). Self-harm and suicidality experiences of middle-age and older adults with vs. Without high autistic traits. *Journal of Autism and Developmental Disorders*, *2022*, 1–13. https://doi.org/10.1007/S10803-022-05595-Y

Wallace, G. L., Budgett, J., & Charlton, R. A. (2016). Aging and autism spectrum disorder: Evidence from the broad autism phenotype. *Autism Research*, *9*(12), 1294–1303. https://doi.org/10.1002/AUR.1620

9

TOXIC

Problematic relationships and victimisation

Any relationship can be twisted into something toxic. That might sound like a dramatic statement, but we believe it to be true. As a society, we are getting much better at talking about abusive intimate partner relationships (though there is still a tendency to ignore the experiences of men who are the victims of these situations). What we need to work on, though, is recognising that any relationship can become abusive. Relationships between family members, between friends, between community members – and yes, between intimate partners. We are going to look at what we know about autistic people's experiences of these relationships as harmful in this chapter, and some of the ways in which abusive relationships can interact to make other types of relationships more difficult.

We want to start by saying something **very clearly**.

Autistic people are more likely to be victimised by people they are in relationships with, relationships being broadly defined. There are aspects of being autistic which contribute to this. That does **not** mean that autistic people are in any way to blame for their victimisation. The blame always and entirely lies with the abuser, the exploiter, the manipulator. Being autistic can make it harder to see these behaviours being used against a person, or make it harder to find ways out of a toxic relationship. We are going to talk about some of the ways autism and abuse interact, but we are not victim blaming, and never intend to do so.

In this chapter, we are going to look at some of the ways in which different kinds of relationships can become toxic or abusive, following a similar pattern as the other chapters – first family, then friends, then romantic and sexual relationships. Many of the autistic people who have contributed to this book, and Sarah, have shared their experiences in this chapter. These are difficult to read about, and even more difficult to have gone through. If you feel that anything around this topic is likely to be distressing for you, please do skip reading it – you have our permission! Chapter 10: Tips and Tricks starts on page 380, so you can go straight

DOI: 10.4324/9781003044536-10

Toxic **215**

there. We do not want anyone to be upset or hurt in any way by what we have written. The book is not going anywhere, so don't force yourself to read something which may trigger or re-traumatise you right now, or ever. Your mental health, well-being, and safety matter more than you reading every page.

Autistic people and negative life experiences

It is worth starting this chapter by pointing out some of what we know about autistic people's negative life experiences, before we look at negative relationships specifically.

Essentially – autistic people have a lot more of them.

In 2019, a new research questionnaire was published called the Vulnerability Experiences Quotient (VEQ). What this does is ask about 60 different negative life experiences people may have had, from car crashes to unemployment, to being assaulted to being in a natural disaster. Over 400 autistic adults, and nearly 300 non-autistic adults, were then asked to say whether they had experienced each of these things. The study showed that autistic adults were more likely to have experienced the majority of the events listed, especially domestic abuse, financial exploitation and hardship, and being involved with social services as parents (because it is often assumed that an autistic parent must require intervention) (Griffiths et al., 2019). With these high rates of negative life experiences as the context for many autistic people's lives, it becomes less and less surprising that there are also higher rates of negative social experiences reported by autistic people. A meta-analysis of papers reporting of victimisation amongst autistic people found that 47% reported severe bullying, 16% being victims of child abuse, 40% reported sexual victimisation, and 84% of autistic adults had been victimised in more than one category (Trundle et al., 2022). We are going to look at some of those experiences in more detail in this chapter, but those are important statistics to keep in mind.

Ella summed up autistic people's experiences pretty clearly when she said:

> We are all living with a certain amount of trauma.
>
> *(Ella, autistic person)*

That trauma can come from lots of different places and causes, but it affects the autistic people and their relationships regardless of the origin.

Adverse childhood experiences (ACEs) are a key category of negative life experience which we know have significant long-term impacts in non-autistic people. ACEs include things like being the victim of abuse, witnessing violence against a parent (specifically a mother in most studies), parental divorce, the death of a parent or caregiver, and severe illness, among many others. They are linked to worse mental health across the lifespan, to worse educational and employment outcomes, to increased risk of substance and alcohol misuse, and increased likelihood of death by suicide (Felitti et al., 1998; Merrick et al., 2017).

216 Toxic

Just as autistic adults are more likely to report more negative life experiences overall, there is some suggestion that autistic children are more likely to have ACEs too (Andrzejewski et al., 2022). Interestingly, their caregivers also report higher levels of ACEs in their childhoods, so there is potentially an intergenerational trauma effect playing out amongst these families. This intergenerational trauma has also been investigated by another research team, who found that parents with PTSD were more likely to report that their autistic child had been the victim of at least one form of abuse (usually by other people), and autistic girls were most likely to have been victims of sexual abuse, and of a higher number of types of abuse (Dike et al., 2022). It has been suggested that autistic children who have a high number of ACEs may face delays to getting an autism diagnosis, because their behaviours are read as a trauma response by clinicians rather than them recognising the intersection between autism and trauma (Hoover & Kaufman, 2018). Traumatised parents can struggle to sufficiently support their child, especially in terms of their emotional development, because they themselves are trying to cope with emotional difficulties. For autistic children who may have emotional regulation challenges, or co-occurring alexithymia, this may end up exacerbating the problems they have with managing their emotions, which feeds into social relationships being more difficult. Combined with a potentially delayed diagnosis, you can see how there is often more than just being autistic which is impacting the relationships of autistic people across their lifespan.

A recent study where over 100 people were interviewed about their experiences of being hurt by people in their lives (friends, family, partners) found that autistic people basically expect to be treated this way, because it is so common for them (Pearson et al., 2022). From childhood onwards, autistic people had been hurt, manipulated, and abused by others, and this became their model for what relationships with other people were meant to be like. It often took them a long time to realise that what had happened to them was wrong, and working through the trauma was difficult, compounded by masking to try to protect themselves from harm in current and future relationships. This led to them being overwhelmed by trying to socialise safely, and eventually contributed to burnout. Participants talked about the relationship between social trauma, masking, and burnout, and the significant impact for the worse these had on their lives – which is a key message to keep in mind throughout this chapter. It is not just the immediate harm which matters, autistic people carry those experiences with them in the same way non-autistic people do, and that means the damage usually continues as well.

Harmful families

At different points in this book, and going forwards in this chapter, Sarah has written about the ways in which her parents' treatment of her was harmful, directly and indirectly, and the lifelong impact this has had on her mental health and relationships. Obviously her experiences are uniquely her own, and will not exactly apply

Toxic **217**

for most other people, but sadly difficult relationships with parents are not that unusual – for autistic people and non-autistic people.

There is, honestly, zero research we could find on this topic – on problematic relationships between autistic people and their parents, where the parents do things which damage their autistic child. There are lots and lots of papers published on how having an autistic child impacts parent mental health, parent stress, parent well-being. There are papers on relationship quality between parents and their autistic children, from the parental perspective. There are no papers on what autistic people think and feel about their relationships with their parents, or the impact these had on them. What is important to remember, though, is this:

> There is such a lot of bullshit talked about blood being thicker than water. It just isn't. Toxicity is toxicity wherever it comes from.
>
> *(Sarah, autistic woman)*

Considering the extent of the work on attachment which we have talked about elsewhere, and the real emphasis placed on the importance of parental relationships for child development and adult outcomes, this is surprising. Let's be honest, considering the amount of work that looks at attachment in autistic children, the fact that there is very little follow-up with autistic adults is deeply frustrating. Obviously there are the papers which look at attachment in adults which we discussed in Chapter 6: Well, Hello There, but these tend to be more about attachment style being measured in adulthood within the context of current relationships – they don't use retrospective qualitative methods to ask autistic people for their reflections on the parenting they received. This means that there is a huge section of understanding which is missing from how we understand the parent–child relationship for autistic people, because we only have the parent side of the picture (which is often/usually a non-autistic side of the picture as well). Forcing an autistic child (or any child) into situations which are distressing for them, ignoring when they are upset about things, or telling them that they are wrong about the way they perceive the world and other people are all ways in which a parent–child relationship can be harmful. It undermines their sense of self, their trust in their senses and their instincts, and leaves them more open to manipulation or exploitation by other people later on in life.

Obviously, parents are unlikely to report that they are bad at parenting their autistic child, in the ways outlined earlier, and so this kind of negative treatment of children is unlikely to appear in the research which only asks for parent views on their relationship with their child. Similarly, behaviour which is considered 'classically' abusive, such as physical or sexual abuse, is rarely reported by the parents carrying it out. We do know from adult reports, though, that autistic children are more likely to be victims of this kind of abuse from adults in their lives, and some of those perpetrators are their parents. Felicity has a study which she is writing up into a publication (as of June 2022 – that gets finished after the book is finished!). In it she asked 25 autistic adults who had been victims of sexual abuse or intimate partner violence

218 Toxic

about their experiences. Of these 25, several had been victims of childhood abuse, including at the hands of fathers, teachers, and older children. A bit more about this study will come in the later section about sexual abuse, but it is worth highlighting here that this can and does happen to autistic children and young people, and by not asking them about their experiences, this harm remains hidden.

Sarah's experiences with difficult family relationships

My memories of immediate and wider family was of a strict and patriarchal structure that was not a pleasant one to grow up in. I distinctly remember at a young age being told by my father that girls were meant to obey their parents, wives were there to support their husbands and daughters were expected to look after their fathers in their old age. Men made the decisions; women and girl children kept quiet if they knew what was good for them. Male children who presented in a traditional way were prized, and unusual girls who did not fit a particular mould, were not. In addition to this, intergenerational bullying, favouritism, and snobbery underpinned my paternal family relationships. According to my father, my uncle was the preferred child and although my grandfather had made a prosperous living from working as a plumber and then investing in rental property, there was an aspirational drive to 'better themselves' in terms of class.

Looking back at the family gatherings at my paternal grandparents bungalow at Kirby Muxloe in Leicester I recognise those tensions and resentments, and although I enjoyed being with my cousins, I also remember feeling bullied and shamed by my grandparents who frequently informed me that I was too large, too loud, and, on one occasion, actually told me that I was disgusting. My grandfather hated noise and there were vague references made about him having had a breakdown at some stage, but, like most things in the family, it was never discussed. He was bullying towards my grandmother, who in turn resented her glamorous sister, who was a successful singer during the war. Lillian entertained troops in the Far East on the same bill as Dame Vera Lynn and was then director of the Leicester Light Operatic Society, having had numerous relationships and several husbands. Lillian chose not to have children and my grandmother felt that by having had a family, she was forever in her sister's far more exciting shadow.

My paternal grandmother may well have also felt overawed by my great-grandmother, who not only independently owned the family plumbing business, which was unusual in itself for a woman at the time, but had also been Churchill's secretary for a while when he was in the Midlands during the pre-war years. My childhood recollections of her was someone who was selectively deaf, extraordinarily good at playing cards, and a stealer of roast potatoes from my dinner plate, but she was also clearly a woman of substance whose social unusualness, I suspect, may well point to her having been autistic. Of course I will never know, but I do wonder if the subsequent patriarchal and bullying attitudes from my grandfather and father were partly fuelled by misogynistic resentment of her success and a desire to reclaim their societally normative male privilege.

My maternal grandparents didn't get much of a look in as they, being proudly working class, were deemed undesirable company, but I do remember visiting their terraced house in the city of Leicester on a couple of occasions. Granddad Ben was kind and gentle whereas Granny Douglas was fierce, stubborn, and 'difficult' and although the more stereotypical autistic traits were more obviously evident in my paternal family I suspect that she too was also probably autistic. The fact that my siblings and I are autistic as well as the majority of our offspring, it is highly likely that the autistic genome has travelled down both the maternal and paternal lines and I am left wondering about just how many lost generations of undiagnosed family members there were throughout the ages.

My parents were unhappy, distant people who were emotionally unavailable to themselves or each other, let alone their children. I remember being at a peer's house and feeling confused at seeing them being kissed goodnight or being hugged. This just didn't happen at home and felt very alien to me. I also remember the way my father treated my mother. She was expected to keep house and to look a certain way and it was made clear that the clothes she felt comfortable wearing were not to my father's taste. He mocked her for needing to frequently dash to the loo because of her ulcerative colitis and although he denies it, he had affairs, one of which was confirmed by a school peer who had seen him hand in hand with another woman who wasn't my mother. There were other tensions that my older brother noticed such as my mother's fierce working class pride which clashed with my father's middle class aspirations so it wasn't surprising when they made the announcement that they were separating when we were living in Worthing.

I will never forget that scene. We were all called into the lounge and the statement was made that our parents were no longer going to live together. I didn't really understand what that meant and became very upset. For many years following this I experienced flashbacks and panic attacks if I went into a room that had the same pattern carpet. It was awful, but what was even worse was that the announced separation did not happen, there was no explanation or discussion and life went on as if nothing had occurred. To this day I do not know why my siblings and I were left in the dark, but I'm guessing our parents considered this the

220 Toxic

> *best course of action in order to protect us from their relational mess. If so, it was a terrible decision on their part. We were all intelligent, intuitive children and to be left with this vacuum and uncertainty was cruel beyond words. The emotional fall out for me was that I began to believe that the family difficulties were somehow my fault, that I was responsible for all the unhappiness, but because expressing feelings was clearly not allowed, it set an unhealthy precedent of internalising any pain that I felt.*

Of course, it can also be the case that parents are undiagnosed themselves, which seems possible within Sarah's family, and this can lead to difficulties just as the clash between autistic and non-autistic children/parents can. Especially if an undiagnosed parent or parents were unsympathetic to the challenges their child experiences, taking an "I coped, you need to toughen up" approach – something which is more common amongst older generations, who grew up not discussing mental health or knowing what autism was – then this may have made the relationship more tense and more likely to devolve into harmful behaviour patterns. This is effectively the opposite of the positive parenting we discussed in Chapter 7: A Family Affair, where autistic parents found that they were more able to understand and support their autistic child because of the insight they had from being autistic themselves.

The same lack of research knowledge applies to relationships with siblings, or grandparents, or any other family relationship. We often have research giving the accounts of the (presumably) non-autistic person, but not so much the autistic perspective on that same relationship – especially among adults. This means that even though we know that conflict with siblings is a major issue for many children and young people which can impact their development and well-being into adulthood, we don't know what that process looks like in autistic people who had difficult or abusive relationships with their siblings – something which is entirely possible and does happen. Understanding this, in light of what research with non-autistic children and young people has shown regarding the way sibling relationships act as models for interacting with peers at school, could be an important insight into the difficulties some autistic children have socialising. If your model for how to behave with other children includes hitting, pinching, pushing, shouting, and general aggression – then it makes sense that these autistic children have more difficulty fitting in and making friends, above and beyond the differences which come with being neurodivergent. But, we do not have research which has investigated this, and so we do not know for how many autistic children this plays a role, or how much of a role it plays.

Toxic friendships

Generally, our friends are people who have a positive impact in our lives – we have talked extensively about the ways in which friendships are supportive and enriching in earlier chapters. Not all peer relationships are so good though, and sometimes they can become outright abusive, just as other types of relationships can.

At various points in the previous chapters, we have talked about the fact that autistic people of all ages and all genders are frequently victims of bullying. Most autistic people, possibly all, will be bullied at some point in their lives, often repeatedly. This bullying can come from parents, siblings, peers, teachers, work colleagues, partners . . . anyone, really, though peers are the most common perpetrators. That is a sad statement, but unfortunately it is true. Sometimes this will be almost unintentional, but often it will be conscious and deliberate. All of it has a significant negative impact on the mental health and well-being of the autistic person who is the victim.

Although bullying is not usually considered the type of experience which qualifies for creating a post-traumatic stress disorder (PTSD) response, for autistic people it very much can do so. Complex PTSD is a form of PTSD which develops due to repeated exposure to a traumatising event or stimuli, rather than because of a single massively traumatic event – although it should go without saying that repeated traumas can also be massively traumatic in that way. There is some evidence that autistic people are more likely to develop PTSD and complex PTSD, with a higher percentage of autistic than non-autistic people saying they have experienced both/either a traditional traumatic event and what is called a "non-DSM-5" traumatic event, that is, one which is not listed in the diagnostic manual but which has the potential to be traumatic (Rumball et al., 2020). This works out as autistic adults being ten times more likely to meet PTSD criteria than non-autistic adults – which is shocking. The fact that a higher number of autistic adults reached the PTSD clinical cut-off, based on a wider range of experiences, is important. That the things which autistic and non-autistic people find traumatising are different is a message which is repeatedly emerging from studies into PTSD – 60% of autistic people say that their most traumatic event was a social one, compared to 20% of non-autistic people, for example (Haruvi-Lamdan et al., 2018). Equally, things like sensory trauma can be significant for autistic people in a way that naturally doesn't apply for non-autistic people (Kerns et al., 2022). This has implications for clinical engagement with autistic people, and for those who care about the autistic people in their lives – there is a reasonable chance that person is dealing with mental health issues which have not been recognised formally and which are deeply significant.

The repeated trauma which causes complex PTSD (also called cPTSD) has also specifically been investigated amongst autistic people, also by a team with Freya Rumball who led the study discussed in the preceding paragraph. Their follow-up study showed that cumulative trauma exposure only seemed to have a cumulative effect in autistic people, not in non-autistic people, and this effect was stronger in autistic people who had memory difficulties. This is possibly because difficulties in this realm interfere with the ability to talk about and process the trauma someone has experienced, meaning that the impact it has on them is more extreme and longer lasting (Rumball et al., 2021a). Other studies looking at this effect have found that autistic people who have PTSD tend to suppress their thoughts about their trauma or their PTSD, which contributed to higher anxiety, and they tended to ruminate more on these thoughts, which predicted higher depression (Golan et al., 2022; Rumball et al., 2021b). This shows how different aspects of mental

222 Toxic

health and autistic cognitive styles interact to exacerbate the difficulties autistic people have long term as a result of traumatic experiences, including bullying.

Bullying, and the effect it has on people, is not truly about a 'toxic friendship', because bullies are not friends, but it is an intensely harmful peer relationship which can have far-reaching consequences. The other form of damaging peer relationship which has had attention in the literature (so far) is the phenomenon of 'mate crime'.

Mate crime is a term used widely in criminal justice circles, in research, and in the media to refer to criminal actions taken against a disabled person by someone, or several someones, who the disabled person believes are their friends. The term 'mate crime' was first used as a play on the term 'hate crime', which is a recognised phenomenon where people are targeted, usually by strangers, based on a protected characteristic. In mate crime, disability is the protected characteristic, but the perpetrator is not a stranger. It also covers the same kind of actions against a disabled person by their relatives. Mate crimes usually take the form of things like acts of cruelty against the disabled person; deliberately humiliating them; forcing them into servitude in some way (e.g. forced domestic work); exploiting them (e.g. tricking them into criminal actions such as being a driver or drug runner, or sexual exploitation); or stealing from the disabled person (e.g. taking their money or belongings by saying that 'this is what friends do') (Thomas, 2011). This is, sadly, something which some of our contributors had experienced:

> The friends I suppose in my tutor group were the wrong type of people and that led to incidents that could be classed as mate crime. I was giving out change or cash to these people, but ultimately not receiving the money back or the favour not being returned in a way that would be appropriate. Perhaps I was naive or gullible enough to assume that people might do things in the right way and I bracketed people into my way of thinking, but it doesn't quite work that way so largely I was known as a bit of a victim.
>
> *(Jack)*

There is one paper looking at mate crime specifically amongst autistic adults, rather than among disabled adults generally. This study was conducted by Dr Amy Pearson, an autistic academic, and she interviewed five autistic people about their experiences, and how these interacted with their ideas about friendship (Forster & Pearson, 2019). Autistic people talked about how struggling to see the hidden meanings or intentions behind the words people were saying meant that they were at a disadvantage socially. This could make them easier targets for those who wanted to exploit or harm them, because the perpetrators played on their difficulty in spotting when they were being manipulated. They also talked about the fact that they tended to be more trusting and to take people at face value, because that is how they expected people to behave, so it could take them longer to realise when someone had malicious intentions and was abusing that trust. Being manipulated this way also left the autistic people feeling embarrassed, and like they should be

Toxic **223**

ashamed of their naivety, which meant that they were less likely to seek help with these situations. That abuse of trust and the internalised stigma which came with it meant that for many autistic people, mate crime is worse than being bullied because it comes with betrayal, whereas you expect a bully to be nasty to you.

We said earlier that mate crime can overlap with domestic abuse in terms of the strategies perpetrators use against autistic people. In the next section, we look specifically at autistic people's experiences of intimate partner abuse and sexual victimisation, as well as at some of the ways in which autistic people can cause harm. Again, if this is going to be distressing for you, please skip it and go to Chapter 10: Tips and Tricks, on page 380.

Intimate partner abuse and sexual victimisation

Before we look at the research on this difficult topic, we want to start with Sarah sharing her experiences. Many autistic people, especially autistic women, will have been assaulted, abused, and victimised during their lifetimes, and her story gives some insight into how this happens, how this feels, and the consequences it has.

Sarah's experiences of sexual violence and abuse

I was an easy target for predatory and abusive males, not just because my undiagnosed differences made me stand out, but also because my upbringing hadn't prepared me in any way for navigating relationships, sexual or otherwise. Men were to be obeyed if I was going to earn their affection, I was socially isolated and there was precious little in the way of sex education or discussions about consent at school. It was a recipe for disaster and over the years I experienced multiple rapes and sexual assaults, the following account of which is an abbreviated version of a piece that was published on the Neuroclastic site in November 2019.

Armed with my set of rules for earning love and approval I discovered one day that I was attractive to someone of the opposite sex. It was exciting and I felt wanted. He singled me out, paid attention to me and was flattering. I believed everything he said and thought that he was genuinely interested in me. Men, of course in my head, made the decisions, took the lead and had to have their needs met, so I allowed him to take me into his hotel bedroom, passively obeying him while he undressed me. I quickly felt out of my depth and wanted it to stop. I tried to verbalise this, but somehow was unable to make myself heard. What I wanted or in this case, what I didn't want, was unimportant and I had to do what the man wanted.

224 Toxic

I froze, shut down and disappeared into myself until it was over. I don't remember much about the aftermath. Leaving the room and going home was a blur. I was fourteen.

I don't recall feeling very much after that for a while. It was a strange numbness. What had happened didn't feel right, but it took some time for me to be able to name it as rape. It didn't feel like rape. I hadn't been dragged into a dark corner against my will, or pinned down screaming, as I imagined rape to be. It couldn't be rape because I hadn't explicitly shouted "no!" or fought him off. I nevertheless knew that deep down, something was wrong. I was terrified that I might be pregnant, told my mother what had happened and was taken to the GP for a test. It wasn't mentioned again and life, as it was, continued. There were other boyfriends, always older, and as a precaution I was put on the pill. Then one day, another family member confronted me, calling me a whore and a liar. He said that I hadn't been raped, that he knew the man I had accused and that if he found out about my lies then I would be in a lot of trouble. He was in a position of authority in the family, therefore he must have been right so I believed I was, indeed, a liar. My feelings were wrong and he was right. I was nothing and I didn't matter. So, the next time a boyfriend forced himself on me, I just sunk into myself until it was over and didn't bother telling anyone. What was the point? I was a liar and deserved to be treated like this. Passive compliance, approval-seeking and an inability to name any kind of need became my modus operandi during my teen years and I became hyper-sexualised, having many boyfriends, but rarely finding sex fulfilling.

Many years later when I began to heal and believe my truth I reported my historical rapes and received specialist support and psycho-education from SARSAS (Somerset and Avon Rape and Sexual Abuse Support). Thanks to Georgie and the team I now understand that my physical and psychological responses to this kind of abuse are recognised fawning reactions and that I was not responsible for the harm that was done to me. It was not my fault and I was not a liar. I was an easy target and I was raped by abusive males.

All autistic people should be safe from sexual predators and given the support, education and guidance from autism and trauma-informed organisations and from those who love us throughout our lives so that we can learn to recognise abusive behaviour and red flags and also experience the fulfilling sexual relationships that we deserve. I now volunteer for SARSAS offering support to other survivors and am an advisor on their Learning Disabilities and Autism Project in the hope that future generations of autistic people will be better empowered to protect themselves from sexual abuse and violence.

As we said at the start of this section, Sarah is far from the only autistic person to have these kinds of experiences. In the general population, almost 100% of women report experiencing some kind of sexual harassment or assault at some point in their lives, around 20% of women report having been the victim of serious sexual assault or rape, and a similar number experience domestic violence. A third of victims of sexual assault and domestic abuse are men, and we have scant statistics for non-binary people but we know that trans people are often at much higher risk of intimate partner violence than cis people.

Among autistic people, it seems like those statistics are all worse. Between 60% and 90% of autistic women report having been victims of a sexual assault, including serious sexual assault, rape, or domestic violence – four times the number of non-autistic women. It also seems that autistic people are more vulnerable to being assaulted earlier – a majority say that the first time they were victimised was before the age of 18, with many the first instance being before they were 15 (Cazalis et al., 2022). Childhood victimisation is much more common for autistic people than non-autistic people, including for sexual victimisation (Weiss & Fardella, 2018). Knowing this, there is a real need for understanding the long-term consequences of this kind of victimisation for autistic people, which is currently lacking, but it likely contributes to the high rates of mental health issues we see autistic people struggle with, especially PTSD (Reuben et al., 2021).

Most of the autistic people we talked to for this book had experienced some form of sexual victimisation or intimate partner violence. We are not going to share graphic details of these here, but a selection of their quotes are here. As before, if reading this will be hurtful to you, feel free to move to the next section.

> At 17 I made the very bad mistake of dating someone I worked with. I was 17 and he was 23 and I was made to feel as though there was nothing wrong with that situation. And then he was quite pushy and I was like "I'm not into this" and we went out for drinks a couple of times as soon as I'd turned 18 and two weeks after I'd turned 18, he turned around and said "bye", which felt very poetic as you're obviously a creep. That was something that caused me a lot of really weird popularity at school dating a 23-year-old which is very fucked up, looking back on it. I was so cool that I was dating someone who was muscly and then very briefly I dated someone at the start of uni who was 23 to my 18. It really gives me the ick as he was a really cruel person. The other 23-year-old was a love bomber and this one was very sarcastic

226 Toxic

and very rude to all of my friends and didn't want me to be around my friends and that was two weeks of WTF. I'm in my first weeks of university, I'm just making friends. Why are you being mean to everyone? I was able to make better friendships with my friends over the bonding of his treatment of them. It's a positive in the darkness of the 23 year old.

(Sarah O, autistic woman)

In the case of the first relationship I felt that my life was in danger and so I had to very carefully plan this out for a few months . . . the gaslighting started to happen. I started to doubt myself on what was right and what was wrong. Looking for his opinion more and more. He had me convinced that I was no good. Then the sexual abuse happened over the last year. I think that it would be unfair of me to say that it was abuse as we were in a relationship and there were times when I didn't really want to have sex, but there were times where there was no consent and at the very very end, my mother was living with us when my father died and when he went to work I got all my Mum's stuff in a suitcase, I got all my stuff in a suitcase and went to the airport. I withdrew as much money as I could from an account that he allowed me to use where we had shared funds. I withdrew as much money as I could without him noticing anything weird was going on. I sent my mum to my sister's and moved to the UK. For all I know, he may still be looking for me. I always say that from everything you learn you know.

(anonymous, 47, autistic male)

I only noticed when it was really intense pursuit from a sociopathic stare from a narcissistic man. At that point I would perk up and think, "oh maybe they are interested" and that is what it took for me to realise that men were interested. So I ended up in a series of relationships with narcissistic and sociopathic men. Totally abusive.

(anonymous, 54, autistic woman)

There are no large-scale general prevalence studies of sexual victimisation and intimate partner violence against autistic people of non-female genders yet, but one study which asked students at four universities in America found that 15% of autistic men said they had experienced unwanted sexual contact, and 23% of non-binary and trans autistic students had as well (Brown et al., 2017). While these numbers are lower than autistic women, they were higher than the non-autistic students of the same genders, and autistic students generally are twice as likely to report being sexually assaulted (Rothman et al., 2021). Importantly this research found that having a strong sense of belonging to a friendship group or a community was protective against victimisation, which emphasises again the points made in the previous chapter.

Small-scale qualitative studies support the themes which we can see in the statistical work. Autistic people of all genders report having been victims of sexual assault and intimate partner violence, and also to have been victimised in childhood. The study Felicity is working on which we talked about earlier, where she interviewed 25 autistic people about their experiences, included seven men and three non-binary people, and their experiences are indistinguishable from those of autistic women. Everyone had been victimised in similar ways, by strangers, by peers, by family, by friends, or most often by partners. Many had been subject to 'classic abuse' in terms of physical and sexual violence from their partner, and talked about how even though they knew that this was wrong, they found it difficult to work out whether it was 'really bad' or the sort of thing that 'just happened' in relationships. Media often portrays violence in relationships as something that couples 'work through', or only shows the most extreme physical abuse. This meant that many autistic people struggled to calibrate how bad what they were experiencing would seem to others, and therefore whether to tell someone or to just 'get on with it'. One person talked to us about this:

> I ended up in a series of relationships with narcissistic and sociopathic men that were really destructive. Totally abusive. I was totally baffled time and time again that these men were lying to me and I didn't spot it. So I would go along with the mask that they put up, the persona that they portrayed up until the point where they, as they would have seen it, captured their prey, and then they would let the mask slip, at which point I was completely flummoxed as to what was going on. And that pattern repeated. . . . As soon as I did figure out what was going on in the abusive relationships, I was out of it, I was gone, but I stayed for too long because of a sense of confusion and bafflement of dealing with the different sides of a charming yet abusive partner.
>
> *(anonymous, 54, autistic woman)*

Autistic people often also feel targeted specifically because they are autistic, because this made them more vulnerable to social manipulation and therefore easier to manipulate or to gaslight into thinking their experiences weren't abuse. Some people also talked about their abuser deliberately triggering meltdowns or doing things which would hurt them via their sensory sensitivities, essentially weaponising autism as a tool of abuse.

> I screamed at him. "Why did you do this?" and he said, "because it was easy" and walked away . . . I couldn't wait to get out. I was afraid for me being on my own with him and it took me a further seven years to get out of that relationship.
>
> *(anonymous, 48, trans man)*

Vulnerability based on aspects of being autistic is something autistic women talked about in terms of their autistic traits in a different study Felicity did as part of her

228 Toxic

PhD. Women who had been victimised in some way said that they felt part of why things happened the way they did was that they struggled to read the hidden messages in other people's behaviours, and that this meant they missed malicious intentions which others could see. They were then easier targets for those predators who were looking for a victim, and they often had fewer friends with whom they could 'check in' about someone's behaviour towards them so they thought this treatment was normal (Sedgewick et al., 2018). They often stayed in abusive relationships longer than they felt they should have done, first because they did not realise that the behaviour was abusive if their partner told them it was ok, and second because they lacked the social support which is so necessary for getting out of domestic violence situations. This chimes with the study by Amy Pearson and her team we talked about at the start of the chapter, that many autistic people feel that being hurt by the people in their lives is normal – and if that has been your model, it can be hard to see when you are being mistreated by your romantic or sexual partners. And that, in turn, makes it difficult to know when or how to get out of those situations.

As part of writing this book, we interviewed Georgie, a therapist who works with the charity Sarah talked about, SARSAS, who are a specialist sexual assault and rape survivor support organisation. They are currently running a project to try to understand the neurodivergent people who come to them better, and to try to improve the support they offer to those people. Her insights are summaries of the things she has seen come up multiple times, working with dozens of autistic survivors. These patterns include:

- Finding it hard to recognise patterns of abuse, and instead trying to work around 'red flag' behaviours
- Internalising blame for how the abuser treats them, and thinking 'this is my fault'
- Many autistic survivors recount having difficult family upbringings, including undiagnosed parents, which means a lack of clear relationship models when young
- Social isolation of autistic people leads to desperation for relationships, so people rationalise being in a bad relationship as better than being alone
- High levels of learned compliance, where someone is used to having to do what they are told and therefore acquiesce to behaviours or treatment which they do not want to take part in
- A tendency towards a freeze or fawn trauma response, rather than fight or flight – which can mean that an abuser continues rather than being scared off, for example
- Not being understood by services or being seen as 'difficult' because of communication differences or need for adjustments, and therefore struggling to access support

All of these points need further investigation by researchers, to try to find ways to support autistic people with these devastating experiences. While Georgie noted

Toxic **229**

that younger clients tended to have better awareness, fewer repeated traumas and assaults, and more ability to talk about what they had been through, the fact that young people are still coming to her shows that this kind of victimisation is still happening. However, she said:

> What gives me hope is that little by little, things are slowly changing.
>
> *(Georgie, non-autistic woman)*

And that has to be what brings us all hope, on such a dark set of topics.

Autism and stalking

We said earlier that we would also look at the ways in which autistic people can sometimes be perpetrators of abuse and harm against other people, especially the people they are attracted to or in relationships with. The most commonly investigated form of harm done by autistic people in the context of romantic and sexual relationships – or any relationships, really – is stalking.

Stalking is defined as when "someone repeatedly behaves in a way that makes the recipient feel scared, distressed, or threatened" (Protection from Harassment Act, 1997), and covers both harassment and stalking. Harassment includes behaviours like cyberstalking/using the internet to harass someone, sending abusive text or phone messages, sending unwanted gifts, or repeatedly calling or visiting someone when this is not wanted. Sexual harassment is versions of these behaviours with a specific sexual tone or which create an intimidating, hostile, humiliating or offensive environment based on sexual identity or orientation, including online. Stalking is the more aggressive form of harassment, and can include regularly following someone in their daily life, repeatedly going to their home or work uninvited, tracking their internet or phone use, or watching or spying on someone. Online stalking and harassment can also include things like revealing someone's private information on the internet, directing other users to harass or threaten someone, sharing photos without permission (usually in the context of 'revenge porn'), or spreading false information about someone to damage their reputation. Unwanted behaviour that happens more than once can be classified as harassment or stalking, and these terms apply whether the two people are strangers or know each other well – someone you have never met who does these things can be classed as a stalker, and so could an ex (or current) partner.

On average, a stalker persists for between six months and two years, and the majority of victims are female while the majority of perpetrators are male – but being stalked can and does happen to anyone, regardless of gender, race, education, or anything else (Sherifan et al., 2003). Stalking is normally seen in the light of what is called relational goal pursuit theory, meaning that people engage in stalking behaviours because they desire a relationship with the target of the behaviours, but that they do these obsessively and persistently despite the distress they cause because a range of cognitive processes internal to the stalker interact and escalate,

230 Toxic

reinforcing each other rather than them accepting the rejection (Cupach et al., 2000). Combining this view with what we know about the difficulties autistic people can have in interpreting social signals, and what we know about monotropic thinking and hyperfocus, it is possible to see why some autistic people may fall into stalking behaviours towards people they are interested in, often without meaning to.

There have been several studies of autistic people and stalking, because this is one of the crimes which autistic people (mostly autistic men) are most commonly prosecuted for. Autistic adolescents and adults are more likely to engage in what the researchers often call inappropriate courtship behaviours (which means harassment and stalking-type behaviours as described earlier), and that they tended to pursue their target longer than non-autistic people did (Stokes et al., 2007). They are also more likely to target celebrities, ex-partners, friends, or colleagues, whereas non-autistic people are more likely to stalk strangers and ex-partners. When asked about why they engaged in these kinds of behaviours, autistic people said that they had not been taught appropriate or effective ways to initiate romantic relationships, that they found it hard to interpret social signals so did not know when someone was subtly trying to discourage them, and that they found it confusing if someone wanted a casual relationship and so could end up engaging in unwanted behaviours based on thinking that the situation was more serious than it was, or becoming aggressive when they found their partners behaviour inconsistent (Mogavero & Hsu, 2020). These difficulties with recognising how their behaviours are experienced by other people, and with understanding when a partner expects something different from the relationship than they do, have been seen in several studies of autistic stalking. Some autistic boys, in particular, lacked insight into the harm they did to their victims, instead being confused and concerned over the loss of a 'friendship' where they thought they had done nothing wrong (Dewinter et al., 2016). Equally, the tendency towards intense interests and obsessive research of these topics can lead to stalking behaviours, if the focus of that interest is a person:

> There was one person who I had become fixated on and couldn't stop phoning him, but on reflection, I now recognise that this behaviour was stalker-like. I didn't realise at the time that this could have been distressing for the person I was repeatedly phoning and even though it wasn't my intention to do any harm, it was damagingly obsessive and I regret it.
>
> *(anonymous, young autistic woman)*

This highlights how autistic people can often engage in harmful relationship behaviours accidentally, but this does not diminish the distress the other person feels, and these two things need to be considered together, rather than an autism diagnosis being treated as a 'free pass' for bad behaviour. That doesn't happen often, of course, but there is an increasing trend online for people to claim that they are allowed to do and say things which upset other people because they are autistic, or at least that they shouldn't be held to account for doing those things. Similarly, being autistic is sometimes used as a mitigating factor in criminal cases, arguing that simply because someone is autistic they can't possibly have understood that what they were doing was wrong. This may well be true in some cases, but in some of the highest-profile ones (such as mass shootings in America) it is hard to believe that an otherwise well-educated and capable person has a specific autistic blind spot when it comes to criminal behaviour. This kind of argument isn't helpful – to the people who are hurt or to the autism community generally. Most autistic people are kind, caring, polite, law-abiding, and empathetic – the few who use their diagnosis as an excuse to be the opposite give autistic people a bad name!

Inter-neurotype difficulties

Another aspect of negative relationships which we haven't yet touched on is the realm of inter-neurotype difficulties. Most of the relationships we have discussed throughout the book have been between autistic and non-autistic people, or at least are presumed to be. The work we have presented about the Double Empathy Theory reinforces the idea that autistic and non-autistic people struggle to communicate effectively with each other, and that this can underlie many of the social difficulties and challenges that autistic people experience in their relationships. The research into this theory also suggests that autistic people automatically get on better with each other, having more insight and understanding, and more instant rapport.

This is all true.

But it doesn't mean that no autistic person ever finds another autistic person annoying. Or that they never have disagreements, or misunderstand each other. Or simply that their personalities never clash.

As we have hopefully made clear throughout this book, autistic people are just as individual and varied as non-autistic people, and there is no group of humans on earth who all get on perfectly. Especially not when the group is as large as 'all the autistic people on the planet'.

There is minimal research out there on conflict between autistic people, rather than conflict between autistic and non-autistic people. Anecdotally, we know that this absolutely happens – Sarah has some examples in her following piece, and our contributors talked about their experiences with this:

> I think it is 'are you a logical neurodivergent or an emotional neurodivergent' and I think the conflict comes when you are with people who are an opposite version of you and it becomes really difficult to have emotional conversations if you don't approach them the way that emotion is expected to be brought to that conversation.
>
> *(Sarah O, autistic woman)*

Equally, there are accounts of autistic people's sensory needs clashing and causing arguments, or of disagreements about appropriate language use online causing

232 Toxic

social media pile-ons which end up with the person in the 'wrong' leaving the platform altogether.

> In the adult autistic world on the twitternet people might have quite mixed views about me because of my relationships with organisations.
>
> *(Jack)*

In Chapter 5: With a Little Help from My Friends, we looked at how important finding the autism community is for many autistic people. It is self-affirming, it builds self-esteem, and it provides a space where many people feel accepted for who they really are. If those spaces end up feeling unfriendly, unwelcoming, or like they require you to put your mask 'back on', that can be devastating. Autistic people who have had this experience say it is doubly hard, because you have spent years feeling like you don't fit in with the non-autistic world, and so you are excited to fit in with the autistic one, but then find you aren't automatically going to get on with everyone there either, which can feel unsettling:

> I get on with some autistic people but not all and that's not something that I thought would happen. When I was first diagnosed I thought that obviously I will get on with all these people because we've got this really major thing in common, but some autistic people are arseholes, just as some non-autistic people are arseholes. It took me a long time to realise that you don't have to like everybody and not everybody has to like you. And that applies to NT people and autistic people so that was a really formative thing for me. Just because you've got something in common with someone doesn't mean you've got everything in common and you're besties.
>
> *(Sarah O, autistic woman)*

The Double Empathy Theory focusses on misunderstandings between autistic and non-autistic people, but misunderstandings between autistic people who have different profiles can also happen, and this can be difficult to manage:

> In my experience it's not just the Double Empathy Problem between NT and ND folk, it's the wheels within wheels of Double Empathy within the autistic community itself.
>
> *(Sarah, autistic woman)*

There is a brilliant piece on the Neuroclastic website by David Gray-Hammond which discusses the need for healing in the autism community, where major divisions can erupt over relatively minor points because everyone involved cares so much (Bullying, In-fighting, and Abuse in the Autistic Community: A Call for Healing, January 2022). When emotions are high, because the stakes feel high, then it is easy for tempers to flare or the situation to become intense – and online communication can remove nuance which helps to lower the tension when people are communicating in-person, so these situations can escalate in ways they wouldn't offline. This is something Krysia talked about in the context of her specifically doing research about autistic people and their experiences of community:

> I know within the autistic community there are some particularly strong characters and I think that some of them do fantastic work but I find I can get completely washed out with people who are particularly strong and drawing those boundaries of "I want to do this or I need some time alone" can be really difficult.
>
> *(Krysia, 30)*

Autistic people can be bullies – they are not always the victims (Liu et al., 2019; Liu et al., 2021; Maïano et al., 2016). While it is much less common, it does happen, and there is the potential for this kind of behaviour to develop online particularly. The power dynamics of the online autism community are different to those in the offline world in many ways – follower count is not related to your social skill, or how physically able you are to stand up for yourself, for example. This means that people who may have had genuinely traumatic social experiences in the offline world find themselves in positions of social power online, and this kind of dramatic change can be difficult to navigate. Using defensive strategies which protected you one-on-one on the school playground, when you are now on Twitter with 30,000 followers and arguing with someone with 16 followers, is a very different – and very new – social dynamic. Twitter isn't that old, and the social 'rules' for good behaviour aren't all that clear necessarily – they definitely aren't written down anywhere. The nice thing about that is that communities get to build new rules for themselves, but that can also result in some significant issues along the way.

Sarah on asking awkward questions

I have written about some of my painful memories of what I experienced growing up in a dysfunctional and damaged family and of course, some of this is down to the narcissism of care-givers and generational toxicity but the awkward reality is that most of my immediate family, from both maternal and paternal roots have or had observable autistic traits and would possibly be diagnosed as being autistic if they were assessed now, and I wonder how much this may have influenced their behaviour. I've discussed this with other autistic people and one, who wishes to remain anonymous, has come up with an interesting theory as to how an autistic person's behaviour towards others could become toxic.

"Most of us have a predisposition towards honesty, but it's very easy to have that kicked out of us. It's very easy for the world to prove to us that

our way is not the way of the world and because we have this monotropic focus of staying in a single direction, we've got a choice of switching direction or sticking to our guns. Some of us switch direction and when that happens, that is when it becomes abusive and dangerous because if you start seeing the lying, cheating, abusing, selfish, cruel way as being the right way, you put yourself wholeheartedly into it and become the worst person."

My friend is not saying that if an autistic person has experienced trauma, then they will inevitably turn to the monotropic dark side, and similarly I am not saying that an autistic person will, because they are autistic, be automatically abusive. The effects of trauma and abuse on behaviour are complex and sadly, autistic people are far more likely to experience abuse and victimisation, but just like any other neurotype on this planet, autistic people can and do behave in harmful ways, sometimes catastrophically so.

It was an autistic person who wormed his way into several Bristol families in order to sexually abuse children and although he was allegedly abused himself, he was rightly convicted for his actions, although the defence tried to use his diagnosis as part of their case to argue that being autistic diminished his sense of right or wrong. He knew what he was doing and the appalling choices he made caused immense damage to many lives.

My brothers and I all suffered because of what I suspect was my father's autistic monotropic focus on achieving the goal of getting a degree, which would, in his eyes, set us up for life. What he neglected or was unable to consider though, was that in order to achieve, a child needs to have strong loving attachments and a sense that they are wanted and this caused all of us relational and emotional difficulties that still resonate today.

I know that I have caused harm to others. I had an affair when I was married to my first husband, have projected anger and bitterness onto my loved ones, and am guilty of many other things that I am not proud of. This isn't intended to be a confessional, but I do know that I have, in my 52 years, behaved badly in some of my relationships.

I've also handed out a fair amount of snark on social media, but I have seen and been on the receiving end of far too many online pile-ons and bullying from autistic people and it often feels like this is a very awkward elephant in the room that may benefit the community if it was addressed. We rightly talk about Double Empathy and communication misunderstandings between neurotypes, but there doesn't seem to be much said about conflict within the autistic community itself. I absolutely agree with the importance of challenging damaging stereotypical media reporting of autistic people being psychopaths who, for example, throw

> *children off the Tate Gallery roof and instead, redress the balance by presenting autistics as being the wonderful, compassionate and empathic people that the vast majority of us are. I also share the desire to challenge the stigma that will automatically blame a neuro-minority for communication breakdown, but I do wonder if as a result, there is less of a desire to challenge the often unpleasant nature of online community disagreement because it doesn't fit with this narrative that suggests that 'everything is awesome'.*
>
> *This is not intended to be tone policing in any shape or form. It is a plea to autistic people in general, and particularly the vocal autistic social media community to yes, understand that we are a marginalised group that has suffered huge levels of abuse, but also to recognise that by lashing out at members of our community in our disputes, we can perpetuate that harm. I do not accept that being autistic gives me a free pass or that because I have cPTSD and have been badly damaged by other people's treatment of me, that this gives me any excuse to then behave in an abusive way to anyone else. I am not the only person who is sensitive to some of the autistic-on-autistic online communications, or who has left online groups because of these kinds of interactions. We do ourselves a disservice if we become bullies or gatekeepers to our own neuro-minority and it would be more healing if we could build bridges instead, or at least try to disagree more kindly.*
>
> *(Deep breath) TED talk over and out.*

There are lots of blogs and Twitter-based discussions out there on the internet about the ways in which the autism community can be a difficult place for some autistic people to be, or about how some autistic people do harm to other autistic people. While it can feel like these writings are setting out to attack, and therefore the natural response is to be defensive, they present important opportunities for reflection for how we all interact with each other, especially online. That is probably a good thing – thinking more carefully about what you are saying and doing, and giving other autistic people the benefit of the doubt, or assuming good faith intentions rather than bad, is unlikely to make the autism community a *less* pleasant place for everyone.

Recovering from harmful experiences

Having talked about many different types of harmful and abusive relationship experiences autistic people go through, we also want to look at the ways in which they recover. Because recovery is possible, and does happen, even if it feels like this might be impossible at times. Knowing about the experiences that happen, and that there are ways to support autistic people who have trauma, is important:

236 Toxic

> A huge part of this is feeling alone and it's hugely important that these experiences are out there to help autistic people realise that they're not the only ones and helping them to know that they are not alone. That they're not the only ones to have experienced this or have been treated this way. It's so important to build those bridges and to build up those damaged people who are like us.
>
> *(anonymous)*

> The stuff that protects from trauma includes community and a lot of us are isolated. We're having a lot of our inner feelings invalidated. We've not been allowed to develop our sense of identity because we had to mask or were shamed.
>
> *(Sonny, non-binary autistic person)*

Earlier on we talked about the fact that autistic people who have suffered trauma tend to ruminate more on their experiences, tend to struggle to talk about their experiences, and tend to have more intense PTSD symptoms which persist for longer than in non-autistic people. This means that their therapy and support needs are also different to those of non-autistic people, for whom almost all existing therapies have been developed.

This need has actually been recognised for about a decade in the research literature, and a variety of small-scale trials of different therapy adaptations have been tried. These include trying to work with core autism traits, rather than ignoring them, and making them part of the treatment plan, for example (Peterson et al., 2019). Recommendations have also included a focus on making sure that the therapy setting works with the sensory needs of the autistic person; adapting communication styles, for example allowing more time for processing, waiting longer for answers, and using more direct questions; asking about and respecting client language preferences, both around being autistic and around their gender identity; and working to give as much clear information as possible as early as possible to reduce anxiety about uncertainty in the therapeutic relationship (Petty et al., 2021; Spain & Happe, 2020). Equally, using measures which have been specifically designed to work well with autistic people is important, as otherwise the clinician or therapist may get an inaccurate view of their current mental health, and potentially the level of risk they are experiencing. A team working on this is led by Dr Sarah Cassidy at Nottingham, who has partnered with autistic people to develop adapted measures of suicidality, having shown that autistic adults interpret standard questionnaires differently than non-autistic people (Cassidy et al., 2020a; Cassidy et al., 2020b). These may all feel obvious as ways to help autistic people feel comfortable and able to engage with therapy, but having the evidence from research means that there is some weight behind requests for these reasonable adjustments – it is not 'just you' asking, the research shows that this will help.

Sarah's experience of therapy

I cannot overstress the difference that autism and trauma-informed counselling and psycho-education made for my process of autistic self-discovery. Deborah helped me to understand that it wasn't my fault that previous therapies hadn't worked for me and had left me feeling even more inadequate. An autistic person who has a lifetime of effectively being told that their way of thinking and being is 'wrong' may not be helped by the premise of CBT that a person's problems are because of faulty cognition. Similarly, an autistic person who processes emotion differently or who finds identifying and expressing emotion difficult due to alexithymia may find talking therapies that focus on re-experiencing traumatic feelings in order to heal from them too difficult. It is becoming increasingly recognised that autistic people require either adaptations to existing therapies or entirely new therapeutic methods to be developed and the good news is that there is some great work being done in this area, much of which is autistic-led or in collaboration with autistic people in participatory studies. For example, the ADEPT (Autism Depression Trial) programme has been developed to help autistic people reduce the depression they feel, and because it was designed with autistic people there were higher rates of staying in the treatment, and so it had better effects (if you want to read about this, Felicity found the reference: Russell et al., 2020).

I would suggest that counselling training also needs to adapt so that not only clients with neurodivergent ways of recognising and processing emotion are validated and accommodated, but that student counsellors are as well. My own experience of person-centred counselling training was initially underpinned by a feeling that my way of reaching and exploring my pain was wrong. I really struggled with the concept that intellectualising or rationalising a problem was considered a defence or barrier to getting in touch with and exploring a client's emotional pain, when this was precisely how I accessed mine. My method of cognitively understanding and analysing a particular situation and its context enables me to reach and identify my feelings, and after months of struggle and journaling I realised that it wasn't myself who was at fault, it was that the model was not designed for my alexithymic brain-wiring.

Unfortunately, none of the changes to therapy for autistic people have yet become widespread, well-known, or generally built into therapeutic practices outside of the research setting. Accessing therapy can be difficult for autistic people:

> We know that there is a basic access problem and we are being told to go away effectively. But we also know that even if we were to get the NHS to

238 Toxic

say "you're not allowed to turn away autistic people anymore" we know that there is a basic problem for autistic people trying to access talk therapies. What we wanted to find out was why was this happening? Is it because counsellors don't know enough? Is it because they think they know enough? Is it something to do with the basic misunderstanding or invalidation? We were kind of exploring which areas could do with more development.

(Sonny, non-binary autistic person)

Individual therapists who set out to learn about autism, neurodiversity, and how best to work with autistic and neurodivergent clients exist, though, and can be hugely beneficial for people, as Sarah talked about:

I found my way to an autistic psychotherapist through Twitter and thank goodness I did. It has been essential for me to have that support to help me to come to terms with the past and to help me understand situations in the present and to see how the past impacts on the present and what about my future?

(anonymous, 62, autistic woman)

There is not yet a "neurodivergence friendly therapist" qualification, or even standardisation of what that might look like in practice, so it is sometimes hard to know whether a specific therapist will understand and work with your needs until you meet them. Therapists who know that adaptations are needed will often try to do so, but their confidence in their abilities varies (naturally), with those who have worked with more autistic people being more confident in doing so again (Cooper et al., 2018). There are a few neurodiversity-informed training courses beginning to appear, mostly online, and hopefully more and more practitioners will take up these opportunities. There are people out there deliberately working to improve the situation:

My own experiences of therapy, both positive and negative, also led into this work. I've had some very negative experiences of mental health services, but counselling changed my life, which is why I am a counsellor now. I worry, for example, about the normative approaches to CBT that we have. I know autistic people who have found it helpful, but framing it as faulty thinking is not helpful. Emotions and understanding of trauma need to be in there too.

(Sonny, non-binary autistic person)

Chapter conclusion

This chapter is the most difficult in the whole book, and it is in many ways a fairly depressing place to end the majority of our writing. It gives the impression that autistic people are always being exploited, manipulated, and abused by almost anyone and everyone they come into contact with.

That isn't the case though – please do not let this chapter override all the positive parenting, genuine friendships, and healthy romantic relationships we have talked about elsewhere. There are bad people out there who will prey on those who are different, including those who are autistic, but this is not the only type of social interaction autistic people have, and does not characterise the majority of their relationships.

A lot of the aforementioned research on therapeutic adaptations, and the contributions from Sarah and others in this chapter, show how there is a growing understanding of the specific counselling needs of autistic people. This is a good thing – we have seen the myriad ways in which relationships, and life in general, can be traumatic for autistic people, so improving the therapies on offer to deal with that is invaluable. People are out there working on making sure that fewer autistic people experience interpersonal trauma, and that those who are better supported in their recovery. That is a message of hope with which to end a very dark chapter, we think.

References

Andrzejewski, T., DeLucia, E. A., Semones, O., Khan, S., & McDonnell, C. G. (2022). Adverse childhood experiences in autistic children and their caregivers: Examining intergenerational continuity. *Journal of Autism and Developmental Disorders*, 1–17. https://doi.org/10.1007/S10803-022-05551-W/FIGURES/5

Brown, K. R., Peña, V., & Rankin, S. (2017). Unwanted sexual contact: Students with autism and other disabilities at greater risk. *Development*, *58*(5), 771–776. https://doi.org/10.1353/csd.2017.0059

Cassidy, S., Bradley, L., Cogger-Ward, H., Shaw, R., Bowen, E., Glod, M., Baron-Cohen, S., & Rodgers, J. (2020a). Measurement properties of the suicidal behaviour questionnaire-revised in autistic adults. *Journal of Autism and Developmental Disorders*, *50*(10), 3477–3488. https://doi.org/10.1007/S10803-020-04431-5/TABLES/5

Cassidy, S., Bradley, L., Cogger-Ward, H., & Rodgers, J. (2020b). *Development and validation of the suicide behaviours questionnaire-autism spectrum conditions in autistic, Possibly autistic and non-autistic adults.* https://doi.org/10.21203/rs.3.rs-48455/v1

Cazalis, F., Reyes, E., Leduc, S., & Gourion, D. (2022). Evidence that nine autistic women out of ten have been victims of sexual violence. *Frontiers in Behavioral Neuroscience*, 136. https://doi.org/10.3389/FNBEH.2022.852203

Cooper, K., Loades, M. E., & Russell, A. (2018). Adapting psychological therapies for autism. *Research in Autism Spectrum Disorders*, *45*, 43–50. https://doi.org/10.1016/J.RASD.2017.11.002

Cupach, W. R., Spitzberg, B. H., & Carson, C. L. (2000). *Toward a theory of obsessive relational intrusion . . . – Google scholar. Communication and personal relationships.* https://scholar.google.com/scholar?cluster=10965206461272016943&hl=en&oi=scholarr

Dewinter, J., Vermeiren, R., Vanwesenbeeck, I., & Van Nieuwenhuizen, C. (2016). Adolescent boys with autism spectrum disorder growing up: Follow-up of self-reported sexual experience. *European Child and Adolescent Psychiatry*, *25*(9), 969–978. https://doi.org/10.1007/S00787-016-0816-7/TABLES/4

Dike, J. E., DeLucia, E. A., Semones, O., Andrzejewski, T., & McDonnell, C. G. (2022). A systematic review of sexual violence among autistic individuals. *Review Journal of Autism and Developmental Disorders*, 1–19. https://doi.org/10.1007/S40489-022-00310-0/TABLES/2

Felitti, V. J., Anda, R. F., Nordenberg, D., Williamson, D. F., Spitz, A. M., Edwards, V., Koss, M. P., & Marks, J. S. (1998). Relationship of childhood abuse and household dysfunction to many of the leading causes of death in adults: The adverse childhood experiences (ACE) study. *American Journal of Preventive Medicine, 14*(4), 245–258. https://doi.org/10.1016/S0749-3797(98)00017-8

Forster, S., & Pearson, A. (2020). Bullies tend to be obvious: Autistic adults perceptions of friendship and the concept of mate crime. *Disability & Society, 35*(7), 1103–1123. https://doi.org/10.1080/09687599.2019.1680347

Golan, O., Haruvi-Lamdan, N., Laor, N., & Horesh, D. (2022). The comorbidity between autism spectrum disorder and post-traumatic stress disorder is mediated by brooding rumination. *Autism, 26*(2), 538–544. https://doi.org/10.1177/13623613211035240

Griffiths, S., Allison, C., Kenny, R., Holt, R., Smith, P., & Baron-Cohen, S. (2019). The vulnerability experiences quotient (VEQ): A study of vulnerability, Mental health and life satisfaction in autistic adults. *Autism Research, 21*, 62. https://doi.org/10.1002/aur.2162

Haruvi-Lamdan, N., Horesh, D., & Golan, O. (2018). PTSD and autism spectrum disorder: Co-morbidity, gaps in research, and potential shared mechanisms. *Psychological Trauma: Theory, Research, Practice, and Policy, 10*(3), 290–299. https://doi.org/10.1037/tra0000298

Hoover, D. W., & Kaufman, J. (2018). Adverse childhood experiences in children with autism spectrum disorder. *Current Opinion in Psychiatry, 31*(2), 128. https://doi.org/10.1097/YCO.0000000000000390

Kerns, C. M., Lankenau, S., Shattuck, P. T., Robins, D. L., Newschaffer, C. J., & Berkowitz, S. J. (2022). Exploring potential sources of childhood trauma: A qualitative study with autistic adults and caregivers. *Autism, 26*(8), 1987–1998. https://doi.org/10.1177/13623613211070637

Liu, T. L., Hsiao, R. C., Chou, W. J., & Yen, C. F. (2021). Social anxiety in victimization and perpetration of cyberbullying and traditional bullying in adolescents with autism spectrum disorder and attention-deficit/hyperactivity disorder. *International Journal of Environmental Research and Public Health 2021, 18*(11), 5728. https://doi.org/10.3390/IJERPH18115728

Liu, T. L., Wang, P. W., Yang, Y. H. C., Shyi, G. C. W., & Yen, C. F. (2019). Association between facial emotion recognition and bullying involvement among adolescents with high-functioning autism spectrum disorder. *International Journal of Environmental Research and Public Health 2019, 16*(24), 5125. https://doi.org/10.3390/IJERPH16245125

Maïano, C., Normand, C. L., Salvas, M. C., Moullec, G., & Aimé, A. (2016). Prevalence of school bullying among youth with autism spectrum disorders: A systematic review and meta-analysis. *Autism Research, 9*(6), 601–615. https://doi.org/10.1002/AUR.1568

Merrick, M. T., Ports, K. A., Ford, D. C., Afifi, T. O., Gershoff, E. T., & Grogan-Kaylor, A. (2017). Unpacking the impact of adverse childhood experiences on adult mental health. *Child abuse & neglect, 69*, 10–19.

Mogavero, M. C., & Hsu, K. H. (2020). Dating and courtship behaviors among those with autism spectrum disorder. *Sexuality and Disability, 38*(2), 355–364. https://doi.org/10.1007/S11195-019-09565-8/TABLES/4

Pearson, A., Rose, K., & Rees, J. (2022). I felt like i deserved it because i was autistic: Understanding the impact of interpersonal victimisation in the lives of autistic people, 136236132211045. https://doi.org/10.1177/13623613221104546

Peterson, J. L., Earl, R. K., Fox, E. A., Ma, R., Haidar, G., Pepper, M., Berliner, L., Wallace, A. S., & Bernier, R. A. (2019). Trauma and autism spectrum disorder: Review, proposed treatment adaptations and future directions. *Journal of Child & Adolescent Trauma 2019, 12*(4), 529–547. https://doi.org/10.1007/S40653-019-00253-5

Petty, S., Bergenheim, M. L., Mahoney, G., & Chamberlain, L. (2021). Adapting services for autism: Recommendations from a specialist multidisciplinary perspective using freelisting. *Current Psychology*, 1–12. https://doi.org/10.1007/S12144-021-02061-3/TABLES/6

Protection from Harassment Act. (1997). UK Government, https://www.legislation.gov.uk/ukpga/1997/40/contents

Reuben, K. E., Stanzione, C. M., & Singleton, J. L. (2021). Interpersonal trauma and posttraumatic stress in autistic adults. *Autism in Adulthood*, 3(3), 247–256. https://doi.org/10.1089/AUT.2020.0073

Rothman, E. F., Heller, S., & Graham Holmes, L. (2021). Sexual, physical, and emotional aggression, experienced by autistic vs. non-autistic U.S. college students. *Journal of American College Health*. https://doi.org/10.1080/07448481.2021.1996373

Rumball, F., Antal, K., Happé, F., & Grey, N. (2021a). Co-occurring mental health symptoms and cognitive processes in trauma-exposed ASD adults. *Research in Developmental Disabilities*, 110, 103836.

Rumball, F., Brook, L., Happé, F., & Karl, A. (2021b). Heightened risk of posttraumatic stress disorder in adults with autism spectrum disorder: The role of cumulative trauma and memory deficits. *Research in Developmental Disabilities*, 110, 103848. https://doi.org/10.1016/J.RIDD.2020.103848

Russell, A., Gaunt, D. M., Cooper, K., Barton, S., Horwood, J., Kessler, D., Metcalfe, C., Ensum, I., Ingham, B., Parr, J. R., Rai, D., & Wiles, N. (2020). The feasibility of low-intensity psychological therapy for depression co-occurring with autism in adults: The autism depression trial (ADEPT) – A pilot randomised controlled trial. *Autism*, 24(6), 1360–1372. https://doi.org/10.1177/1362361319889272

Sedgewick, F., Crane, L., Hill, V., & Pellicano, E. (2018). Friends and lovers: The relationships of autistic and neurotypical women. *Autism in Adulthood*, 1(2), 112–123. https://doi.org/10.1089/aut.2018.0028

Sedgewick, F., Crane, L., Hill, V., & Pellicano, E. (2019). Friends and lovers: The relationships of autistic and neurotypical women. *Autism in Adulthood*, 1(2), 112–123.

Sheridan, L. P., Blaauw, E., & Davies, G. M. (2003). Stalking: Knowns and unknowns. *Trauma, Violence & Abuse*, 4(2), 148–162. https://doi.org/10.1177/1524838002250766

Spain, D., & Happé, F. (2020). How to optimise cognitive behaviour therapy (CBT) for People with autism spectrum disorders (ASD): A delphi study. *Journal of Rational – Emotive and Cognitive – Behavior Therapy*, 38(2), 184–208. https://doi.org/10.1007/S10942-019-00335-1/TABLES/3

Stokes, M., Newton, N., & Kaur, A. (2007). Stalking, and social and romantic functioning among adolescents and adults with autism spectrum disorder. *Journal of Autism and Developmental Disorders*, 37(10), 1969–1986. https://doi.org/10.1007/s10803-006-0344-2

Thomas, P. (2011). Mate crime: Ridicule, hostility and targeted attacks against disabled people. *Disability and Society*, 26(1), 107–111. https://doi.org/10.1080/09687599.2011.532590

Trundle, G., Jones, K. A., Ropar, D., & Egan, V. (2022). Prevalence of victimisation in autistic individuals: A systematic review and meta-analysis. *Trauma, Violence, and Abuse*. https://doi.org/10.1177/15248380221093689

Weiss, J. A., & Fardella, M. A. (2018). Victimization and perpetration experiences of adults with autism. *Frontiers in Psychiatry*, 9, 203, 2013. https://doi.org/10.3389/FPSYT.2018.00203/BIBTEX

10

TIPS AND TRICKS FOR GOOD RELATIONSHIPS WITH AUTISTIC PEOPLE

At the end of every interview we did with autistic people for this book, we asked them for their tips for how non–autistic people could build better relationships with the autistic people in their lives. We also asked if they had tips for autistic people as to how to find good relationships. Lots of people said very similar things, so this is a summary of what they said.

Sarah's tips and reflections

I hope that my experience of developing close adult friendships is encouraging for any autistic people who may be reading this. I have now got friends 'across the neuroverse' and have found that if non-neurodivergent people are comfortable with and embracing of difference and have an open-minded and inclusive attitude to life and people, then the chances are that they will make great friends and will appreciate your qualities. My top tips are to look out for folk who are kind, honest, self-aware, generous, funny, empathic, and non-judgmental. There are a lot of people who meet these criteria, so take a risk getting to know the good people out there who are worthy of you.

Relationships of any kind can be difficult, and for autistic folk they can be especially fractured, but sometimes these wounds can be healed and futures can be hopeful. To illustrate this I want to include this Facebook post from my friend Jacci Brady as it makes me cry happy tears. I hope it encourages you too.

> *I've rebuilt my relationship with my adult offspring and after most of my life in conflict with my Mum and her conservative values, there was a peacefulness in that relationship in the last two years of her life that I'm grateful for. This feels like full bodied hope.*

DOI: 10.4324/9781003044536-11

Tips for non-autistic people

1   Be patient, and give autistic people space. This avoids autistic people feeling pressured into socialising in ways which they don't want or which are upsetting.
2   Listen to autistic people about what they experience and what they need, and respect that. Non-autistic people often have a lot of advantages you aren't even aware of.
3   Show trust, and that you can earn it. A lot of autistic people are carrying trauma or negative experiences with them, so be consistent and reliable to show that they can trust you not to be like those people.
4   Be understanding and forgiving. Autistic people can be blunt, or say or do the 'wrong thing', without meaning to. Talking through why something was hurtful and how to avoid it again helps to make the relationship better for both of you – though if this is repeatedly or deliberately mean, obviously this should be challenged.
5   Think about ways to make the relationship easier for the autistic person. How can you help reduce their anxiety? Can you make the way you spend time together better, or even nice, for their sensory needs? This will mean that they can spend time with you more easily and you can both have more fun. Ask them what will help.
6   Offer to help, not to do things for someone. Supporting an autistic person's independence and autonomy is important in building a balanced relationship, so find ways that they want you to help rather than taking over.
7   Don't expect your friendships and relationships with autistic people to look exactly like the ones you have with non-autistic people. And remember that is ok!

Tips for autistic people

1   Be yourself. Try to get comfortable with liking yourself, as you are. It is a cliche, but it is much easier in the long run and it means that you will know that people like you for who you really are.
2   Be authentic, as much as you can. Don't just mirror the people around you, or pretend to be happy when you are not.
3   Work out what your communication needs are, and how you can explain these to other people. This sets up the rest of the relationship as positively as possible and helps avoid miscommunication and misunderstandings.
4   Be clear and ask for clarity from other people – if both of you can make and keep to explicit rules, to help reduce anxiety or uncertainty.
5   Take your time. It can be tempting to want to know everything about someone immediately, or to want them to be your best friend right away. This kind of intensity is hard for a lot of people though, and a relationship can be stronger if time is taken over getting to really know each other – and it means you avoid trusting someone early who it later turns out you should not have trusted.

244 Tips and tricks for good relationships with autistic people

6   Invest in the people you want to invest in you. Effort is an important part of building and maintaining any relationship, and while this can be hard work, it helps to keep someone you care about involved in your life. It shouldn't be all one way, either all you or all them, and you both should work on keeping in touch for example.

7   Avoid putting too much emphasis on external models which tell you how to interpret people, for example personality types, love languages. These are often gimmicks, or based in bad science, and don't tell you much about someone as an individual.

8   Don't project your feelings onto other people, or blame them for things like your mental health difficulties. Some people are genuinely mean or will upset you, but if you are feeling bad one day that is not always someone else's fault, sometimes it is just anxiety or brain chemistry.

Tips for everyone

1   Talk about it! If something goes well, or badly, try not to ruminate on it alone. Talk to each other and work out what you want to repeat, or not repeat, so that you can both have a good time.

2   Respect each other. Respect in a relationship needs to go both ways for both people to feel valued and fulfilled. It can look different for different people, but it is important for everyone.

3   Learn to repair your relationship. Every relationship will have difficult times, but this does not have to mean that everything is over. Find the negotiation and resolution strategies that you can both work with, and use them.

11
CONCLUSION

In this book, we have taken a tour through the highs and lows of autistic people's social lives, from birth through to old age, and even looking at death.

That's pretty ambitious! And hopefully, we have done it well, and done justice to the autistic people who have shared their stories to help us tell you about what autistic people experience.

It isn't all easy reading, we know that. We have discussed some of the darkest and most difficult ways in which people treat each other, and particularly treat autistic people. There are sections looking at stigma and prejudice, pathologisation, bullying, isolation, and abuse. These are real parts of most autistic people's lives, especially those who are adults now and grew up in a world which knew only the worst stereotypes when it came to autism. For those who spent most of their lives without a diagnosis, struggling with picking up unwritten social rules and being punished for 'not getting it', building and maintaining relationships has often been one of the hardest and most upsetting things they battle with. It causes difficulties at school, at university, at work. Problems with friends, family, romantic partners, colleagues. When anyone you come into contact with has the potential to be a negative interaction which leaves you feeling confused, sad, or scared, it is hardly surprising that many autistic people have anxiety or depression, or both. This is a defining feature of autistic people's lives in so many ways.

Equally, we have tried to show so many of the ways in which autistic people can thrive socially. Autistic people can and do have fulfilling friendships and romantic relationships. They have warm, secure attachments to their parents and their children. They bring those positive relationship models into their friendships at school and in adulthood, into their love lives, and into their community building. There is no reason to automatically assume that an autistic child has to have bad social experiences, that they will always be bullied, or always feel lonely. Throughout this book we have tried to emphasise the ways in which acceptance of autistic people's

DOI: 10.4324/9781003044536-12

246 Conclusion

way of interacting with the world and the people around them – and more than acceptance, celebration – builds good self-esteem, good mental health, and good relationships. The lessons we can learn from understanding Double Empathy Theory in practice, and by watching the autism-friendly spaces autistic people build for themselves, should set the aspirations for anyone who has an autistic person in their lives. Hopefully it also sets the expectations for autistic people reading this book – there are people and places out there who will support you to thrive, and you deserve to find them.

There are transitions and changes throughout our lives. The most predictable thing in life is change. Changes to your setting, from home to school to work to retirement. Changes to your relationships, as you grow close to people and then apart from them. Changes to what you want out of your friendships and relationships, and find that something which felt perfect no longer is, or something which seemed unappealing is now exactly right. Everyone needs support with those times of transition, to help them navigate new situations and relationships. That is even more true for autistic people, who can find change scary and for whom those ever-adapting social skills come less easily. Being, and teaching, understanding of this need for support can help both the autistic person and the (often) non-autistic person in any relationship to have a better time together – which is usually what both are looking for in the first place.

For a long time, autism research only looked at the first dozen or so years of autistic people's lives. Researchers, professionals, and policymakers saw them as children, and fixed them that way in their minds forever – they assumed that they did not change, because they were not looking for those changes. For something which considers itself developmental psychology, autism research wasn't actually very interested in development.

That is changing – the wealth of research from the last five years or so, and the speed at which new papers are coming out, show that. This new research is more and more often done with autistic people rather than to them. It is more and more often led by autistic researchers and follows autistic community priorities. That shift, more than anything, is leading the huge change we see in the field, and we believe it is a change for the good.

That is the message we would like to close the book with. One of hope, for autistic people's social lives and for autism research as a discipline. There are challenges out there, undeniably, and they are not small. But they are also not insurmountable. People are working on improving autism awareness, building acceptance, and making the physical and social world friendlier for autistic people. Things are better for autistic children born today than they were for autistic children born 20 years ago, and they will be that much better again in the next 10, 20, 30 years too.

We can all be part of that positive change, and we hope that this book is part of that progress.

RECOMMENDED READING LIST

There are so many great autism resources and reading materials available now that this list feels almost impossible to compile. The following suggestions are resources that I have found to be really helpful during my autistic journey so far and, in the case of online resources, access regularly. There are many, many more that could also be added, but I haven't managed to get to them yet, or indeed, with regard to books, focus on them long enough to have been able to complete!

Online resources

Neuroclastic: *https://neuroclastic.com/*
NDSA (Neuro Diverse Self Advocacy): *https://ndsa.uk/content/*
The Mighty: *https://themighty.com/*
The Thinking Person's Guide to Autism: *https://thinkingautismguide.com/*
The Autistic Self Advocacy Network: *https://autisticadvocacy.org/*
Monotropism: *https://monotropism.org/*
Science on the Spectrum: *www.scienceonthespectrum.net/*
Autistamatic: *www.autistamatic.com/*
Purple Ella: *www.purpleella.com/category/autistic-spectrum/*
Ann's Autism Blog: *http://annsautism.blogspot.com/*
Autistically Sarah: *https://autistcallysarah.com/blog/*
LEANS Project Resources: *www.ed.ac.uk/salvesen-research/leans*

Books

Anxiety in Adults, Luke Beardon, Sheldon Press 2017
Aspergirls, Rudy Simone, Jessica Kingsley 2010
Autism and Masking: How and Why People Do It, and the Impact It Can Have, Felicity Sedgewick, Laura Hull and Helen Ellis, Jessica Kingsley 2020

248 Recommended reading list

Autism, A New Introduction to Psychological Theory and Current Debate, Sue Fletcher-Watson and Francesca Happé, Routledge 2019

Avoiding Anxiety in Autistic Adults, Luke Beardon, Sheldon Press 2021

"But you said . . . ?!" A Story of Confusion Caused by Growing Up as an Undiagnosed Autistic Person, Emma Wishart, Amazon 2020

Camouflage. The Hidden Lives of Autistic Women, Sarah Bargiela, Jessica Kingsley 2019

I'm Just Me, Kenzi Jupp (this can be found on the Etsy shop KenziK)

Neurodiversity, Autism and Recovery from Sexual Violence, Susy Ridout, Pavillion 2021

NeuroTribes: The Legacy of Autism and How to Think Smarter About People Who Think Differently, Steve Silbermann, Allen and Unwin 2016

Odd Girl Out: An Autistic Woman in a Neurotypical World, Laura James, Bluebird 2018

Safeguarding Autistic Girls, Carly Jones, Jessica Kingsley 2021

Spectrum Women: Walking to the Beat of Autism, Edited by Barb Cook and Dr Michelle Garnet, Jessica Kingsley 2018

Supporting Spectacular Girls, Helen Clarke, Jessica Kingsley 2022

The Autism-Friendly Guide to Periods, Robyn Steward, Jessica Kingsley 2019

The Autism and Neurodiversity Self-Advocacy Handbook, Barb Cook and Yenn Purkiss, Jessica Kingsley 2022

The Electricity of Every Living Thing, Katherine May, Orion 2018

Trauma, Stigma and Autism, Gordon Gates, Jessica Kingsley 2019

Truly Yours, Sabrina Guerra, *https://drive.google.com/file/d/1EXzIkPjRgU – UMkUk1L pEpyvMJ5RDHL/view*

Wintering, Katherine May, Penguin 2020

Women and Girls with Autism Spectrum Disorder, Sarah Hendrickx, Jessica Kingsley 2016

INDEX

ableist 118, 121, 123, 132
abuse: child 21, 215, 218; domestic 215, 223, 225 (*see also* intimate partner abuse); sexual 216–218, 224–226; substance 91, 215
academic: development 8, 28, 38, 100; expectations 84, 115
acceptance: among peers 68; desire for 59, 63, 95, 119; genuine 131–132, 134, 246
activity 33, 41, 60, 93, 125; *see also* sexual activity
adaptive 13, 206
ADEPT (Autism Depression Trial) 237
ADHD (attention deficit hyperactivity disorder) 113, 122–124, 183, 207–208
adolescent: dating 83, 95; friendships 55, 58 70, 72 93; relationships 84–85, 91, 93, 101; sibling interaction 23, 25, 29
adult: elderly/aging 189, 197 (*see also* elder care); families 170; friendships 66, 70, 106, 109, 116; late diagnosis 67, 114, 119–120, 140–141; non-autistic 8, 46, 109, 185, 203, 215, 221; relationships 17, 22, 88, 119, 125, 139
adverse childhood experiences (ACEs) 215–216
ageing *see* parent, ageing of; lifespan; life expectancy; retirement
aggression 25, 72–73, 124, 187, 220
Ainsworth, Mary 14–16, 22
alcohol 41, 191–192, 215; *see also* substance abuse
Alcorn, Alyssa 52

ambivalent 15, 21–23
America 14, 50, 88, 100–101, 226, 231
Andrew (participant) 64, 101, 114
anxiety: attachment-related 22–23; bullying 64–65; increased levels of 19, 23, 66–67, 73, 76; internalised 3, 17, 24, 40, 49, 61, 220; social 6, 76, 91, 173, 203
Applied Behavioural Analysis (ABA) 17
approval 223–224
asexual 98, 163
Asperger's syndrome 120
attachment: adult/adulthood 22, 140; ambivalent/resistant 15, 21–22; avoidant 15, 21–22, 141; long-term impact 20–21; parent/child 17, 19; research 18; secure 15–16, 18–19, 28, 141, 245; style 17–18, 21, 23, 95, 140, 145, 217; testing 28; theory of 13
Attachment Behaviour Form 19
attitude: gender-type 40, 100; sexual 87, 164; sibling 24, 186; stereotypical 125, 129, 132, 153, 178
Australia 76, 180
autism spectrum disorder 109; early years 12, 27–28; identity 98, 133–134; lifelong disorder 197; narratives about 18, 111, 179; teenager 64–65, 68 (*see also* teenagers); traits 68, 85, 101, 117, 141, 152, 200
Autistic Adult Choir 128
autistic boys: emotional responses 36; sexual behaviour 86, 96, 230; social environment/skills 44, 68, 71

250 Index

autistic girls: masking/camouflaging 68–70; social experiences/skills 36, 44, 56, 71–72, 85; suicidality/self-harm 65–66, 73

autistic women: abuse of 223, 225; dating and relationships 142–144, 147, 163, 165; health concerns 85; late diagnosis, impact of 119, 124; masking/camouflaging 67–68; menopause 205–208; pregnancy 177; research findings 4, 110–111; suicide rates 199

autonomy 87, 92, 96, 164, 175, 211, 243

avoidant attachment 15, 21–22, 141

Baron-Cohen, Simon (et al 1985) 4, 110–111

behaviour: antisocial 38; sexual 86, 95–96, 102; social 56, 69

belonging, sense of 59, 113, 128, 134, 202, 226

bereavement 158, 160; *see also* grief

binary/non-binary 39, 41, 64, 98, 111, 120, 225

biographical illumination 119

bisexual 98–99, 101

bond/bonding: emotional 12–13, 19, 38, 55, 70; pair/attachment bonds 22–23, 28, 179; relational 89, 93, 117

borderline personality disorder 5

Botha, Monique 100

Bowlby, John 13–14

Bradford, Jill 128

breakup: effects of 91–92; recovery patterns 155

Brennan, Kathy 22

Broad Autism Phenotype (BAP) 140–141

Brownies 43, 48

bullying: social 46, 52, 64–65; victim of 73, 118, 222, 234

camouflaging: defined as 24 (*see also* masking); in friendships 67–69

Camouflaging Autism Traits Questionnaire (CAT-Q) 68

career(s) 47, 111, 146, 159, 176

caregiver: nursery 13, 16, 27–29, 180; primary 12–14, 29, 215

Cassidy, Sarah 20, 236

cheating 92, 234

Chevallier, Coralie 49

childbirth 176

cognitive: development 1, 13, 27; skills 33; style 155, 222

cognitive behaviour therapy (CBT) 120, 154, 237–238

commitment 145–146

communication 92; good, form of 150; lack of 184, 187; online 232, 235; written 74, 88, 118

community: autistic 9, 126–127, 134, 201–203, 232–234, 246; church/Christian 128, 132; online 116, 133; RockFit 129–131

companionship 38, 153

complex PTSD (cPTSD) 122–123, 202, 221, 235

confidence 19, 49, 66, 74, 107, 119, 123, 172, 190; *see also* self–confidence

connection: emotional 17, 46, 144; social 110, 117, 204

coping 121, 192, 206

counselling: person-centered 121, 237; training 203, 237; trauma–informed 237–239

COVID-19 pandemic 75–76, 109, 180

creativity 32, 131

criminal: actions 222, 231; justice 156, 222, 231

cyberbullying 75, 118

cybermonitoring 93

cybersexual/cybersexuality 146

cyberstalking 93, 156, 229

dating 83; online 88, 116, 143; teenage 90, 95–96

death: parental 121, 191–193, 215; by suicide 162, 215

dementia 197, 207

depression: anxiety and (*see* mental health); levels of, varying 66, 109–110, 200; menopausal 205, 207; post-partum 177; study 237

detachment 153–154

diagnostic criteria 1–3, 5, 9, 110, 209

different: as being 3, 115, 162; patterns/behaviours 3, 19, 22, 26, 36, 50, 68, 94, 102, 190

difficulty: of expression 36, 97, 143; narrative of 45, 57, 107

discrimination 67, 100, 133–134

divorce 88, 149, 157–160, 215

double empathy problem 48, 133, 232

Double Empathy Theory 7–8, 58, 111, 135, 186, 231–232, 246

Douglas, Rob 149, 171–172, 175–176

Douglas, Sarah: adult friendships 106; awkward questions 233; childhood friendships 42; community, experiences of 126; death/dying 160; early relationships 16; menopause 207; parenting 171; puberty/dating 94; reflections 183, 201, 237, 242; relationships 147, 218; self-discovery/friendships 120; sexual violence 223; teenage friendships 60
Down's syndrome 64, 185–186
Dunphy, Dexter 89

education 174 (*see also* secondary school); early years 28, 64; sex (*see* sex education); special 47, 64
elder care 197, 209–210
Eleanor (participant) 34, 72–73
emetophobia (fear of vomiting) 121, 171
emotional: distress 73, 159; investment 55; response 22, 36, 66, 155; support 112
emotions, regulating 13, 21, 26, 33–34, 190, 216
empathy 35–36, 40, 48, 133, 164, 179
employment 215
environment 49, 52, 75, 129, 143, 173, 210–212, 229
epilepsy 198
exploitation 75, 88, 118, 215, 222
Extreme Male Brain Theory 4, 71, 111

Facebook 3, 75, 117, 126, 128–130, 146, 242
family: dynamics 25, 188–189, 193; relationships 170, 183–184, 188, 191, 218
feminism 40
Fletcher-Watson, Sue 52
Friendship Questionnaire (FQ) 46, 110–111
friendships: adult 106, 114, 184, 242; childhood 32, 42, 88; cross-gender 91; online 44, 74, 116–117; same-sex 88; teenage 44, 56, 111; toxic 220, 222

gay 98–101
gender: differences 36, 39, 70, 72, 111; dysphoria 99; identity 24, 39, 42, 77, 101, 236; non-female 120, 226
Georgie (participant) 224, 228
girls, non-autistic 36, 68, 71–72, 83; *see also* autistic girls
goals 33, 75, 150
Google 37, 192
Gould, Judy 2

grief 154, 158, 160, 191–192
group: focus 205–206; friendship 70, 93, 147, 226; online 128, 130

Hampton, Sarah 176
Happe, Francesca (et al 1994) 5
Hazan, Cindy 22
health: mental 5, 27, 32 (*see also* mental health); physical 109, 197, 205, 211
healthcare: barriers 198–199, 201; professionals 123, 177, 180, 198–199
heterosexual: adolescents/teenagers 93, 98, 101; experiences, adult 145–146, 156, 160, 165
higher education 115, 174
homophobia 100
homosexual 40, 100
Howlin, Patricia 139
Hull, Laura 68
human/humanity 77, 130, 173, 204
hyperfocus 9, 155, 173, 178, 230
hypersensitivity 145

identity: autistic 98, 133–134; gender 24, 39, 42, 77, 101, 236; minority 133, 185; sexual 98, 100, 185, 229
imagination 2, 32
independent 19, 110, 170, 185, 188, 210
individual: experiences 5, 12, 85, 209; relationships 28, 89, 145, 163, 186
Instagram 75, 93, 141
interaction: harmonious 113; social 2–5, 7, 26, 34, 131, 211, 239
interests: as complex 46, 48; shared 58–59, 114, 150, 183, 210; special 2, 70
intervention 27, 50–51, 56, 86, 102, 209
intimacy: building 94, 101, 153; emotional 22, 58, 152; physical 90, 92, 150, 159
intimate partner abuse/violence 139, 217, 223, 225–227

jobs 12, 14, 121, 184
Jones, Carly 88
Jupp, Kenzi 26, 45

Kapp, Steven 126
Knapp Development and Dissolution of Relationships model 89
Knapp, Mark L. 89
Krysia (participant) 64, 132–133, 233
Kyle (participant) 148–149, 171–172, 175–176, 202

252 Index

late diagnosis 114, 119–120
LEANS (Learning About Neurodiversity at School) project 52; *see also* neurodiversity
LGBTQ: adolescents/teenagers 93, 101; community 101, 145, 184; people 100, 145, 156
life expectancy 193, 198–200
life experiences 16, 191, 215–216
lifespan 22–23, 40, 111, 140, 155, 184, 202, 209, 215
long-term: attachment, impact of 21; effects of COVID 77; relationships 35, 91, 143, 146, 149–150, 153, 166
Louise (autistic woman) 34, 45, 72
lying 143, 151, 227, 234

male brain 4; *see also* Extreme Male Brain Theory
marriage 17, 60, 152, 157–159, 176
masculinity 120, 155
masking/camouflaging: behaviours 68, 134, 206; engaging in 36, 70, 206
mate crime 72, 222–223; *see also* intimate partner violence
medical neglect 160–161, 202
medication: Prozac 121–122; Sertraline 122, 208
menopause 205–207
mental health: issues 20, 24, 27, 52, 73, 91, 199, 221, 225; suicidality 20, 65, 91, 99, 200, 205, 236; support system 18, 24, 42, 56, 70, 94, 109
Michael, Cos 197, 211
middle childhood 20, 39, 41
migration 88, 184
Milton, Damien 7
Minecraft 45, 75
monotropism 8–9, 190
mothers: autistic 19, 177–178; of autistic children 15, 84–85, 182; non-autistic 19, 177; role of 12–13, 16, 20
Multiple Minority Stress Theory 100, 133
Murray, Dinah 8–9, 190, 192
Murray, Fergus 192
music, as therapeutic 108, 129–130, 203
Myalgic Encephalomyelitis/Chronic Fatigue Syndrome (ME/CFS) 122–123, 131, 149, 176, 207–208

National Health Service (NHS) 121, 237
Neale, Laura 128
neurodivergent people 49, 107, 113, 126, 151, 228; *see also* LEANS

neurodiversity: informed 18, 36, 58, 115, 179, 238; movement 18, 126
neurodiversity informed schools (LEANS project) 51–52
neurologically typical (NT) 113, 151, 232; *see also* neurotypical
neurotypical: relationships 64, 101, 151; social status 38, 47, 64, 127

online: dating 88, 116, 143; gaming 75, 93, 117–118; manners 117; relationships 74, 141

parent/parenting: ageing of 187, 189–190; autistic 178–179, 181; death of 163, 191–192, 215; fatherhood 182–183; motherhood 177–178, 180
partnership 147, 170; mutual 153–154
Pavlopoulou, Georgia 26
Pearson, Amy 222, 228
peer/peers: dating and 96–98; non-autistic 20, 45, 57, 64, 72, 83, 96; puberty and 83, 87, 91, 94; rejection 50, 73; relationships 21, 29, 46, 60, 65, 143, 220; sexuality 98
periods (female) 84–87
personality 20, 69, 112, 148, 244
phobia (fear) 17, 21, 43, 62, 65, 100, 107, 121, 171
Photovoice 26
polycystic ovary syndrome (PCOS) 85
pregnancy: childbirth and 176–177; experience of 86, 171, 177–178
Program for the Education and Enrichment of Relational Skills (PEERS) 50
PTSD (post-traumatic stress disorder) 216, 221, 239; *see also* complex PTSD
puberty 41, 83, 94, 205; *see also* dating

quality of life 109, 117, 122, 125, 164, 203, 212

reactive attachment disorder (RAD) 21
recognition: autistic 110; emotion 3, 35
reinforcement, positive 24, 40
rejection 17, 21, 92–93, 130, 230; *see also* peer/peers
relationships: abusive 214, 220, 227–228, 235; breakup 90, 92, 145, 147, 154, 157; child-parent 19, 183, 187; inter-neurotype 231; long(er)-term 35, 66, 90–91, 97, 110, 143, 149, 153, 166; neuro-mixed 152, 154; reflections

Index **253**

and tips 16, 147, 183, 201, 237, 242; romantic 22, 83, 88, 91, 98, 139, 141; sibling 24–27, 184–186, 193, 220; toxic 139, 214
residential care 139, 202, 209–211
respect 51, 95, 126, 150, 160, 243–244
retirement 197–198, 246
risk 28, 40, 62, 73, 86, 192, 199

Sarah O (participant) 37, 46, 65, 72, 84, 114, 120
sarcasm 72, 173
SARSAS (sexual assault/rape survivor support) 203, 224, 225, 228
school: friendships 55, 114; high school 56, 60, 72, 88, 91, 115, 154; primary 42, 46, 48, 56, 173; readiness 28; secondary 55–57, 113
Sedgewick, Felicity 24, 56, 60, 71, 76, 110, 124, 150, 201, 217, 227, 237
self-advocacy 116
self-authentic/true 69, 101, 120, 134
self-care 202, 208–209
self-confidence 22, 176
self-control 5, 33
self-discovery 120, 123, 175
self-esteem 24, 58, 84, 92–93, 95, 115, 133, 156, 232
self-harm 73, 91, 123, 200
self-identity 48, 156, 182
self-soothing 34
sensory: experiences 9, 124, 171; needs 113, 119, 231, 236, 243
sex: biological 39; education 86, 96, 142, 223; lack of interest 87, 159
sex and relationships education (SRE) 86–87, 101
sexting 93–94, 146
sexual: abuse 216–218, 225–226; activity 97, 143, 165; experiences 87, 96–98, 101, 143–144; violence 176, 203, 223, 227
sexual behaviour 86, 95, 102
sexuality: healthy 88; non-heterosexual 98, 100
Shaver, Phillip 22
siblings/sibling relationship: autistic/non-autistic 25, 184; brothers 16–17, 23, 60–61, 161, 174, 184, 234; conflictual/tangential 185; sisters 23–24, 26, 84, 186
social: challenges 115, 210; development 20, 25, 27–29, 50, 156; hierarchies 57,
74; intelligences 8; isolation 73, 76, 153, 228; norms 90, 97–98, 115, 155; services 116, 177, 215, 238
social media: cyberbullying 118, 231–232; dating/relationship formation 93, 142, 146; groups/chat rooms 126–127; online friendships 74–76, 116–117
Social Motivation Theory (SMY) 6, 9, 26, 49
social skills: building 33–34, 36, 49, 59, 75; interventions 50; lack of 6–7, 75, 111
Solomon, Marjorie 15
special education 47, 64
spouse 110, 160
Stages of Play 32–33
stalking 229–230; *see also* cyberstalking
Strange Situation 14, 18–19, 21–22
strangers 222, 227, 229–230k
stress: disorders (*see* complex PTSD; PTSD); hormones 202; relief/outlet 76, 117, 128, 186; response 18, 100, 180
studies: large-scale 2, 111, 181, 226; small-scale 205, 227, 236
suicide 124, 158, 162, 199–200, 205, 215; *see also* mental health
survival mode 95, 121, 202
survivorship bias 200

technology 45, 75, 93, 142, 146, 155
teenager: dating 83; friendships 55, 57–58, 65; masking/camouflaging 68–69; pandemic, effects of 76–77; sibling relationships 25–26; social media/online activity 74–75
Theory of Mind (ToM) 4, 7, 35, 87, 164
therapy 17, 121, 202, 236–238
TikTok 117
Tillman, Henry 128
Tomkins, Ian 128
toxic: actions/reactions 67, 124; family members 162, 176, 183; friendships 220; relationships 95, 214
trans 39, 41, 77, 99, 120, 160, 225–226
transitions 211—212, 246
trauma: intergenerational 17, 216, 218; recovery 123, 235; release of 73, 130; response 216, 228
Twitter 41, 75, 93, 117, 127, 133–134, 233, 235, 238

University of Nottingham 20
University of Edinburgh 8
University of York 124

254 Index

values 38, 48, 60, 150, 242
victimisation 139, 214, 225, 234; *see also*
    intimate partner violence; bullying
video games 44, 75, 117
vulnerability 75, 84, 88, 130, 215, 227
Vulnerability Experiences Quotient
    (VEQ) 215

Wakefield, Andrew 2
Weak Central Coherence Theory 5, 8
well-being: adolescent 74, 91, 95, 97, 99;
    general 24, 56, 65, 109, 117, 124; mental
    health and 99, 109, 131, 174, 221
Wheelwright, Sally 111
World War II 14, 200